THE
ACCIDENTAL
EVOLUTION
OF
ROCK 'N' ROLL

A Misguided Tour
Through Popular Music

CHUCK EDDY

DA CAPO PRESS • NEW YORK

To Sherman,
for keeping your playpen half of our office
as disorganized as my word-processor half.

Library of Congress Cataloging-in-Publication Data
Eddy, Chuck.
  The accidental evolution of rock'n'roll: a misguided tour
through popular music / Chuck Eddy.
     p.   cm.
  Includes index.
  ISBN 0-306-80741-6
  1. Popular music—History and criticism. I. Title.
ML3470.E33   1997
781.64'09—dc21
                                                    96-39638
                                                         CIP
                                                          MN

Published by Da Capo Press, Inc.
A Subsidiary of Plenum Publishing Corporation
233 Spring Street, New York, N.Y. 10013

Manufactured in the United States of America

Contents

Welcome to the Junkyard:
Square Pegs in Round Holes

The big genres of kids at my high school (West Bloomfield, Michigan, 1974–78) were "jocks," "burnouts," and "granolas" (the latter wore earth shoes and carried backpacks and cross-country-skied and listened to John Denver), and I didn't much fit in anywhere. When my German class went to Germany junior year, Chris Heckert (whose little brother dated my Bryan-Adams-fan little sister eight years later) wound up as my roommate; he kept singing "Hotel California," and he asked me what kind of music I liked. I told him "all kinds," which really meant "no kinds." I was an equal opportunity chicken—scared of jocks and cheerleaders exactly as much as I was scared of burnouts and kids who went to band camp. Teenagers are supposed to hate their teachers, so I might have amnesia, but I'm pretty sure I preferred most of the teachers to most of the kids.

I vaguely remember we had another clique called "freaks," who were apparently different in some important ways from "burnouts," but I didn't attend enough parties to find out *how* they were different—maybe their dads had cheaper lawnmowers, or maybe they subscribed to the *Detroit News* instead of the *Free Press*. Or maybe it had something to do with disco. The primary attribute of freaks in disco and funk songs would seem to be deviantly kinky sexual appetites—think of Betty Davis's "He Was a Big Freak" (where big-Afroed Betty gets dominant on her male sub with a turquoise chain), Rick James's "Super Freak," Phreek's "I'm a Big Freak (R-U-1-2)," and Was (Not Was)'s "Out Come the Freaks," if not Chic's "Le Freak" (which was about a kinky dancestep instead). Phreek themselves were a (not very musically memorable) project of Patrick Adams, the guy behind Musique's irresistibly innuendoed 1978 gumbo-disco hit "(Push Push) In the Bush"; Phreek's album cover depicted a green martian woman with pointy ears and a long tail and high-heeled feet dancing with a dapper dogfaced man. The cover of Silver Convention's 1976 *Madhouse* album ventured even further into freakdom, with a mansion full of wolfboys, Icarus boys, octopi, devils, dog ladies pulling naked ladies on leashes, and a pinhead with a parasite pinhead sprouting out of his forehead; its song "Fancy Party" was an invitation to preachers dressed up as clowns, ragged beggarbears, drug dealers, Mona Lisas hitting on Casanovas, and "couples making love in plain sight." Most of these aren't hippie freaks—they're more like the circus hermaphrodites and caterpillar men in Tod Browning's 1932 cult movie *Freaks*, or like the French maids having a nasty orgy in the ancient obscene prison toast "Dance of the Freaks." The Ramones' "Gabba Gabba Hey" pinhead, the sideshow deformities on the cover of *Exile on Main St.*, and the big-top geek asking a grey-flannel straight arrow how *he* feels to be such a freak in Bob Dylan's "Ballad of a Thin Man" are rock equivalents. And the only song I ever liked by T-Bone Burnett, who converted Dylan to Christianity, was "The Sixties," where some yuppie brags, "I'm a sports freak, I'm a jazz freak, I'm a video freak." So obviously any post-new-jack hack who bills his-or-her-self nowadays as a freak (Adina Howard) or even an expert at so-called "freaking" (Jodeci—does anybody in the *real* world use "freak" or "sex" as verbs?) has a long freaky history to live up to.

Anyway (getting back to the *first* freaks I ever ran into), high schoolers often base the kind of music they like on the kind of clique they want to belong to, instead of the other way around. And of course that's perfectly normal—shared leisure tastes are something friends have in common. Subcultures wind up being very protective of their tastes, and of the basis for their tastes—I personally have been told by punk, heavy metal, disco, *and* hip-hop people that I have no right analyzing their music because I'm not part of the in-group that uses their music in the "right" way. And I've told them all to go to hell.

But I understand where they're coming from. Everybody wants to feel special, and now that they belong to a clique that considers their color or sexual preference or awkwardness or hair or bad attitude an asset instead of something to make fun of, why *shouldn't* they protect that clique from outsiders who might threaten it? This is what the Beach Boys called "being true to your school." Nonconformists join a genre, name their genre "grunge" or "alternative" or "lo-fi" or "trip-hop" or "Mods" or "rockers" or "rock criticism" or "Socialism" or "literary theory" or "burnouts" or "grits" or "people who read *Sassy*," then become conformists; the new boss winds up the same as the old boss, and if you're not down with the program, you're "perverse" or "politically incorrect" or "a geek" or "a glam fag" or "overproduced" or "using outmoded discursive techniques."

Anyway, I don't know who invented the idea of "genres" within music, but he must have been a party dude, because genres are part of what makes music fun. They give us a periscope to look through, and if they were different, we'd hear the music differently. Some people say you should define genres by the audience that listens to the music; others by the type of people who make the music; others by what the music sounds like; others by what it "says." Or maybe by where record stores file it, or what kind of radio stations play it, or which *Billboard* charts it shows up on. (Most people never even think about such things, obviously, and good for them. May they lead healthy adult lives.)

I like genres because when I was little I didn't want to be a zoologist so much as a taxonomist—the guy who determines what phyla and orders and genuses and species and breeds animals and plants belong to. I was always making charts and diagrams, and I was always especially fascinated by those flora and fauna that didn't fit perfectly into any one group—that existed either on a cusp between two groups or that existed somewhere outside of any of the groups. Elephants and aardvarks were genres unto themselves. Other creatures proved the fallibility of the system: platypuses (egg-laying mammals), lungfish (fish with lungs and gills both), so on and so forth.

Then I was going to be a sportswriter—that's what I went to journalism school for. I subscribed to *The Sporting News* and *Baseball Digest*, but I wasn't really a fan in terms of caring who won or lost; I just liked the math. And I pored through the sports pages not for batting averages so much as for who got traded to whom, and who played a position they weren't supposed to play, and what old-timer got boosted to whose front office position—I just wanted to keep my baseball cards organized. I thought it was great when the Oakland A's hired track star Herb Washington as a "designated runner," just because it made him such a weirdo—if you categorized your cards by position, he'd be the only one in his pile. (Player-coach cards were neat that way, too; in 1965 the Cubs had a "head coach" instead of a "manager." And so were Seattle Pilots cards, since the team only existed for one year.) Unfortunately, I did stuff like crossing out "catcher" on my 1959 Yogi Berra and writing in "coach," which kind of decreased its street value.

I'm now told making lists and inventing categories is a very male concern. Boys collect bubblegum cards more than girls, after all; boys also tend to excel in clear-cut objective math-style subjects that don't require much imagination. So if you're lacking a penis you might wanna skip ahead a few chapters, but don't expect me to apologize, okay? Besides, I think the *idea* of genres can be way more interesting than the genres themselves.

The "lightening" of genres is sort of like how there's lemon yellow and sea green Crayola crayons, but it's more controversial: Many heavy metal people would consider Def Leppard too light to be a heavy metal band. In fact, late guitarist Steve Clark once told *People* magazine that Lep *can't* be heavy metal, because "I mean, we *read*. We can *think*." (Whereas later in the thrash/grunge '90s, the metal norm was to *try* to pass yourself off as a deep thinker.) Other metal bands say "we're just a rock band," not unlike how a number of rock critics have denied over the years that they're rock critics. (Since they serve no purpose in the world, rock critics understandably have trouble believing they exist.)

Similarly, highly respected and incomprehensible French discourse doofus Michael Foucault denies he's a structuralist in the foreword to his 1970 taxonomical treatise *The Order of Things*. He admits that he and structuralists have this or that in common, "but it is only too easy to avoid the trouble of analyzing such work by giving it an admittedly impressive-sounding, but inaccurate label." Yet if you ask me he still *looks* like a structuralist, and *smells* like a structuralist. And if you squeeze him, you'll get structuralist juice. (By which I might just mean he talks in circles and uses dorky words—Structuralism's pretty damn Greek to me. Or maybe French.)

Foucault's smarter when it comes to classifying *other* things. "There is a middle region which liberates order itself": he's talking about platypuses and player-coaches, right? He knows that "ceremonial" means of order can be a means to hide "tangled paths, strange places, secret passages, and unexpected communications." He even praises a Chinese encyclopedia that subdivides the animal kingdom into groups like animals "belonging to the Emperor" and "stray dogs" and animals "drawn with a camelhair brush" and animals "having just broken the water pitcher" and ones "that from a long way off look like flies"!

In the May 1991 issue of the science magazine *Discover*, an article about the African wild dog *Lyacon pictus* contains the following observation from UCLA geneticist Robert Wayne: "Like wolves in the United States, which used to be in every state, they're viewed as vermin. They aren't one of the 'disco' animals, like elephants or cheetahs, so not much attention has been paid to them." This passage raises a number of questions, not least of which is when did taxonomists start classifying animals by names of musical genres? (The cover of the 1978 album *Disco Circus* features an elephant, hippo, giraffe, lion, tiger, gorilla, bear, kangaroo, and two ostriches disco-dancing, but no cheetah, wolf, or wild dog.) If wolves and wild dogs aren't disco animals, what are they—funk animals? Singer-songwriter animals? Klezmer animals? And why does this mean so much less attention is paid to them? It *does* seem unfair.

"I don't wanna classify you like an animal in the zoo," Pete Shelley sings in "Homo Sapien," but he can't prevent the inevitable. Frank Kogan's song "12 Varieties of Worms" puts forth such classifications as the "I grew up in the Bronx worm," the "he did me a great favor by letting me wear his T-shirt worm," and the "worm that buys lots of records and belongs to a band." An article in *Seventeen* magazine in the late '60s asked which kind of girl you consider yourself: "glamorous," "trendy," "wholesome," "down to earth," or "ultra-cool." You could easily use the same adjectives to subdivide popular music, especially bubblesalsa girl groups. (Exposé would be wholesome and trendy, Seduction would be glamorous and ultra-cool.) Nintendo's Doctor Mario game lets you pick between two video-game-muzik subgenres, "chill" or "fever" (or you can just opt to turn the sound off).

When you get down to it, there are only two kinds of heavy metal, too: metal for girls and metal for boys. (The girls' stuff is almost always preferable.) But is "the stroll" a musical genre? Is "superstars"? " '70s rock" is definitely a genre *now*, but was it in the '70s? If you wanted to, you could say there are five musical genres, one for each of the five senses (with each tastebud a distinct substyle). Or seven, one for each of the seven deadly sins. (I'd do it myself but I can't remember what "avarice" means.) Or how about genres based on cloud types: cumulus concetus (grey and billowing like Neil Young); cumulonimbus (towering, angry, and severe like Metallica); nimbostratus (monotonal and sun-blocking like Joy Division); cirrostratus (high, transparent, and able to put a halo around the moon like Debarge); cumulous (fluffy and white like Abba).

The rap group the World Famous Supreme Team divide their *listeners* into two genres: "Some people listen for history, some listen 'cause they wanna hear a mystery." The earlier rap group Funky Four Plus One More (worms who grew up in the Bronx) go much further on their 1979 "Rappin' and Rocking the House," subdividing their listenership by ten sociologically ingrained reasons a person might travel to a house party to hear them—to be shocked, to dance, to get new ideas, and so on. Thus, they demonstrate that they belong to *all* musical genres; at one point, they call their style "punk rock" (not as rare a claim for early rappers as you'd think—Time Zone did it in "The Wild Style"; Spoonie Gee in "Love Rap"; Solid C., Bobby D., and Kool Drop in "Wack Rap"). Another line even has Funky Four Plus One More presaging the "sasquatch sound" of lousy '90s Seattle bands such as the Melvins and Alice in Chains.

Which was especially strange at a time when, to anybody outside of New York City, "funk," "disco," and "rap" were basically indistinguishable, or at least they all belonged to the *same* genre—as late as 1984, after I'd already been writing about music for money in my spare time for a year or so, a staff duty NCO I was working with in the Army commented to me that music kept going back and forth between "funk" and "disco," and I thought it was completely bizarre that he drew any line in the sand at all between two things so blatantly similar.

(Even weirder, in retrospect, was how, a couple years earlier, as defined by K-Tel's *Rock 80* compilation, "new wave" meant Gary Numan, the Pretenders, Sniff 'N' the Tears, Joe Jackson, Blondie, Pat Benatar, the Knack, Cheap Trick, and M—acts who shared almost no distinguishing traits whatsoever! Listening to radio in Detroit in 1980, I deduced that Iron City Houserockers' blues-rock was new wave and Herman Brood's blues-rock wasn't, but history proved me wrong on both counts. About the only generalization you could make is that new wave somehow subverted punk rock by letting in dance beats that punk had previously banned. But when it tried to subvert disco, it froze.)

Smart musical acts have been known to inadvertently create their *own* genres. "Folks, you have seen the heavy groups, now you will see Morning Maniac Music," proclaimed Grace Slick at Woodstock, introducing Jefferson Airplane's "Volunteers." Ray Daniels, in his notes for Vaughan Mason's 1980 *Bounce, Rock, Skate, Roll*, writes that "this album offers Funk, Ballads, and Roller Skating Music." "The rhythms played on *Emerald City* are called 'Sha Sha a La Fum,'" Teena Marie claims on that album's inner sleeve; she has also referred to "Jesus Music Heaven Sent." But in "Too Many Colors (Tee's Interlude)" on 1980's *Lady T*, she addresses the near-infinite nature of race-related subgenres and her frustration at her inability to blend them all.

New genres are very important, because old ones don't stay interesting very long. By the time an abstract trait ("punk," "jungle rhythm," "anthemicness," "emotion," "speed," "nostalgia," "outrage") becomes a genre, that trait has usually more or less been depleted as such. (Which isn't to say that people in other genres might not have success by somehow tapping into the trait.) Most relevant genre movements (psychedelica, metal, dub reggae, punk, rap, house, Latin freestyle, power balladry) seem to stay exciting for approximately three years tops. Maybe genres are like the exhaust system in your car: when any part of the system fucks up you have to replace the whole system. They never *completely* "exhaust" themselves, but they sure do wear down.

So does music criticism (a genre in its own right, as I've pointed out). Ever since tastemakers started writing long boring books about it in the mid-'60s, rock'n'roll has been governed by an anachronistic canon cast in stone, and every new pop "revolution" (punk or rap or grunge or "world music" or "techno-rave") only makes the canon stodgier: with rare exceptions, blandness is preferred over color, restraint over vitality, predictability over surprise. Caution and tastefulness and detached oblique Robyn Hitchcock nonsense pass for intelligence.

Okay, those might well be unfair generalizations. I'm sure critics see the music they like as ambitious, and obviously some of it is. But rock writers have always insisted on blindly equating "purity" with "integrity," and they increasingly look down their noses at anything that's fast and catchy with intelligible words. Critics delude themselves by assuming, say, that brightly hairdoed '90s bubblepunk bands (Rancid, Green Day, Offspring) lack the depth or originality of whatever deadly serious art-blues ripoff is being regurgitated this month. Metal-identified hard rock and post-disco dance music, the two most vital musical genres of the 1980s, weren't embraced by critics until they'd forfeited almost all of their giddiness and ghostliness and galvinization and glow. By 1995, way too many Krishnas were being brainwashed into spiritual fullfillment by music that barely existed at all: "drum and bass," "electronica," "lo-fi," "acid-jazz," "post-rock." Who comes up with these hokey titles anyway? I even went into a record store and saw a section labeled "rare groove," but when I told the man at the counter that I prefer my grooves medium rare, he just stared at me funny.

Maybe the problem is that all these revolutions are just figments of somebody's imagination, and maybe that's why so few records I care about are ever honored by Hall of Fame plaques or critics' polls. Maybe my favorites just didn't come along in the right place at the right time. If they were extremely popular, as many of them have always been, maybe they didn't conform to arbitrary rules laid down by the Holy Rock Academy—in lots of cases, what entertains me most intensely is the stuff punk or grunge or hip-hop supposedly rebelled *against*.

So I decided to put together a history-cum-buying-guide-cum-jokebook-of-lists where I could make connections between what seem to *me* like the greatest records ever made. I wanted to decipher unknown languages, plot trajectories through hidden labyrinths until I'd locate light at the other end, search for clues amidst the Cheetos hidden beneath sofa cushions. I wanted to prove what I've always suspected— that music evolves by accident; that sounds and words that might've seemed routinely expedient at the time, even to the musicians making them, can change the world forever. I wanted to figure out how pop genres *really* worked, and I wanted to make a total adventure out of it. I failed miserably, no doubt. But decide for yourself.

Introductory Soapbox Speech: Why It's Good to be a Hack

When Bruce Springsteen puts over a believable song, he does it the same way John Waite does—by accident. (In fact, Bruce acknowledges this axiom himself in his non-album 1985 rockabilly B-side "Stand on It," where Columbus discovers America "even though he hadn't planned on it.") Rock'n'roll was *invented* by accident, when Ike Turner's amp fell off the back of a truck in 1951 on the way to the studio. You can't *plan* this stuff.

Def Leppard wrote their most rap-music-like hit "Pour Some Sugar on Me" during a fifteen-minute coffee break. (So I guess it's the coffee talking. It doesn't want to be black.) It went number-two in the summer of 1988, and summer was perfect for it. As a summery song that became a hit by accident, it ranks with such on-the-spot impromptu knock-off jobs as: Chuck Berry's 1955 debut hit "Maybelline" (actually an on-the-spot name-change of the old Bob Wills country-fiddle standard "Ida Red" he'd auditioned for Chess Records with); the Champs' Mexican-rhythmed 1958 instrumental classic "Tequila" (recorded to fill B-side space at the end of a studio session by an ad-hoc group); the Surfaris' equally classic 1963 instrumental "Wipe Out" (another B-side could-abeen, composed by accelerating the A-side's riffs and getting rid of the words); Claudine Clark's 1962 lonely-girl classic "Party Lights" (another session-ending get-it-over-with one-take, meant to be the B-side of a big ballad); the Troggs' 1966 Neanderthal-metal milestone "Wild Thing" (B-side again); Tommy James's 1966 double-entendre dance-rock classic "Hanky Panky" (words made up extemporaneously, who listens to B-sides anyway, right?); and Salt-N-Pepa's 1987 double-entendre girl-rap classic "Push It" (originally the non-LP B-side of "Tramp" until a San Francisco deejay started spinderelling it on the air). And "Pour Some Sugar on Me" is sort of a cross between "Hanky Panky" and "Push It" if you want it to be. Which just goes to show that there *is* a collective unconscious, and that great rock'n'roll doesn't have much to do with hard work and malice aforethought. Or at least it *sounds* like it doesn't.

I like music that doesn't feel like too much second-guessing went into it. (John Schlesinger, film director, on his ex-X-rated 1969 *Midnight Cowboy*, which I prefer to *Drugstore Cowboy* and *Urban Cowboy*: "We didn't think, 'Oh we're being very ground-breaking on this' . . . There's a lot to be said for ignorance, you know.") The same sudden hunches and lightbulbs over heads that make music sell can make it fun. This is entertainment made for monetary ends: it's product by definition and better for it, because corporate corruption and rock'n'roll go hand in hand—in fact, corruption pretty much *caused* rock'n'roll.

Mass-producing music and peddling it for profit has never necessarily compromised "risk" or "emotion," and lots of so-called "teen exploitation music" weathers the years in better shape than important classics cast in bronze. Rock seems to work best when greedy kids on the make, ones who don't mind *looking* like they're on the make, contemptible bastards who'll serve up any tossed-off perfunctory garbage their audience will swallow, inadvertently let their humanness leak out. And the most happening rock usually doesn't seem to have the slightest idea what it's trying to accomplish, or why.

Intellectual sophistication, poetic artifice, "nimble use of language" (as defined by creative-writing teachers), all that Cole Porter bushwa, is what rock reacted *against* (which isn't to say that Porter's bawdily punned *Kiss Me Kate* songs aren't more rock than most of what passes as rock, because they are). Bruce Springsteen has his moments, but he usually doesn't have a whole lot to do with rock'n'roll. Like Rick Wakeman or Pete Townshend, he plays art-rock. By which I mean his muse can't be separated from his ego; he's too palpably concerned with how he'll be documented in the history books. If post-conscious rock has visionaries, they're guys and gals who don't spend their whole careers trying to *prove* it, no matter how much ground they're breaking. And most great rock'n'roll records are the only great records the performers who made them will ever make.

Conscious-to-the-point-of-cautiousness non-party-turning-out rock isn't *direct* enough, and that's why bubblegum and pop-metal and disco formula-mongers generally have more to say than "artists" making "statements." Ignorance of aesthetic integrity, of where the "edge" is, keeps people honest: "Idealism" limits music more than commercialism does. And though we pretend the difference between genius and idiocy is one of miles, really it's one of inches. The widely accepted recurring theme where a singer or band or movement comes along and miraculously saves the world, and keeps saving the world over and over again, contradicts the anyone-can-do-it democracy (which is a myth in its own right, but what the heck) at the music's core.

Serious rock performers should probably only be analyzed in a completely ridiculous way (though I suppose it's okay to be serious about the ridiculous guys). Only fools spew solemnities over what is primarily trivial doo-doo. (Sometimes I'm a fool.) In rock'n'roll, it ought to make sense to dismiss music for being *too* relevant, to say that the very cultural influence a Bruce Springsteen (or even a Michael Jackson or Madonna) exerts is what precludes them from being "great" artists. The mere way they're able to be dealt with so sobersidedly might negate whatever rock'n'roll importance they'd otherwise have. Is it really possible for your eyes to pop out over a Bruce Springsteen (or Beatles) record, when you've been taught to expect more than you'll ever get? Isn't it possible their genius has been hyped into nothingness? When we con guys like Lou Reed and Chuck D and Axl Rose and Kurt Cobain into believing their genius tag is true, they destroy themselves.

Alleged alternatives to the mainstream speak to an incrementally smaller audience, climbing further and further up their own butthole everyday. (Unless they actually *become* mainstream that is, like the Butthole Surfers themselves when they hit with their surprisingly stomachable psychedelic rap song "Pepper" in 1996, suddenly allowing their obscene name to be pronounced over the airwaves when a couple years before you couldn't even write it in a newspaper. But in that case they're not really alternatives anymore, now are they?)

If you went to high school in the '70s, Alice Cooper's "I'm Eighteen" and "School's Out" became part of your life and language whether you cared about rock music or not. You probably can't say that about any of the revived grunge of the last few years, even "Smells Like Teen Spirit"—Alice's lyrics were direct where Nirvana's and Pearl Jam's are oblique and muffled. So I'm not entirely convinced the big Seattle bands communicate all that much to their *own* audience, much less beyond it.

Insularity leads to an inevitable cynical fatigue and frustration, so for years now the "rock underground" has mostly just been one big predictable in-joke. If music's going to matter anymore, it's got to stop sucking up to *any* tradition, including the worn-out tradition-of-bucking-tradition—Protesting history at this point is no less a limitation than wishing history had stopped in 1957. We need pop for the present, not for posterity.

By the early '90s, the liveliest, weirdest, most surprising kinds of pop music—Bang Tango, Gipsy Kings, Garth Brooks, Amy Grant—were rooted in styles rock critics had always either derided or ignored—respectively, early '70s space-glitter shlock, late '70s flamenco-disco shlock, early '80s countrypolitan-crossover shlock, mid-'80s AOR-ballad shlock. That is, in styles you could just about completely define in terms of the *compromises* they let themselves make. Not too long ago (when both artists were making the best music they'd ever make) most people thought Madonna was just another New York disco dolly, Guns N' Roses just more Hollywood haircut-metal shnooks. They should've taught everybody a lesson, but hardly anybody learned.

Rock fans who want their music to survive should stop being such snobs and start tuning into commercial radio and accepting unlistenable crap at face value, intertwining their heartstrings with the heartstrings of the hacks on the records, surrendering to supposed stupidity like any average commuter. We've got to stop insisting, as is too easy to do these days, that all meanings present themselves complexly;

we've got to reconnect to mass-crass pop's unique potential to make all the puny stuff that goes right and wrong in life more bearable.

I mean, that's what it's *there* for, right? If we're gonna settle for lowest common denominators, we might as well settle for an LCD that doesn't disguise itself as something bigger. So more and more, the only valid way to critique rock music is through an aesthetic of what used to be called "guilty pleasures." Not all shlock is good shlock: like any rock'n'roll, hackpop should aim high (preferably in a vulgar/playful way rather than an epistemological/melodramatic way, but why not both at the same time?) And like any music, hackpop should be unstifled, urgent, sexy, catchy, and fast. Or else just real pretty—innocuousness is as noisy as noise, in its own way.

In The Beginning

Once upon a time, back when Def Leppard was still the most popular rock band on earth, this entire book was going to revolve around their umpteentuple-platinum *Hysteria* CD from 1987—chapters would correspond to individual tracks, even. I changed my mind when daring grunge bands (like, you know, Nirvana and Ugly Kid Joe) came along and knocked pop-metal acts like Def Lep off their MTV pedestal. But I can still *start* with *Hysteria*, can't I? Like the Book of Genesis, *Hysteria* begins "in the beginning," a really good place to start. (Compare the indecision of Elvis Costello's 1979 *Armed Forces*, his last worthwhile record really, which starts "I just don't know where to begin.")

Lep's song is "Women," about the creation of the universe. It rewrites the story of the Garden of Eden, just like a song called "Let There Be Rock" had ten years earlier: "In the beginning," Bon Scott of Australia's ale-boogie fivesome AC/DC had started, "back in 1955, man didn't know that a rock'n'roll show, and all that jive." His grammar doesn't compute, and he recreates history to suit his whims, even rolling over Chuck Berry's "Roll Over Beethoven." "The white man had the stops [or 'shorts,' or maybe 'shlock'], the red man had the blues." (He must mean '50s feedback grandpa Link Wray, pure Cherokee, or '20s Delta blues founder Charley Patton, a half-breed with straight brown hair.) Then, Bon claims, Tchaikovsky came along and invented light, sound, guitars—and finally, rock itself.

Sixteen years earlier still, yet another happy-go-lucky fivesome, namely L.A. R&B clowns the Coasters, whose lyrics were written by Jewish bohemians named Jerry Lieber and Mike Stoller, had suggested a creation scenario similar to AC/DC's, only reversed. "In the beginning," a deep voice intones between hollow church notes, rock was the only thing around. Then early technological advance (i.e.: wheels!) gave the rock its roll. Lead comedian Carl Gardner starts describing horns swinging like hatchets, "honkin' like a [Harlem-style] fuck," a simile Bon Scott could appreciate. (Both AC/DC and the Coasters lusted after exotic dancers—in

"Soul Stripper" and "Little Egypt.") "That is Rock & Roll," the song title informs, but the music doesn't *sound* like rock'n'roll. Too rural. There's a banjo, and more than any other '50s rock song, this one sounds like something medicine-show graduate Will Shade and his Memphis Jug Band might've played at ballgames or at fish-fries not far from Beale Street, entertaining white city slickers way back in the *'20s*. Acting drunk and buck-dancing on rollerskates maybe.

You can imagine AC/DC covering the Memphis Jug Band's 1930 "Everybody's Talking About Sadie Green"—"when she dances she don't move her head, but moves everything else instead." But the Jug Band might be most notable for inventing rap music, in a staccato verse in 1928's "Whitewash Station Blues." So now might be a good time to explain *AC/DC's* relationship to rap music. I won't get into the musicological stuff—the whole vocal-beats-over-rhythmic-riffs thing. No, I'm talking weirder stuff, all on 1976's *High Voltage*—how Bon calls himself "Public Enemy number one," how his claim that "by the time I was half alive I knew what I was gonna be" forecasts Ice Cube's 1990 memories (in "The Product") of life inside his dad's testicle. And most notably, how his "hotel, motel" chant in "It's A Long Way To The Top" sets the table for the Sugarhill Gang's "hotel, motel, Holiday Inn" just three years later.

AC/DC's spiritual big brothers were Slade, Bovver-booted '70s British skinheads in plaid trousers who merged hard rock with music-hall lewdness and jolly boogie-woogie beats. Slade's most notable contribution to the development of rap music comes from spelling so many song titles wrong: "Gudbuy T'Jane," "Mama Weer All Crazee Now," "Look Wot You Dun." Plus, on their 1972 concert album *Slade Alive*, leader Noddy Holder gets his audience to participate by enjoining, "everybody raise your hands in the air, everybody everywhere." Early rap groups like the Sugarhill Gang ("throw your hands up in the air and party hardy like you just don't care") and Grandmaster Flash and the Furious Five ("I want everybody to put their hands in the air if they have a birthday"—hey, I do!) would follow suit. Of course, *they* never told the crowd to "get your boots up!" like

Noddy does. And they never let a fan on stage to belch into the microphone, maybe. But in the end, it was the same kind of celebration.

Throwing your hands in the air isn't always a party, though. For Marvin Gaye in "Inner City Blues," it meant desperation: "Makes me wanna holler, throw up both my hands." And when do people tell you to "stick'em up"?—when they're robbing you with a gun, right? But desperation, protest, and violence can *be* a party. For a while, rap was the best place to find out.

And the Memphis Jug Band, it turns out, might not have invented rap alone. In 1996, Yazoo Records archivally revived a pile of very-old-schooled 78s on a disc called *The Roots of Rap: Classic Recordings from the 1920's and 30s*. You could draw direct lines from Blind Willie Johnson's ugly grunting through to '90s stars the Wu-Tang Clan, or from battle-of-sexes dialogues in tracks by Butterbeans & Susie or Kansas City Kitty & Georgia Tom through to Positive K's early '90s rap duet "I Got A Man."

In 1928, the same year the Memphis Jug Band recorded "Whitewash Station Blues," a white man from Greenville, South Carolina named Chris Bouchillon battled his wife Ethel in another proto-rap novelty duet. He used a style called "talking blues," which he himself had coined a few years earlier when an ear-aching Columbia Studios A&R director had begged him to recite some of his amusing lyrics without trying to sing them. The banter is all flirty one-liners: a woman just got fired from her last job for kissing the boss, so a man wants to hire her as a stenographer. She offers to work for 30 dollars a week, asks if her figure suits him, and he says it's perfect. The song was reissued in 1993 on a compilation called *White Country Blues, 1926-1938: A Lighter Shade of Blue*. Bouchillon's title returns us to the beginning, the beginning not only of rap, but of the entire human race again: "Adam and Eve (Part 2)".

Intermission (Time For Popcorn)

Woody Guthrie's '40s folk-rap "Talking Dust Blues" eventually introduced popcorn to rap music; his old Ford starts "goin' pretty fast and I wasn't even stoppin', a bouncin' up'n' down like a popcorn poppin'." Slim Gaillard's '40s bebop jive "Poppity Pop" quickly followed suit, and within a couple decades popcorn actually became a rap necessity for a while, as witness the Sugarhill Gang's "Rapper's Delight" ("Jiffy Jiffy Pop dada pop dada don't dare stop") and "Apache" (they promise to rock us like "maize—what's that? hot buttered popcorn"). Moog pioneers Hot Butter had gone top-ten in 1972 with "Popcorn," a crazed synth instrumental sonically foretelling the technodisco boom of later that decade, mainly by sounding like a theater's popcorn machine on overload. James Brown hit the Top 40 with no less than *four* popcorn songs between June 1969 and January 1970, and a few years earlier the Supremes did "Buttered Popcorn" (once labeled a "handjob classic" by no less a handjob authority than rock critic Dave Marsh). And don't forget country feminist Loretta Lynn: she confessed once that "if they had the pill when I was havin' babies, I'd be eatin' 'em like popcorn."

Working-Woman Rock from Sigmund Freud to Simon Frith

In 1971's ovariesy "One's on the Way," a pill-less and therefore pregnant Loretta Lynn swatted flies and changed diapers and slapped kids's hands in Topeka while libbers marched on New York and *Better Homes and Gardens* offered her worthless advice. A year later, Loretta's fellow country diva Donna Fargo drove an hour west from Topeka to "Manhattan, Kansas," where she was a single mom washing restaurant dishes so she could afford milk for her baby, and because all that Palmolive helped her clean away memories of touching Junior's no-good dad. (Anita Ward washes dishes in her 1979 disco number-one "Ring My Bell," too, but she's at home and her hubbie relaxes at the time. Ray Parker, Jr.'s "Bad Boy" is the only song I know where a *husband* offers to do dishes. He promises to take the trash out, too!)

"Housewives now leave the rock'n'roll station on when they do dishes; that's ambient, and so is disco," Lester Bangs fretted not long before his 1981 death, but if he would've listened closer to said housewives' soundtrack instead of settling for boring old John Lee Hooker LPs, he might've found a better kind of blues. (By the way, housewifery is very hard work—I oughta know, being a housewife myself. Rock criticism's just my *hobby*.)

On the album it came from, Fargo's "Manhattan, Kansas" was immediately preceded by her first pop hit, the seemingly oblivious-to-feminism "The Happiest Girl in the Whole U.S.A." But even that song had Donna and the man-she-was-standing-by fixing each others' lunches in between her skippidydoodahdays, indicating they were most likely a two-job couple. Within a decade, Dolly Parton was mixing disco into country and dealing Marxist propaganda: Mere weeks after Ronald Reagan was elected in 1980, her "9 to 5" miraculously took complaints about slaving to put money in the bossman's pocket to the tiptop of the charts.

Simon Frith, who is a British sociologist and therefore only wrote one paragraph on the topic as far as I know (which is

still one more than everybody else in the world put together), theorized in the late '80s about a genre called "career woman pop." He said it was rooted in mainstream pop
and country, especially songs like Abba's "The Day Before
You Came" and Sheena Easton's "Modern Girl." His late '80s
favorites were Tanita Tikaram and Nanci Griffith, who've
never clicked with me for some reason (too obtuse, too retro,
too lazy to listen to 'em?). But I like his description of how
Tikaram "seems to have stepped out of a *Cosmopolitan* feature," how her genre relies on the "overblown romance and
wry cynicism" of *Cosmo*-type magazines.

Me, I'm too intimidated by *Cosmo*'s buxom covers to read
the articles. But I love how the independent-lady-taking-care-
of-herself in Sheena's "Modern Girl" kicks her bed partner
out of her house before she grabs a tangerine to munch on
the morning train to work, and I dig Abba's "The Day Before You Came," too: over a glacial cabaret-like melody, a
woman reaches her desk around a quarter to nine, reads
business letters and signs important papers, leaves around
three and has dinner. The potentially reactionary upshot is
that Some Guy Saves Her From All This (mundanity, routine, insomnia), but she doesn't talk about the Guy, just the
This, which is more interesting. Abba had other songs along
the same lines—"If It Wasn't for the Nights," for instance,
where either Agnetha or Frida attends high-stress appoint-
ments and loses her temper all day long. By 1983, Frida was
scoring solo with "I Know There's Something Going On,"
monstrous cascading jilted-wife rock with echoing metal guitars and Phil Collins pummelling drumheads like John Bonham and Frida standing on Alpine peaks yelling at her husband three peaks away. And when Agnetha Faltskog went
solo on 1988's *I Stand Alone*, she sounded like she was giving
up the PTA meetings, the picture window, the outdoor barbecue, all those labor-saving devices the Maytag man never
has to fix. The emotion was slow-mapped and snow-capped—
a sweet Swede soap opera.

Among the countless Europeans Abba inspired was British
chantoozie Hazell Dean, who dresses in leather but regularly
dances the Upper Middle Class Romance-Shred, clinging to

despondency amid banks of fracturous Fairlights. Her 1988 "Whatever I Do (Wherever I Go)" starts cartoonish, the singer playing electro-jai-alai at the club, but then she gives herself the green light and heads for the frontier like Isaac Hayes in "By the Time I Get to Phoenix." Somewhere around Albuquerque, a liquid sky of synths opens up, and archangels battle demons atop the precipices for Hazel's self-affirming soul. Like Erma Bombeck says: the grass is always greener over the septic tank.

On her 1970 album *Angel of the Morning/That Kind of Woman*, Merilee Rush sang about career women who had become "victims of the night"; in fact, "Working Girl" itself is still one of the only rock songs (at least good ones) to address sexual harassment—her boss is Mr. Jones, who knew something was happening but didn't know what it was in Dylan's "Ballad of a Thin Man" (so his wife dumped him for Billy Paul so he wound up cruising the barrio for Hispanic chicks with Counting Crows), but he could just as well be Clarence Thomas. Donna Summer's "Working the Midnight Shift" (which panders way less than her later "I Work Hard for the Money") and Nanci Griffith's "Looking for the Time (Working Girl)" are apparently about prostitutes (ditto "the working girls in the county jail" in Steely Dan's "My Old School"), which I kind of doubt is the sort of career Simon Frith had in mind. The Chordettes' 1959 "A Girl's Work is Never Done" is a funny Coasters-like bopper about a teeny who has to launder her dad's "1500 dirty shirts" and mop up the mud her little siblings drag in. "Working Girl (For The)," written by Bernie Taupin and sung by Melissa Manchester, talks about smokestacks and meat racks and not getting laid in Detroit and Des Moines, so that's probably more Simon Frith's speed. As is Brown University country slummer Mary Chapin-Carpenter's 1993 "He Thinks He'll Keep Her," wherein a woman hits 35, leaves her hubby, and winds up "in the typing pool at minimum wage."

An Okie cowgirl married at 21 then divorced when she got sick of sitting around the house so much, '90s C&W diva Reba McEntire's best songs are mostly stay-at-home regardless—in "For My Broken Heart" she helps her worser half carry his packed boxes down the hall. But in 1992, Reba made a mini-movie video called "Is There Life Out There" about a working mom going to nightschool; Huey Lewis (!?) plays her husband, and when her kid spills coffee on her *Great Gatsby* term paper, she tells the brat "I DON'T NEED ANY MORE ACCIDENTS IN MY LIFE," but she gets an "A." (She also did a spouse-abuse number a few years before Garth Brooks got booted off the Nashville Network for depicting the same in his own mini-movie "The Thunder Rolls." Spouse-abuse debate: the best anti-abuse song I know is Yvonne Chaka Chaka's South African blues-guitar disco "I'm Suffering," where she progresses from "I have to fight to stay alive and to survive" to heated revenge like "I can bring you pain." But creepily enough, from '30s delta bluesman Robert Johnson's beating-until-satisfied "Me and the Devil Blues" to Jackie Gleason's 1954 "One Of These Days—Pow!" to Dion's face-slapping 1962 "Little Diane" to Lou Reed exclaiming "you better hit her" in "There She Goes Again" to the Intruders chasing girls and beating 'em up in their 1968 beach-soul hit "Cowboys to Girls" to the "wifebeating has been around for 10,000 years" headline fronting Guns N' Roses *Lies*, those in favor seem more prevalent. "Don't Let Me Be Misunderstood" by the Animals and/or Santa Esmeralda, where the singer begs for forgiveness for losing control of his rage, might fit here too.)

Anyway, up against Reba McEntire, '60s-rock-bred big city escapee K.T. Oslin comes off both more ribald ("Younger Men") and prouder of the bras and bridges she used to burn (" '80s Ladies") in her best country hits. She growls like Janis Joplin or Phoebe Snow, but she reminds me of a divorced old Army buddy my wife and I had named Tanya Puchalski, who's probably a Major by now. ("Ground Control to Major Tanya: commencing countdown, engine's on ya . . .") Like Reba, Oslin is more suburban than rural—critic James Hunter imagined her "behind the steering wheel of a station wagon in Atlanta, though not necessarily enroute to Kroger's." But despite a gratutious stab at sexual harassment in "You Can't Do That," K.T.'s lyrics don't go into labor much.

I doubt that makes much of a difference, actually. Because career-woman pop shouldn't necessarily be music *about* career women; it should be music *for* career women. Which might mean it should be anything you want, but certain records do seem tailored in that direction—more than lyrics, the determining factors seem to be production and voices. Which voices would generally tend to be female themselves, though not necessarily. I expect the demographic that made REO Speedwagon's *Hi Infidelity* 1981's biggest album intersected appreciably with the one that made Kim Carnes's "Bette Davis Eyes" the year's biggest single. So REO (maybe even their Bo Diddleyed do-si-do in "Don't Let Him Go" and Troggsy garage sleazing in "Follow My Heart") must be career-woman pop in a way, because "Bette Davis Eyes" just about *defines* the style, soundwise: bedraggled swallowing-lit-cigs croon protected by dreamily anxious Eurosynths and classy strings and maracas. If Laura Branigan's rock-guitared disco "Self Control" is career-woman pop, then Lou Gramm's disco-synthed rock "Midnight Blue" is. They're both energetic semiballads boosted by heavy-hearted all-out emotion and elegant polish.

By my estimation, Lesley Gore invented the *hausfrau* sound and attitude with her violin and vocal outpouring in "You Don't Own Me" in 1964, ostensibly sung to a boyfriend but to me it sounds like she's married. Dionne Warwick sweetened it in hits like "Reach Out for Me" and "Wives and Lovers" (about husbands who stay too long at the office) and "I Say A Little Prayer" (where Dionne actually refers to her "coffee-break time," which probably means she has a job) in the '60s. Then she updated it in her 1972 album track "Hasbrook Heights," which will make you want to buy a house with a pool and lots of screen doors.

Dusty Springfield's sultry bossa-nova-syncopated stringsoul and choral choruses on 1969's *Dusty in Memphis* figure too, and she's even done a Barry Manilow number called "Sandra" where a housewife accidentally (she says) slits her wrists because her wifely and motherly duties won't allow her time to establish her own identity. And there's also proto-Sheena-Easton Glaswegian Lulu (who played house for real with Bee

Gee Maurice Gibb for a while) with "To Sir With Love" in 1967, and maybe Roberta Flack killing you softly with Lemon Pledge (in preparation for the Fugees killing you softly with kung fu). I'm sure a few working wives had a taunting affection for househusband rock (my roots!) like Bobby Goldsboro's 1971 "Watching Scotty Grow" (if not his far superior if sorta bring-me-my-crackers-and-beer chauvinist 1968 "The Straight Life") and Bobby Russell's 1971 "Saturday Morning Confusion" (which has pregnant dogs and grill-swiping neighbors tormenting a hungover dad who just wants to watch the game of the week). And the Fifth Dimension's bridesmaid ("Wedding Bell Blues") and breakfast breakup ("One Less Bell to Answer") singles are at least as important as the displaced proto-thirty-something neuroses on Carole King's record-breakingly purchased 1971 *Tapestry*. Maybe even early Olivia Newton-John (who, like Dionne and Dusty, reportedly partakes in gender-preference proclivities which might tend to preclude real-life housewifehood): clippity-clopping country box-steps with worn-down but hopeful moods when she was good, by which I mean not just certified classics like "Have You Never Been Mellow" and "Please Mr. Please," but for instance "Sam," where a recent divorcee seeks out a recently divorced male pal.

Olivia managed to keep the tradition alive longer than her eventual disappearance from the charts suggested—1988's *The Rumour* had a trebly bell-ringing sparseness from ex-Top-40-apologist-pop-critic producer Davitt Sigerson, plus AIDS and ecosystem and might's-not-right messages. One Latin-lilted number rhymed "muddle through" with "BMW," but our lowland-Aussie lassie turned most ambitious when she got post-nuclear-familial, blowing the lid off technoburbia's shopaholic sprawl. Livvy plays a discouraged divorced ma of a latchkey brat in "It's Not Heaven," goes off on her jobless househusband whilst he clangs dishes around (you can *hear* 'em!) in "Get Out." Here you got bills-to-pay tension, Olivia echoing the honeyed harmony of producer Sigerson's touching 1982 Christmas hymn "It's a Big Country" then reverting back to a *real bitch*, yelling at her husband how she's "just working to keep us off the skids," swearing Ozzie and Harriet's white picket fence was an illusion.

Still, Olivia has plenty of competition for the career-woman-queen-of-the-'80s-and-'90s crown: Martha Johnson of Toronto's Martha and the Muffins, who claimed "my job is very boring I'm an office-clerk" in their 1980 new wave hit "Echo Beach"; Susanne Sulley, who works as a waitress in a cocktail bar when Phil Oakey picks her up in the Human League's "Don't You Want Me," WHICH WAS ACTUALLY INSPIRED BY AN ARTICLE IN A WOMAN'S MAGAZINE; blind Georgia countrypolitan singer/pianist Terri Gibbs, whose Top-20 1981 hit "Somebody's Knockin' " put gravel-growled paranoia about a single gal meeting a blue-jeaned devil at her door over a Donna Summer "I Feel Love" electropulse (and her seemingly lesbian "Ashes to Ashes" sounded even darker); alto-sax-bleating Oregon seafood mama Rindy Ross of Quarterflash, whose yuppie anthems looked back at female-bonding art-school flings ("Valerie") and looked down on households with too many kids ("Welcome to the City"); sellout-from-God Amy Grant, whose uncharacteristally arch "Hats" is about a working mom balancing roles; Trisha Yearwood, whose "XXXs and OOOs (An American Girl)" has a unmarried mother climbing her father's old-boy-network corporate ladder whilst juggling demands of romance and finance.

The Real Roxanne is too hip-hop to *sound* like career-woman pop, but her 1988 rap singalong "Early Early (La La)" qualifies here for the way it shows (like nothing since BTO's "Taking Care of Business," and far more than Shelly Thunder's comparable 1989 rap "Working Girl") how getting up in the morning to make music can be a drag just like any other vocation ("but it's my *job,* it's my livelihood.") And Japan's Shonen Knife don't feel career-womany either (way too peppy), but in *real life* their jobs are velly bolling they're an office crerk, and songs like "Summertime Boogie," "A Day of the Factory" and "Lazy Bone" say employment's no fun and make it sound like a revolutionary discovery. Which, especially in the Land of the Rising Sun and Loyalty to the Organization Above All, it probably is.

Recent career-woman-pop-not-about-careering landmarks include Karyn White's leggy 1988 breakfast breakup "Superwoman" and Lorrie Morgan's pungent 1992 lingerie-shopping operetta "Something in Red." They're both about marriages that need saving, they both seem closer to each other (and to "One Less Bell to Answer") than to the "R&B" and "country" the industry aligns them with, and they both give me chills. Another matched pair: Faith Hill's 1994 "Wild One," where a newly teenaged girl begins to dress sloppy, date bad boys, defy rules, and run wild and free, and its 1995 Helen Darling sequel "Jenny Come Back," where Wild Jenny gets good grades till she's fifteen, then her eyes glaze over when she learns gentlemen prefer airheads. She falls for a dumb jock and quits school; he dumps her after college, and she winds up in a tedious job. It's a case study in American class and gender sociology: why do certain kids start hanging out in bad crowds and burning out to Alice in Chains and their best friends don't? And why do smart girls in ninth grade suddenly stop raising their hands in class? That Helen Darling (who has a bachelor's degree in organizational communications, plus a radiologist dad and a tenured journalism professor husband) defines working in a movie theater as failure is smug and condescending. She forgets that, in rock'n'roll, getting lost and falling through the cracks can be what makes life worth living. But she sings like she's a missionary on a mission, venturing onto the wrong side of the tracks to save a life.

Conversely, Gail Ann Dorsey's 1989 yuppie-racing-the-clock journal entries "No Time" and "The Corporate World" cannily address women in high-power executive positions, yet seem somewhat subdued by all that upscale weight on their shoulders. (And the Gang of Four's "It's Her Factory" and Au Pairs' "Diet"—and probably Androids of Mu's "Bored Housewives" if I ever hear the damn thing—are just your usual dorky early-'80s anti-housework artpunk kvetches. Though the verse where the slaving-over-a-hot-dryer mommy in "Diet" addicts herself to pills is firmly in the tradition of the Stones' "Mother's Little Helper.")

Guess we should wrap this up with ladies wrapping it up themselves; i.e. *mad* housewife rock, a.k.a. the *Thelma and Louise* syndrome. Which is what Olivia's "Physical" and Sheena's "Strut" represent to the respective singers' *singing* careers (good girls going bad in other words), and which phenomenon has also been addressed in stepping-out numbers like Reba's "Little Rock" and Sammi Smith's "Help Me Make It Through the Night." And more depressingly in Glen Campbell's somewhat condescending 1968 suburban-country waltz "Dreams of an Everyday Housewife," wherein an aging domestic goddess stares at her wrinkles in the mirror and reminisces about the good life she gave up for Glen. A couple songs go even farther: in demure-British-thrush-gone-ragged Marianne Faithfull's spooky 1979 "The Ballad of Lucy Jordan," children's-book author Shel Silverstein's words document a weary matron who turns 37 and goes nuts so she runs naked and screaming through the crêpes-suzetted backstreets of Paris; in L.A. Ph.D.-punk band Bad Religion's atypically keyboard-hooked 1983 "Chasing the Wild Goose," a woman disrobes then does herself in to escape four walls her spouse (the louse) has boxed her inside.

Way back in 1893, in his *On the Psychical Mechanism of Hysterical Phenomena*, Sigmund Freud naturally blamed such odd distaff-half disturbances on suppressed perverse sexual desires. Which makes Def Leppard's *Hysteria* one of the only rock albums in history ever named after a figment of Sigmund's imagination.

Freud Rock

Sigmund Freud's influence on rock has, to my knowledge, never been charted, but he's at least as important as Robert Johnson when you get down to it. Certainly his theories on dreams (see "Playground in Your Mind" chapter) and the superego (Cheap Trick's "Dream Police" and Amy Grant's "Wise Up") figure prominently. "Old Man's Dream" by the art-pinko band Red Krayola has a shrink saying a dreamt-about millionaire represents his patient's dad; "Talking World War III Blues" has Bob Dylan consulting a psychiatrist after dreaming about doomsday. Iggy Pop even renamed Freud's "death instinct" the "death trip."

And it makes perfect sense to divvy up rock songs (or maybe rock history) into oral, anal, phallic, and latency stages. X-Ray Spex dealt with anal-compulsiveness in their punk power ballad "Germ Free Adolescents" ("cleans her teeth ten times a day"). Groups like Boston and Def Leppard have demonstrated anal-compulsiveness in their squeaky-clean *music*. And there have actually been songs *about* Freud, such as "Sigmund Freud's Impersonation of Albert Einstein in America" by Randy Newman, "Sigmund Freud's Party" by '80s Belgian proto-techno cyborgs Telex, and the far catchier (and shorter) "Freud in Flop" by late '70s New York no wave gremlins Teenage Jesus and the Jerks.

Freud's Oedipus and Electra Complexes (or misapprehending variations on same) have been explored by the Doors ("The End"), Prince ("When Doves Cry"), George Michael ("Father Figure"), Richard Meltzer's '70s punk band Vom ("I'm in Love With Your Mom"), Mott the Hoople ("I Wish I Was Your Mother"), Sophie B. Hawkins ("Damn I Wish I Was Your Lover" where she quotes Mott and "Carry Me" where she dreams about seducing her mom), the Kendalls (country dad/daughter duo who sing cheating songs about each other), Frank and Nancy Sinatra (singing "Something Stupid" to each other), Lee Hazlewood and Nancy Sinatra (he tells her "about Phaedra and how she gave me life and how she made it in" in their 1968 hit "Some Velvet Morning"), Gilbert O'Sullivan (singing about marrying a kid he's babysitting in his 1972 hit

"Clair"), Serge and daughter Charlotte Gainsbourg ("Lemon Incest"), Chuck Berry (switching "Memphis" into a love song to a six-year-old then getting arrested for transporting a minor across state lines), John Lennon (all those idiotic songs where he calls Yoko "Mommy"), Bruce Springsteen (all those idiotic songs where he calls grown women he's dating "little girl"), and Bobby Goldsboro (who talks about his dead wife like she's a dead daughter he bought a puppy for once in his 1968 hit "Honey.")

Freud has also inspired any number of rock'n'rollers to blame the fact that they are total fuckups in life on the way they were raised by their parents. (Obviously Sigmund didn't invent that particular idea, but he certainly went a long way toward popularizing it in the public eye and turning it into an all-purpose excuse.) Real-life traumatic experiences directly affecting the music itself include Axl Rose attributing his homophobia and general hatred to the fact that he was incestually abused by his father since he was three years old, and the more amusing case of Milli Vanilli's Rob Pilatus, whose lipsynching antics and $8485 in unpaid traffic tickets have been excused by friends as byproducts of a difficult childhood spent largely in Bavarian-mountain orphanages. Also, if indeed as tykes Michael Jackson was sexually molested and Kurt Cobain had uncles shoot themselves, their chances of repeating said patterns would of course be increased, assuming Oprah shows I've seen are accurate.

Rock *lyrics* have an even longer history of Menendez-type psychic-injury defenses. Trauma-to-failure connections have been established in the Rolling Stones' "19th Nervous Breakdown" (kid neglected by tax-delinquent mom winds up turning his back on people); Guns N' Roses' "Right Next Door to Hell" (kid neglected by young scared mom winds up dropping Freud's name in the song and all his friends are bad too and "we don't even have ourselves to blame"); the Pagans' "Boy Can I Dance Good" ("I've got psychological problems, my parents are to blame"); Bobby Bare's "Up Against the Wall Redneck Mother" ("he ain't responsible for what he's doin' cause his mother made him what he is"); Johnny Cash's "A Boy Named Sue" (sissy name parents gave him forces Sue to learn to fight); the Temptations' "Cloud Nine" (son of lazy disrespectful dad who treats his kids like dirt resorts to evil drugs); the Limeliters' "Gunslinger" (Native American children are mean to cowboy who comes from a "broken home on the range" so he grows up to kill 130 men in an immature bid for attention); "Gee, Officer Krupke" from *West Side Story* (juvenile delinquency traced to junkie moms and drunk dads who won't even give a puff of their marijuana to their offspring).

Also: Cher's racial pride statement "Half Breed" ("My father married up your Cherokee, my mother's people were ashamed of me" so she's on her own at nineteen) and "Gypsys Tramps and Thieves" (Mom's an gogo stripper and dad sells snakeoil so sixteen-year-old Cher drives to Memphis with some punk and "Daddy woulda shot him if he seen what we did"); the Supremes' "I'm Livin' in Shame" (rich woman worries about winding up like her tacky old mom) and "Love Child" (girl born dadless in tenement slum worries about being an unmarried mom); the Roches' "Runs in the Family" ("I'm holding the bag just like my mama did, just like her mama did"); Harry Chapin's "Cat's in the Cradle" (son ignored by too-busy dad grows up only to be too busy for dad); Andrew Gold's "Lonely Boy" (his new baby sister means he's not an only child anymore like Mom promised so when he's eighteen he moves out); Prince's "Sister" (blames her for his bisexuality); the aptly-named Offspring's 1997 "Way Down the Line" (all of the above); Frank Kogan and the pre-Pillowmakers (who have a drummer named Jack Freud!)'s "12 Varieties of Worms" ("I grew up in the Bronx so I'm entitled to hit people"). In their 1994 comeback "Get Over It," the Eagles threatened to kick the asses of all such depraved-'cause-deprived victims' inner children. Don Henley naturally came off a smarmy hypocrite blowhard, but I kinda agreed with him anyhow—anytime you maim/kill/rape anybody, you're obviously simply acting on everything that happened in your life *before* you went bad. But just because people have no control whatsoever over their actions doesn't mean I have to put up with their crap, does it?

Faster Pussycat's "House of Pain" says a boy should have a daddy growing up, as does Naughty By Nature's 1992 rap hit "Everything's Gonna Be Alright" (a.k.a. "Ghetto Bastard"), where a kid grows up two blocks from South Shit where the sun never shines and he knows he'll never make it so he calls his absent dad a "fag" over sweet Boney M samples. (Caption under cute baby picture on the CD single cover: "He never knew his dad.") And no doubt there's any number of interminable singer-songwriter ballads (like Elton John's "Ticking," where a real quiet boy grows up and starts pulling guns and knifing black people) that try to psychologically analyze nutso lunatics, but they're too impersonal and unmusical and I don't have patience for them. Merle Haggard, philosophizing semi-autobiographically about winding up serving a life sentence at 21 after his dad died when he was a kid in his powerful 1968 country number-one "Mama Tried," is one of the only artists ever to actually swim against the determinist tide and take some responsibility for himself: "Her breeding I denied, so that leaves only me to blame."

In Schoolly-D's "Saturday Night," his mom pulls a gun on him and fucks up the room. In one song on Poison's *Open Up and Say . . . Aah!*, Bret Michaels's parents say he's crazy and the doctor says he's cracked; in the next one, his daddy says he's crazy and his boss swears he's losing his cool. (And if you flip the record over, his mama don't dance and his daddy don't rock'n'roll!) Sister Sledge did "We are Family" and sounded like a happy one; Isaac Hayes did "One Big Unhappy Family" about *pretending* to be a happy one; the Ramones did "We're a Happy Family" but sounded dysfunctional; Frank Kogan's "Baby Doe" has him predicting his kid will grow up to hate him and chanting "We are not family! We are not family! We are not family!" Sly and the Family Stone's "Family Affair" is the most Caribbean-sounding and least arty (most back-to-the-family-tree) track on *There's a Riot Goin' On*, and it has one kid growing up to be a winner and another growing up to be a loser. Madonna's "Keep it Together" is the most Caribbean-sounding (even more so in its 12-inch mixes) and least arty track on *Like a Prayer*, and it has one kid learning to clown around and be different to get attention and everybody getting along when things go bad.

The Shaggs' late '60s cult favorite "We Are Parents" claims "parents are the ones who really care," but the Wiggins sisters sing out-of-key and out-of-mind to an extreme that suggests Mr. and Mrs. Wiggins locked them in a closet until they were thirteen, passing in bread and water through a laundry chute. D.J. Jazzy Jeff and the Fresh Prince's "Parents Just Don't Understand" has their parents taking them to Center City Philadelphia's Gallery Mall and buying them *Brady Bunch* pants then scolding "if they were laughing you don't need 'em 'cause they're not good friends." But the album it's from, *He's the DJ, I'm the Rapper*, nonetheless won the 1988 Parents' Choice Award as album of the year! Panelists included Barbara Bush and Kitty Dukakis.

Unforgettable Memory
Rock Moments

Amnesia rock like Dion and the Belmonts' "Where or When" (which at least remembered Hal Kemp's chart-topping 1937 version) and repressed-memory rock like Barbara Streisand's "The Way We Were" ("what's too painful to remember we simply choose to forget") might be Freudian too. And there's *planned*-amnesia rock, like the Doors' "Soul Kitchen" ("light another cigarette/learn to forget") and Frank Kogan and the pre-Pillowmakers' "Baby Doe" ("I could take a gun and kill 1961 and grammar school is dead, it's out of my life," then he offs 1968—eighth grade and hatred—with a razor blade). The Anti-Nowhere League's "(We Will Not) Remember You" even anticipates future amnesia.

Anticipating future memory is far more common: Poison's "I Won't Forget You," Amy Grant's "I Will Remember You," Merle Haggard's "Someday We'll Look Back," the Doobie Brothers' "What a Fool Believes" where they try "to recreate what had yet to be created," Chuck Berry's "Baby Doll" where he predicts "we'll sing the old alma mater and talk of things that used to be."

Additional archetypal memory-rock milestones include the Drifters' "Sand in My Shoes" (mnemonic-device rock, where sand serves as something like a string around your finger), Eddie Money's "I Wanna Go Back" (impossibility-of-reverse-time-machine rock), Bryan Adams' "Summer of '69" (intentionally ambiguous nostalgic double entendre), Slade's "Thanks for the Memories" (=mammaries), Tommy Conwell's "I'm Seventeen" (routine memory song pretending memory isn't a memory yet), and the Beach Boys' "When I Grow Up" (memory of anticipation-of-then-future-now-present song pretending memory *still* isn't a memory yet).

"Roots rock" bar bands from Hootie and the Blowfish and Son Volt backwards to Creedence Clearwater Revival and the Band codify memory into an entire musical genre; Kool Moe Dee's "Way Way Back" and D.J. Jazzy Jeff and the Fresh Prince's "Summertime" are roots-type good-old-days nostalgia in a rap context. Memories materialize as tangible objects in Martha and the Vandellas' "Come and Get These Memories" and John Cougar Mellencamp's "Rain on the Scarecrow" ("son I'm sorry there's just memories for you now"). Don Henley's "Boys of Summer" and Steely Dan's "Reeling in the Years" treat memory as an implicit subject of general treatises on aging, and Sam Cooke's "Only Sixteen" ("I've aged a year since then") revolves around a memory of *past* aging.

I'm afraid I can't remember what the Rolling Stones "Memory Motel" was about, but Richard Meltzer once calculated that on *Between the Buttons* in 1967, the Stones used the word "yesterday" 25 times. The album came out way too many yesterdays ago for me to feel any need to go back and doublecheck his figures.

Repetition Repetition Repetition Repetition Repetition Repetition

Music *depends* on memory—the notes you're hearing now won't mean anything if you can't connect them with notes you've already heard, and remembering past notes helps you predict future ones. Yet though rhythm demands that you anticipate the next beat, if you're not surprised or jarred once in a while, you'll get bored. The more daring rhythm is, the more it'll jar you, but if it gets so daring that it flies without a safety net, people will stop paying attention. Or they'll sit down.

This is a sort of paradox, obviously, and coping with it occupies many a musician-hour. Music's recurring part is called a "groove," as in Madonna's "Into the Groove" or Teena Marie's "Behind the Groove" (which is where she says Xanadu is), both of which titles connect repetition with sex, a linkage James Brown knew well, too: He wouldn't call a song "Sexy"; he'd call it "Sexy, Sexy, Sexy." And he did "Spinning Wheel" on his *Sex Machine* album because wheels and machines imply perpetual recurrence, and he'd say "one more time" 100 times in the same song. And he kept naming songs "Popcorn This" and "Popcorn That."

With 1967's "Cold Sweat," Dave Marsh has observed, James invented "music in which chord changes were superfluous." His groove could last forever—"The beat is getting stronger, the music's getting *longer*, too," his disciple Sly Stone put it in 1969. Or "on and on til the break o'dawn to the beat the beat the double beat beat and ya don't stop," as so many hip-hop disciples later put it. Chuck Berry, who did a presciently near-forever (10:35) "Chuck's Beat" with Bo Diddley around 1964, said it first: "reelin' and rockin' til the break of dawn."

Chuck is also a repetition god in the sense that all his songs sound basically the same (until you listen closer and notice all the ethnic parts). He treated repetition as a theme in "Around and Around"; many later pop and rock acts (Edgar Winter, Aerosmith, Ratt, New Order, Ish) changed the title to "Round and Round." The Aerosmith one ends with Steve Tyler repeating the line "round and round and round" scores of times, like a tapeloop. Early '60s hard rock idol Freddie Cannon's top hit "Palisades Park" has ferris wheels, merry-go-rounds, and loop-de-loops in it, all of which put round-and-roundness into joyful action; in "If You Were a Rock'n'roll Record," Freddie demonstrates how repetition is an intrinsic part of the home listening experience, since *records* twirl around and around. Sonny and Cher summed it all up with 1967's "The Beat Goes On," and the drum that kept pounding rhythm to their brains was so unstoppable that even rappers Public Enemy wound up conceding two decades later that "the beat is for Sonny Bono."

Dusty Springfield's 1969 "The Windmills of Your Mind" refers to tunnels leading through tunnels to dark caverns, snowballs growing as they roll down hills, wheels within circles, clock hands turning, puddle ripples, ever-revolving doors, "and the world is like an apple spinning silently in space." An even more lysergic 1969 hit was Tommy Roe's "Dizzy," where Tom's drummer fabricated a proto-disco drumtrance to demonstrate what Tom meant by "like a whirlpool, it never ends." But the trance Diana Ross enters into in her 1984 disco-metal comeback "Swept Away" reassures us contradictorily that, though "the rise and fall is endless," "nothing lasts (repeated three times) forever."

Sometimes it could seem to, though, at least to certain people, and at least if "it" was disco. Disco-sucks propagandists always complained about how the beat never changed and the lyrics never did either, and they kind of had a point—Silver Convention's 1976 "Get Up and Boogie" is basically four words repeated with very little respite for six-and-a-half minutes over an incrementally changing stripped-to-the-gears synthesizer pulse; Donna Summer's 1977 "I Feel Love" is mainly three words repeated for eight minutes over machine beats that weigh even less. But these are also two of the greatest records of their time, and Munich's the only place they could've come from. Kraftwerk's German 1975 synth-loop hit "Autobahn" convinced disco producers to use voices as synths too, but Donna's voice was no monotone: it had *sex* in it, and so did Giorgio Morodor's electronics. "I Feel Love" must have been a hard record to make—chanting was one thing, but nobody else had ever *sung* that way before.

"I Feel Love" is the windmills of *my* mind. There's actually two synthesizer figures—one like a giant spinning helium Slinky spring the other one passes in and out of. The singing feels like helium, too. And the big spring encircles the inner perimeter of whatever room you're listening to it in, a circle within a square, and you *feel* every time the shapes intersect, because the pitch changes for a split-second. Or maybe the shapes don't really intersect; maybe the spring just skims the surface of the walls, ceiling, and floor and keeps right on moving. And sunlight keeps peeping in and out of the clouds, through your window and into your room, getting lost then reappearing.

Munich disco like Donna's saw itself as part of German art-rock, united in rebellion against Nazi oompah beerhall Liederkranz: Silver Convention "belongs to a new generation of artists who have broken with the established image of German music," the notes to their 1975 *Save Me* assert. Yet Kraftwerk had never made any music so *fast*; judging from their earliest "rock"-oriented noise, it's clear that Kraftwerk had learned too many tricks from fellow Baader-Meinhof buddies Can and Faust, *musique concrète*-and-free-jazz-and-tone-cluster-and-Kurt-Weill-folk-opera fans whose best music wasn't much more than clumsy and inept acid-damaged-Eurotrash-artboy attempts at Miles Davis fusion-grooving. To this day, Eurodisco-rooted drone bands (Depeche Mode, Duran Duran) manage a fleshful velocity that Eurorock-rooted drone bands (Laika, Stereolab, Unrest) tend to miss out on; Public Image Ltd.'s 1980 *Second Edition* is one of the few successful attempts to bridge the two sensibilities.

Kraftwerk were hardly the first arty types to revel in repetition. "At Pomona College, in response to questions about the Lake Poets, I wrote in the manner of Gertrude Stein, irrelevantly and repetitiously," John Cage wrote in the late '50s. "I got an A." Since then, eggheads from Philip Glass to Yoko Ono have made careers of using repeating-sound motifs as a crutch. Classical-metal bore Glen Branca learned about repetition by hearing the Kinks' "You Really Got Me" and Paul Revere and the Raiders' "Just Like Me" on the radio as a kid. Brian Eno named a song "The True Wheel" and made it sound like one, claiming "repetition is a form of change." But repetition can also just mean you lack *imagination*, as so many unbearable '70s mud-sweat-festival drum solos proved. Way too often, the emphasis on trance-as-such (without even help from a decent dance beat) leaves arty repetition cold, de-energized, moot: how pre-Kraftwerk German groups (Faust, Can, Neu!, Amon Düül) combined electromultiduplication with unhealthy guitar parts generally suggested tin rocket hatches being slammed again and again in outer space, but never catching, *ad infinitum*.

In the mid-'80s, a number of continental Europeans (Yello, Propaganda, Nena, Telex, Laid Back, Trio, Falco, George Kranz, Alexander Robotnik, the Off, Flexx, Belfegore, 16 Bit) managed to inject PiL's Krautdrone into bubblegum Krautdisco, pioneering the breathy/guttural rap-growls and grinding techno-hypnosis which would soon be shrunk into "industrial rave" tedium on Chicago's Wax Trax record label (then into Moby and Nine Inch Nails). "Electrica Salsa" by the Off, about making old percussion sound new, has the most deadpan sheep-accent ever: "Don't half to ask you to get up you do eet on your own baa *baa* baa baa." It employs R&B horns too, as do Robotnik and fellow circa-1985 Italian "fuzzdance" groups (Naïf Orchestra, Myra and the Mirror), who hid pachyderm sax-wailing inside illegally catchy staccato synth-stuttering, yielding a giddiness indebted at least partly to Donna Summer's "Romeo," on the 1983 *Flashdance* soundtrack.

If it seems like a drastic leap of faith to connect James Brown to Giorgio Morodor and beyond, that's only because I haven't mentioned the middleman, Isaac Hayes. On *Hot Buttered Soul* (1969), *The Isaac Hayes Movement* (1971), and *Joy* (1973), this bald and bechained graduate of the Stax Records studio stable developed the idea of using a deep and doggedly mesmeric wah-wah-stacked murmur of post-hamhock concentricity as a means toward extreme length in a non-art-rock genre—he'd take a schmaltz standard by the likes of Jimmy Webb, make it slaver with monologues full of silk-sheet wannafuck ursine machoman rapturing and narrative turnaround and over-a-bottle-of-ripple seduction languor, and he'd keep it purring for 9:55, 11:11, 12:00, 12:30, 15:15, even 18:40 (in the eternally eternal "By The Time I Get to Phoenix," where he buries so deep into the song he digs himself a subway to the desert). He started disco's tradition of tossing anything-you-want on top: soap opera strings, sound effects, saxophones, gospel response, organs, orgasms, orchestrally massed ribjoint guitar, showbiz patter ("there's some deep meaning to this toon," "I'm gonna bring it on down to soulsville"). This was the era of symphonic R&B by the likes of Marvin Gaye, but it was the Black Moses who truly stretched soul atmosphere and polish to untold dramatic extremes of foreplay-act-and-afterglow—basically, Isaac was doing the same thing Miles Davis was doing on LPs like *Bitches Brew* and *Jack Johnson* at the time. Except he did it as "music," which tends (in my house anyway) to be preferable to "jazz."

Isaac's sustained-length moves were anticipated and/or mirrored by any number of interminable James Brown jams, obviously, but also by time-for-the-disc-jockey-to-shit-shower-and-shave epics by any number of late '60s and early '70s album-rock acts—Uriah Heep's "July Morning" lasted 10:36, the Stones' "Goin' Home" 11:18, the Doors' "The End" 11:35, Velvet Underground's "Sister Ray" 17:25, and Iron Butterfly's "Inna-Gadda-Da-Vida" a half-hour, for instance. All of these bands, along with others on the art/metal cusp (Black Sabbath, Neil Young and Crazy Horse, Can, Hawkwind, Pere Ubu, Patti Smith Group, Television, Leather Nun, Fairport Convention doing their marchtimed folk-unto-metal "Sloth," etc.) basically expanded on a technique developed by Bob Dylan in 1965 and 1966 that suggested you could you use recurrence and increasing musical intensity to stretch rock music toward infinity, and that you could keep the groove from getting boring by seasoning it with extraneous stuff (which in Gothic dirge-metal terms would mean fuzztone, feedback, and electronics). For example, Dylan's music in "Stuck Inside of Mobile with Thee" keeps returning to the same place (Mobile, I guess), establishing a grooval/modal mobile Memphis blues inside which Bob stuck jokes, meanness, meaninglessness, politics, harmonica notes, keyboard phrases, guitar solos, slurred stuff you can't make out, monotonous poetic allegories that just go on and on. "People just get uglier and lose their sense of time," he says; so does the music.

Bob used more or less the same technique while composing "Desolation Row," "Tombstone Blues," "Bob Dylan's 115th Dream," "It's Alright Ma (I'm Only Bleeding)," "Absolutely Sweet Marie," "Visions of Johanna." With "Sad Eyed Lady of the Lowlands," he was the first person to stretch a song for a whole album side (even though, at 11:23, it wasn't really an album-side's worth of music.) The Velvet Underground (whose songs like "Here She Comes Now" and "There She Goes Again" swiped the James Brown concept of having similar titles to each other) drew on Dylan's ideas by having John Cale play "96 Tears"-type garage plinks on the organ and letting Moe Tucker's unchanging drum pulse pull more than it pushed, then by putting guitar noise and post-Yardbird middle-eastern minor keys and crosstalk and long lewd gross shaggy-dog stories with surprising twists in them on top. (On their first two albums, that is—by their third, they were chamber musicians hooklessly codifying stuff that either "Sister Ray" or Simon and Garfunkel had already done better.) "In the context of repetition, novelty is a surprise," Richard Meltzer says. Dave Marsh has astutely suggested that the use of mood shifts and dramatic buildup in Derek and the Dominoes' 7:10 1970 "Layla" might have paved the way for disco 12-inches, but then again so did the Velvets. (Even Uriah Heep.)

Early attempts to fuse Dylan/Velvets punkpoem grooval stretch with James Brown funkjam grooval stretch include various Jimi Hendrix tracks ("Voodoo Chile" for instance) plus Lightnin' Rod's 1973 *Hustler's Convention*, an album-long ghetto-jazzed R&B opera about gambling and murder, but its music works better than its vocals, and if you're not fully attentive you'll lose track of the story. Rapper Spoonie Gee developed a purer and more extreme hybrid in his '80s singles

"Spoonin' Rap," "Street Girl," and "The Godfather": he keeps rapping faster and louder as the groove progresses, and his voice echoes more and more, as if he were leading you by the wrist through some darkened tunnel, and it gets claustrophobic in there. By the end, he's rabid, spitting out words, turning "r"'s into growls, flailing, slamming his punching-bag mouth beats against the stadium bricks—real mean. Spoonie turned song-length into a self-actualizing obsession: in his 1981 Sequence collaboration "Monster Jam," he chants "I will not stop, I must keep on rockin'," like a marathon runner hitting the Wall. (Best rock approximation of such Spoonie-obsession—Alternative TV's 1978 "Another Coke," though the Fall's "Music Scene" and "Various Times" come close. All three feature dark guitars and unexpected violence over an insistent beat, plus spoken vocals often working as rhythm. But "Another Coke" gets the nod because both it and "Spoonin' Rap" have verses about guys being molested in public restrooms.)

Before Dylan and James Brown, extreme brevity was taken for granted: at 3:09, the Flamingoes' "I Only Have Eyes For You" is the *longest* of the 40 pre-1963 rock'n'roll classics on 1973's definitive *American Graffiti* soundtrack. *After* Dylan and James, in prog and dance circles especially (though hardcore punk did make tiny ditties fashionable for a couple months in 1981), extreme brevity almost had to be a conscious move in its own right: the two less-than-a-minute tracks on Yes's 1971 *Fragile*; the 12 New Zealand artpunk bands in 12 minutes on the 1991 Xpressway Records 7-inch *I Hear the Devil Calling Me*.

Minimalist art grooves can be silly, accidentally or on purpose. Teenage Jesus and the Jerks' "Red Alert" has Lydia Lunch repeating the same seven-note razor-guitar blitz 17 times in 32 seconds (which computes to something like 222 beats per minute.) And the Jerks' fellow New York no wavers DNA have a quickie called "32123" where they play a theme then repeat it backwards just like the title suggests, and one called "Not Moving" where they jog in place for two-and-a-half minutes.

Similar tricks work for Mark E. Smith (who says he's "the Mick Jagger of right now") and the Fall, who named their first 45 "Repetition," named another tune "Neighborhood of Infinity," and peaked repetition-wise with the aforementioned 5:16 "Various Times" (about imagining you're a Nazi, among other things) and 8:04 "Music Scene" (which has various and sundry incidental keyboard crashes and radio signals and sax signals). Mark E. says the three R's are "repetition, repetition, repetition." In lots of songs he just repeats a title over and over. Which can be a drag—certain spans of dry didacticism leave me unmoved, un-anythinged. There's too much proto-Sonic-Youth quiet-unto-loudness cornballism and elevator-horror mood music.

On the other hand, lots of Fall stuff is the raw gnaw of discontent, the loather's leap into something infallible—rough wraparound murk-blues-unto-excelsis drone with mundane household words spasmodically and (sort of) rhythmically spoken or shouted or declaimed or poeticized or laughed or squealed or panicked, with new slang and pronunciations invented on the spot. All over syncopation with a real grasp of history: doowop, rockabilly, garage bands, gunk-metal, Kraut rock, Beefheart, Lennon, Dylan, dub reggae. The Fall turned Diddley/Stooge grooves into dirge progressions ("Elves") and hooks from Status Quo's "Pictures of Matchstick Men" (or Jeff Airplane's "We Can Be Together"?) into hopped-up hillbilly music ("How I Wrote 'Elastic Man'"). They tried Jackson Five beats and disco ones, too.

When the Fall stumbled on a groove, they *rocked* it. They were at least as rock'n'roll, and certainly no more arty, than Prince. (Anyway, nobody says you can't be both.) In the high-strung early days (1977–1979), their rhythm already had a fairly straightforward Farfisa-punk push. But it improved into a dense, drastic, and anything-but-immobile pore-congestion when they instituted a double-drum (plus keyboards/voice/bass/zither/percussion) rhythm format on their 1981 "Lie Dream of a Casino Soul" single and 1982 *Hex Enduction Hour* album.

The Fall have been fairly influential in '90s indie-rock circles, supposedly inspiring Pavement (whose vocals and rhythm section are basically wet noodles) and definitely inspiring Girls Against Boys (who have an extremely appropriate name, I figured out at the opening Kansas City stop of the 1996 Lollapalooza tour after some apparent ex-Deadhead with burgeoning middle-age-spread asked me what they were called: "That's *great*! Girls are *always* trying to do shit better than boys!—*fuck* that!!" Girls Against Boys' ranted power-chord groove was tough enough for moshdudes but also had enough fuckability in it [as did their cleancut pretty-boy hair] for cute non-dudes to gyrate hips to. An all-blond high school cheerleader squad even came on stage for one number. When some pushy skinhead type started slamming where he wasn't wanted, a boyishly-haircutted 24-year-old record-store-employee named Molly with a sociology degree from my alma mater University of Missouri gallantly tossed her cupful of water at the dork, but it accidently soaked me instead).

Years before the Fall, though, '60s bands made repetition kick even harder. The Shadows of Knight came up with a bent-calculus system of technocratic guitar loops in their mid-'60s garage nugget "My Fire Department Needs a Fireman" which later wound up in almost every rock song Brian Eno ever wrote (starting with "Paw Paw Negro Blowtorch" in 1973), then eventually was handed down to Public Image Ltd. ("Memories"), Giorgio Morodor ("Love Theme From Flashdance"), Dinosaur ("Kiss Me Again"—by Arthur Russell's indie-disco Dinosaur not J. Mascis's indie-rock Dinosaur), Tiffany ("I Saw Him Standing There"), plus assorted Ut, Feelies, Pavement, 3Ds, Death of Samantha, Red Dark Sweet, Stranglers, and Siouxsie and the Banshees numbers.

In late '60s songs like "Goin' Home" and "Midnight Rambler" (verbally) and "Monkey Man" and "Sympathy for the Devil" (polyrhythmically), the Rolling Stones pioneered the use of James-Brown-like eternally-dittoed-stretch in a hard rock sphere. And the Who were fond of Spirographed embellishments: 1965's "Anyway, Anyhow, Anywhere" climaxes with a whole bunch of atonal stuff happening seemingly randomly at the same time that Pete Townshend enters a kind of mantra saying "way I choose" over and over; a similar spiral is the "can't have it"-vs.-"I want it" trance amidst "Magic Bus" 's salsa-like syncopation.

On 1970's *Who's Next*, maybe deriving the idea from the Stones' "Gimme Shelter," Townshend used his ARP synthesizer as a melodic tool for a sort of minimalist rainbow-in-curved-air effect, rather than for souped-up classical-rock melodrama. In "Baba O'Riley" and "Won't Get Fooled Again," he programmed the machine to one catchy hookline of just a few notes, then let it savor over that hook for seven or eight minutes on end. Many a canny semi-metal act (the Sweet, Foreigner, Manfred Mann, AC/DC, Loverboy, Girlschool, Kix, Van Halen) later picked up on Pete's loops as an excuse to use dancey electronic keyboard frills without coming off too blatantly "disco" about it.

Slade's "mama mama mama mama" mess in "Mama Weer All Crazee Now" is stutter-repetition after the manner of Roger Daltrey's in "My Generation." Later famous stutter-rock landmarks include David Bowie's "Changes," Bachman-Turner Overdrive's "You Ain't Seen Nothin' Yet," the Bee Gees' "Jive Talkin'," Stacey Q's "Two of Hearts," the Oak Ridge Boys' "Bobbie Sue," Def Leppard's "Foolin'," and quite a few S-S-S-Samantha Fox songs. (Sad to say, rap record-scratch production techniques have more than likely turned stuttering into something of a cliche by now.)

On "Born to Be Wild" on *Slade Alive* (1972), Slade foiled the whole "authentic live album" myth about a half-inch from the end of the side by locking into a maddeningly interminable closed-groove-thing (or maybe my record just has a gash) that know-it-alls might blindfold-test as the German cult act Faust, or maybe as feedback from 100 police sirens. Also, Def Lep's "No No No" ends *High N' Dry* in a surprisingly *Slade Alive*-like way, with somebody saying "no" 44 times. (Their "Another Hit and Run" and "Billy's Got a Gun" have similarly echoey endings. Supposedly the Beatles did it first, on *Sgt. Pepper's* somewhere.)

Before "No No No," there was "Nobody But Me," a 1965 top-ten frat hit by Cleveland's Human Beinz, who started up by saying their "no" 26 times. Elvis's 1955 "Baby Let's Play House" begins with 15 or 20 "baby"s plus one "buh-buh-buh-

buh-buh" tossed in in the middle. The Skyliners' 1959 doo-wop hit "Since I Don't Have You" ends with a virtual sonata created from the word "you."

Redundancy rock has been mastered by Wings ("in this world in which we live in"), John Cougar Mellencamp ("I cannot forget from where it is that I come from"), Elvis ("the future looks bright ahead"), and Young MC ("hoping you can make it there if you can"). And Grandmaster Flash's confusingly titled 1983 cocaine protest "White Lines (Don't Don't Do It)" has one part where deep altered voices repeat the "don't"s so many times that you can't tell whether you should snort or not anymore.

And speaking of drugs, Jefferson Airplane drummed up a bloodshot-eyed dribbly-gravel-hauling-truck-repetitive grumble in 1968's "Crown of Creation" which in the '70s was both stolen by hard rockers (Black Sabbath's "Children of the Grave," Alice Cooper's "School's Out," Uriah Heep's "Look At Yourself," David Bowie's "John I'm Only Dancing," Cheap Trick's "Elo Kiddies") and synthesized by Giorgio Morodor, first in "Son of My Father" in 1972, then in Blondie's huge "Call Me" from 1980's *American Gigolo* soundtrack. "Call Me" was supposedly an instrumental called "Metal Man" (as in Sabbath's "Iron Man"?) at first, but it might also have been directly inspired by Nick-Gilder-led Canadian glamsters Sweeney Todd's use of the "Crown of Creation" groove in their 1976 B-side "Rue De Chance" (featuring a then-unknown Bryan "Guy" Adams), seeing how both Blondie and Gilder spent lots of time having studio knobs fondled by Mike Chapman.

Also in the '70s, drawing on the Stones and Who (and perhaps on such forgotten fraternity masterpieces as the McCoys' 1965 number-one "Hang on Sloopy"), the Stooges and Pere Ubu did their best to swell your basic hard-rock buzz toward incidentally trancelike and potentionally everlasting besiegement, using Iggy Pop's and Crocus Behemoth's voices as rhythmic boosts in ways most arty New York and German protopunks hadn't figured out yet. Later, around the same time as the Fall, Frank Kogan's New York bands the Pillowmakers and Red Dark Sweet reincorporated hillbilly jangle and falsetto-blues train-whistle hooks into a loud post-post-Dylan repetition-excavating-deep-caves context.

Quarterflash, a supposedly soft-rock '80s sextet led by a married pair of ex-school-teachers, arranged exploratory sax appeal and belted thirtysomething transitory-love plaints around obsessive vamping picked up from Eurodisco, salsa, and Fleetwood Mac for up to eight minutes (the epic Friday-night-in-Portland depiction "Williams Avenue"), building clam-restaurant-bopfolk force and tension without collapsing into jazz-fusion noxiousnes.

For a long time, Dylan's "Like a Rolling Stone" was the longest *single* ever. But early '70s hits (Don McLean's mighty "American Pie," Cashman and West's rancid "American City Suite") climbed toward eight minutes; then with 12-inch singles, disco instigated the idea that individual songs could have the scope and autonomy of a whole album, if not symphony. Love and Kisses' 1977 debut LP is a single and album at the same time, seeing how it only has two songs, "Accidental Lover" (17:20) and "Love (Now That I've Found You)" (16:14). (The A-side repeats the phrase "love you" about 500 times.) Since Funky Four Plus One More's 1980 debut 12-inch "Rappin' and Rocking the House" has a 16-minute A-side version and a not-one-iota-similar 14-minute B-side version (both fully extemporaneous and live-in-studio, it sounds like), you can call that record an album, too. And Greil Marcus writes that New Order's 1982 "Temptation" uses "repetitions [that] deny an ending"; i.e., it lasts *forever.*

Actually, to me, New Order were more like *in-a-rut* rock. Starting their career as Joy Division, they had a song where Ian Curtis droned "when will it end, when will it end, when will it end?": my sentiments exactly. He also kept saying "love will tear us apart *again*," which after a few "agains" made me stop sympathizing. Ian's band didn't really get the repetition idea down pat until long after he hung himself in 1980. Like many new wavers, they were attracted to disco for its repetition, and eventually as New Order they learned to surrender to some of its pleasures as well. As disco goes, they weren't much—they'd steal an obsessive electrobeat from "Into the the Groove" or Shannon's "Let the Music Play," then Bernard Sumner would start whispering and you'd wonder where the obsessiveness went. Their 1987 remix collection *Substance* contains some gleefulness in its curlicued synths and strums, but if I had to pick a lyric on it that best underscores the band's swoony sonic mission, I'd go straight for "It seems like I've been here before."

Repetition can be mere assembly-line *automation*. Kraftwerk, who usually acted like life was one big tapeloop, named one song "Music Non Stop" (inspiration for the Afrika Bambaataa "Planet Rock" line "you gotta rocket don't stop") and another one "The Man Machine"; U.K. oildrumbangers Test Dept. named one "Total State Machine." Post-Kraftwerk electrodisco Germans Silver Convention were smarter—they recorded "I'm Not a Slot Machine," with prettiness and a jackpot of clanky Atlantic City sound effects, denying they were pinball machines as well.

Eurodisco repetition no doubt has certain roots in avant-classical new age pioneers like Terry Riley and Steve Reich (maybe via the minimalistic studio-swirls in such late-'60s/early-'70s rock chestnuts as the Beatles' "She's Leaving Home," Wings' "Another Day," 10cc's "Rubber Bullets," Eno's "Paw Paw Negro Blowtorch," David Essex's "Rock On," etc.). But disco electrodes made those mathematical modulations *move*, and not by accident, as titles like Gino Soccio's "Running in Circles" and Love Deluxe's "Here Comes that Sound Again" (and again and again, for *17* minutes) should make clear. Thanks to remixing, disco acts could do a single song an infinite number of ways. Dance-rap guys like Mantronix and Schoolly-D always do "improved" sequels of their own songs or each others', blatantly fluctuating old themes into new-'cause-we-say-so contexts, raising nonchalance to an untold urgency level and filler into a way of life: "Get Stupid 'Fresh' Part I," "Listen to the Bass of Get Stupid Fresh Part II," "Get Stupid III," "Gangster Boogie" (Schoolly 1984), "Gangster Boogie II" (Schoolly 1988), "Gangster Boogie" (Mantronix 1988), "Gangster Boogie" (Schoolly 1989). (All from before "gangsta rap" happened!)

So What Else is New?

"Let's do it again!" the Showmen exclaimed in their 1961 New Orleans rock'n'roll-will-never-die proclamation "It Will Stand," "I feel good let's do it again!" The Staple Singers had a hit with "Let's Do It Again," and "Do It Again" is one of the only Steely Dan songs I like because it's sort of a salsa or mambo and I think it's about obsessive-compulsive-type addiction (to gambling or cheating on your wife or whatever), even though one of my friends swears it's about suicide. (But why would you want to do *suicide* again? Isn't once enough?)

Here's Herman's Hermits in "I'm Henry VIII, I Am" (which was first popularized in 1911): "Second verse, same as the first." So rock'n'roll has always prided itself in its redundancy, always equated eternal recurrence with eternal life.

"Depth" and "originality" can definitely be tools that help make good music, but they've never been mandatory, and as often as not they just get in the way. Conversely, unoriginality can be an asset as long as the musicians in question are stealing from music I *like*; in fact, I'd go so far to argue that more new bands *should* rip off my favorite records. The best album I heard in 1995, Rancid's . . . *And Out Come the Wolves*, was dismissed (accurately!) by spoilsports as a mere Clash wannabee, which ignores the fact that the Clash don't get wannabeed nearly enough. I'm pretty sure I've never had an "original" idea in my life—I just accumulate what other people say, shuffle it all up, and spit back what makes sense. Rock works the same way: "Plagiarism is a time-honored tradition," Mike Saunders of the Angry Samoans told me once.

The Four Tops' "It's the Same Old Song" sounds like the same old song as their "I Can't Help Myself," as does the Stones' "Under My Thumb," as does XTC's "Life Begins at the Hop." The Funky Four Plus One's first two singles ("Rappin' and Rocking the House" and "That's the Joint") sound exactly the same as each other and are two of the greatest records ever made; if their next two singles ("Do You Want to Rock" and "The Mexican") had sounded the same, they'd be among the best, too. (Though actually, if their "The Mexican" was much like Babe Ruth's or Jellybean's versions, it might be among the best *anyway*.) Rock records are made by recycling and recombining sounds and words that have already come and gone, and smart songwriters have no delusions about their (or anybody's) originality. To wit:

—Syndicate of Sound "Little Girl," 1966. "Other girls did it, you didn't think up nothing new."

—Byrds "Mr. Spaceman," 1966. "Out into the universe, we don't care who's been there first."

—Strawberry Alarm Clock "Incense and Peppermints," 1967. "Beatniks and politics, nothing is new."

—Rod Stewart "Every Picture Tells a Story," 1971. He decides it's pointless to quote Dickens, Shelly, or Keats, " 'cause it's all been said before."

—Carole King "So Far Away," 1971. "One more song about moving along the highway, can't say much of anything new."

—Wings "Silly Love Songs," 1976. About how there's already lots of 'em, but what's wrong with that? So here he goes again.

—David Allen Coe "Mississippi River Queen," 1978. On the pseudo-originality of Manhattan bohemian subculture: "New York City you can't show me anything I haven't seen at least 100 times before." Echoed by Frank Kogan in his Lower East Side insider critique "Stars Vomit Coffee Shop," c. 1985: "Wanna see something different, so different that it's the same."

—X-Ray Spex "I Am a Cliché," 1978. The *title*, stupid.

—Fatback Band "King Tim III (Personality Jock)," 1979. The first rap record ever: "We ain't doin' nothing new."

—John Cougar "Cheap Shot," 1980. "I bet you've heard this song before." And as a matter of fact I *did*; it was called "Radio, Radio," and Elvis Costello ended *This Year's Model* with it in 1978 just like the Coug ends *Nothin' Matters and What if it Did* with it here. And Cougar's "Don't Misunderstand Me" on the same album used to be called "Miracle Man" when Elvis did it, and "Ain't Even Done With the Night" used to be "Mystery Dance." But John's versions are grimier—I respect that.

—John Mellencamp "Crumblin' Down," 1983. "Ain't no news here, it's the same old song you've been hearing for years." And "Small Town," 1985. "Another boring romantic, that's me."

—Teena Marie "Lovergirl," 1985. "Touché olé, my opening line might be a bit passé." And in the notes to *Starchild*, on which "Lovergirl" appears: "No one's new or innovative except the Creator." (But "Once is not enough once is not enough once is not enough," she explains on *Emerald City*. Then in the next song: "Once is not enough when you've been satisfied." Get it?)

—MTV promotional spot, 1991. "You see it here first. And then you see it again."

—Metallica "Ain't My Bitch," 1996. "Headstrong, what's wrong? I've already heard this song before." (Yeah, but oddly enough, you'd never actually heard it from Metallica, since on *Load* they'd suddenly evolved into a not-quite-as-pompous-as-before boogie band. And inside their CD booklet they were male-bonding shirtlessly and flaunting Freddie Mercury coiffures and glam makeup, a notably gutsy sellout for San Francisco guys who'd never exactly specialized in songs about sex with women.)

—Local H "Bound for the Floor," 1996. "Born to be down, I think that I've said this before now." And "Nothing Special," 1996. "I know I'm nothing different." Bubblegrungers from Zion, Illinois (who really oughta cover "Rivers of Babylon": "where he sat down, and there he went, when he remembered Zion"); totally unoriginal in that they sound a lot like Nirvana (except way better), but also totally original in that they're only two guys (one white, one black), and when they play live some roadie jogs out on stage every few songs to honk kazoo or whatever, then turns around and ducks his head and rushes off in a theoretically inconspicuous roadie-type ducked walk (as opposed to *duckwalk*, which would be Chuck Berry. This kid's more like *Bruce* Berry, the working man who used to love that econoline van).

The Power Ballad Revolution

If unoriginality is indeed the essence of rock'n'roll, and if unoriginality can be measured in degrees, then it stands to reason that the most unoriginal kinds of rock are the truest to the form. And if you polled 100 people about what kind of rock'n'roll was the most unoriginal, there's a good chance that a plurality would vote for the pop-metal power ballad.

Adolescent females have the best pop-music taste in the world, usually, and hard rock performers have *always* done slow songs for them. Elvis did "Love Me Tender," the Beatles did "Do You Want to Know a Secret," the Troggs did "Love is All Around," the Stones did "Angie." The Beach Boys' confessional teen-utopia glee-club ballads ("Wouldn't It Be Nice," "Don't Worry Baby," "All Summer Long") hold up better than fast frat cheers like "California Girls." (None of which explains Nelson, by whom I mean Rick Nelson's famously blond twin sons Gunnar and Matthew, who have the most female audience of any "rock" unit of the '90s, but blow bigtime anyway. So let's forget them.)

Slow songs have more to do with pre-rock gloop than with what most people think of as rock'n'roll, but pre-rock gloop is an intrinsic *part* of rock'n'roll—part of what makes rock'n'roll rock, in fact, because if everything rocked what would we be able to compare it to? In the mid-'60s, Frank Sinatra's "adult" "That's Life" could coexist peacefully with the Buckinghams' "teenage" "Kind of a Drag" because they were both syntheses of Farfisa organs with easy-listening swill; even (especially?) in the Beatles' wake, pure Tin Pan Alley middle-of-the-road ice-cube-down-your-back heaven music (by the Carpenters, Sandpipers, Bread, Climax, Poppy Family) could easily be accepted by brave rock fans at emotional face-value.

In the '70s, "soft" rock by Fleetwood Mac rocked harder than "hard" rock by Cactus (just like how, in the '90s, "soft" rap by Vanilla Ice and Gillette rocks harder than "hard" rap by Warren G and the Notorious B.I.G.). Rock'n'roll could not survive *without* lovely lovey-doviness; when it expels it from its world (as hardcore punk and speedmetal do), it turns itself into something *other* than rock'n'roll. Something dumber.

In the 1982 movie *Fast Times At Ridgemont High*, Sean Penn or somebody presents the theory that Led Zeppelin's fourth album is the ultimate makeout music, but that's probably just because he hasn't heard much Smokey Robinson or Roberta Flack or DeBarge or Dionne Warwick or Dusty Springfield or Chi-Lites or Stylistics. And Murray the K didn't name his '60s doowop-and-oldies compilation *Golden Gassers for Submarine Race Watchers* for nothing, you know; he took it for granted that "In My Diary" and "Will You Love Me Tomorrow" and "A Sunday Kind of Love" would be French-kissed to. Street-corner R&B evolved out of the effect European harmony and black Baptist church singing had on '40s black vocal groups like the Mills Brothers and Ink Spots and Platters, and its most swoonable singers were always ones with high voices. (I only sing that well when I'm in the shower, and nobody else is listening.) Cleancut early '60s Italians whitened the sound, and you can draw a line from them through the Four Seasons and Beach Boys to the first metal era, where the smoochiest ballads aren't Zep's art-rock ("Going to California," "The Rain Song") or lesser attempts by Black Sabbath so much as crass wimpitude by less angular rockers—Especially Kiss's "Beth," Nazareth's version of the Everly Brothers' "Love Hurts," and two by Alice Cooper: "I Never Cry" and "You and Me."

These all charted in 1976 or 1977 ("I Never Cry" hit number 12, the other three went top ten), so I guess power ballads were invented at the same time as punk rock. The Eagles, whose rural harmonies and clippity-clop jangle-hooks and sad cocaine-cowpoke misogyny loom equally large in the realm of Nerf-metal inspirations, had actually been topping the charts for a few years by 1976; but since almost *all* Eagles songs were ballads ("Take it to the Limit" was a *waltz*!), they don't really fulfill the power-ballads-as-changes-of-pace criterion. Lynyrd Skynyrd had had "Free Bird" and "Simple Man" and "Tuesday's Gone," but those were too *complex* to be power ballads—too blues, too, truth be told. "All the Young Dudes" by Mott the Hoople was too literary, "Dream On" by

Aerosmith was too Gothic, and the Raspberries sounded too much like the early Beatles covering Rachmaninoff. But "Beth" had Kiss whining to their girl like Pete Townshend in "The Kids are Alright" that "me and the boys will be playing all night." (They didn't specify *what* they'd be playing. Records? Charades? Poker? Spin the Bottle? No way to tell. Can't be Nintendo 'cause it hasn't been invented yet.)

More important, "Beth" had lots of *strings*. As did the Alice Cooper ballads—he orchestrated them to the skies. He put acoustic guitars in there too, and it'd make perfect sense to draw an analogy between his ballads and Madonna's ballads if you're so inclined; similar balance-out-the-shocking-and-rocking-stuff motivation, and they both come from Detroit. "You and Me" was about being everyday people; "I Never Cry" was about drinking too much. Both talked about watching television.

Nazareth were four Scots with an unappreciated knack for taking brutal blues-metal with a humongously swinging (almost "harmelodic" but not boring enough; e.g. "Too Bad Too Sad" sounds like a fast Police B-side six years early) rhythm section and making it alternately beautiful, witty, literate, and explosively loud, with thick twang, surprising cover versions (Woody Guthrie, Little Feat, Joni Mitchell), and high-pitched drawls diverging into drunk-rough histrionics. For years Nazareth were assumed by critics to be utter cavemen; weird, because on the back of their 1977 *Hot Tracks* compilation, one guy's wearing a somewhat fruity knitted sweater, one looks exactly like Al Franken from *Saturday Night Live,* one looks like some jetsetting *New York Times* photographer, and they're all carrying shoulder bags!

Anyway, "Love Hurts"'s dramatically strummed and cymbaled opening turns into a thin waltzy repeated riff under sad sweet ragged mushmouthing that's Axl-Rose-like in the way it never touches down, just admits how young it is and learns from life's foulups and grabs ahold of that bluebird of happiness and *goes.*

As J.D. Consadine predicted in his 1981 *Village Voice* review of REO Speedwagon's megaplatinum *Hi Infidelity,* power ballads' big innovation wound up being guitars serving purposes violins used to in pre-rock days. Consadine rightly compared Gary Richrath's distorted soloing in "Keep on Loving You" to a Nelson Riddle string arrangement, but his warning that music like this might result in a generation that would mistake the mere presence of a particular guitar and drum sound for rock'n'roll "substance" seems pretty darn quaint by now (especially since that's exactly what *punkrock* wound up leading to, in pre-Nirvana college-radio days). Powerchords have *always* been mere hooks, even in Motörhead songs; power balladry simply helped make the chords *expressive* again. Still, J.D. was no doubt prophetic in figuring the sound could unite heretofore opposed AOR and MOR factions. (It was "compeletely inoffensive," as rock critics enjoy saying—by which they invariably mean it offended them!) By 1982, critic Ken Tucker was pegging Diesel's "Sausalito Summernight" and Loverboy's "Working for the Weekend" as prototype light metal: "a creation of the u/c [for 'unlistenable crap'] marketplace."

Truth is, the first Loverboy album was a very strange animal—as weird as, to pick a better-remembered example also from 1980, the Stones' *Emotional Rescue.* The beat was hopped-up AOR-going-disco, often favoring synth over guitars; the vocals were tumbling suburban new wave. The words could be heard as so-what macho crotch-rock "freedom" arias, but to me they come off more like Flashdance-disco escape-from-working-class-rut, with sexual preferences open to interpretation: "On my knees making love to whoever I please" indeed. Minimalist Philip Glass whorls swell into deep phallic funk, beats pogo around in a jumpy/hyper dance-oriented fashion, riffs work as rhythm, and there's incomparably sprightly stopoffs at Paul Rodgers AOR-blues muscle, Rush-like pomp, trash-organ garage rock, hiccupping Cheap Trick-gone-Elvis glamabilly, full-on goofily-snotnosed snide-nihilistic bubble-punk ("Teenage Overdose") not far from what Loverboy's fellow Vancouverites the Young Canadians and Pointed Sticks were doing at the time. After the last song seems to end, there's even a freebie Police-ska parody/tribute, complete with a Sting imitation and could-be-jazz sax solo.

I wrote in my college newspaper back then that the worst song was probably "The Kid is Hot Tonite," which tries to be un-trendy by making fun of new wave, all the more despicable since Loverboy's press kit described *them* as sounding "new wavey" and since they wore color-coordinated play clothes, like those Garanimal-brand kids' ones where parents just had to match the giraffes or hippos. (On five people: three red pants, three red shirts, one black shirt, one black pants, one yellow shirt, one yellow pants. But only two members wear the *same* color shirt and pants—a brain-teaser!) "Maybe they figure they can have their cake and eat it, too," I complained. "And, due largely to the gullibility of the record-buying public, they probably can."

I was a total retard then. (In rock'n'roll, wanting to have your cake and eat it too is the *whole point!*) I also sandblasted REO Speedwagon so bad I got threats on my life over the phone. My lead: "REO Speedwagon, the epitome of Midwestern heavy metal crud, visited the Hearnes Center Saturday night and delivered less than two hours of monotonous, compromised, and gutless music." (And this was Missouri, with REO's Champaign, Illinois homebase within hogcalling distance.) But in 1985, I heard "Can't Fight this Feeling" on the radio, and like the millions of other music lovers who made it number-one for three weeks, I knew it was something special. Maritime Michael-Row-Your-Boat-Ashore melody, marchtime drums, acoustics giving way to electrics making the song grow bigger and better, Kevin Cronin drawling about love making him throw up on the floor and come crashing through your door, and enough strings to suggest they'd taken J.D. Consadine's "Keep on Loving You" comments to heart—hey, if this is confusing form with substance, count me in!

Besides being the blueprint for hillbilly Poison ballads like "I Won't Forget You" and "Every Rose has its Thorn," "Can't Fight this Feeling" would seem to be one of two records that truly signified the coming world domination of the power-ballad genre. The other one was John Waite's "Missing You," a chart-topper in the summer of 1984. John had a new-wavey brushcut and used to sing for the Babys, whose proto-Def-

Lep twixt-AOR-and-powerpop rip-it-up yielded some excellent hits in the late '70s, most notably "Isn't it Time," "Every Time I Think of You," and the hilarious "Midnight Rendezvous." "Missing You" basically updated "Every Time I Think of You"'s wimp cool with immaculate mall-blues strums taken from "Every Breath You Take" by the Police, plus teardrop irony in the tradition of George Jones's "She Thinks I Still Care" and glorious premonitions of communication breakdown along the AT&T lines. Waite sounded tense and intense, like these worries were just piling up in his head making him shiver. And he turned the extra trick of involving individual radio listeners: he told us he was "sending out a signal tonight" (*a la* Golden Earring's "Radar Love," the Five Americans' "Western Union," Donna Summer's "On the Radio.")

There was no doubt in my mind that John Waite *meant* what he was singing in "Missing You" AT THE EXACT MOMENT HE WAS SINGING THE SONG. And even though I now realize he was just a guy standing in the studio trying to maximize his record company's investment, the song still hits me like the God's Honest Truth. Trust it, or forget it— same with, say, how you have to believe the finality of Jani Lane sighing "I don't think I'm gonna love you anymore" in Warrant's 1991 end-of-the-lost-highway ballad "I Saw Red." Sometimes you just have to go ahead and accept the mystique, believe in Santa Claus.

Anyway, I wasn't the only one who felt that way, because "Missing You" begat the deluge. At the end of 1984 came Foreigner's gigantic "I Want to Know What Love Is," a genre unto itself (the only *gospel*-metal power ballad), an awe-inspiring fusion of European and African-American church musics with a healthy dose of easy-listening violins to boot. And before we knew it, love letters came in from Mötley Crüe, Poison, Vixen, Bryan Adams, Whitesnake, Richard Marx, Cheap Trick, Slaughter, Firehouse, all those guys. (Where do you draw the line: Mr. Mister? Tiffany? Tommy Page?) By decade's end, guitar rock in every other conceivable corner was turning itself into either nostalgia or a stupid inside joke, but to the people in (and fans of) the haircut-metal franchises hogging Dial MTV time, rock'n'roll still *mattered*. And when the trustworthy ones tracked down a workable lyric and hook, they believed so hard that they made me believe too, at least for as long as I was singing along.

In 1988, Lita Ford's "Kiss Me Deadly"'s title sketched a lineage through the punk band Generation X to Mickey Spillane, and the words snuck the phrase "gettin' high" onto quality car radios everywhere. The hooks skimmed the shit off Bruce Springsteen's "Thunder Road" only to find a Ronettes mood underneath; the song also had Lita borrowing ten bucks from Dad and getting in a fight instead of getting laid. And there was Jon Bon Jovi, turning into Levi Stubbs with the chorus and Pete Townshend with the screams at the end of his souped-up rustic slow dance "I'll Be There for You." Heroically swirling fuzzgloss bent apologetic platitudes toward paralysis until Jon finally let on that his honey packed her bags because he forgot her birthday (sort of like what happens to Molly Ringwald in *Sixteen Candles*.) But those five words he swore to us also worked as a pledge of loyalty to Bon Jovi fans. Jon was a man with a vision, and his muse and conscience wouldn't let him walk the other way.

Summer, 1989: Mike Tramp of the Long Island shag troupe White Lion stands up in the middle of "Little Fighter" and screeches "don't stop believing!," and the fact that he's stolen the sentiment from Journey only makes it more credible. In the winter, Jani Lane mixes string parts and "Strawberry Fields Forever" lines about blue suburban skies into Warrant's touching boulevard ballad "Heaven," and reveals every power-balladeer's modest but hardly insignificant goal: "I don't want to be the king of the world as long as I'm the hero of this little girl."

And he was. At least until "More than Words" by Boston's too-respectable-for-their-own-good Extreme came along in 1991 and tried to turn power ballads into folk-harmony trivia. If Nazareth started it all by *covering* the Everly Brothers, Extreme ended it all by trying to *be* the Everly Brothers. Mr. Big's late-'91 "To Be With You" was more of the same, which meant people were missing the point—the best power ballads had always been more like halfway (never *more* than halfway!) to the *blues*. Cinderella's "Coming Home" was bluesier than Faster Pussycat's "House of Pain," which was bluesier than "Sweet Child O' Mine," which was bluesier than Skid Row's convertible ode "I Remember You," which was bluesier than "Heaven," but they all shared a certain loose and lush spirit: they were wimpy white altar boys in love, but they weren't *anorexic*. The real blame might go to Tesla, whose 1990 *Five Man Acoustical Jam* was (paradoxically or oxymoronically or just-plain-moronically enough) the first heavy metal album with no electric guitars.

Or maybe it started with the mid-'80s trend for metal bands to do epic songs cowboy-philosophers could roast marshmallows to over an open flame ("Every Rose Had its Thorn," Bon Jovi's "Wanted Dead or Alive," Ratt's "Wanted Man," Tesla's "Modern Day Cowboy," Def Lep's "Billy's Got a Gun"). Which can be traced back through earlier AOR campfire-fugitive hymns by Thin Lizzy ("Cowboy Song"), Elton John ("Roy Rogers"), Mountain ("Theme From An Imaginary Western"), Eddie Money ("Gimme Some Water"), Aerosmith ("Draw the Line"), Styx ("Renegade"), Bob Seger ("Jesse James"), Bad Company ("Bad Company"), Billy Joel ("Close to the Borderline" and "The Ballad of Billy the Kid"), Christopher Cross ("Ride Like the Wind"), and Alice Cooper ("Desperado"), not to mention the whole idea of a band called the James Gang. '70s hard-rock country moves (Aerosmith's "Chip Away at the Stone," the Stones' "Fool to Cry" and "Far Away Eyes," Elton's "Country Comfort," Zep's "Hot Dog") no doubt play a role here as well. And all those old Saturday matinees where American boys learned all about heroes and bad guys and the dirty frontier—the fart scene in 1974's *Blazing Saddles* figures prominently.

Yeah, but cowboy-metal was a laugh and a half, whereas folk-metal is just a tasteful drag (unless the singing's really out of tune). Extreme's and Mr. Big's early-'90s skating-rink ditties castrated power-ballad metal into sexless wispiness, so before long power ballads became the sole province of cowboy music, where old Journey/Kiss fan Garth Brooks hatched repeated ingenious plots to overthrow neotraditional honky-tonk by rethinking it as the spawn of '70s bubbleprogrock melodrama. Whenever I checked in 1992, Garth had three albums in the pop Top 30, and though he didn't acknowledge much debt to country's past, he did climb rope ladders and wear snazzy sport shirts, which was far more interesting. Billy Ray Cyrus, likewise, loaded his 1992 debut *Some Gave All* with electrokeyboarded background sighs, shlock-symphonic piano filigrees, and swoops stolen from half-forgotten Styx hits. Toward the end of "Could've Been Me," he slipped into tear-jerking philosophy ("dreams move on . . . if you wait . . . too long"), and without warning he was Brad Delp in Boston's "Foreplay/Long Time," saying he's gotta keep chasing a dream because time doesn't wait for him, it keeps on going.

In the mid-'90s, teenage girls started swooning over alleged alternative MTV ballads like Blind Melon's "No Rain" and the Red Hot Chili Peppers' "Soul to Squeeze," and only their older sisters who'd graduated to VH-1 still cared about aging '80s pretties of the Bon Jovi/Def Leppard ilk, who by now were scoring with *only* ballads. Their faster cuts never even got released as singles; same went for aging post-Springsteen hacks like Richard Marx, Bryan Adams, and Meat Loaf. By late 1994, *black* guys on acoustic guitars were the hot MTV trend, showing up in videos by Madonna, Eric Clapton, Babyface, and Hootie and the Blowfish. I figured Richie Havens must have been waiting in the wings.

But then next thing I knew, MTV was blessing us with fake grunge bands (Candlebox, Collective Soul, Stone Temple Pilots) who tended to be notably catchier than genuine Sub-Pop-record-label-rooted Seattle grungers of Pearl Jam's and Soundgarden's ilk—since said bandwagon-jumping posers were frequently just converted haircut-metal twerps ripping off the "now sound of the '90s," they had hooks imbedded deep in their psyches no matter how hard they tried to suppress them with fashionable noise. No "real" Seattlites came up with a misfit-anxiety nugget as free from baloney as Ruth Ruth's party-crashing '60s-riffed 1995 shimmy-stomp "Uninvited," or a sex song as flat-out rocking as Collective Soul's concise '70s-riffed 1995 chugger "Gel." (In 1996, however, bitter ex-power-balladeers Warrant did combine "Gel"'s guitar swagger with vocal growling straight out of Pearl Jam's toughest tune "Not For You"; they named the track "A.Y.M." for "Angry Young Man," and the words were a devastating parody of all things Seattle: "Gennnnn-eration X/Weeeeee are complex...")

As for Candlebox, you would've fallen for their bittersweet 1994 ballad smash "Far Behind" if you were in junior high, too: a girl's fair-weather friends let her so-called-life fall apart, her boyfriend can't bear to watch her suffer, so they all leave each other far behind. (Actually, the singer claimed it was about some buddy of his who had overdosed on drugs, but I never heard it that way.) The guitar solo twists up, up, up, and Kevin Martin's warbling climaxes by growing up to be Axl Rose.

Like "Molly," the big cute fancy dramatic Molly Ringwald tribute a summer later from Detroit one-hit-grungers Sponge, "Far Behind" was basically about (in Sponge's poetic words) "16 candles down the drain." Which might explain what a candlebox is for, unless it's what their teen-girl fans hold up in the air when the band plays "Far Behind" live. Cigarette lighters will never die, but we'll always need sad music to keep us warm.

The Great Sellout Debate

"Selling out" (by starting to do power ballads or otherwise) is a hallowed pop tradition. In fact, rock'n'roll's first big sellout was rock'n'roll itself! "In the fifties, the critics of mass culture regarded rock and roll as one of its horrors," Ellen Willis wrote in "Can a Man Who Hates the Jukebox Love the Beatles?," her early-'70s answer essay to sociologist Charles Reich's *The Greening of America.* "In contrast to 'real people's music' like blues, rock was ersatz, mechanical, relying for effect on electric guitars and echo chambers rather than the talent or skill of the performer; it was black music watered down to sell to the white middle class; its lyrics substituted teenage fantasy for real emotion; it was cynically foisted on youth by profit-hungry businessmen who bribed disc jockeys to push it; its popularity showed that we were passive consumers whose taste had been corrupted; and so on." So Milli Vanilli and Vanilla Ice have something in common with Elvis after all, see?

Willis goes on to admit that said critics' observations were mainly *right*—early rock hits were written by songwriters no less professional (Lieber and Stoller) and no less teenage (Chuck Berry) than Irving Berlin. Producers screwed around with voices and instruments in the studio until they got a saleable sound, and if that meant their audience was brainwashed, so be it. But as Willis points out, the profit motive made rock *better.* Short songs, tight arrangements, and gimmicky hooks helped sell records, but also made the music more immediate, and constituted a more vigorous revolt against outmoded urbane standards. I submit that very little has changed since the beginning, or at least less than most people admit—Vanilla Ice probably was more responsible for "Ice Ice Baby" than Frankie Ford, a squeaky white teen hunk from Mississippi with similar appeal, was responsible for his comparably furious 1959 black-dance-music hit "Sea Cruise." Ace Records president Johnny Vincent took the basic "Sea Cruise" track from his charges Huey Smith and the Clowns; Frankie just sang over it. At least Ice stole his music (from

Queen and David Bowie) and words (allegedly from a black college fraternity) himself!

Basically, "selling out" means changing your music, usually by opening it up to previously unpermitted sounds, to reach a new, larger audience and perhaps to challenge the cult that used to love you. You do it knowing full well that your new fans might not be as devoted as your old ones, but it has no necessary connection to your music's quality. To assume evil corporations water down music by fiddling with artists' intentions is to fall prey to the fallacy that artists have any idea what makes their music good in the first place. Lots of underground bands *improve* by selling out, but that's usually just because they were so awful in the first place that they've got nowhere to go but up (the Cult when they went "metal," Soul Asylum when they started sounding like Bon Jovi's *Slippery When Wet* minus synthesizers). Others (Pere Ubu, Sonic Youth, Pavement) fall flat on their faces, mainly because their pop moves place them in a realm they've got no aptitude for, and the Warrants and Taylor Daynes of the world make their hooks sound trite and inefficiently arty by comparison. (Well, I guess that means those bands didn't sell out *enough*. Pavement's early Burger-King-drive-through-loudspeaker imitations on the tiny Drag City label were better than their later stuff on Atlantic-distributed Matador because the Drag City records were so noisy you couldn't hear the hokey words or ho-hum vocals. Their EPs and singles work better than their albums because you don't have time to become completely bored by their inability to keep a beat. *Newsweek*'s John Leland might say bands like Pavement are "obsessed with surfaces in the CD age." I might too, if I knew what it meant).

Altering your sound isn't the only way to piss off fans and influence people, of course. You can suddenly become irresponsible like aging Partridge Family psuedo-bassist Danny Bonaduce beating up transvestites or New Kids on the Block urinating in airplane aisles or former Nickelodeon Network kids'-TV star and dance-pop teen Alanis Morissette yelling fellatio in a crowded movie theater ("You Oughta Know," 1995). Or you can suddenly become respectable by doing benefit concerts or going through drug rehab in order to make bad Aerosmith albums.

Plus, pop music has a long, proud tradition of selling out to the advertising world. The Memphis Jug Band used to play on the backs of trucks advertising Colonial Bread and Shlitz Beer in the '30s, and everybody from Jan & Dean to Ray Charles to the Four Tops to the Jefferson Airplane made soft drink commercials in the '60s, and in 1970 leftist ranters the MC5 sang that "rock'n'roll music is the best advertisin'." So when people like John Mellencamp whine about the evils of corporate sponsorship, claiming "there's no battle zone anymore: it's not us against them," somebody really ought to give them a quick history lesson. (Mellencamp used to give free plugs to Tastee-Freez chili dogs and Bobby Brooks jeans in his songs back when he was called John Cougar.)

Directly and indirectly, one of rock'n'roll's main reasons for existence has always been to sell Clearasil and new cars. In his 1958 song "Green Christmas," anti-rock satirist Stan Freberg sang cynically about decking the halls with advertising; he went on in the early '60s to *work* in advertising, spinning jingles for Chun King Chinese food, Sunsweet Prunes, Jeno's Pizza Rolls, and so on. His commercials won 21 Clio Awards. Anyway, I think it's about time somebody documented a History of Rock'n'Roll Sellouts. I elect myself.

The Big Sellouts

Vernon Dalhart: Conservatory-trained Texas opera singer who hits on hard times in New York in the early '20s trades in Puccini for hillbilly music. Covers Henry Whitter's "The Wreck of the Old '97." It sells six million copies, the best-selling 78-rpm country record ever. In photos he looks uncannily like Garth Brooks, who would grow up on opera numbers like "Bohemian Rhapsody" and "Dust in the Wind" a half-century later.

Louis Armstrong: Starts out by helping invent Dixieland jazz and worldbeat (with "King of the Zulus" and "Cornet Chop Suey"), and leads the way toward R&B and rock'n'roll by using zesty hooks and fast dance rhythms in a small-band format in rambunctious Hot Five and Hot Seven songs like "Georgia Grind" and "Muskrat Ramble"; by 1929, no black musician anywhere is more popular. Winds up four decades later doing happyface swill like "Hello, Dolly!" and "What a Wonderful World," succumbing to icky European-bred song structure.

Memphis Jug Band: Forced to keep up to date with changing trends, they sell out from earlier blues-jug novelties to scat-jazz hokum in 1934. A major improvement—they started swinging faster, with more yowzah; "Little Green Slippers" and "Insane Crazy Blues" might be their wildest music ever. This was an especially canny switch given how most Southern blues was turning so bland during the early-to-mid-'30s (maybe because of the depression, who knows)—in terms of energy, humor, hooks, rhythm, strangeness, and vocal personality, the music Robert Johnson (who debuted in 1936) made was no match for the post-minstrel/pre-blues traveling-show dance-novelty songsterism that peaked circa the mid-to-late '20s (Beans Hambone, Bogus Ben Covington, the Memphis Shieks, etc.). White hobos like the Anglin Brothers ("Southern Whoopee Song," 1938) and Wesley Long ("They are Wild Over Me," 1936) seem to be the main people who kept silly craziness from completely dying off during the lean years—they were the Beastie Boys of their day.

Elvis Presley: Sacrifices rockabilly power for pop slickness when he moves from Sun Records to RCA in 1956; sells out later to bossa nova, Stephen Foster stuff, patriotic stuff, Christian crap, show tunes, ballads based on "O Sole Mio," dance numbers about clams, you name it. He defined rock'n'roll by being the furthest thing from a "purist" rock'n'roll has ever known.

Sam Cooke: Sings in choirs for years, then makes his sacred-to-secular sellout, first under the assumed name "Dale Cook" for Specialty Records in 1956; a year later, tops pop charts. Then at Harlem Square Club in 1963 he sells out from pop proto-soul to hard rock (or maybe his smooth soul records were *always* a sellout of his wild live performances.) Then he gets murdered in a motel room. Sam set the stage for such later sellouts-from-God as the Staple Singers, Stryper, and especially Amy Grant (who wound up 1991's *Heart in Motion* praising convicted defrocked heretic astronomer Galileo). All of these performers got better; too bad they're doomed to be engulfed in demonic flames for eternity. What a price to pay for success. (And in fact, *any* kid in a church choir who grows up only to wind up singing pop music is a sellout to his or her true heritage!)

The Beatles: Abandoned original grimy Liverpool hoodlum audience by adopting image as adorably well-shorn Little-Lord-Fauntleroys-next-door who Shea Stadium teenyboppers or your mom or Leonard Bernstein could love. Became more popular than Jesus Christ, turned rock respectable, changed the world.

Bob Dylan: The most scandalous sellout in rock history, July 25, 1965—wears motorcycle jacket and fancy boots at the Newport Folk Festival, starts playing his electric guitar, backed by the Paul Butterfield Blues Band. It's so loud the acoustic-purist audience can't hear him. They boo him off stage.

Gilberto Gil: In Saõ Paulo, Brazil in 1968, his performance crashes to a Dylan-at-Newport-style conclusion when he demonstrates how bossa nova is due to evolve into *Tropicalismo*, a multi-hybridized and partially ironic world-Beatlemaniac pretension-movement addicted to history, bricolage, racial pride, campy tangos, and zodiac signs. Humorless leftists tell him to get lost, then rightists who figure he's subversive toss him into solitary confinement for three years. As you'd expect, he becomes a legend, then a superstar, then a city councilman.

San Francisco: Greil Marcus in the *San Francisco Chronicle* in 1987, on the bands of the Summer of Love: "Commercialism was condemned and selling out was a horror, but every San Francisco rock'n'roller had to decide whether to sell out or change the world, and most decided they could do both at once." For example Jefferson Airplane, who did Levi's commercials, then went on to sell out to future spaced-out generations by changing their name to Jefferson Starship, then just plain Starship, then John Starship Mellencamp, then M.C. Starship Hammer, then just plain Starship Hammer. In 1987, I heard either Grace Slick or a perfect facsimile doing a radio ad for Flintstones vitamins: "One pill's shaped like Barney, and one pill's shaped like Fred . . ."

Albert Ayler: Free-jazz noise-saxist has sense enough to try some R&B on his late '60s *New Grass* album. It sucks anyhow.

10cc: English arch-popsters give up angular ironic cult-world shlock for straightforward ironic realworld shlock with "I'm Not in Love" in 1975 and "The Things We Do For Love" in 1977.

Blondie: New wave garage-retroactivists (who'd already paved the way for late '80s bubblesalsa with "The Attack of the Giant Ants" on their 1976 debut album) "go Eurodisco" with "Heart of Glass" in 1979 and "Call Me" in 1980, then "go rap" with "Rapture" in 1981. All three climb real high on the charts.

Lionel Richie: Jumps ship from funk-rock Commodores to solo success and Fantasy Island calypso and red-clay country-politan soul ballads in 1981. Rapper Def Jef once put a picture of the "12 apostles of funk" on an album cover, guys like James Brown and George Clinton; he said Lionel would be Judas.

Herbie Hancock: Jazz-fusion twerp makes electro move with "Rockit," 1983, actually managing to weasel his way onto MTV's heavy rotation. He's still twerpy, but now almost *likably* twerpy.

Gloria Estefan and Celine Dion: Torch-dance divas gradually switch from respective foreign languages (Spanish and French) to reach U.S. audience in late '80s and early '90s, softening and lightening their original semi-ethnicity for the same reason.

Soul Asylum, Urge Overkill, Green Day, Cracker, Rancid, etc.: Ensembles like these graduated from indie-rock insularity to pop stardom in the mid-'90s, and all of them had old fans who thought they turned "too rock" and wished they weren't on MTV.

Lollapalooza: The traveling-carnival-tacked-onto-a-rock-festival was pretty much always a heavy metal fest; it was even founded by art-metal airhead Perry Farrell, whose Jane's Addiction were logged in the early '90s Lolla loud-guitar annals alongside Alice in Chains, Pearl Jam, Soundgarden, L7, Rage Against the Machine, Primus, Nine Inch Nails, Ministry, Faith No More, Red Hot Chili Peppers, and Smashing Pumpkins. So when accusations of integrity-loss started flying upon Metallica's addition to the 1996 roster, the only conceivable explanations were fishing-for-headlines, conspiracy theory, or short-term memory loss.

Chemical Brothers: Trip-hop (or something) phenoms compromise sound-effect-instrumental integrity in late 1996 by putting out a boring record ("Setting Sun") whereon some Oasis idiot recites actual sentences. So propeller-headed kids rename them the "Comical Brothers" instead, albeit cutting them a little slack (this rule works with D.J. Shadow too) seeing how they have "really cool CD covers."

Chuck Eddy: I've sold out several times—when I switched from mostly writing about noisy independent-label post-hardcore bands to mostly writing about Debbie Gibson, when I unsuccessfully sued the Beastie Boys for breaking into my hotel room, when I agreed to write advertorial copy for Columbia Records about bad speedmetal groups I can't even remember the names of. For the right price, I'll write like the most vacant hack on earth.

Records That Say Selling Out is a Virtue

Louise Tobin and Benny Goodman "There'll Be Some Changes Made," 1939. New walk, new talk, new name. Strut your stuff.

Chuck Berry "Sweet Little Sixteen," 1958. "Tomorrow morning, she'll have to change her trend." Like it's only natural.

The Kingston Trio *Sold Out*, 1960. These guys sold out folk-revival stodginess years before Dylan—they did lots of fast dance-beat music (hulas, mariachis, square dances, flamencos), tossed silly jokes into murder ballads, and could sound as crazed as rock'n'roll. This album topped the pop charts for twelve weeks.

Lesley Gore "You Don't Own Me," 1964. Imagine she's a pop star (which she was), singing to her *audience* (who really knows?).

Bob Dylan "Positively Fourth Street," 1965. Supposedly directed at Irwin Silber, from the folkzine *Sing Out!*, who'd complained that Bob's move toward the mainstream at Newport meant he'd "lost contact with the people," meaning, of course, *Sing Out!*'s people. So Bob tells Irwin that he used to run in that crowd but not anymore, that any faith Irwin claimed to lose was never there in the first place. Pro-sellout was a Dylan theme at the time: "They say sing while you slave and I just get bored," "He not busy being born is busy dying." (And in "Bob Dylan's Blues" he says most modern folk songs are written in Tin Pan Alley, but not this one—it's from the U.S.A.!)

The Seekers "Georgy Girl," 1966. About releasing the other Georgy trapped deep inside every one of us: "don't be so scared of changing and rearranging yourself." Dress like a slut, babe!

Rolling Stones "Sold Out," 1967. An apparently unhappy song off the Stones' first somewhat wimpy album, *Between the Buttons*, and not long after they'd begun doing violin, dulcimer, and sitar ballads. So maybe they were just on the defensive.

The Who *The Who Sell Out*, 1967. Complete with homemade radio commercials, and therefore a predecessor of: (1) Run D.M.C.'s 1986 "My Adidas" (recorded only two years after they rapped that they didn't want Calvin Klein's name on their behinds); (2) Einstürzende Neubauten's 1988 "Jordache" (subtitled "sell out"); (3) Yvonne Chaka Chaka's 1990 "Umqomboti" (a beer commercial, basically, whether the title's really the name of the African beer brand the lyrics say it is or not—bombastic soul-disco singer beckons us to come and drink her magic beer, Soweto chorus chants the title in the background); and (4) Nirvana's 1991 "Smells Like Teen Spirit" (named for a brand of deodorant, appearing on an album with a drowning baby chasing a dollar bill on its cover, sung by guy who thought it was real daring to put "Corporate Magazines Still Suck" on his T-shirt when he got photographed for the cover of *Rolling Stone*). On the other hand, in 1949 New Orleans pianist Professor Longhair had recorded a song called "Hadacol Bounce," named for a brand of over-the-counter old-age medicine, and even though Mercury Records deleted it real soon after its release to avoid legal tangles, it might be considered the grandad of all of these.

Mothers of Invention *We're Only in it for the Money*, 1968. Might be true—they certainly weren't in it for the music!

Mark Lindsay "Arizona," 1970. Former Paul Revere and the Raiders singer (i.e., a garage band guy selling out to adult contemporary pop) tells his new hippiechick girlfriend to get rid of her rainbow shades, hobo shoes, and Indian braids, and stop acting like such a teenybopper and follow him instead.

Dr. Hook "The Cover of 'Rolling Stone'," 1973. The price of beauty and truth: "10,000 dollars a show." He's got his dad driving the limo, teenage blue-eyed groupies, Indian gurus, all the friends money can buy. He's lovin' every minute of it.

Glen Campbell "Rhinestone Cowboy," 1975. "There's been a load of compromisin' on the road to my horizon." No shit:

like Leon Russell, Seals and Crofts, and David Gates of the group Bread, Glen started out by playing on wild early '60s rock'n'roll hits by Jan & Dean, Freddie Cannon, and the Crystals. Then he and his fellow session musicians went solo and mellowed out.

Wild Cherry "Play That Funky Music," 1976. The true story of white rock boogieboys converting, then converting the world, to disco: "First it wasn't easy, changing rock'n'rollin' minds."

Lynyrd Skynyrd "Am I Losin'," 1976. About being abandoned by old friends who think dollar signs in your eyes have turned you phoney. Ronnie Van Zant sounds as uncomfortable with stardom, and as doomed, as Kurt Cobain ever would. He died in 1977.

Crystal Gayle "Don't It Make My Brown Eyes Blue," 1977. Nerf-country with a melody recommended to Axl Rose, about the effect of contact lenses on black singers' pop-crossover ambitions.

Cheap Trick "He's A Whore," 1977. "I'll do anything for money." And anyone who's heard "The Flame," their awful outside-written number-one single from 1988, knows they weren't fooling.

Joe Walsh "Life's Been Good," 1978. Former Eagle drives his Mazerati at 185, charges hotel damage to his C.P.A., displays his gold records: "Everybody's so different, I haven't changed."

Public Image Ltd. "Public Image," 1979 ("I'm not the same as when I began") and "Albatross," 1980 ("getting rid of the albatross, still the spirit of '68"). Johnny Rotten kills punk.

The Fools *Sold Out*, 1980. This Boston bar band fares fine here, but where they *really* sold out was a year later on *Heavy Mental*, as hard-rocking an album as new wave produced. In "Around the Block," Mike Girard wails through his whine like Axl Rose before his time.

Minor Threat "Cashing In," 1983. As sarcastic as "The Cover of 'Rolling Stone'," and these clean-living D.C. punks' most powerful moment despite itself—turns into homesickness out of *The Wizard of Oz*, then into classical minimalism.

But they feel guilty about it: the proof is Fugazi, the self-righteous monk-cloister community singer Ian MacKaye formed after this one collapsed, where he made staying-indie-no-matter-what his life's calling.

Garth Brooks "Shameless," 1991. "I'm shameless when you need to be satisfied." Compromising, he's just decided, is cool.

Michael Jackson "Black or White," 1991. About why Karma Chameleon Michael's color doesn't matter, and how pious hypocrites (John Fogerty in "Soda Pop," the Pretenders in "How Much Did You Get For Your Soul?," brother Jermaine in "Word to the Badd!!") kick dirt in his eye. Coinciding with his lucrative Pepsi endorsements, Michael's racial/facial makeover was an even more visible sellout than Dylan in '65. In "Black or White" he's like John Lydon in "Public Image," asking his old fans whether they only loved him for his hair color.

Cracker "Get Off This," 1993. Having given up dumb bowling jokes for Peter Frampton voicebox hooks, ex-Camper-Van-Beethovens defend their honor against titty-ringed grunge brats who liked them back "when no one knew your name and you were pompous."

Records That Say Selling Out is a Sin

Stan Freberg "The Great Pretender," 1956. A Little-Richard-like screamer instructs a beleaguered jazz pianist to play the same notes over and over again if he wants to get paid; if he doesn't, he can forget about teenagers buying any of his music.

Shangri-Las "Out in the Streets," 1965. "He don't do the wild things like he did before." (Tone-Loc would interpret that to mean he's now celibate.) He even stopped wearing black boots, and these three streetwise chicks hold themselves responsible.

The Byrds "So You Want to be a Rock 'N' Roll Star," 1967. Their reaction to the Monkees, supposedly: "You sell your soul to the company, who is waiting there to sell plasticware."

Mott the Hoople "All the Way from Memphis," 1973. Eternal myth, or the truth?: "As your name gets hot, your heart grows cold." Rephrased by Guns N' Roses in "Right Next Door to Hell," 1991: "As your arms get shorter, your pockets get deeper."

Parliament *Funkentelechy vs. the Placebo Syndrome*, 1977. To George Clinton, if you were black and didn't own any Frank Zappa records, you weren't worth much. I'll take the placebo.

The Clash "White Man in Hammersmith Palais," 1978. A great self-righteous reggae tune about sellouts of all different kinds: black musicians adopting Vegas-revue stage shows, punks licking boots and wearing suits, British voters inching toward fascism.

The Clash "Death or Glory," 1980. Yeah, them again, bitter and fork-tongued: "He who fucks nuns will later join the church."

The Brains "Money Changes Everything," 1980. Rocking Georgia new wavers, moving from an unknown indie to a major label: "We think we know what we're doing, but we don't pull the strings."

Malcolm X with Keith Leblanc "No Sell Out," 1983. One of the first pretentious hip-hop records to sample a dead person.

Shannon "Let the Music Play," 1984. The social context of being let down: when Shannon's beloved alters his music, the world changes with it, and he winds up with a new partner.

Public Enemy "Caught, Can We Get a Witness?," 1988. Chuck D ends this rap with a roundtable discussion debating whether his group should sell out; unfortunately, they decide not to.

Cynthia "Change on Me," 1987. "Out in the Streets" updated as electric salsa: "Why did you have to change on me?"

Too Much Joy "Hugo," 1988. Overprecious powerpop about the Clash making *Combat Rock* and Lou Reed hawking motor scooters: "We renounce what we once loved to prove that we can rise above."

3rd Bass "Pop Goes The Weasel," 1991. "So You Want to be a Rock 'N' Roll Star" updated as Vanilla Ice criticism (really envy), catchier than it deserves to be. 3rd Bass pretended to be the authentic white face of black entertainment, but really they just toed the party line and dressed as old homeless men.

Rancid "Disorder and Disarray," 1995. Friendly boys with mean mohawks imagine their crucifixion by hand-shaking businessmen offering big numbers: "Say goodbye when you see me sign."

Blues Death

To my knowledge, no rock song (no good one, anyway) has ever sold out the whole farm by denouncing *all* quests for moral integrity and equating roots music—by which I specifically mean the blues—with garbage. Still, a few have come close: in her top-ten 1976 disco hit "Turn the Beat Around," Vickie Sue Robinson tells a blues player to keep on playing blues chords, "but you see I've made up my mind about it, got to be the *rhythm*, no doubt about it." Similarly, in her 1992 hit "Good for Me," Christpop superstar Amy Grant thanks her guardian angel thusly: "When I start to sing the blues, you pull out my dancing shoes."

Annoyingly pretentious rappers the Jungle Brothers opened their 1987 "What U Waitin' 4" (one of only two memorable songs they did in their whole career) with a joyful command to "freak or hustle" because said Bros "ain't in the mood to be singin' no blues"—a wholesale rejection of rap music's distant ancestor in favor of, well, its more *recent* ancestor: disco!

Nonetheless, for me, no post-old-school rappers ever came closer to matching the spirit of disco-era hip-hop than a pair of teenaged Miami girls separately named Tigra and Bunny and collectively named L'Trimm. In 1988, they made cars go boom with *Drop That Bottom*, one of my five favorite rap albums ever. The track "Heaven Sent" (over a beat that gets more carbonation out of the Tom Tom Club's "Genius of Love" than Grandmaster Flash and the Furious Five did in "It's Nasty" or Mariah Carey and Ol' Dirty Bastard did in "Fantasy") lays out L'Trimm's own Book-of-Genesis-type theory on how the world was created. They say "God" did it; they even thank him in their liner notes.

But it took *humans* to murder the blues: back when "leaves were high fashion," L'Trimm say, "the world was full of mystery, oral harp action." Everybody wanted to have parties, but harps just weren't funky enough, so instead everybody just chilled and ate and hummed the same tunes over and over again. But when the drum was invented, history was born anew! I guess it's possible these words are meant to argue African drums' primacy over European harps. But what they're really doing is affirming rock or funk or whatever as progress from the blues, which after all is where "oral harp action"—i.e., harmonica solos—rule the roost. In rock and rap, which usually view the blues as something superior to be revered, this qualifies as downright subversive. If L'Trimm had come right out with a track entitled "The Blues Sucks, It's Boring And Too Slow, And It Doesn't Have Enough Instruments," they would've made exactly the same point.

On *Goodbye Yellow Brick Road*, Elton John boos the blues *twice*: in "Your Sister Can't Twist" ("Throw away them records 'cause the blues are dead") and the title cut ("This boy's too young to be singin' the blues"). Then in "Right Next Door To Hell," the first of three or four songs on Guns N' Roses' 1991 *Use Your Illusion* to actually *refer* to *Yellow Brick Road*, Axl Rose theorizes that "when your innocence dies you'll be singing the blues." In other words, blues belong to *old people*, get it?

Garden of Eden Rock

The Garden of Eden was the *first* place anybody's innocence died. Son-of-a-preacher-man Axl Rose knows the place well— On *Use Your Illusion I*, he even wrote three songs about it: "The Garden," "Garden of Eden," and "Bad Apples." These songs are mostly art-metal shtick; one has an Alice Cooper guest vocal that's supposed to sound ominous but of course doesn't, plus flowery backup flourishes. Alice discusses losing virginity; Axl likens Eden to a graveyard. Then in "Bad Apples," referring back to the Osmond Brothers' "One Bad Apple," he sells fruit like the Great Depression's back. No great shakes, except one line as the tempo speeds toward hardcore overdrive in "Garden of Eden": "It's not a problem you can stop, it's rock'n'roll."

If Axl's right, maybe rock'n'roll *dates* back to the Garden of Eden; maybe it's something *in* us, an invincible kind of fear or rage or violent energy or mirth. I doubt it, but Neil Young might not. "Rock'n'roll is reckless abandon," he told *Written in My Soul* author Bill Flanagan in the late '80s. "Rock'n'roll is the *cause* of country and blues." (Similarly, the Bellamy Brothers' "Old Hippie" and David Allen Coe's "Willie, Waylon, and Me" suggest how rock might have evolved *into* country after the '60s ended. And in the '80s, Neil Young temporarily gave up loud guitars for first country, then blues.) Thing is, if your rhythm sections are as wimpy as Neil's have always been, maybe your abandon isn't reckless *enough*. In 1990, Virgin Records co-president Michael Ayeroff told *Rolling Stone* the following: "If you started learning about it ten years ago, rock'n'roll is MTV. Madonna is rock'n'roll. Neil Young isn't." Ayeroff went on to take back his words somewhat, saying he'd always liked Neil and always will, but I think he was right the first time.

Anyway, rock has been fascinated with Eden since the very beginning, or earlier. In their beatific 1959 hit "I Only Have Eyes For You," which had actually been a bigger hit for some unknown named Ben Selvin in 1934, Chicago doowop fivesome the Flamingoes expressed existential confusion: "I don't know if we're in a garden, or a crowded avenue." (I pick the garden.) The same year, in "Way Down Yonder in New Orleans," pounded out as an homage to Fats Domino–style piano boogie, white teen dream Freddie Cannon likened Crescent City to the Garden of Eden; the song was first written as jazz, down yonder in 1922.

Rock lost its innocence in the mid-'60s, when Bob Dylan and the Beatles turned it into art, which worked okay for a month or two. Inside the Gates of Eden, Dylan theorized, there was no sound, no trials, no truth, no kings. By the end of the decade, some people felt something was missing, so they started taking drugs and stuff. Which worked okay for a month or two.

"Woodstock," written by Joni Mitchell and a hit for both Ian Matthews and Crosby, Stills, Nash, and (Neil!) Young, says, "We've got to get ourselves back to the Garden"; in 1968's "In-A-Gadda-Da-Vida," the prototype San Diego heavy metal band Iron Butterfly kept repeating the mantra "in a Garden of Eden baby" for more than 20 minutes, but never once could they get the pronunciation right (though when the German act Disco Circus covered the song in 1979, they rectified the situation). In "Diamond Dogs," David Bowie *reveled* in his loss of innocence, dared you to be decadent too, to "come out the Garden, baby." By 1976, in "This Ain't The Summer of Love," in the wake of Altamont and Vietnam and Nixon, Long Island metal cynics Blue Öyster Cult just plain gave up: "This ain't the Garden of Eden, there ain't no angels above." So they paid the devil his due.

In 1971, the Osmonds had reassured Eve that one bad apple don't spoil the whole bunch girl. But after that, from Bruce Springsteen's "Adam Raised A Cain" to Aerosmith's "Adam's Apple," rock mostly took it for granted that Eden was a lost cause. To remember its sense of wonder, rock'n'roll had to be born again, as *disco*, of all things. Boney M, a German aggregate fronted by four flying-saucer-uniform-clad West Indian fashion models whose names go uncredited on album covers (and svengalied by Frank Farian, who later achieved infamy as the mastermind behind Milli Vanilli's Memorex), even *sang* about being born again. In

"Children of Paradise," their voices managed a kind of wonder that (fig)-leaves even the Flamingoes in the dust.

The song's melody comes from the black hills of Bavaria, probably; the rhythm is childlike and electronic. The voices sing about having starry eyes full of innocence, about not having a care, "in the early morning glow, and it all began with Adam and Eve." Yet somehow, maybe in the way the sour stratospheric chords keep turning icier, you know a fall from grace is coming.

Suburbia

Dig this: First your jungle is the Garden of Eden, and it's as primitive as can be so therefore it's a perfect state of un-fucked-with bliss. But then (by the Wailers' lovely and dreary 1972 blues-reggae dirge "Concrete Jungle," Grandmaster Flash and the Furious Five complaining "it's like a jungle sometimes" in their watershed 1982 protest-rap "The Message," Axl Rose saying you can have anything you want but you better not take it from him in "Welcome to The Jungle" in 1987) the jungle turns out to be a place of horror and claustrophobia—a city, say. Still like Robinson Crusoe as primitive as can be, so therefore *also* as fucked-up as can be. What makes the paradox plausible is that part of rock'n'roll is that fucked-up-ness *is* perfect bliss; that's where the music's tension (and therefore its power) comes from often as not. Axl Rose escaped *to* the jungle—classmates in Indiana called him a faggot, so he went someplace where he could be free to be different. Thing is, when he gets there, his idea of Uto-pia changes. He wants to go back home to "paradise city, where the grass is green and the girls are pretty." He starts bawling, homesick, "so *faaar* away, so *faaar* away . . ."

Suburbia can be a kind of Garden of Eden, I think, a way to leave the concrete jungle behind, to go back to some-where less *tainted*, clean and bright and vegetated with the right kind of flora but not the wrong kind of fauna, with nothing manmade blocking the sun. The young families who flocked to the outskirts in decades following World War II have been accused of trying to leave behind the same demo-graphic changes that were then giving birth to rock'n'roll: i.e., rural southern blacks moving to urban areas, consorting with young whites. But really, suburbia helped make rock'n'roll possible. If it was the industrial revolution and the institution of public schooling and child labor laws that created the heretofore unheard-of social class known as "teenager," it was postwar affluence that gave those kids lei-sure time. All these prosperous veterans were having kids, and that's who suburban houses were built for; they bought TVs, and teens were suddenly perceived as an open market by advertisers. Who sold them *Mad* magazine and James Dean and Marlon Brando, and most of all Elvis Presley.

Yet suburbia *really* was a garden—an idyllic, peaceful, well-mannered place to do your barbecuing, solipsistic and private from the country club to the enclosed cubicles on the freeway. (Gary Numan, 1980: "Here in my car I feel safest of all, I can lock all my doors.") It was a *dream*, the *American* dream. Robert Fishman titled his late 1980s history of suburbia *Bourgeois Utopias* for the same reason John Lydon equated "shallow spreads of ordered lawns" with heaven in Public Image Ltd.'s 1980 treatise "No Birds"—it didn't even seem like a *real world.*

On the other hand, I've never believed that "white flight" (as it's been labeled) was fully, or even primarily, a racist development—there's nothing especially "racist," I don't think, about wanting your kids to get a better education or breathe better air, nothing racist about wanting to own your own space, or about wanting to feel safe walking down the street at night, or even about wanting to separate the place you live from the place you work. It's just *common sense* is all, and frankly I'm glad my parents had it. For teenagers especially, what could be better than a place where you *run the show*, a place where life really can revolve around station wagons and high school football games, K-Marts and 7-11 parking lots? (One reason white people in New York City have such stupid lopsided tastes in music is because there's no white *kids* there—only miniature adults, and scads of talented young blacks and Latins.)

The one thing I don't get about suburbia is why there's so few great rock songs about it. Well, okay, *all* great rock songs are about it if you ponder 'em enough, and from "Summertime Blues" to "Smokin' in the Boys Room" to "Parents Just Don't Understand," lots of songs *seem* to be set there. Most everything the Dictators and Beastie Boys ever did seemed to be, and they came from New York! But I'm talking *specifics.* "No Birds," Rush's "Subdivisions," and the Monkees' "Pleasant Valley Sunday" (with platitudinous guff about "Status Symbol Land," etc.) are kneejerk (if somewhat sympathetic) dismissals by non-Americans (or at least non-United-States-of-

The Disco as Bigtop. (Note absence of African wild dogs.)

The woodwork squeaks and out come the super freaks.

Shonen Knife: the politics of being a razybone, I mean lazybone.

Suburban C&W career woman K.T. Oslin featherdusts her furniture.

Suburban C&W career woman Lorrie Morgan loads her wheelbarrow.

Repetition visualized: here come those threshers and cigarettes again.

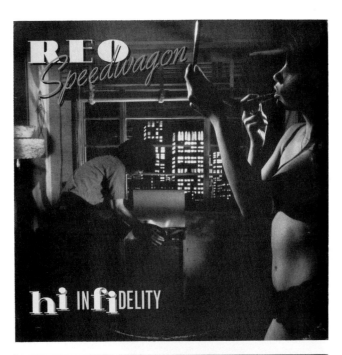

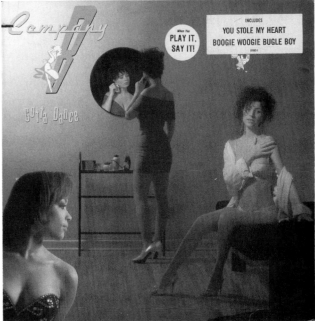

The '80s were obviously an excellent decade for underwear.

Hootie (with Blowfish) . . .

... and Garth: what power ballads hath wrought.

Heroes-of-little-girls Warrant, wondering where the down boys went.

On the other hand, maybe they just meant no tickets were left for sale.

Lionel Richie: funk's Judas crouches in wait for his southbound train.

If Amy Grant starts gasping "Ohmigod!," will it be sinful or sacred?

Laura Branigan (left) and Taylor Dayne (below): when mouths mattered.

Bunny (left) and Tigra of L'Trimm: too cute to be singing the blues.

Americans in Rush's case) who know not of what they speak. So they don't count.

Most self-righteous and suburbophobic song I like anyway: "There But For The Grace of God Go I," written by talented NYC Latino August Darnell, especially in its 1981 salsa-metal version with Kid Creole and the Coconuts, where somebody hunts for a home in a faraway place without Jews or blacks or homosexuals. August talks about a girl growing up and "digging that rock'n'roll," and there's noisy guitars, so he's probably being sarcastic. His 1978 version with Machine isn't quite so mean—in that one the ship-jumpers merely move to "where only upper-class people stay." (Wait: come to think of it, "Movin' Out" from 1977 by NYC's Billy Joel—"Who needs a house out in Hackensack?"—is the same damn song! Maybe done better.)

Most of the greatest blatant suburbia odes, from Bobby Russell's "Saturday Morning Confusion" and Dionne Warwick's "Hasbrook Heights" on down, are about being a *grownup* there! Only exception I know of: "Suburbia" by the Pet Shop Boys, who (like the Monkees and Public Image Ltd.) come from England, where if suburbs exist at all, they're not *real* suburbs. But the "Suburbia" suburb feels real to me—Neil Tennant makes it sound *vicious*, full of mad dogs, lying policemen, broken town hall windows. He sees suburbia as this place that was supposed to lead us not into temptation, but he knows the evil stuff can't help but be there. Just like in any other Eden.

Flashdancing Through Nowhere

For a while during Ronald Reagan's early '80s reign, back when *Time* was doing cover stories on "America's upbeat mood," the pop hits you'd hear in suburbia's malls all seemed to gloat in a decidedly prosperous optimism, suggesting we could see all the obstacles in our way, and we would dance over them. If you find such an idea deluded, and if history proved you right, bully for you: whaddaya want, a medal or a chest to pin it on? But when I hear those records—starting roughly with Survivor's number-one "Eye of the Tiger" in July 1982 and peaking with Billy Ocean's number-one "Caribbean Queen (No More Love on the Run)" in November 1984—I don't hear the optimism; I hear the obstacles, the driving rain, the restlessness. The two biggest pop hits of 1983, Michael Jackson's "Billie Jean" and the Police's "Every Breath You Take" (". . . I'll be watching you"), were both about paranoia, just like Men At Work's "Who Can it be Now?," which had topped the charts the autumn before. The third biggest hit, "Flashdance (What a Feeling)" by Irene Cara, addressed escaping "a world made of steel, made of stone."

Flashdance (as I'll call the Survivor/Cara/Ocean sound) was a legitimate genre, I think (unlike most of the genres in this book, which are bastards!). Many of its songs seem to be played in minor keys, and most seem to combine fast synthetic syncopation with loud AOR-radio guitar solos. The singers might be black or white, men or women. But they weren't notably rooted in the church, except inasmuch as soul music has been sifted through hard rock and Europop— the biggest vocal influence is probably Donna Summer, then maybe Stevie Nicks, Lou Gramm, or late Tina Turner. From there you can trace the gutbust passion back through Cher's and Three Dog Night's '70s hits to forgotten middle-Nixon-era classics like "Brandy" by Looking Glass and "Thunder and Lightning" by Chi Coltrane: torch-rock.

Hard to tell where the style started; my guess is it snuck over from Europe via gay danceclubs, but as with most genres, to say this one came from any one place would be oversimplifying things. Four months before "Eye of the Tiger," Stevie Nicks herself just missed the top ten with "Edge of Seventeen (Just Like a White-Winged Dove)," which has obvious connections to Anne Murray's early '70s bird-migration pop, but its Euro-veiled teenage dread certainly fits in the flashdance scheme as well.

Flashdance's queen was Laura Branigan, a parttime actress from New York who scored five top-20 hits between mid-'82 and mid-'84. Laura sang about hearing voices, and her own voice was hoarse and VERY BIG—even as operatic pop, "Gloria" went *way* overboard (and in 1996, foperatic British popsters Pulp combined its melody with guitars from Elton John's "Saturday Night's Alright For Fighting" and words about a woman friend who used to ignore the singer in high school, sort of like the mom and dad on my all-time favorite TV show *My So-Called Life*). In "Breaking Out," Laura's "caught in the trap of the workaday world," but breaking free at night; in "Self Control," basically Joy Division's "She's Lost Control" made more lurid, she lives "among the creatures of the night," pacing the streets of her soul. The near-metal "Heart" comes from "the hour of nighttime when the demons come to call," when sleep is the only way out.

Branigan contributed another of her more heavily guitared songs about forsaking the perils of real life for "the other side," "Imagination," to *Flashdance*, the 1983 soundtrack album from which the flashdance genre derives its name. And also its themes—in the extremely high-grossing movie, a Catholic girl of eighteen welds Pittsburgh steel together during the day and go-go dances at night, hoping someday to switch to ballet. The soundtrack LP sold so many copies that it was credited (along with Def Leppard's *Pyromania*, the Police's *Synchronicity*, and above all Michael Jackson's *Thriller*) with lifting the music industry out of its early '80s doldrums. This was a pivotal year for the record biz—the first year prerecorded cassettes outsold longplaying vinyl. And like those other '83 blockbusters, *Flashdance*'s success was based on musical compromise: where Michael stepped back from disco rhythms and hired Eddie Van Halen and Paul McCartney, where Lep added a Fairlight synthesizer and pretty harmonies from "the Leppardettes," *Flashdance* found an unexplored white-trash middle ground where rockers and club dancers could see eye to eye.

Flashdance produced two number-one hits. In May came the title track, from Donna Summer mimic Cara, whose two previous hits had come from the 1980 movie *Fame*; like Branigan, she was an actress, and her "Flashdance" character wanted to "have it all"—an '80s deathwish if ever there was one. The Police supplanted it in the number one spot with their paranoia song, which stayed there eight weeks. Then came the Eurythmics' "Sweet Dreams (Are Made of This)," where Annie Lennox cooed cynically about "everybody looking for something." (In 1996, Goth uglies Marilyn Manson would shtick Lennox's sweet-nightmare abuse-or-be-abused cynicism into a dumb hit cover version.) Then it was *Flashdance*'s turn again: specifically, "Maniac," by ex-Stevie-Wonder-sessionman Michael Sembello. His maniac was the steeltown girl from the movie and from Cara's song—everybody calls her crazy, she dances her ballet into "the danger zone." Which danger zone turns out to be her mind.

These songs are about being trapped all day, then going nuts at night; their corny assumptions about romance in urban darkness date back to Gothic late '70s Eurodisco. And even when flashdance words reject the more ghoulish aspects—in Bonnie Tyler's "Total Eclipse of the Heart," Pamala Stanley's gay metaphor "Coming out of Hiding" (though maybe not her cover of "Rhiannon" by Fleetwood Mac), Taylor Dayne's huge post-flash "Tell It to My Heart" and *Can't Fight Fate* album—the sheer size and slickness of the vocal and guitar drama insures a certain old-country technopassion. On the other hand, there's nothing inherently more corny about this bombast than about, say, Bruce Springsteen's, which dabbles in similar themes. In fact, one of the most prominent flashdance-rock *boys* was Corey Hart, a Montreal-born/Spain-and-Mexico-raised Bruce mimic who always wore his sunglasses at night and had eight top 40 hits between 1984 and 1988. And *Flashdance* also inspired bigger fishies in the pop pond, for instance Lionel Richie (with

"Running with the Night"), Manfred Mann (with "Runner"), and Bryan Adams (with "She's Only Happy When She's Dancin'").

In "She's Only Happy When She's Dancin'," from 1984, a girl who works 9-to-5 all week to make ends meet waits for Friday night, when she heads down to the Ball and Chain and loses herself in her fantasies, going insane until Monday. The girl who's only happy when dancing is Abba's dancing queen, who looks for a place to go on Friday nights and has the time of her life to the beat of the tambourine. But then again, she's also David Bowie's "rebel rebel," who loves bands when they're playing hard and likes dancin' and looks divine. And she's the girl in Van Halen's "Dance the Night Away," "'cause dancin' gets her higher than anything else she knows." And she's everybody listening to Detroit hard rock stations at 5 p.m. quitting time Friday, when they play Ted Nugent's "Weekend Warrior," and everybody listening to Philadelphia dance stations at the same time, when they play Debbie Deb's even more impatient Miami classic "Lookout Weekend." (There's a real arrogance to Deb's giddiness. She just closes her eyes, plugs her nose, and jumps in the pool. She's a knee-powdered flapper entranced by "jumping music, slick DJs, fog machines and laser rays." Or maybe "fuck machines and razor blades," as somebody once told me they heard it.) But mostly, Bryan Adams's gal is all the kids in Loverboy's "Working for the Weekend," Canuck white-trash dance-metal from two years before *Flashdance*, where the whole junior class plans all week to "go off the deep end," eager "to be in the show." (Three years earlier still, in their blatant Black-Sabbath-metal parody "Teenage Jail" on *The Long Run*, the Eagles had *also* talked about people who "wait for the weekend to go off the deep end"!)

So the 9-to-5 girl's working for the weekend in more ways than one. And I wouldn't be so sure she's happy when she's dancing, either, because I know people like her. I know people older than me who go to bars every night and get blasted and smoke dope like 10th graders, and watch bands they've been told they're supposed to like. And it's no fun, just another routine—most probably, they just don't have any-thing *better* to do.

Or maybe I'm just a poor sport. My friend Frank Kogan has written that music in the '90s (unlike music of historical periods depicted in old Western movies) fails to provide a context in which adult Americans can lead an active social life, and though for a long time I agreed with him, now I'm starting to think he's dead wrong—it seems everybody I meet outside of music circles these days has a more active life than me, and music *always* seems to be a part of it. They go line-dancing to Shania Twain songs, or they go see Hootie and the Blowfish or some bad Jersey Shore blues-cover bar band (or bad White Zombie/Nine Inch Nails cover bar band) after drinking too much, or they go to a party or wedding where music's playing, and they dance to it. They tape concert guides to the fridge and spend their hard-earned on CDs. They flirt or fight at shows and talk about it the next day and get asked out on dates or wish they did or wish they didn't. Or they get a keg and have a rowdy asshole Stanley Cup party on our street, and they blast "Rock and Roll Part 2" and "Na Na Hey Hey Kiss Him Goodbye" out their car speakers. These people are *participating* in their music, mak-ing it an active part of their world. Well so am I, I guess, but sometimes I wish I knew how to use it more like they do. Going to concerts is a *big event* for most people.

Obviously, I really need to get out of my room and stop being a deadbeat and go drink up the world—to attain the adventure and romance and energy I want in my music and my writing, I probably ought to get some in my *life*. But it might be more work than it's worth, especially when every-body's always telling me how "easy" it is. What originally made me give up going to live shows in the late '80s was my sudden brainstorm at an Ann Arbor gig by pre-Nirvana Se-attle grungers Mudhoney that concerts were *more* a social ac-tivity than a musical one, and *my* main activity tended to be standing around waiting for them to *end*. So maybe I should just take up golf instead.

Going out to dance can be a source of stress and strife. Lots of boys are just plain *afraid* to dance—think of Marvin

Gaye (a wallflower at parties " 'cause I was too nervous to really get down," "Got to Give it Up," 1977) or early British artpunks Alternative TV ("D.J. man he played records all night as I stood in the corner shivering from fright," "Lost in Room," 1979). And there's girls who'd rather just cry (Lesley Gore, "It's My Party," 1963: "play all my records, keep dancing all night . . . ")

And there's boys who'll turn dancing into a competitive boxing match (Michael Jackson in "Bad," New York Dolls in "There's Gonna be a Showdown," L.L. Cool J in "You Can't Dance," Human Beinz in "Nobody But Me," the Pagans in "Boy Can I Dance Good," John Travolta in *Saturday Night Fever*, "too much fighting on the dancefloor" in the Specials' "Ghost Town," Axl Rose in "Shotgun Blues": "I just like to dance, how's that for provocation?"). And girls who turn dating into a catfight (Yvonne Chaka Chaka in "I'm Winning," Vanessa Williams in "Save the Best for Last," Blondie in "Rip Her to Shreds," New York Blondie descendants the Goops in their 1996 "You Wish"). And boys who worry they're not very coordinated (Eddie Money in "I Wanna Go Back": "First slow dance, hoping that I'd get it right.")

Stodgy rockers who boys like always fear colorful rockers who girls like are phony hypes "reducing" music to an ass-wiggling contest. In fact, in 1992 brutish redneck throwback Travis Tritt used almost those exact words complaining about newly number-one country hunk Billy Ray Cyrus. It made sense to some people: here was a real handsome devil, with soap opera cheekbones, surfer tan, anchorman blow-dry, George Michael (or Nixon?) stubble, Springsteen biceps, gym shoes, tight jeans, tight ponytail, loose shirttail. Billy would sing with his legs spread and knees bent, do a Chippendale's striptease, and Victorias tossed their secrets. The video to his big hit "Achy Breaky Heart" had an all-female audience (seven to seventy) shrieking while Billy danced so fast you expected his hips to fly into the cheap seats. He was plainly too sexy for your Nashville. But Travis's lazy-reasoned whining conveniently forgot that shaking your healthy butt is one big reason music *exists*.

So, apparently, did Dave Marsh, who wrote in his usually much smarter *The Heart of Rock & Soul: The 1001 Greatest Singles Ever Made* that since Madonna's ghostly "Live to Tell" is sung from the point of view of an abused child, the material girl therefore "has earned the right to party." Ouch! Talk about working for your weekend!! So if my parents didn't slam me against walls and smack me with belt buckles and lock me in a freezer, does that mean Dave is gonna make me stay home like Claudine Clark in 1962's "Party Lights," staring at mom's hair curlers while there's a party raging across the street?

And anyway, going out to parties can be abuse *too*, right? You can't dress sloppy like at home, can you? Some people spend hours plucking eyebrows, picking out the right shirt, combing hair. John Mellencamp looks back in 1987's "Cherry Bomb" to days when "dancing meant everything," and "everything" includes bad stuff as well as good, obviously. Iggy Pop dances to the beat of the living dead, Axl Rose dances to the tension of a world on edge. York University student Shannon accuses her boyfriend in her seminal top-ten 1984 hit "Let the Music Play" of acting as if a dance is just a dance, but she knows better.

"The smart artist brings terror and conflict to the party because he thinks it will make a better party, not to make the party more 'realistic,'" writes disco intellectual Frank Kogan. So just because disco lets the party be the main thing doesn't mean the terror's not there. When the trio of Latin New York dolls called Pajama Party sing in their 1989 "Surfing in Babylon" that "You gotta keep your sanity or else you'll lose your mind," it sounds more like "vanity," and means more that way: they thank their hair-stylist on the album cover. But this is a song about a girl trying to get her friend to try something dangerous—heroin maybe, or lesbian sex. Or maybe just a cigarette. Guitars and strings add noisy ornamentation as the singer stands "on the edge." Her pal says "jump in, the water's fine," but as soon as the singer dives into iniquity, the friend disappears. Surfing in Babylon means playing with fire, and getting burned.

Never Mind the Bullocks–T-shirt-wearing frisky Frisco fluff-disco floozy Stacey Q surfs through Babylon in "Incognito" on 1989's *Nights Like This*. Like Pajama Party, she talks about standing on the edge, "checkin' out the other side, taking a ride." She pushes herself as far as humanly possible, but wants to go further. She walks the streets until early morning, exclaiming, "Look at me!," but nobody can recognize her. This is a recurring theme in Stacey Q's music. There's "The Edge of Love," where she's on a high cliff chanting, "Don't-look-down look-down-below it's a long way down." There's "The River," where memories of cinnamon, distant eyes, and North Carolina skies make her dizzy, then she's "going down completely" with no one to turn to, so she begs to be rescued and halfway through lets her Eurodisco thicken into a dope-drowned dub, at which point she mumbles something about Led Zeppelin's *Houses of the Holy*, which has nothing to do with the rest of the song. Weirdest of all, on her debut LP, there's a sarcastic, fog-fuck-machined statement about how discos send out "a special invitation to anyone who looks like you"; she calls it "Dancing Nowhere."

"Nowhere" is a very popular place, it seems—one of the only listenable folk albums of the '80s was 1981's *Going Nowhere Fast*, by Peter Stampfel and Steve Weber, formerly of acid-beatnik jokesters the Holy Modal Rounders. In the *San Francisco Chronicle* on the 20th anniversary of that city's Summer of Love, Greil Marcus wrote that "'San Francisco' described a utopia as well as a place—and 'utopia' derives from the Greek for 'not a place,' i.e., nowhere." In "The Land of Nowhere," on the 1988 ZYX Records Eurotechno compilation *New Beat Edit 1*, a guttural foreign man named Kähli-T first tells you there's no wars in his land, his beautiful land, but then he starts ranting like Johnny Rotten: "get *out* of my world, my beautiful wonderful world!" "I'm so grateful to be nowhere," the Clash sing in "Hateful" on *London Calling*. Rock critics say bands from Seattle or Minnesota or Athens or New Zealand "come *out* of nowhere." "It gets me nowhere to tie you up," chirps Olivia Newton-John in "A Little More Love"; two tracks later on her second greatest hits album, she does a song called "Tied Up."

I guess it all goes back to Dion in "The Wanderer" in 1961, bragging that he's "as happy as a clown with my two fists of iron and I'm going nowhere." But the Drifters countered in 1963's "On Broadway" about how when you're wandering hungry on the street "the glitter rubs right off and you're nowhere"—you lose your illusions and you're a complete unknown with no direction home like a rolling stone, in other words, and flashdancers certainly have plenty of glitter to rub off. The Beatles chided their "Nowhere Man" in 1966, but if they couldn't appreciate that making nowhere plans for nobody was as rock'n'roll as you can get, who needed them? It really wasn't until disco that anybody figured out how to make nowhere seem like a scary place. Thank the Bee Gees in "Stayin' Alive," from John Travolta's 1977 dance-contest movie, which paved the way for *Flashdance* in more ways than one: "Somebody help me! I'm going nowhere!"

Contrary to what you may have read, the Bee Gees did not "dilute" disco by turning it frivolous and white. They were always a very fatalistic band, kicked around since they were born, as they put it in "Stayin' Alive"—their first single, "New York Mining Disaster 1941," was sung in the voice of a man buried alive. With the Moorish moodishness of "Holiday" and the totally creepy Latin chanting in "Every Christian Lion-hearted Man Will Show You," they set the stage for '90s Enigma-style Gregorian disco way back in the '60s. In 1968 they had their first top ten hits, "I've Gotta Get a Message to You" and "I Started a Joke"; both discussed dying. (The latter was later used to startling effect at the end of the movie *Penn and Teller Get Killed*.) When they turned to disco, their dejection only accelerated: nobody gets too much heaven no more.

The Bee Gees' younger brother Andy Gibb had less jarring peaks, maybe, and his songs had more background-music proclivities; for example string washes where his siblings might've used subdued wah-wah guitars. But the music had a very sad bent, perhaps exemplified best by the lonesome smokiness of 1978's "Our Love Don't Throw it Away" and the curdling Mediteranean blues of 1977's "Love is Thicker than Water." In 1984, ex-Bee Gee Robin Gibb made the uncharacteristically gleeful "Boys Do Fall in Love," full of dizzy Miami popcorn-disco tricks and stolen breathy moments. But by the late '80s, Hispanic kids in New York were combining Bee Gee gloom with an equally frail sorrow they'd picked up from British synthesizer bands: disembodied crooning, bleak melodies, ascending factory rhythms.

Willie and Gil's 1990 "Time" got its eerie feel from Andy Gibb's "Time is Time," Culture Club's "Time (Clock of the Heart)," and the Zombies' "Time of the Season." Anything Box based their self-explanatory 1991 "Living in Oblivion" on remnants of the Bee Gees' prophetic 1979 "Love You Inside Out": "Too many lovers in one lifetime ain't good for you." A boy named Noel, sounding more nervous and haunted than any of the rest, suddenly woke up in 1987's "Silent Morning" to find *his* lover an AIDS casualty.

People danced to this stuff, and there was more: on his 1990 debut album, Latin Lothario Coro gave us Dark Ages titles on the order of "No Way Out" and "My Fallen Angel," mixing salsa castanets and barrio-bistro blues saxes with horror-kitsh violins and Joy Division death guitars. And the same year, a registered Fresno, California locksmith named Timmy T (real last name: Torres) broke up with his gas-station-cashier girlfriend. He was bumming, man. So he took his $80 Moog, $500 drum machine, and $1600 digital sampler to the recording studio, payed $181 for time and tape, and recorded an end-of-my-rope rubber-ball-beat dance dirge with a weepy vocal hush that suggested he'd swallowed a whole pill bottle's worth of Depeche Mode's morose minor chords. Eventually Timmy paid another $500 and made a ballad, "One More Try." It was the most brazen whipped-male mush you ever heard, and a few months later it was the first number-one-in-Billboard independent-label single in a decade.

Depressiveness and nihilism are old stories in teen shlock. The Shangri-Las' mid-'60s girlpunk morality plays rank with the most morbid music ever: "Leader of the Pack" is death-rock pure and simple; the minor-key melodrama in "I Can Never Go Home Anymore" and mullahs moaning in the desert in "Out in the Streets" are the precursor of Black Sab-

bath and Joy Division both. (And that's called "sad.")
"There's so much evil around me that I feel I could die"
howls teen-idolized Clearasil wimp Dion like Al Jolson as he
waits for his name to be called by St. Peter in 1962's "I Was
Born to Cry," a dense New Orleans blues-wake funeral dirge
with sax blurting like the farts of God and a backdrop of intoning monks. Levi Stubbs booms operatically in the Four
Tops' 1967 "Seven Rooms of Gloom" that he lives in emptiness in a house that's just a hiding place.

In 1970's "Band of Gold," Freda Payne waits in the darkness of her lonely wedding suite, "filled with gloom" instead
of filled with groom, paving the way for such later impotence rock landmarks as Kid Creole and the Coconuts' "Mister Softee" and Elastica's "Stutter." (On Adam VIII Records'
1973 *Soul Train Hall of Fame* TV-mailaway sampler, "Band of
Gold" is appropriately-if-accidentally followed immediately by
the Chairmen of the Board's Four-Tops-like "Give Me Just a
Little More Time," where the singer rationalizes his flaccid-
ness with "You're eager for love but don't you worry, these
things don't come overnight.")

"Darkness all around me . . . emptiness has found me,"
goes Gladys Knight and the Pips' 1973 "I've Got to Use My
Imagination," and what Gladys has to use it for is to come
up with good reasons not to kill herself. The housewife singing Abba's 1976 "Knowing Me, Knowing You" might not be
so lucky. She walks teary-eyed through her empty nest, remembering kids who used to play in the rooms, saying the
story of her life ends here. The music is an elaborate waltz,
with pretty vocals sung as a round: "Now there is only emptiness, nothing to say."

Abba initiated a whole genre of such suicidal stuff. In
1987, two scrub-skinned blond Italian flirts named Fun Fun
put out a record called "Baila Bolero," using an Abba-man-
que melody and alluding to Abba's "Take a Chance on Me"
in the lyrics. The cover to their *Double Fun* album was a sick-
ening sort of Doublemint flashback, and the sound first
struck me as sexless and shallow: anonymous cloud-nine harmonies riding rice-paper-thin synths over eternally jiggly choral hooks, not even very fast, with Ventures riffs and ballpark

organ now and then. Mostly it was like strobelight sound-tracks in lousy TV movies—nothing jarring or unpleasant; in fact, no "personality." I was left wondering how actual human beings could stoop to such blankness.

But the lush and relentless 12-inch remix of "Baila Bolero" was *about* blankness; it was *proud* of its anonymity. Fleshed-out vocals and bottom end helped orchestrate it unto hypnosis with synbass triplets, claps, horn charts, castanets (that's the "bolero" part), lute strums. "A never-ending desire will never know your name" laments the key line; the twins (?) are afraid of waking up to find out their dream is gone, so instead they just "dance the night away," accelerating that last line as if dancing is some inescapable toil or compulsion they'd rather not be reminded of. The emotion sounds drugged, frozen.

According to Susan Orlean in her essay collection *Saturday Night*, people now are driven by something called the "fun imperative"; not living it up on Saturday night is often thought to be indicative of a "major failure and possible character flaw." "Don't wanna stay home on a Saturday night all alone," laments Will To Power's Elin Michaels in "Clock on the Wall," stuck there with her rented videos. As an Army officer in the '80s, I was required to attend monthly Saturday dinners called Hail and Farewells, ostensibly meant to boost morale and give everybody a chance to let their hair down; we called them "forced fun." And forced fun exists in civilian life, as well—in his 1991 *Atlantic Monthly* cover story "Waiting for the Weekend," Witold Rybczynski discusses how the weekend has progressed as an institution from its late 19th Century London country-house beginnings and its earlier Saturday night music hall and Sunday go-to-meeting roots, to the point where people take their leisure time more seriously than "real" work. So "playing tennis" becomes "working on your backhand," and the Protestant work ethic puts on a new disguise. (In 1980's "Return the Gift," Leeds *Communist Manifesto*-up-their-rectum "punk-funk" do-gooders the Gang of Four ask God to please send them "evenings and weekends." Poor Marxist shmucks, they don't know what they're getting themselves into!) "The freedom to do anything has become the obligation to do something," Rybczyn-ski theorizes. "The need to do something well, whether it is sailing a boat or building a boat, reflects a need that was previously met in the workplace."

In "Working the Midnight Shift" from 1977, Donna Summer's work and others' pleasure seem interlinked—I assume she's a prostitute, though she never explicity says so. She says she's dying inside while her friends have "all gone out dancing, having fun." She's like the Velvet Underground in "Sweet Jane" ("Some people like to go out dancing, and other people they gotta work") and in "Afterhours" ("All the people are dancing, they're having such fun, I wish it could happen to me")—I think this is where flashdance gloom started. Rock fans assume dance music is all happy-go-lucky pleasure; they call it "escapist." Well, it's *escapist*, alright, but sometimes the only escape is sticking your head in a gas oven. Both the Velvets and Donna knew and sang the oblivion their lonely urban night people were sentenced to: "Say hello to never." "Faster and Faster to Nowhere."

Playground in Your Mind

The Donna Summer album with "Working the Midnight Shift" and "Faster and Faster to Nowhere" (her best ever) is *Once Upon a Time*; it also has songs called "Fairy Tale High" (about euphoria, not high school) and "Happily Ever After." The liner notes depict a woman/girl living in fairytales, fleeing to dreams like flashdancers flee to the dancefloor—to escape the ugliness of real life. When her dreams end every a.m., she feels let down. (Compare Teena Marie's 1987 *Emerald City* notes: "Once upon a time there lived a little girl named Pity who decided more than anything in the world she wanted to be green...", then stuff about persecution of blacks in 1850 and Jesus-followers in Jordan.) In Donna's title track, she's singing about the girl over shlock-classical piano-and-string figures out of Henry Mancini's "Theme From Love Story," and the music gets darker, more intense, like an Isaac Hayes monologue, until "bitterness surrounds her." Next song, the dream's turned into a nightmare that doesn't even go away when daylight comes.

The same girl with the same nightmare shows up in Helen Reddy's 1974 number-one hit "Angie Baby." (The song was written by Alan O'Day, who three years later had his own very notable number-one with "Undercover Angel," about sex with a succubus—*wet* dream rock, like the Everly Brothers' "All I Have to do is Dream," or maybe like Gordon Lightfoot's 1974 "Sundown," which refers to "a sailor's dream.") In "Angie Baby," a friendless teenager lives vicariously through the songs she hears on a rock station. Angie dances in her head with boys, but when she pumps up the volume on her transistor, the music we hear gets real loud and noisy too, and the evil boy next door disappears into thin air. It's insanity in sheep's clothing.

The girl in Janis Ian's mopey top-five 1975 folkie classic "At Seventeen" invents lovers too (she talks to them over the phone, when she's not being chosen last for basketball or cheating at solitaire). So I adamantly reject the claim that rock'n'roll has anything inherently to do with "real life"—it can mean solipsism, too. The idea that you and everything else are nothing but figments of my imagination is a proud legacy dating back to doowop days: to the Harptones' "Life is but a Dream" and Chords' "Sh-boom" ("life could be a dream . . .") (or earlier, to "Row Row Row Your Boat": "life is but a dream").

Handsome boys were dreamy, capable of being dreamboats. The public domain is full of songs like Bing Crosby's "Dream a Little Dream," Bobby Darin's "Dream Lover," and Jiminy Cricket's "When You Wish Upon a Star" ("your dreams come true"). Patsy Cline's "Sweet Dreams" was a country hit after she died in 1963 and a hit movie eighteen years later. And muzakbilly blowhard Roy Orbison had all those allegedly "haunting" candy-colored sandmen in "In Dreams" (as used too damn heavy-handedly in the movie *Blue Velvet*) and in "Dream Baby (How Long Must I Dream)".

"There's a Freudian aspect to all this," Dave Marsh says, which would probably make sense to Bob Dylan, who actually went so far as to consult a psychiatrist about the problem in "Talking World War III Blues." He dreamt a *lot*, and his dreams (though perhaps not as literally as the dream in "Cheeseburger in Paradise" by Jimmy Buffett) were generally in the tradition of Bogus Ben Covington's race-music novelty "I Heard the Voice of a Porkchop," recorded in Chicago in 1928, where Ben falls asleep under a shady tree and dreams of his favorite food.

Dylan dreamt in "Bob Dylan's Dream" and "Motorpsycho Nightmare," then in "Bob Dylan's 115th Dream" about discovering America with Captain A-hab, going to jail for harpoon possession, talking to cows, getting asked for collateral then yanking his trousers down, and feet coming through phone lines and kicking him. (I don't know how he knew it was his *115th* dream. Maybe he kept a log, like I tried to do once until I had dreams I was too embarrassed to write down.) The dreams in Eric Burdon and War's 1970 "Spill the Wine" and Daddy Dewdrop's 1971 "Chick-A-Boom" are in the Dylan lineage; when Leo Sayer talk-sings over New Orleans piano about being a hobo forced to dance like Fred Astaire for his caviar in his 1975 top-ten "Long Tall Glasses," he's doing a Dylan dream as disco, almost.

Mid-'70s rock songs frequently verged on dream-disco territory—Aerosmith's "Dream On" builds disco strings and towering minor chords and tense stuttering drumbeats to a climax that urges you to "dream until your dreams come true." Fleetwood Mac's "Dreams" picks up on bewitchy "crystal visions" Stevie Nicks had already tapped in "Rhiannon" and would tap more in her solo career, but space cadet Stevie keeps her visions to herself. Gary Wright's 1976 washroom-stoner ballad "Dream Weaver" has a woozy elixir of whooshes carting you away to Cannabis seas of tranquility on the other side of the moon.

Heart's 1976 *Dreamboat Annie* almost undoubtedly *influenced* disco, and vice-versa. *Dreamboat* opens with "Magic Man," where synth and congas meld into an obsessive pulse progressing toward funk; Ann Wilson passes the peacepipe under the moon with a swarthy hunk she'd first met in a dream. Then comes "Dreamboat Annie," subtitled "Fantasy Child" to match a liner-note poem Donna Summer would certainly understand: "She's a fantasy child tonight, skimming the mirror waves, heading out somewhere." The music is incandescent, barely even there. (Not unlike their Bernie-Taupin-penned 1986 chart-topping power ballad "These Dreams," where Heart croon about walking through stained glass walls without a scratch.) On the rest of *Dreamboat*, they use *silence* a lot, including once right after Ann says "no silence"—so sometimes the music *literally* isn't there. After the title track comes "Crazy on You," the most brazen explosion of clitoral lust in folk-metal history, about ear-kissing, going crazy, and love fluids as a life force. "What're you gonna do?," Ann winds up taunting her gent, just like Teena Marie (who read Heart's liner notes too, I bet) would in "Lips 2 Find U" in 1986.

The dreams in "Dream On" and *Dreamboat Annie* share roots in Led Zeppelin, people say (possibly in the crazy Honolulu Hoochie-Koo-dancing dream Robert Plant has in "The Song Remains the Same"). Same with Boston, I'm told, and they dreamt all the time. There's "Long Time": "I gotta keep chasing a dream." And in "More than a Feeling," Brad Delp wakes up and finds the sun gone, hides in his music and forgets the day, dreams of a girl he used to know, closes his eyes and she slips away—if this sounds familiar, it's because it's exactly what happened to Angie Baby in that Helen Reddy song. This theme—people who just poof! *vanish*, don't even so much as drop you a postcard—pops up in more pop music than you might think.

Another Boston song, "A Man I'll Never Be," has the singer's girl "disappearing way back in her dreams." It's what Stacey Q wishes on her enemy in her epic "The River": "Sometimes I wish you were not there, dissolve you into air." Anne Murray originally ventured into the dissipation-of-self realm with her top-ten version of the Beatles' "You Won't See Me" in 1974, then plunged further with 1979's "Shadows in the Moonlight." (Shadows pass in and out of existence, and Anne dances with hers through the Milky Way—what Andy Gibb called "Shadow Dancing" in his huge hit from the year before.) Then Anne fled completely into the land of Nod with her 1980 rethinking of the Monkees' "Daydream Believer," where a former homecoming queen sleeps her whole life away, haunted by alarm clocks.

The cease-to-exist thing also happens to Fleetwood Mac's "Rhiannon" ("a woman taken by the wind") and to the lady in the white T-bird who keeps appearing for seconds then eclipsing from Richard Dreyfuss's sight in *American Graffiti*. It happens in the Carpenters' devastating 1971 "Superstar" (where a lonely woman awaits the return of a one-night stand who we assume is a famous rock star) and in Lydia Murlock's gossip-worthy 1983 "Superstar" (a completely different song where the disappearing rock star is Michael Jackson and Lydia is Billie Jean and the music is taken from "Billie Jean"). And in the Sweet's "Ballroom Blitz" ("I softly call you over and when you appear there's nothing left of you") and the Electric Prunes' "I Had Too Much to Dream Last Night" ("then came the dawn and you were gone gone gone"). So I gather it fills some *deep-seated human need*!

It's also what keeps happening to Boston's music. Boston cared nothing for roots—"Where the people who make up this band called Boston came from is irrelevant to who and where they are now," the liner notes to 1976's *Boston* say; the band even brags about being unknown in its own hometown. And though by all accounts guitarist/technician/recording-equipment-inventor Tom Scholz was a demon on the basketball court (maybe if he would've given lessons to Janis Ian she wouldn't have been chosen last all the time!), Boston also cared nothing for masculinity; one song was called "A Man I'll Never Be," and "Peace of Mind" argued that competing with other people is unhealthy. Inside the gatefold of 1978's *Don't Look Back*, Tom wears all white like the Man from Glad, and Brad Delp wears his wrist on his hips and his bar-cruising mustache like a real, well, *open-minded person*, let's say. In one song he even says he's "kind of shy."

After getting his Master's from MIT, Tom spoke of music in purely technical terms, like British synthesizer players later would in the '80s. He had seen the future of rock'n'roll, and it was *antiseptic*. The spaceship on the cover of *Don't Look Back* houses a clean new outerspace city, full of skyscrapers, enclosed in a pollution-free/crime-free/blues-free plastic dome, like Michael Jackson's oxygen tent. The first two album covers both have big drawings of guitars that look like spaceships. Tom Scholz wanted his guitars to *sound* like spaceships.

Album-oriented dream-rock (Boston, Fleetwood Mac) is apparently a big influence on Miami's Will To Power (who have songs called "Dreamin' " and "Fading Away"), but it's not the only one—basically, they've founded their own school of libertarian dream disco, with individually sprayed notes fading into layer upon underweight layer of light bright elevator-classical beauty above (reverberating man/woman repartee floating up toward the sky or dribbling down a stormdrain, extended sax sustains, polymelodic power-ballad guitars, whispered Greek chorus asides) and all manner of dinky little tricks and embellishments below (minimalist Euro beats, dub-reggaeish basslines, subtly violent corner-turning surges, rhythm breaks that suggest worn-down breakpads). The usually female voices, all but devoid of soul roots, obsess on the perils of middle-class twentysomething romance; the occasional male voice belongs to songwriter/producer/Führer Bob Rosenberg, who quotes Nietzsche and Solzhenitzyn, insults "knee-jerk liberals," demands relaxed gun-control laws, and says he won't let his anger linger because it'd be bad for his aim and his trigger finger—honest!

Most of Grandmaster Flash and the Furious Five's singles boast of the presence of member Raheim in all the ladies' dreams. But he was lying—some ladies dream about the end of the world instead. Nicknaming herself Nena, a skinny cheerleader-skirt-clad West German fraulein named Gabrielle Kerner just missed reaching the pinnacle of the U.S. charts in 1984 with "99 Luftballons," about sitting between hilltops in the Fulda Gap (near what was still a border at the time), pondering nuclear armageddon. I was in the Army just near Frankfurt then, and Reagan had joked about bombing Russia only months before, so for me this was no novelty record—it was, how 'bout that, real life. Nena trills in an intense girl's gutterals, above straight high-speed Eurodisco done as symphonic Motown-modeled rock. In the weepy final verse, she confesses she's dreamt of red balloons 99 times, and every time after the war's over she winds up "standing pretty in this dusty crumbled city," looking for a souvenir to prove to herself that there really was a world once. Nena's second-best song was called "Just a Dream."

Of course, though it *helps* to be a German to dream your city's crumbling down, it's hardly mandatory. You can live on Long Island, like Debbie Gibson. The snazziest words on Gibson's smash 1987 debut *Out of the Blue* concern being trapped in a suburb where you constantly fall heels over head and go weak in the knees for people who basically don't care (or maybe even know) you exist. Oodles of dreams that don't come true, looking for the perfect love-at-first-sight stuff. NO SLEAZE. "Only in My Dreams" is spiritedly slinky, with bongobeats and girl-group backdrop adding credence to a somewhat ambiguous situation where the Debster's whole mall-world falls apart as she bemoans the loss of a guy who was apparently never hers to begin with—a no-baloney teen-life predicament, and you can't assume her dreamtext has anything to do with birds and bees. In the "Only in my Dreams" video, Debbie wears pajamas.

Deb's not Helen Reddy's Angie Baby—she's Rosie and the Originals' Angel Baby. She sings kind of restricted, but in a pleasant, unassuming, even meek way, with long vowels doing the cha-cha-cha. She's at her bubbliest over a quasi-maraca nurserybeat that's real spry but not sexual or anything. In the "Shake Your Love" video, she wears a miniskirt (in only one shot, so watch fast!), smiles crooked, and does a funky hand-jive that looks like referee signals. "Shake Your Love," the song, has a prefornicating id-level triple-entendre title, an exuberant domino-effect rhythm, some underlying synthbuzz, some google-eyes syncopation, some inspired phrase repetition, and one cute part where Debbie telephones her desired one, hangs up, and cries. And though "Out of the Blue" has this sweet sixteen Lawn Guyland hoodsie calling her boyfriend a "dream come true," her nightmare number is "Foolish Beat," a surreal chart-topping torcher about abandoning a place (really, a TIME IN YOUR LIFE) where you could wish on four-leaf clovers for a dusty crumbled city of "broken hearts and broken dreams."

Debbie was dream-disco's commercial triumph. She paved the way for important teenydream hits like Color Me Badd's beautifully bilingual lambada ballad "I Ador Mi Amor" and the Party's holographic "In My Dreams," which has desperate guitars and an "I Feel Love" opening supporting sirens, insomnia, an all-encompassing *Degrassi Street* aura, and a sarcastic rap indebted to Madonna's pretentious side. These songs both came from groups who look like rainbow coalitions—they've both got members of just about every racial stock known to anthropology, and they thereby fulfill Martin Luther King's "I Have a Dream" speech dream, sort of. (Though, to be fair, not even Martin could've predicted Color Me Badd—one guy with George Michael's haircut, one guy with George Michael's whiskers, one guy who looks like he should be in Milli Vanilli, one guy who looks like Arnold Horschack on *Welcome Back Kotter*!) Along with Metallica's unintentionally silly "Enter Sandman" and the Geto Boys' truly foreboding "Mind Playing Tricks on Me" (not to mention such British hypes as My Bloody Valentine who were trying to treat "dream pop" as an end in itself, having heard

Suicide's "Dream Baby Dream" once and having thereby determined deadweight vocals sound menacing and new-age drones equal art), these acts helped make 1991 a dreamy year indeed.

Kids Know Best

Debbie Gibson came along right when we needed her most. For most of the '80s, rock had been getting too damned grown-up—just scads of stonefaced egos bonovoxing all over the place. (Actually, I suspect Menudo had a couple of swell tunes, but I never listened to them much.) But by 1987, with Debbie and her country cousin Tiffany and Lisa Lisa's suburban Hispanic "Head to Toe" and Poison's nursery-rhyming "Talk Dirty to Me," then New Kids on the Block and Vanilla Ice in the early '90s, bubblegum was finally a major pop genre in its own right all over again—it was the first time since the early '70s that we were really inundated with *Tiger Beat* teendream singing idols.

By the mid-'90s, sadly, even the new teen dreams bonovoxed stonefacedly—e.g., Australian 15-year-olds Silverchair (who did at least moan ridiculous words about bathrooms with no sinks but water from taps there being very hard to drink anyway—so where the hell was the tap, in the bathtub?). Green Day were basically Poison without makeup, but something was still *missing.*

See, I remember being in a classroom. Around fourth grade or so, stuck in the middle of an end-of-the-year school's-out-for-summer cake-and-ice-cream party, the Magnavox switched on with "Simon Says" by the 1910 Fruitgum Company and "Yummy Yummy Yummy" by the Ohio Express coming out . . . Girls were dancing fast. I didn't know it then (or care—this was my rude awakening to something hormonal), but both bands had the same singer, a guy named Joey Levine. They sprang from the fertile imaginations of Buddah Records prexy Neil Bogert and the production duo of Jerry Kasenatz and Jeff Katz, a think-tank that satiated busting-out pre-pubertal passions the world over in the late '60s by building an empire of cynical condescension and naming it "Bubblegum." There had always been "Hanky Panky"s and "Da Doo Ron Ron"s and "Iko Iko"s and "Hippy Hippy Shake"s and other monstrosities of ingratiating meaninglessness to keep the candystore contingent smiling (gubblebumminess as a sound dates back to "Sweet Sixteen" by

'20s banjoker Charlie Poole, *about* a teenygirl fond of gum), but Kasenatz/Katz were the first to align kiddiepap into a (gumball)-machine-marketed commodity.

Bubblegum was terrific! Because unlike all of the astral-weakling acidwreck dreck teenagers were soon burning out to, gum laid all its cards on the table, not disguising itself as anything (i.e.: "smart") it wasn't. As Jim Bickhart puts it in his notes to the early '70s TV-mailaway compilation *Super Bubble*, it was "music that sticks to the bottom of your shoes and the roof of your mouth." Mostly it just strung lots of very obvious hooks together on a non-skewed straight line (unlike the skewed line that unpopular powerpop-without-the-power airheads like Big Star would initiate a couple years later, thus making way for the travesty which, in the '80s, we laughingly referred to as "college radio"). You didn't have to study these hooks paramecium-like under a microscope or anything; they were so incontestably cute on the surface you just wanted to tickle 'em under the chin.

Also, bubblegum songs had preposterous words that didn't make any sense nor pretend to, though sometimes the gob-bledygook hid some quite ribald sentiments. There were plenty of lines about "chewing" and how "sweet" people were (an idea expanded on years later in "Taste of Cindy" and "Just Like Honey" by Limey noisemakers the Jesus and Mary Chain). The most immortal gumtune, and (therefore!) the biggest seller, was "Sugar Sugar" by the Archies, a group who were nothing more than Saturday morning cartoon charac-ters. Basically, something's genuine bubblegum only if you can imagine Betty of the Archies shaking a tambourine to it. "Sugar Sugar" had tic-tac-toe-branded redhead Archie An-drews repeatedly telling his main squeeze that she was his "candy girl," asking her to coat his body in sucrose. Interpret this cryptic demand as you will. (Def Leppard sure did, un-less they came up with the sentence "pour some sugar on me" after hearing the "throw some water on me" part in "Fire" by the Ohio Players. Which is doubtful: Lep's Joe El-liott says "Sugar, Sugar" was the first record he ever bought as a kid.)

Now, lots of octagenarians have asserted for years that all this good clean fun kicked the bucket around the time my classmates and I were switching to the FM dial—which is more-or-less also when countercultural marijuana festivals and Yes's mountains-coming-out-of-the-sky-and-standing-there were becoming major enterprises. Some even say it's self-destructive to keep searching for this callow ingenuousness we once knew, because we've lost it forever, and to deny that is to deny our own consciousness. Well, I've always figured that obituary garbage was just a lie perpetuated by lazy '60s snobs. What I know for sure is that wonder and bliss are out there somewhere (and I don't just mean music-wise, either) for anybody who's got guts enough to hunt around instead of settling for the delusions of lethargy and necrosis we're offered these days. If I didn't believe that, I might as well kill myself, or at least give up writing about music and go to law school. I'm here to tell you that bubblegum lives, even if Kasenatz-Katz are already dead.

Early '70s gum had a symbiotic relationship with K-Tel Records, which regularly put out cut-rate compilations of AM-radio pop—as distinguished from FM-radio rock, which was busy fabricating medieval poetry or looking back to Robert Johnson, suddenly obsessed with its own authenticity. FM fans had dubbed commercialism a mortal sin; rock was something serious, to be "appreciated," not used up and then disposed of like everything else in American culture (though, ironically, decades later it's the "disposable" stuff that hasn't been used up, that still sounds smart, where the "permanent" stuff's been worn out for years!). As documented on Rhino Records' essential 15-volume 1990 *Have a Nice Day* compilation, the Top 40 succumbed to teenybop wimps, to studio musicians disguised as singers. But in hack shlock like the Defranco Family's "Heartbeat (It's a Lovebeat)," there's a *zeitgeist* at work, and an aesthetic. The *zeitgeist* says everything is beautiful; the aesthetic says everything's allowed: gimmicks can be good things after all!

As the '70s progressed, bubblegum became more an attitude than a genre, a sticky perky feeling that performers (or producers—Mike Chapman and Nicky Chinn of Suzi Quatro/Sweet/Nick Gilder fame were the Kasenatz/Katz of the me-decade) could draw on, as everybody from K.C. and the Sunshine Band to Mötley Crüe has done. Gumlike concoctions thrived with the glam and nouveau-Merseybeat movements (explicit reactions to rock-as-art) of the early '70s, with disco and powerpop in the late '70s, with contemporary hits radio's mid-'80s girl-group mini-revival. Arthur Baker's 12-inch remix of "Girls Just Wanna Have Fun" by Cyndi Lauper sounded like Olive Oyl turning feminist in a house of mirrors, with spinach gumballs tossed at her by Popeye.

Anyway, what unites the best '70s/'80s/'90s bubblegum songs is feel, sound, and words. By "feel," I'm talking playful and unschooled, the more kindergarten-worthy the better, with a whitebread gentleness and purity that's the gentle underside of the violence that's supposedly at the heart of "street" music but mostly is just a load of crap. The tunes only last a couple minutes, during which time their stolen hooks make you pound your steering wheel real hard. Fast tempos are common, ditto for high-register (like they haven't changed yet) vocals, with even higher surf/Beatles-type background harmonies; fuzztone riffs and drum thunder are encouraged, but only if they conceal a confectionary center. Lyrics are either of the playpen-bound ga-goo-ga-ga variety, or something only slightly more mature: about parents or cars or rock-as-religion or (usually) boy-girl predicaments free of adult neuroses: playing footsie, having crushes, going steady. All the most exciting things in the world until some imbecile tells you they're corny and you should only care about carnal knowledge, at which point it is my belief that you have started to stop living and begun to die.

Late bubblegum seems to divide itself naturally into three basic gumstrains, the first of which is real cheesy trash that exists exclusively to exploit you. Examples: Bay City Rollers' 1975 "Saturday Night" (a brogue spelling lesson from Tartan-clad Scottish lads who've got a date and just can't wait). Shaun Cassidy's 1977 "That's Rock 'n' Roll" (you're sixteen, sick of school, Keith Partridge's little brother. You buy a Farfisa, get the fever, get down and get with it). Abba's 1979 "Does Your Mother Know" (some tender hoodsie's hitting on either Bjorn or Benny at a bash; he says scram, but the riff-vroom—a snowmobile pillaging Scandinavia—tells her to stick around). The Knack's 1979 "My Sharona" (salacious sleaze-balls drooling about what's running down their thighs, mixing Beatle suits with John Bonham drums. Some people hated it. Some people have no sense of humor).

Post-'60s bubblegum's second strain primarily consists of nostalgic tributes to a supposedly simpler epoch, an endeavor which can risk both hyper-respectful quasicerebralness and smirky contempt, but can ring almost as true as the real thing if the performance is generous enough to be taken at face value. Such as it sort of is in: The Raspberries' 1972 "Go All the Way" (a restoration of pre-*Pepper* Lennon/McCartney via an airy chorus, a boogie kick, and the tiptop adolescent dilemma) and Nick Lowe's 1978 "Rollers Show" (dynamite semi-satire about going to see Tartan-clad Scottish lads, shouting noisily, and really giving it to 'em. Welsh critics' darlings the Pooh Sticks later applied the same idea to New Kids on the Block, to far lesser effect).

The third and final non-oldie bubblegum subgenre is bubblegum from isolated lands (in the far East, continental Europe, South America, etc.) where music is apparently still thought of as an opiate for the masses with no aesthetic strings attached. Since I can't understand the words (even if they're in English!), records like these tend to come off as nonsensical as "Yummy Yummy Yummy" and "Da Doo Ron Ron," and I can never tell whether they're trying to be funny or not: Plastic Bertrand's 1978 "Ça Plane Pour Moi" (how the Ramones would sound if they came from Belgium and wanted to imitate Brian Wilson in French but didn't know how); Naïf Orchestra's 1985 "Check-Out Five" (impiously infectious and interplanetarily offbeat sequencers and saxes, and Gianni Sangalli sad 'cause her Suzy's busy bagging vermicelli on a Sunday and can't see her); etc.

Might as well face it: If I tried hard enough, I could probably convince myself that *any* old tripe is terrific. Three years on the continent (1982–85), I tolerated Naïf Orchestra's sort of Eurodinkiness in every *Gasthaus* and record shop I killed time in (even remember Aryan kids breakdancing on Frankfurt sidewalks to it). So I'm well aware it's a zero-level reduction, the ultimate bastardization of rock'n'roll, a flimsy millimeter removed from Muzak. I originally associated yonder technopulse with stuff that had always repulsed me for no reason other than my own heteroboy repression, so you can chalk my tastes for such stuff up as a willfull fascination with an acknowledged annoyance if you want. I like music that's vacuous, contrived, absolutely redundant, okay? Sue me. The way I look at it, unlike vacuously contrived redundancies from Springsteen to Soundgarden, Eurobeat bubblegum has no aesthetic delusions. So it's free to be free.

The Bubblegum/Disco Connection

Eurodisco is easily bubblegum rock's truest successor. '60s-to-early-'70s gum was dance music created in the studio by producers, and an awful lot of it used an automated-sounding rhythm that anticipated disco's electronic pulse. In his liner notes to Rhino Records' excellent *The Best of the Ohio Express and other Bubblegum Smashes*, Harold Bronson says bubblegum's two primary factors were basic Midwestern rock and "a 1960's New York disco get-up-and-dance spirit." (By which he of course means *discotheques*, which predated "disco.") The 1910 Fruitgum Company's "Indian Giver" uses its organ, bass, and drums as pre-synthesized synths—the tom-tom hits are unchanging and unspaced, a steady automatic machinelike buzz, assisted by electricized hand-claps as well. Tony Orlando and Dawn's castanet-and-horn rhythm in their 1970 smashes "Candida" and "Knock Three Times" is an ancestor of the flamenco-disco hybrids of Santa Esmeralda and Gipsy Kings. The proto-Eno beat in the Shadows of Knight's "My Fire Department Needs a Fireman" is skittery but unyielding, like a ticking time-bomb, and in "Shake" they break into a gallant attempt-at-Latin-percussion break.

"Mercy" by the Ohio Express seems to have explicit elec-trobeat solos in the middle, almost serving as embellish-ments atop the main rhythm; their more famous hit "Yummy Yummy Yummy" shares its hook with Claudja Barry's 1979 disco hit "(Boogie Woogie) Dancin' Shoes." The Archies' "Jingle Jangle" opens with a ferocious grunt, then switches to a natural mambo-like swing featuring fast and curt basslines that anticipate Chic, then ends with deep voices doing blues calls. Toss in the expert percussive counterpoint (and title) of the Jaggerz' 1970 number-two "The Rapper" and the conga and electro parts in plenty of hits by gum/glam-cuspers the Sweet, and the gum factor winds up at least as important in disco's makeup as soul music itself!

Ram Jam's 1977 one-shot "Black Betty" was bubblegum, disco, and everything else. A cover of an age-old Leadbelly blues, produced by Kasenatz/Katz with huge kick drums and stomping glam-metal chords played in a way that approximates classical progressions, it passed as punk in *Time* magazine (where a '70s feature on said subculture included a picture of a girl in a torn "Black Betty Blam-De-Lam" T-shirt) even though the band included Billy Joel's old bassist and the guitarist used to do '60s pop with the Lemon Pipers. In 1989, Epic Records put out a house music remix. In 1994, it became a hit in France.

Disco hits by the Sylvers ("Hot Line" and "Boogie Fever"), K.C. and the Sunshine Band ("Keep it Comin' Love"), Taste of Honey ("Boogie Oogie Oogie"), and Dan Hartman ("Instant Replay") were bubblegum pure and simple. As Robot Hull and some pals pointed out in *Creem* in 1979, many disco groups were functional ad-hoc concoctions just like bubblegum acts used to be. It's no mistake that, in "Special Delivery," the 1910 Fruitgum Company used a gang chorus that sounded exactly like Village People in "Y.M.C.A." or "Macho Man," ten years early—Buddah (then Cameo-Parkway) Records '60s-gum magnate Neil Bogert wound up as a major disco magnate at Casablanca, home of Donna Summer, Village People, and *Thank God It's Friday*. And Barry White, whose Love Unlimited Orchestra helped invent disco from silk-and-string residue of Isaac Hayes's hot-buttered-soul-stained sheets in the early '70s, had his first taste of fame by writing "Doin' the Banana Split" for the Banana Splits a few years before.

Like the Archies, the Banana Splits had their own cartoon show. Only, they weren't teenagers—they were a dog, bear, elephant, and gorilla. (And which came first, anyway—Isaac's 1969 "Hyperbolicsyllabicsesquedalymistic" or the Splits' cereal box B-side "Caliopasaxaviatrumparimbaclarabassatrombophone"? We'll never know. "Supercalifragilisticexpialidocious," I guess.)

Nursery-Rhyme/Kiddie-Game/ Bedtime-Story Rock

Babytalk (the most bubblegum language of all) is most surprising and useful when it's just sort of stuck in there unexpectedly and it has nothing to do with the rest of the song, as opposed to a merely obvious aren't-we-being-cute move. Nursery rhymes have cohabitated with rock'n'roll ever since Chuck Berry quoted "Hey Diddle Diddle" in "Roll Over Beethoven," or maybe earlier: Ella Fitzgerald scored a big hit with "A Tisket a Tasket" in 1938, and Louis Jordan's 1949 "School Days (When We Were Kids)" incorporated parts of "Mary Had a Little Lamb," "Little Jack Horner," "Peter Peter Pumpkin Eater," "Humpty Dumpty," and "Simple Simon." Bo Diddley's Latinized 1960 "Nursery Rhyme" and Chubby Checker's calypsofied 1963 "Mother Goose Limbo" were similar montages. (On the other hand, O.C. Smith argued in 1968's "Little Green Apples" that Mother Goose, Doctor Seuss, and nursery rhymes don't even *exist*, if and only if O.C.'s wife doesn't love him. But she does.)

The lullaby rhyme "Hush Little Baby" is used in Bo Diddley's "Bo Diddley," Ian Dury's "Reasons to be Cheerful, Pt. 3" (thanks to its "nanny goat" reference), the Shangri-Las' "I Can Never Go Home Anymore," and Carly Simon's and James Taylor's "Mockingbird"; also, rap songs like the Funky Four Plus One More's "Rappin' and Rocking the House," Grandmaster Flash and the Furious Five's "Superrappin' No. 2," and L'Trimm's "Low Rider," where if your Mercedes breaks down you take the Seville, then Caddy, then Stutz, then Rolls, then train (or, in L'Trimm's case, "if you ain't got a low rider then go 'head and ride the bus") are essentially variations on Diddley's "Hush Little Baby" diamond ring/nánny goat/mockingbird motif, which was in turn a variation on '30s/'40s playground/cottonfield chants called "Hambone" and "Chevrolet." As, most likely, was Rufus Thomas's "Jump Back," where he kept swapping a horse for a bull for a dollar for some grass for a hoe, and Donovan's

"Hey Gyp," where he offered to buy his gal a Chevy, then Mustang, then Cadillac.

"Mary Had a Little Lamb" shows up in the Hombres' "Am I High" (melody scatted in the middle), Otis Redding's "Mary's Little Lamb," Snap's "Mary Had a Little Boy," and Stevie Wonder's "Fingertips—Pt. 2" (a couple furious bars of it, blown on the harmonica). Pig Latin, Double Dutch, atthay ort-say of ing-thay: Another Bad Creation "Playground"; Das EFX "They Want EFX"; Leadbelly "Dog-Latin Song"; Frankie Smith "Double Dutch Bus" (gruff 1981 Philadelphia rap-as-vaudeville-as-disc-jockey as-*Sesame Street* novelty hit). Unidentified rope-jumping song: K.T. Oslin "80's Ladies" ("C my name is Connie, I'm gonna marry Charlie, we're gonna sell cars, and live in California"). "The Wabbit Kicked the Bucket" (by Elmer Fudd): The Fall "Slang King" ("twip wiwah!"); Kix "Yeah, Yeah, Yeah"; Nena "99 Red Balloons" (probably accidental—the English version goes "soopah skoowy caw the twoops out in a hoowy"); Real Roxanne with Howie Tee "Bang Zoom Let's Go-Go!"; Roxanne Shante "Wack It."

And then there's tough guys inspired by prison cells or Barnacle Bill poopdecks or the "bully" section of schoolyards on the bad part of town on the wrong side of the tracks who take words from nursery rhymes and change them so they're *dirty*—Funkadelic in "Loose Booty" and Slade in "Did Ya Mama Ever Tell Ya," then Blowfly and Andrew Dice Clay and maybe Das EFX (hard to make out their words). Schoolly D even had Mary of lamb fame share a joint with Little Miss Muffett once, and his "Gangster Boogie II" had "Tarzan and Jane sittin' in a tree, F-U-C-K-I-N-G" (but nothing about a baby carriage). In "Gucci Time" he made Baa Baa Black Sheep a whore—I think he might've been listening to "Rock'n'Roll Nigger" by Patti Smith that day. Then he blew her brains out, "and now she in jail on a ten-year bid." I never knew they put *dead* hooved mammals behind bars!

Meaning Streets

Joe Elliott of Def Leppard told *Request* magazine in 1992 that "there's nothing wrong with being deep and meaningless," which is what he says Def Leppard (not to mention the Police's "De Do Do Do, De Da Da Da" and Gene Vincent's "Be-Bop-A-Lula") are, and by which he means "we're not a band that preaches about the ozone layer or the Brazilian rain forest." Lots of people credit Bob Dylan with first introducing politics to rock'n'roll (which is silly—politics was in in the Coasters and Chuck Berry and the Silhouettes' "Get a Job" and Elvis Presley's hips already). But from what I can see, the best stuff on *Bringing it all Back Home* and *Highway 61 Revisited* was more like some meaninglessness-disguised-as-meaning-as-mindfuck-on-purpose, same sort of pasttime Rammelzee vs. K-Rob instigated rapwise with "Beat Bop" in 1983, Sonic Youth made loud empty mood music with later in the '80s, then Nirvana made so much money with in 1991. Once an interviewer asked Dylan what his songs were about, and he said "some are about four minutes, some are about five minutes, and believe it or not, some are about 11 or 12."

Which sounds right to me, so I guess I'd say that when "to mean" means "to matter," music *must* "mean" to "matter." (My favorite songs sure mean a lot to me.) But where "to mean" means "to have words translatable as something important," music must not necessarily "mean" to "matter" (though sometimes it helps).

Songs become meaningful when people use them in their everyday lives. "Aboutness" isn't as mandatory in rock as in country, where frequently it's the only interesting thing you've got. Robert Christgau wrote that more "well-meaning bad records" scored in 1992's *Village Voice* Pazz and Jop critics' poll than ever before, but I figure what else is new? Aren't well-meaning bad records the reason rock critics' polls were *invented*? Anyway, here are some musicians' own thoughts on the subject:

Blues comedian Blind Blake, 1929: "I wish somebody would tell me what Diddie Wah Diddie means."

The Delfonics, Philadelphia falsetto-soul prototypes, went to number four in 1968 with "La La Means I Love You."

Carly Simon scolds in 1972's "You're So Vain" that "you probably think this song is about you." Which is often the case with songs that move you deeply—you can relate to them better.

New York Doll David Johansen, in *Creem*, 1973: "We use those guitars to make sounds that mean something to us. We don't make sounds that would mean anything to a bunch of hillbillies."

Frankie Valli's 1978 soundtrack-slime number-one "Grease" claims "grease is the word" (dissenting from the Trashmen, who in 1963 claimed "*bird* is the word"). And their chosen word "has groove, it's got meaning." (Then again, so does "motherfucker.")

"Truckload of Art" by Lubbock cowboy aesthete Terry Allen (1979) instigates an inferno of influential avant-garde on the shoulder of the interstate, "but nobody knows what it means."

Public Image Ltd's 1980 "Careering" commands, "There must be meaning behind the moaning." (But what about *good* singing?)

Halfway into Taana Gardner's 1981 disco classic "Heartbeat," she suddenly admits, "Now you know this don't make *no* sense."

Double Dee & Steinski's 1985 proto-sampling-barrage collage "Lesson 3" ends by asking "Say children, what does it all mean?"

In 1986 in "Expressway to Yr Skull" (alias "Madonna, Sean and Me," alias "The Crucifixion of Sean Penn"), Sonic Youth go West in search of "the meaning of feeling good." I'm sure they were overjoyed to learn Madonna has similar epistemelogical neuroses, as demonstrated by her 1990 title "Justify My Love."

The Bellamy Brothers named an '80s song "When the Music Meant Everything," suggesting it no longer did. Back in 1976, when they'd philosophized in their huge "Let Your Love Flow" that "there's a reason why I'm feeling so high," their music (or *life itself!*) had some higher purpose. (Unless by "reason" they meant a "prior cause," as opposed to a "higher cause.")

Heavy D's 1989 New Jack Wobble smash "We Got Our Thing" insists that "there's always a meaning to a Heavy D statement," but he probably really means "a Heavy D raincoat" instead.

Mark IV's 1989 house single "It's a Mean World" follows the title by explaining what they *mean* by a mean world: "You've gotta mean what you say, mean what you do." Whatever that means.

Nirvana's 1992 hit "In Bloom" mumbles about a guy who sings along to pretty songs "but he don't know what it means." Proving that their fans get no more out of Nirvana songs than I do.

Mouth Instruments

Rock's roots in James Dean and Marlon Brando long ago asserted that the purpose of vocals is most importantly to *sound* cool. Whether you can make sense of them is generally immaterial.

There's intentional incomprehensibility moves like *Exile on Main Street* and (note title) Wire's "French Film Blurred," but all they do is draw yellow highlighter-pen circles around mumbling that's always been there. "You guys wanna sell a few records?" Stan Freberg murmurs like Montgomery Clift to his understudies in his #14 1954 version of "Sh-Boom." "Then stick some old rags in your mouth and take it from the top." "Funniest sound I ever heard," croak doo-wop weirdos the Rivingtons in "Papa-Oom-Mow-Mow," "and I can't understand a single word."

Come 1964, the Kingsmen's "Louie Louie" was officially dismissed, following a federal investigation designed to determine whether its lyrics had something to do with boners in a girl's hair, as "unintelligible at any speed." James Brown's music tended to be just a bunch of disconnected sentences with lots of grunts and screams trying to work as rhythm. And years later, in no-wave 1979, David Thomas's yowling and shrieking panics on Pere Ubu's *Dub Housing* and the New York band Mars's high-MPH-motored marblemouthing in "Helen Forsdale" were almost undeniably *improved* by your not being able to understand them.

Dub reggae makes obscuring words a major tenet of Rastafarianism. (Visual equivalent: how reggae toaster U-Roy obscures his face with bong smoke on the cover of 1975's *Dread in a Babylon*.) And hip-hop carries on any number of rock and dub unintelligibility traditions to this very day, and not always in the labored way that "Native Tongue" art-simps like De La Soul and Tribe Called Quest (or the not-finished-chewing-their-lunch way that oafish speech-impediment posterboys like Wu Tang Clan and Notorious B.I.G.) do it, either: Naughty By Nature's 1991 "O.P.P." revived the old "Tutti Frutti" principle of using a secret teenage-only code to disguise filthy language; in "Mind Playing Tricks on Me," the

Geto Boy rapping the second verse apparently says "I live by the swamp," which could make sense since the music is a kind of plantation blues, but he rhymes "swamp" with "paranoid," so maybe he's saying "I live by the *sword*," which might be more poetic. And in yet another great rap cross-over of 1991, D.J. Jazzy Jeff and the Fresh Prince's barbecue pit soundtrack "Summertime," Will Smith says either that the smell of a "grill" or a "girl" can "spark up nostalgia."

The 496 most *famous* examples of recent unintelligibility, of course, can be found in Nirvana's 1991 "Smells Like Teen Spirit," a song that came out of "nowhere" (a.k.a. Seattle) when it did and hit as big as it did in a way as absurd as what happened to the Knack's "My Sharona" in 1979 (six weeks at number one!). We were all watching and smirking with our mouths hanging open the Knack time, and we were all doing the same the Nirvana time, and kids who bought Nirvana's hype already look back at it with the same be-mused affection that people my age look back at "My Sharona." So "Smells Like Teen Spirit" will never die.

In 1992, Weird Al Yankovic blessed Nirvana with damn near the only honest rock criticism they ever received: "What is this song all about, can't figure any lyrics out" in "Smells Like Nirvana," the most dead-on parody of mangle-mouthed singing since Freberg's "Sh-Boom." Not until my wife and I threw our first party in thirteen years of wedded bliss in 1995 (four years after the song) did I finally realize that "Teen Spirit"'s words are actually about a little-group-that's-always-been of geeks (albinos, mulattos, mosquitos, my libido) who feel less geeky at nighttime since when the light's out it's less dangerous, so they all go out together looking to be entertained—who cares if my interpretation isn't exactly what Kurt had in mind?

Whichever way you hear it determines how it affects you, so whichever way you hear it is right. "A man hears what he wants to hear and disregards the rest," Simon and Garfunkel deeply philosophized in "The Boxer," 1969. So Elton John (who proved with his dada poem "Solar Prestige a Gammon" that he can make even *intentionally* idiotic nonsense stick to your gills) had some great lines when I was growing up:

"Since the day when I was born a naked man"; "I get high in the evening sniffing Pop Tart glue" (you know, that sticky icing they put on top). Same with Bruce Springsteen: "Working in the fields, Alligator Blackburn"; "I don't give a damn if the same old flame outsings me." Here are a few more such rock'n'roll success stories:

—Darlene Love, "Today I Met The Boy I'm Gonna Marry": Smooches boy and feels "his sweet sensation, this time it wasn't just my emasturbation." Thinks we're hearing "imagination."

—Debbie Gibson, "Lost in Your Eyes": "I get weak in the glands, isn't that what's called romance?" She means "glance."

—The Police: "A year has passed since I broke my nose."

—Merilee Rush, "Angel of the Morning": "Wash my feet before you leave me" or "Brush your teeth before you eat me"? (Which perhaps refers to the good-hygiene reminder that rock's ultimate bad-hygeine combo the Velvet Underground used to open "Sweet Jane": "Standing on the corner, toothbrush in my hand.")

—I always thought the line "Roland on the river" in Ike and Tina Turner's "Proud Mary" was about Roland Parker, one of the only black kids I knew when I was in fifth grade.

—And in Bob Seger's version of Ike and Tina's "Nutbush City Limits," when he says "get in jail," I always thought it was "Get Indian Trail," which would make sense since Indian Trail is this place in Northern Oakland County, Michigan, that Bob probably would've known about since he lived around there.

—Proof (from "No Woman No Cry") that Bob Marley smoked too much ganja: "I remember when we used to sit in another dimension in Trenchtown." No weed in a "government mansion"!

—REO Speedwagon on the Protestant Reformation, in their 1978 AOR hit "Time for Me to Fly": "I've had enough of the falseness of a worn-out religion." Which sure beats "relation."

—Sam the Sham and the Pharoahs' 1965 hit "Ju Ju Hand" repeatedly includes the line "Yoko Mott the Hoople backwards sure is grand," even though neither Yoko Ono nor Mott would begin their recording careers until a few years later.

—In "Rockaway Beach" in 1977, the Ramones try to complain about music on a slow "bus ride," but their tongues get twisted: "Punk rock goes too slow/They blast out the disco on the radio."

—Sister Sledge's 1979 hit "He's the Greatest Dancer" mentions "the kind of body that would shame Madonna's," four years before bodybuilder Madonna debuted in "Burning Up" by boasting she feels "no shame." (See also "Visions of Johanna," Bob Dylan, 1966: "Madonna, she still has not showed." Which is actually what he *meant* to say!)

—Jorge Ben's Brazilian (Portuguese?) "Ponta de Lanca Africano (Umbabarauma)" can be heard as a mantra about Nintendo's Super Mario Brothers game: "Stomp anotha goombah, Marr-ee-oh."

—Noisy guttural songs that try hard to sound primitive can be about just about anything you want. Brit sheet-metalheads (or maybe just sheet-heads) Test Dept.'s 1983 debut single "Compulsion"/"Pulsations" has a chant that goes "Sandra Bernhard! Sandra Bernhard!," though she wasn't a famous comedienne yet.

—When my son Linus was little, he thought we couldn't go visit any animals because he'd heard in a TV commercial that it was the "Destroyed Zoo." He didn't realize it was in Detroit!

—And in the Christmas carol "Winter Wonderland," do we "expire" or "perspire" as we sit by the fire? No cheating, now.

What these various and sundry instances of mispronunciation and/or misinterpretation suggest is that, unless they want to lose sleep worrying about smart-alecks like me, rock and pop singers might well be better off just *not saying any words at all*. Which is sort of what scat-singers like Louis Armstrong did, playing around mouth-wise without "communicating" or "expressing" anything. For instance, Neil Sedaka's 1963 "Breaking Up Is Hard to Do" ("comma comma down doobie doo down down") is explicitly-scatted-punctuation-mark rock, a real rarity.

But that's still just (quasi)-improvisatory time-filler material, nice in its own way no argument there but nowhere near as fun as when the singer picks out an instrument in the big parade and imitates *that*. And I don't mean ho-hum Bobby McFerrin showoff-for-the-garden-club crapola; I'm talking as part of an otherwise reasonably justifiable-on-its-own-terms *song*—like, for instance, how either James Brown in the '60s or some African guy centuries ago invented the old-school-rap rule that voices should always be percussion. Or like how:

Fleetwood Mac (the "baow baow-b'bow-baow"s in "Second Hand News") and Sly Stone ("bum bum BUM bum bum"s in "M'Lady") have used vocals as basslines. Acapella bells range from dainty "bom bom bom" church-altar ones (Dionne Warwick's "You'll Never Get to Heaven," the Association's "Windy," Madonna's "Crazy for You," Debbie Gibson's "Only in My Dreams") to rejoiceful "dingalingadingdong" ones (the Willows' 1956 doowop "Church Bells May Ring") to big scary "DING-DONG! DING-DONG!" Notre Dame churchtower ones (the Del-Vikings' 1957 doowop "Whispering Bells," Patti Smith's "Gloria"). Voices-as-drums can ratatattat (Vickie Sue Robinson's "Turn the Beat Around," Shep and the Limelites' "Daddy's Home") or barumpabumbum ("Little Drummer Boy," which has been renditionized by Boney M, Joan Jett, New Kids on the Block, Bob Seger, and David Bowie with Bing Crosby). (And Beck did "Little Drum *Machine* Boy.")

"157 Riverside Avenue" used to be a highlight of REO Speedwagon concerts because of its innovative scat-as-guitar break. (It's even on their live album.) In 1949, Fats Domino gave his "The Fat Man" an extended high-pitched vocal Delta-blues wah-wah guitar part at more or less exactly the same time that his fellow New Orleans piano deity Professor Longhair was using his whistling as a damn-near-second-bank of barrelhouse ivory in "Mardi Gras in New Orleans." The Belmonts open "I Wonder Why," Dion's first hit (1958), with an audaciously complex acapella Morse Code keyboard solo, but their "wop, wop, wop-wop-wop"s are more like drum wallops, not to mention a sly comment on their Italian heritage—they probably had the best vocal-rhythm section *ever*. The Four Seasons' "Who Loves You," the Five Americans' "Western Union," Shonen Knife's "An Angel Has Come," and Gipsy Kings' "Este Mundo" have vocally telegraphed dit-dit-dats, too. The Offspring open their 1994 hit "Self-Esteem" with a vocal-harmonized *Beavis and Butthead*-style version of Black Sabbath's "Ironman" guitar riff. And in between such interjected asides as "How come these words don't rhyme?" and "Oink!" and "You're playing with your meat!," the Rats' 1965-or-so punk rumble "Rat's Revenge" features rock's only known acapella *Jew's Harp* part.

Van Morrison used to use his voice as horns, bells, pianos, guitar riffs, the whole shebang (listen to "Brown Eyed Girl" or "Jackie Wilson Said," not so much his boring interminable speaking-in-tounges puke), what with all those shangalanga-langalangalangalangalangs and bip bop bip bop bips. He knew the voice is the most versatile instrument in rock'n'roll, the one with the biggest capacity for giving music a distinct personality—it's as important as all the other instruments put together.

Four Words to the Wack:
Stay the Hell Back

Rap music is the culmination of vocals-working-as-drums, but rap groups did not invent rapping. To appreciate why, the first thing you have to understand is this: *all* songs rhyme, almost. What makes rap rap is *how* it rhymes. Namely: nonsung, steady-cadenced, word-emphasized. Usually. So though lots of pre-rap crap (scat, doowop, Barry White, Richard Pryor, etc.) shares this or that with rap, most doesn't share enough. But some does. And what does dates back some four-score-and-seven years, to such potty-mouthed post-slave prison tales as "Jody Grinder" and "Shine Swam the Titanic," wherein anybody can have yo mama for a 10¢ glass of beer. Some unbroken thread runs from this stuff through Blowfly to N.W.A. and 2 Live Crew and especially Schoolly-D, whose *Smoke Some Kill* has a thing called "Signifying Rapper," based on Schoolly's dad's copy of Rudy Ray Moore's dirty "party record" "Signifying Monkey." Never heard that version myself, but Smokey Joe Waugh's 1955 Sun single version has unhealthy growling, and there's plenty of poontang in Tom Ellis's rendition, recorded behind Missouri bars in 1966.

Record collectors with longer attention spans than me think the post-"Shine"/"Jody" dirty-dozen-thang peaked with Lightnin' Rod's streetologically explicit black-wax poker-to-electrocution B-flick *Hustler's Convention* (1973), which plopped beaucoups pushers, callgirls, nymphs, and pimps atop jazz wobble; Lightnin' Rod also once praised a pocket-picking prostitute in "Doriella Du Fontaine," a raunchy rap backed by Jimi Hendrix. Lightnin' Rod was one of the Last Poets, whose early-'70s proto-protest-rap was unfortunately really more a mere "free"-verse-atop-avant-bongos deal, descended from Malcolm X and H. Rap Brown and Muhammad Ali. Not to mention from Amiri Baraka, who slings double-dipping pun-rhetoric (too pretentious to rhyme much) over David Murray's hard-to-take horn-honk on an album-you-shouldn't-waste-money-on called *New Music New Poetry*. Last-poetry fans also groove on how Gil Scott-Heron's 1974

"The Revolution Will Not Be Televised" dissed Spiro Agnew, Jed Clampett, "hairy-armed women liberationists and Jackie Onassis blowing her nose."

Reggae Toasting's a protest rap subset if you can make out the words: Tapper Zukie has a song called "Message to Pork Eaters"! Dave and Ansil Collins's 1971 U.S. novelty hit "Double Barrel" is a weird Jamaican radio-deejay duet with backwards R&B rhythms and James Brown grunts, and Dillinger's 1977 "Cokane in My Brain" is illogic by a guy who spells "New York" with silverware and keeps asking where Jim is, but can't find him. (So it's a duet with only one person singing!) As for Linton Kwesi Johnson, he's too bogged down in history and propaganda to think straight (i.e.: too much "integrity" for his own good).

Fact is, none of the post-dozens stuff I've listed sounds *that* much like rap proper. But Pigmeat Markham's "Here Comes The Judge" (famous thanks to *Laugh-In* on '60s TV) does. Likewise, court-jester Pigmeat's "I Got the Number" could pass for a Staxier Run-D.M.C. even though it was New York's Lotto theme in the '40's and was recorded for Chess Records in 1968. Starting with white guy Harmonica Frank in the early '50s, Chess (which struck up an oddly appropriate reissue contract with seminal rap company Sugarhill in 1980) was the first great Novelty Rap label—like "I Got the Number," Bo Diddley's 1958 "Say Man" basically just consisted of two clowns trading off insults.

Later Novelty Raps can be heard halfway through the Jackson Five's 1970 "Goin' Back to Indiana," all the way through Napoleon XIV's insane-in-the-brain 1966 "They're Coming To Take Me Away, Ha-Haa!," at the beginnings of the Pipkins' 1970 top-ten "Gimme Dat Ding," Steve Martin's 1978 "King Tut" (the vocal cadence of which became a major Miami-bass influence), and Paper Lace's 1974 "The Night Chicago Died." The latter, by five happy hacks from England, has the distinction of being the first rap record ever to top the charts in what the record refers to as "the land of the dollar bill"—seven years before Blondie's "Rapture," twelve before Falco's "Rock Me Amadeus," sixteen before Vanilla Ice's "Ice Ice Baby." And being about Al Capone, it obviously qualifies as Gangsta Rap as well: cops even get killed in it!

In fact, the forgotten Pipkins/Paper Lace/Hurricane Smith Charleston revival of the early '70s made a good argument for hip-hop being the invention of vaudeville comics as much as of carnival barkers, medicine men, or AM radio deejays. Freddie Cannon, who'd included the prophetic line "pop a hippity-hop hop a hippity hop pop" in his 1960 "Chattanooga Shoe Shine Boy," does a guest rap in "Outrageous" on the 1975 album *Disco Tex and his Sex-O-Lettes* where he actually *boasts* rap-style, saying you've never had it better than Freddie C, "the boom-boom boy from Talahassee, baby ball me." And Disco Tex (alias Sir Monti Rock) himself tosses in prescient "everybody go woo!" commands plus a rap in "Boogie Flap" that quotes "Hit the Road Jack" by Ray Charles then predicts the return of the Roaring '20s.

Ray Charles's primal pianistic yell-and-response attack "What'd I Say" (1959) doesn't so much resemble a rap as a couple copulating in a cottonfield, but how about let's dub it forerunner of R&B/funk-type proto-rap anyhow—first Rufus Thomas's robbers-and-bedbugs spiel "Jump Back" in 1964, then not so much James Brown (whose groovalistics were too expansive to be truly "rapped" to, by him anyway) as his backup band Fred Wesley and the New JB's, who were blabbing full-fledged rapstyle (albiet Southern-fried in lard grease) in 1974 with "Little Boy Black" and "Breakin' Bread." And Isaac Hayes (whose "raps" were usually just seductive monologues) had a real one with "Good Love 6-996" in 1971, and the Jimmy Castor Bunch did *plenty* of no-question-about-it garrumphing-guitar 'Fro-disco proto-raps: "The Everything Man" in 1974 (a brag about being a Cancer/Gemini-cusp one-man band); "Hallucinations" the same year (sugarcube-groove disco newsflash about the end of the world); "Bertha Butt Encounters Vadar" in 1978 (which turns *heavily* metallic).

Plus, Parliament's "Chocolate City" gets called "the precursor of modern rap" on the back of their *Greatest Hits*, but if Tom Vicker was observant he'd've so-named "Take Your Dead Ass Home" on 1977's live *P-Funk Earth Tour* instead, given its naughtily rapped limerick that rhymes "penis" with "Venus" and "goo" with "Peru." Which disturbingly enough makes this as appropriate a time as any to unveil my Parliament-Funkadelic problem, so I will. They made a couple *Best Of* anthologies worth of okay singles, even a few great ones—"Can You Get to That," "Cosmic Slop," "Flashlight," "One Nation Under a Groove." And with "Maggot Brain" and "Lunchmeataphobia" they perfected the use of the heaviest possible blues-metal guitars as non-rocking but lovely easy-listening schmaltz. But especially as far as their pre-disco-era stuff goes, P-Funk were basically an arty retro band, mixing 1965 James Brown revivalism with 1967 Frank Zappa stupidity. (*Creem*, 1970: "Everything they do seems to be a parody of something.") They were slow and unstructured, and their music festered when it should've moved, not least because they preferred logjammed thumping to actual propulsion. Their mouth-bullshit wandered too aimlessly to work as musical parts of speech, even good musical nonsense. And as usual with denseness hyped as "intense," the melodies weren't worth much.

So forget P-Funk. Instead let's dive way back to the '20s, to caboose-stowaway traveling-tent-show hucksterism like Lonnie Glosson's amusing "Arkansas Hard Luck Blues," which talks about a family with so many kids ("seven boys, eight girls, and two other children") that they have to decide which ones they want to get rid of in the river. Lonnie, who the liner notes to Yazoo Records' indispensable 1996 *Roots of Rap* CD claim later achieved fame peddling harmonica lessons in ads on back covers of comic books, says he's "lost all I had and part of my furniture," so he's a standup comedian if not a standup guy. *Roots of Rap* populates itself otherwise with song collectors, jug jazzers, church sermonizers, self-classified practitioners of "strut" and "jive" (such as cleaning-woman-falsetto-boast-rhyming budding female impersonator Frankie "Half-Pint" Jackson), pinetoppers poeticizing over revolving ragtime rhythms, even a bluegrass-breakdown combo—Seven Foot Dilly and his Dill Pickles, whose fast-fiddled "Pickin' Off Peanuts" is both a spiel and a reel.

The Blue Ridge Playboys, Western Swingers featuring future honky-tonk heroes Floyd Tillman on guitar and Moon Mullican on piano, did a ribald hillbilly rap called "Give Me My Money" in 1936; it had lines about gals living across the hill who won't but their sisters will, plus the singer kept demanding his "dime back," foreseeing Chuck Berry's later "Too Much Monkey Business" payphone travails. By the '40s, Woody Guthrie was chanting absolute, undeniable hobo/dada/Pinko rap with "Talking Columbia" and "Talking Dust Blues," being quite cynical about Ay-tomic bedrooms and how (no kidding) "that old tractor got my homeboys." A generation later, Woody's kid Arlo tried to rap in "Alice's Restaurant," but couldn't get dad's beat right. But Harmonica Frank (who stole chunks of lyric from Lonnie Glosson, from late '20s blackface minstrel Emmett Miller, from who knows who else) could: said Mississippi mystery-train wanderer's randy 1951 "Swamp Root" had him necking with a hussy and introducing the second verse as "the second verse" and ending with an insanitized hiccupping yee-haw yodel, and his similarly recited "The Great Medical Menagerist" from the same year was almost as speedy and maniacal.

With the botherating complexity of "Too Much Monkey Business" ("pay phone, something wrong, dime gone, we'll mail it, oughta sue") in 1956, Harmonica Frank's Chess successor Chuck Berry set the dada-rap standard until Bob Dylan wed Woody to Chuck (and Bo Diddley) in 1965, adding hammy harmonicating and confusing leaders-and-parking-meters advice in "Subterranean Homesick Blues." The cadence of which eventually led directly to stanza #6 of "The Message" by Grandmaster Flash (which also owes something to the Temptations' 1970 Dylan/funk hybrid "Ball of Confusion": "rap on, brother, rap on"). Three decades later, in MTV hits like "Loser" and "Where It's At," post-indie wiseguy Beck would folkify hip-hop vocal and dance rhythms in much the same way Dylan had once folkified R&B vocal and dance rhythms, to certainly entertaining if infinitely less original effect.

Woody Guthrie can also be held responsible for the entire genre of country rap—Jerry Reed's "When You're Hot You're

Hot," Roger Miller's "My Uncle Used to Love Me but She Died," Johnny Cash's "A Boy Named Sue," Lorne Greene's "Ringo" (which actually concerned a "posse" with guns!), Jimmy Dean's "Big Bad John," Commander Cody's "Hot Rod Lincoln," C.W. McCall's "Convoy." And especially Dylan sideman Charlie Daniels's 1973 top-ten "Uneasy Rider," with a cadence and KKK-tavern storyline that soul-singer-turned-foul-mouth Blowfly modified only slightly in *his* one great record, 1980's "Blowfly's Rapp." (Charlie's *A Decade of Hits* almost qualifies as an entire C&W-rap *album*.)

In 1967, the Hombres, a Memphis garage-frat foursome with blood-alcohol levels too high to drive, had a one-shot rap hit with "Let it Out (Let it all Hang Out)." It opens with what almost sounds like a digital sample, namely a preacher railing against "John Barleycorn, nicotine, and the temptations of Eve." Then somebody farts, then a guitar riff taken from the Shadows of Knights' "Gloria" kicks in and is repeated hip-hop-style through the entire song. The singer anticipates how Beck records would sound in the distant future by drawling a ridiculous Dylan parody that compares Galileo to an Eagle scout and warns against parking near sewer signs. On their album, the Hombres performed "Gloria" itself (which they turned into "Eight Miles High" when nobody was looking) and tried two additional Dylan-dada raps.

The Hombres were about as punk rock as you can get, but eventually the other punk rock happened, and then in 1979 (same year the Sugarhill Gang and Fatback Band first put hip-hop-proper on the map with "Rapper's Delight" and "King Tim III") England gave us such rap-like curiosities as "Pop Muzik" (a worldwide number-one re: international travel and doing it in your car in the middle of the night) by M; "Crap Rap 2/Like to Blow" (re: smack, sex, and poop) by the Fall; "Reasons to be Cheerful, Pt. 3" (re: porridge oats, equal votes, nanny goats, and squawky saxophone solos) by Ian Dury; and "Amnesty International Report on British Army Torture of Irish Prisoners" (re: getting "beaten in the face, stomach, head, and genitals") by Communists the Pop Group (who on their just-as-charmingly-titled *For How Much*

Longer Do We Tolerate Mass Murder? covered a Last Poets poem.)

Later seminal pre-"Pour Some Sugar on Me" Brit-rap landmarks include Queen's dub-minimalist 1980 "Another One Bites the Dust," Evasions' Cockney-proper 1981 "Wikka Wrap" (later alluded to in '90s Coolio and Warren G hits), Captain Sensible's Cockney-bawdy/Queen-basslined 1982 "Wot," Malcolm McLaren's square-dancey 1982 "Buffalo Gals," and Wham! U.K.'s dole-embracing 1983 "Wham! Rap." Weirdest of all has to be the 1982 MTV hit "Shiny Shiny," by London Antpeople called Haysi Fantayzee who dressed hobo-style as "Dickensian Rastas." Everything in this song—opening Kate Bush murmur, saxnoise solo, turntable scratch, do-si-do fiddle break with calls swiped from Bob Wills's 1947 proto-rap squaredance "Sally Goodin," playground games swiped from Shirley Ellis's 1965 "The Clapping Song," Vietnam namedrop, "the city is a pity because I dress divine"—is just stuck in there with disregard for everything else. 100% pure What-Were-They-Thinking? Rock.

Everything Rock Vs. Collage Rock

As recently as 1990, Haysi Fantayzee's quiltwork was still a fresh-enough memory that sampled soundbites and musical snippets could seem like the most interesting parts of a rock or rap album; now they're almost always just an annoyance. In 1987, there weren't many precedents for a sugar-metal band like Def Leppard sampling a Ronald Reagan speech about retaliating against Libyan terrorists (in "Gods of War"). But before long, the use of newsbites and similar post-hip-hop pastiche tidbits on loud-guitar CDs by Slaughter, Guns N' Roses, Living Colour, Queensrÿche, Riot, and so forth made the move commonplace.

I say "post-hip-hop" because that's the habitat this stuff proliferated in: the habitat created when Grandmaster Flash used parallel turntables to mix pieces of Spoonie Gee, Chic, Blondie, Queen, a *Flash Gordon* episode, and a skit where somebody tries to sell you dope into his 1981 collage symphony "Adventures of Grandmaster Flash on the Wheels of Steel"; the habitat made inescapable when otherwise ignorable British vague-pop entities A.R. Kane and Colourbox (as M/A/R/R/S) sampled Trouble Funk, the Last Poets, Eric B. & Rakim, crater monsters, and Israeli star Ofra Haza into their 1987 NASA montage "Pump Up the Volume."

But hip-hoppers didn't really invent it. From Def Leppard's vantage point, the Beatles probably did. The 1967 singles "I Am the Walrus"/"Hello Goodbye" and "Penny Lane"/"Strawberry Fields Forever" are four sides of quilted bricolage. "Walrus" mixes Dylan's meaninglessness-as-meaning nonsense with warped 20th-century classical whatever, plus cartoony penguin/walrus juxtapostions (see: Tennessee Tuxedo and Chumley), a mumbling old man at the end, and evil ho-ho-ho-hee-hee-hee-ha-ha-ha laughs (swiped by Black Sabbath in "Am I Going Insane" on their ahead-of-its-time 1975 montage album *Sabotage*, then later by Flipper). "Hello Goodbye" is mood music with some out-of-synch vocals colliding against each other, a dead stop, then Hare Krishna chants. "Penny Lane" is a quasi-nonchalant mundanity move with double-entendres and marching band sounds; "Strawberry Fields Forever" is perfect clatter-beat/altered-vocal kazooband art-pop, ebullient but dark, again stopping dead at the end for a ten-second spiel of off-key backwards experimental whatsis. (You've heard 'em all before right? The last three are kinda pretty.)

Still, the Beatles didn't invent collage-rock, either. Collages had always been implicit in rock music, in *all* music—songs are made up of pieces of other songs. "The total Beach Boy aesthetic is still aggressively wholesome: schizoid rather than eclectic," wrote R. Meltzer in *The Aesthetics of Rock*. "In the '60s 'eclectic' was rock criticism's first cliché," suggests Robert Christgau. And it still is one—plenty of music, including just about all sample-collage stuff, rests on the assumption that recombining all different branches of sound is doing something radical. When really, schizoid everythingness is simply the natural order of things. *Leadbelly's Last Sessions*, recorded casually and spontaneously in folklorist Frederic Ramsey, Jr.'s apartment during three nights in 1948, has standards, hollers, nursery rhymes, reels, pig Latin, musical comedy, rags, murder ballads, ramblin' blues. "Leadbelly, when he got going, had a routine that was like that of the record collector who, with a large library to choose from, spends an evening pulling out his favorite discs in sequence both varied and suggestive," Ramsey observed. Similarly, the notes to Charley Patton's *Founder of the Delta Blues* say the illiterate and usually drunk '30s blues grumbler made songs out of just about anything, especially anything dirty; he'd shuffle verses, add new ones, steal other people's at random, change them if he forgot the right words. Some of his tunes even drew on British and Oriental folk music. Phil Spector, according to Nik Cohn in *The Rolling Stone Illustrated History of Rock and Roll*, "stole from every source he could—Wagner, Leonard Bernstein, Broadway shows, a thousand or a million other singles, past and present." And Italian '20s-to-'70s New-Orleans-to-Vegas dance-band leader Louis Prima (who despite *sounding* rock'n'roll wasn't *considered* such because parents listened to him instead of kids) had a scope documented by Scott Shea thuswise in notes to Capitol Records' *Collectors Series* CD: "tarantellas interwoven with Dixieland jazz, medleys of reworked standards, altered lyrics befitting Prima's dialect." That's not the half of it. In "Embraceable You"/"I Got It Bad and That Ain't Good" on his 1958 *Las Vegas–Prima Style*, Louis's wife and partner Keely Smith sings sultry and serious, but Lou keeps dropping gags like "call for an appointment" and (when she denies her heart's made of wood) "waddaya think mine's made of, lasagna?" Live with Sam Butera and the Witnesses on *The Prima Generation '72*, he rocks oldies: "As Time Goes By," "Lazy River." But he's incapable of doing a song straight: He'll slip into an Al Jolson nasal thing, or he'll scat, and the songs will speed up. What he calls "Sympathy for the Devil" (and credits to Jagger/Richards) is completely unrecognizable and maybe a prank, an old-folks-outdoing-the-kids move with organ solos amidst funky bass and horn clatter from 40-ish guys with post-'60s sideburns, building to an acid-rock climax then cooling off then building a little more, no words—it's like Prima's band is saying "that teenage hard rock shit's all noise to us, so let's pretend we're doing it, but let's *really* make noise." On the same album, Prima turns "I Left My Heart in San Francisco" into Esperanto jibberish: "I'ma gonna go becka to Santa Franscheesekah but dowza some da-nay upindah, forget allah about itta. I wanna takea ridea onna cobbala karza, costa five cents or ten cents . . . ," after which plaid-clad Louis and his combo knock off a heroically overorchestrated carnival-organ version of "Love Story." And "Rose Garden" starts almost normal, give or take the trumpet honking, then turns into jokes about Louis trying to hug his date, but she doesn't like it ("whatsa matta fo you?"). He buys her dinner and peanuts and Crackerjacks "and a little kibbutza too" to show her he has class. Song ends ("thank you too much"), then into a hard-basslined instrumental jazz-rock workout on the Edwin Hawkins Singers' 1969 pop-gospel hit "Oh Happy Day," complete with a heavy-metal wahwah solo.

The lesson of Louis is that, by presenting your work as plain old "entertainment" instead of the more specialized and confining "heavy metal" or even "rock'n'roll," you leave your options open, and you can get away with anything. That's why traveling Edwardian troubadors juggled while they sang, and why morning drivetime deejays tell dumb one-liners. On his 1962 *The New Fugg*, comedian Redd Foxx mixed up shaggy dog yarns and blue banter with jump boogie numbers like "Knock Me a Kiss"; back when he came up, you had to sing *and* dance *and* be funny (and he kept doing it all years later on *Sanford and Son*).

Likewise, Joe Dolce got away with the Italian-accented/misplaced-accordion-solo R&B-cum-polka-cum-Tex-Mex-cum-ska-cum-shlock on his 1980 *Shaddap You Face* by calling it "musical theatre" and filing it in "comedy" sections of record stores. But the real successors of Louis Prima's and Keely Smith's male-butt-of-jokes/straight-woman battle-of-sexes were probably TV stars Sonny and Cher, whose shtick roped together funky garage rock, camp vaudeville, and folk melodies with no distinctions admitted. Cher's early '70s solo hits united country, cabaret, Navaho tomtom beats, torch singing, Spanish guitars, showtunes, waltzes, and classical music. She was a gipsy, tramp, *and* thief!

At least in the '70s, disco's ubiquitous willingness to costume itself, to admit it's *pretending*, helped open up similar possibilities. By calling Jimmy "The Everything Man" and covering "Everything is Beautiful to Me" and switching from Bertha Butt bump buffoonery to the sappiest swoon tunes, for instance, the Jimmy Castor Bunch were simply tying into the centuries-old tradition of the one-man band. But disco's most immortally tawdry variety show was undoubtedly the one on *Disco Tex and his Sex-O-Lettes*, Chelsea Records, 1975. Basically, Sir Monti Rock III quit his lucrative hairdresser position and renamed himself Tex even though he came from Puerto Rico, "where the poor are destined to live or die" (or so says his translator). On the album, a "Jam Band" chants every which way, improvising merengues and jazz gumbo and soul revues on a groove, sort of like Sly and the Family Stone only not so *shy* about it: "Wam, bam, thank you ma'am, here comes the disco man." Sir Monti keeps switching into Ricky Ricardo pidgin-Spanish, then over to "DIG MY RHINESTONE TAP SHOES!" or "Rock'n'roll is here to stay!"

In Disco Tex's world, *anything* can be rock'n'roll, that's his whole point. HE REDEFINES THE TERM, and thanx primarily to his Sheer Unbounded Love of Mankind, he gets away with it. "I Wanna Dance Wit'Choo" turns from Jimmy Durante "dinkadoo"s into Frankie Valli green-cheese doo-wop; the juicy Gatsby-rock hootchie-koo "Shirley Wood" switches to and fro between Mae West and Amazon-drummed tribal flapdoodle and wailing green-card mariachi taunts. It's the land of 1000 dances, every last one racing by so speedy-gonzales you're not sure what they're called: "boogaloo and bubblewalk, flapparock and camelhump, boogiedown and boogiejump." "Chugalug chugalug, jitterbug jitterbug." The album starts with crowd noises out of some bong-burnt all-day '70s mud-choogle festival, but before you know it you've got brassy Latin syncopating, Gatling-gun grunts, 12 or 15 microphones firing at you from all directions, layer upon dense layer of irrelevant asides ("Hello Sherry!"), a gruff gargling maestro of ceremonies (Jerry Corbetta from the hard rock band Sugarloaf) promising you a "heavy load of rock'n'roll."

Obviously, Disco Tex was an extreme case. But in dance music, variety of an only slightly less twisted sort has long been the norm. Everything was permitted, if only because nobody ever got around to excluding corny stuff. Robin Scott, better known as M (of "Pop Muzik" notoriety), observed that "disco was the rock'n'roll/blues/jazz/country/soul recipe." Teena Marie (not exactly disco, but in the neighborhood) holds vowel notes for opera-house lengths, then switches into monkey squeals or random screeches, bouncing-on-the-beat raps, wild scats imitating horn or guitar parts, Hispanic accents for rhythm, British ones for irony, runny-nose toddler talk for sarcasm. What makes her rock also makes her mush, but her mush knows how to rock you.

The clue's in how she stirs styles (Broadway schmooze, supper club bebop, halfway-house soul, hard funk, harder metal, mail-order-orchestra strings, samba, bossa nova) together—not one after (or on top of) another, but all ladled bowlwise so every ingredient oozes amorphously, so they work as *emotion*. "I am upper suburbia and I am Venice Harlem, I am one in a million contradictions to my complacent life," the liner to 1980's *Lady T* reads. ("Complacent"?!) A parade of album jacket poses, starting with Lady T: sequined opera prima donna, baseball tomboy, flower child, synagogue matron, bank robber, teen angel, paisley punkette, glamour nomad, nose-ringed Nile princess.

Well, anyway. Even in the case of collages *per se*, the Lovin' Spoonful's 1966 "Summer in the City," Janis Ian's 1967 "Society's Child," and Jefferson Airplane's 1967 "A Small Package of Value Will Come to You Shortly" (complete with cutup chat and atonal piano and what sounds like a television left on in the background) would have made the whole collage rock idea *explicit* even if the Beatles hadn't. Or you can start even earlier—with Buchanan and Goodman's mid-'50s "Flying Saucer" novelties, which had a newscaster on the scene of a UFO sighting being answered by little scraps of current teen hits. Or with the Five Discs' early '60s Italian doowop "Rock & Roll Revival," which contained portions of oldies by the Monotones, Dovells, Edsels, Angels, Frankie Lymon, Dion, Buddy Holly, and Bobby Freeman. It was published by Lasagna Music (shades of Louis Prima!), but what the hell was left to "publish," I wonder?

Or if you want to impress people, start with John Cage (who theorized on his 1959 comedy masterpiece *Indeterminacy* thuswise: "My intention in putting 90 stories together in an unplanned way is to suggest that all things, sounds, stories and, by extension, beings are related."). Or with turn-of-the-century American tone-clusterer Charles Ives. (Once we were in a car and two radio frequencies overlapped into noise, so my brother-in-law Marvin said "Hey, they're playing Charles Ives"!) Or with actual tape-recorder and electronic-oscillator composers: French guy Pierre Boulez, German guy Karlheinz Stockhausen, American guys Edgar Varèse and Vladimir Ussachevsky. Or with inheritor-of-adding-machine-fortune William Burroughs, who cut up *something* or other in his writing, I'm told. (Don't ask me, 'cause I've never been able to finish any of his books.)

Or with the Situationist International, European art dweebs who convinced themselves they were clever kids in the '50s when they "detourned" mass media images into statements for their misguided cause, which held that capitalism made people passive consumers. ('50s teens danced and screamed for Elvis and sang along with Chuck Berry's observations about growing up in a world of fast cars and refrigerators full of Coca-Cola *passively*? Yeah right.) Here's how the Sits reviewed Def Leppard, in *10 Days that Shook the University*: "The consumption of *Hysteria* has become a principle of social production, but one where the real banality of the goods keeps breaking to the surface."

Okay, maybe I lied. They were talking about hysteria, not *Hysteria*. But anyway, they'd change words in newspaper-cartoon bubbles, sorta like *Mad* turning Mona Lisa into Alfred E. Neuman, in other words, but more "revolutionary," supposedly—just like how, today, Negativeland "postmodernly deconstructing" U2 and getting sued by U2's label for it or Laurie Anderson doing semantic juxtaposition crap (if "Language is a Virus," shouldn't she cover her mouth?) is more highbrow-respected than Weird Al Yankovic doing a Nirvana parody. Even though Weird Al is funnier and has better taste in shirts, even though his *target* is the meaninglessness of Nirvana's silly post-Burroughs songwriting shtick, making him *far more intelligent as well*.

Still, the Sits did indeed take pieces of disparate puzzles and put them together wrong as a means of "subversion." And in the Beatles' wake, art-rock troupes like the Mothers of Invention, Can, Faust, Black Sabbath, Queen, Roxy Music, 10cc, and Pere Ubu (and even comedy troupes like Firesign Theatre) regularly incorporated such art-world mosaic techniques onto their albums—for example, a Can track might switch from boring jazz noise to boring ethnic steals to boring electronic effects or *musique concrète*, while Ubu's 1979 "The Book is on the Table" incorporates part of a French-lesson tape (a technique later used by monotone-mouthed rap mama's boys De La Soul). Pink Floyd collaged too, of course, and their spiffy merger of Beatles-pastiche with dancish beats on 1980's "Another Brick in the Wall" was probably an important Def Leppard influence. In 1979, Frisco Bay eyeball screwballs the Residents did a twitty medley of proto-industrial/underwater-electrocution versions of '60s teen dance hits, naming it *Third Reich 'n Roll* and dressing Dick Clark like Hitler on the cover. By the turn of the '80s, we were putting up with preacher-and-witchdoctor-recycling chop-funk like Brian Eno and David Byrne's *My Life in the Bush of Ghosts* and Was (Not Was)'s *Was (Not Was)* and "Wheel Me Out"; I still harbor a nostalgic new-wave skinny-tie soft-spot for those two Was discs' B-movie dialogue, free-jazz sax, flipped-over-chemistry-class-beaker sounds, and scientific guitar yammer.

But regardless of all this stuff that came before, when a midwestern hip-hop wannabee named D.J. Romancer played me "The Adventures of Grandmaster Flash on the Wheels of Steel" over his car tapedeck in Missouri in '81, I thought I was hearing music from Mars. Maybe I would've reacted differently if I'd grown up in the South Bronx, where back in '70s house-party days, the first rap stars were DJs not microphone commandos. Grandmaster Flash used his record player's stylus as a percussion instrument, making lines repeat, bleeding in pieces of records where they weren't expected; he also used it as a noise instrument. "Adventures" has a part where a fiftyish white man starts telling how he was born in North Dakota, but now he's here; some kids ask what happened in between, and the guy says "something like this," at which point there's suddenly this super-angry classified-document-shred barrage of needle-scratching.

Six years after music from Mars came music from M/A/R/R/S—"Pump Up the Volume" works because Alex and Rudi Kane and their buddies don't really play the musical quotes *as* quotes; you don't even need to know they're quotes to be rocked by them. But by the middle '80s, jazz critic Gary Giddins was already saying he was fed up with "neoclassical postmodern eclecticism" (apparently referring to combos like the Art Ensemble of Chicago) after ten years of the stuff. And before long, some music on pop radio wasn't so much songs as fragments, and it could get real aggravating, especially when pundits attributed it to all that bunk about culture splitting into tiny shards corkscrewing into self-conscious halls of mirrors. Infotainment-era attention spans, geared to the split-second stimulus overload of MTV videos, Super Mario warp worlds and satellite-dished soundbites, supposedly demand music that does their increasingly nervoused nervous systems justice. So with concreteness giving way to incoherent mixology, between rap (De La Soul, 3rd Bass) and industrial (Ministry, KMFDM) and metal (Mordred, Living Colour) and noisy jazz-puke (John Zorn, Bill Laswell) and even select geezers (Malcolm McLaren, Rush), linearity was out the window.

I even bought the line myself for a while—in 1990, the first year since before the Beatles that no rock bands topped *Billboard*'s album chart and a year when the biggest industry surprises came from beatnik-metal bands like Faith No More and Jane's Addiction, output from Top 40 and thrash and college radio circles alike convinced me that guitar rock's future would entail quick-change hip-hop bricolage ideas or else. Seemed like a pretentiously eclectic diversion so far, but I figured that once it turned into catchy pop tunes, I'd start loving it. Yet within a year after I made my prediction, the montages were feeling even more useless than the guitar riffs themselves.

A few dance-oriented can't-make-up-your-mind-music CDs—by Coldcut, KLF, Snap, Information Society, D.J. Shadow, Army of Lovers, Meat Beat Manifesto, South Indian soundtrack-scorer Vijaya Anand—actually struck me as fairly shrewd the first few times through, but in the long run their cutups inevitably wound up distracting from their songs, assuming they had any. Meanwhile, perhaps set in motion by the Butthole Surfers' flatulent 1985 "Lady Sniff" or cyberfunk Pop Group refugee Mark Stewart's dense and mentally fucked but nonetheless disposable mid-'80s noisedub dispatches, any number of less dancey "lo-fi" art bands (Pavement, Sebadoh, Boredoms, Unrest, Guided by Voices, Thinking Fellers Union Local 282) revived dippy old hippie-era anti-linearity-as-applecart-upset poses. New York's Cop Shoot Cop and Switzerland's Young Gods even clanged samplers like metal-machine guitars. Their discs were omnivorous by definition, and now and then had amusing bits.

But they all gave up their surprises right at the start, and since unexpected juxtapostion is all most "deconstruction" is good for in the first place, the fun tended to run dry fast. Something real similar tends to happen with the film dialogue and offhand studio effects filling up post-*Hysteria* collage/*concrète* arena-AOR experiments like Queensrÿche's *Operation: Mindcrime* and Extreme's *Pornograffiti*. A single at a time (Snap's "The Power," S-Express's "Theme From S-Express," Kon Kan's rose-gardened "I Beg Your Pardon," Cameo's spaghetti-westerned "Word Up," Edelweiss's Abbaed-and-yodeled "Bring Me Edelweiss," maybe one Beck track per album), collage music might make for fairly savvy recreation. But mostly I don't wanna know about your record collection (like I should talk) or relationship to fancy gadgets anymore—I just want a song to sing. (Though then again, Boney M did claim in 1985's "Sample City" that "all the finest songs are hidden in a chip." And it was a pretty fine song at that.)

The trick, I guess, is to see how big a variety of junk you can pack into a small space without making it sound like you're just *trying* to pack a ton of junk into a small space: songs which, by virtue of passing through more changes and permutations than you can shake a stick at, encompass the whole world yet (this is important) remain 'songs' instead of detached 'collages' in the long run, are unexpected treats indeed.

Best example I can think of is "Square Biz," a 1981 R&B hit by Teena Marie: Teena slides down some piano keys, screaming *"Wheee!"* She tells everybody to get up. First verse has words like *"kismet"* and *"suave de bone"* in it; chorus is some kind of bebop slang. Second verse, second chorus reiteration, and third verse break this bebop slang down into several component parts. There's a short discussion with Rick James. Teena switches into an adenoidal kiddie voice, repeats the main chorus line six times straight. Then she stops singing and starts rapping. She calls herself Vanilla

Child, says she lives on expensive cuisine, then admits she's lying. She outlines her musical and literary influences, which range from the European classical tradition to contemporary black fiction to the rock she grew up on to the black spirituals she might've instead if her first introduction to music hadn't been singing "Ave Maria" at Catholic weddings when she was eight then going to Italy to study opera when she was sixteen. Then she falls into a trance, but the trance is in a hardboiled Brooklyn accent. Many small children sing along.

Sophisticated Boom Boom

It was Jerry Lieber and Mike Stoller who first blatantly introduced classical music to the rock'n'roll lexicon when they used
four violins and a cello in the Drifters' first pop hit, "There
Goes My Baby." The orchestra was too big for the Atlantic Records studio. Truth be told, though, classical-pop hybrids had
existed for decades (Hoagy Carmichael's symphonic/min-
strel/rube/jazz/Tin-Pan-Alley/Coney-Island-washboard/down-
home-jug/boho-piano/racist-innuendo Americana, for instance. And Kurt Weill's orchestral/sax/German-music-hall.
And Gilbert and Sullivan's instructions to modern major gen-
erals, not to mention various rhapsodies in various colors by
George Gershwin and Aaron Copland or whoever. Hey, don't
expect me to even *pretend* to know what I'm talking about).
And rockers like Jackie Wilson and Elvis had already displayed
a marked light-opera influence and even stole melodies from
sonatas now and then. As would such soon-come Italians as
Dion DiMucci and Lou Christie and Vito and the Salutations,
who grew up listening to Mario Lanza albums (and/or Dean
Martin *bel canto*) during pasta dinners.

Ray Charles, to jeers from his sorry blues-servile peanut
gallery, sold out in the best way, literally inserting "modern"
violin sounds into country-and-western music. Phil Spector
made "little symphonies for the kids." And classical rock
"progressed" (ha!) through instrumental hits (1962's Tchaikovsky remake "Nut Rocker" by B. Bumble and the Stingers,
1963's "The Lonely Surfer" by future *One Flew Over the
Cuckoo's Nest* scorer Jack Nitzsche), toward *Pet Sounds*, *Sgt.
Pepper's*, King Crimson, Kansas.

When the Drifters/Spector classical rock turned into the
Beatles/Kansas classical rock, a capitalistic-hunger/coopta-
tion move devolved into an "art" move. Though lots of classical rock falls in between, of course: think of *Jesus Christ Superstar*, or Electric Light Orchestra, or Focus's ridiculous op-
era-metal yodeling in their Dutch-born 1973 one-shot "Hocus
Pocus," or Australian neo-garagers the Hoodoo Gurus turning guitars from "Hocus Pocus" and arachnids from the
Who's "Boris the Spider" and Stones' "The Spider and the

Fly" into a semiclassical "Little Miss Muffet" rewrite in their 1996 goofoff "Mind the Spider." Or Allan Sherman's 1963 number-two "Hello Mudduh, Hello Faddah! (A Letter from Camp)" (based on Ponchielli's "Dance of the Hours"). Or Kraftwerk's "Franz Schubert," or Madonna's classical bracketing of "Papa Don't Preach," or Jackie and Janie listening to Tchaikovsky by the fire in the Velvet Underground's "Sweet Jane." In a sense, classical *hard* rock started when the Byrds' mid-'60s raga fugueing enabled greaser groups like the Seeds and Amboy Dukes and Electric Prunes to move away from R&B-beat structures, toward lavish Wagnerian whiteboy freak-outs, cool!

But in England, where kids allegedly grow up real cultured, Deep Purple and the Moody Blues got buddy-buddy with orchestras. Despite a few commendable exceptions (the most ubiquitous being Queen's "Bohemian Rhapsody"), rock-guys almost invariably wound up dealing with all those immortal piano-lesson melodies as either dignified "taste" (ELP), parodic "irony" (the Sex Pistols doing a symphonic "Anarchy in the U.K."), or both (Sumner Crane of the New York no wave outfit Mars, whose 1981 clangorizing of Mozart's *Don Giovanni* remains unplayable). Never as *music*.

Disco was different. It used classical music like it used ethnic exotica and protest lyrics and metal guitars and big-band swing and everything else: as an emotional/visceral boost, not as an eclectic/cosmopolitan badge. Just don't credit the two Walters, okay? Walter Carlos, whose eventual submission to the castration knife (after which he became Wendy Carlos) puts every subsequent rock gender-bend (give or take Wayne-to-Jayne County) to shame, didn't really give "Jesu, Joy of Man's Desiring" and "The Well-Tempered Clavier" a more mobile beat on 1968's *Switched-On Bach*; his use of synths was explained in *audiophile* terms, seeing how Moog electrodes offer the utmost in "bright sonorities, terraced dynamics, and high relief of voices" (read: elevator music). And though Walter Murphy and the Big Apple Band's "A Fifth of Beethoven" went number one in 1976, it wasn't all that disco, either—no match for, say, the garish classical-porn of Cerrone's "Love in C Minor."

In 1981, Louis Clark and the Royal Philharmonic Orchestra compressed an unbelievable 106 theme-nibble synopses onto *Hooked on Classics*, but its disruptive remote-control-roulette format obliterated climactic progression. Three years later, though, Malcolm McLaren's "Madame Butterfly" transformed Puccini's aria into a many-splendored thing, with sloe-gin rapping and a sleazy Nagasaki narrative. In 1985, Austrian glitz-king Falco's number-one "Rock Me Amadeus" raised Mozart to züpertzar level via metal riffs, perverted Krautspeak about Immanuel Kant, and dope studio-prestidigitation. 1988 saw Jack E. Makossa's chesty "The Opera House" initiate yet another inevitable fusion—why do you think they call disco singers "divas," anyway?

As Public Enemy publicist Harry Allen would inform you even if you didn't ask, Beethoven was a black man. So I guess that makes him a regular guy or something, but as for all his honky cronies, it's about time somebody booted them off their aristocratic stallions, and classical disco does the job. The world's sweetest melodies were around ages before McCartney/Lennon or Bacharach/David, and with some nonwallflower rhythm behind them, they regain the oomph that put them on the tiptop of *Billboard*'s baroque charts in the first place. Once again, these breathless swoops can be the celebration or circus or copulation they started out as. Disrespect can breed respect, and allegiance to shrunken postindustrial attention spans can occasion the opening of the American mind. Or something.

No doubt that's what Malcolm McLaren had in mind, but it should be noted here that Malcolm wasn't doing anything new; he never has. Classical music has always been implicit in disco's core, whenever a producer adds violins, whenever a Eurodisco act whistles a continental tune. Amanda Lear's 1977 "Alphabet" begins with "Prelude in C by J.S. Bach"; Frankie Knuckles and Satoshi Tomiie's 1989 "Tears" is opera-blues with magnificent electronic keyboards like big fat lumps in your throat. And the shuffled noise-salsa "A Fifth of Beethoven" that opens Judy Torres's 1990 12-inch "Please Stay Tonight" isn't only better than Walter Murphy's version—it's better than the original! (But then, Eddie Palmieri uses a two-piano/three-cello dirge as a salsa intro in 1978's "Colombia Te Canto," and it feels even *more* radiant than in disco. He identifies his symphonic swipes as Cuban *Danzon*, so who knows what else is out there?)

As far as I can see, the point where this hybrid actually began is the Shangri-Las, coincidentally one of the groups Lieber and Stoller supposedly dropped the Drifters in 1963 to start producing, though the Shangri-Las' actual producer wound up being Shadow Morton, if that makes sense. They had a song called "Sophisticated Boom Boom" that could give classical disco a new name, they did mini-operas like "Leader of the Pack" and "Out in the Streets," and they inserted rococo splendor into "I Can Never Go Home Anymore" and especially "Past Present and Future" (where it's the best part of the song, a real magic moment, right after one of the girls asks "shall we dance?")

Most of the Shangri-Las' hits came out in 1965, a banner year for classical girl-pop. A high school trio from Jamaica, New York known as the Toys went to number two with "A Lover's Concerto," a goddesslike ditty based entirely on Bach's "Minuet in G"; they also appeared in a movie called *The Girl in Daddy's Bikini*. And though not quite as orchestrated, the Supremes' "I Hear a Symphony" had a title at least as explicit in its intentions. The pendulum shifted to Dusty Springfield ("with accompaniment") and her ostentatious "You Don't Have to Say You Love Me" in 1966, but by 1967 the ball bounced back to the Supremes' court. No doubt conceived at least partially in reaction to the psychedelic new delusions of grandeur from snob-rockers like the Moody Blues, Procol Harum, and especially the Beatles, the Supremes' 1967-to-1969 singles, by adding what sure sounds to me like an hypno-electronic pulse under the gilded-cage strings, effectively served as a link between the classically inclined girl-group stuff and classical Eurodisco.

When they started going really overboard lavishnesswise was right around when they started billing themselves as *Diana Ross* and the Supremes, Diana obviously being the archetypal disco diva no matter how stuck-up she turned out in real life. (Flo Ballard was replaced with Cindy Birdsong in

1967; Diana flew the coop in 1969.) "Reflections" was dazzling teary-eyed looking-back sap with forwardlooking rocket effects; "The Composer" swooped high with congas underneath; "I'm Livin' in Shame"'s corny pregnant-college-girl-ashamed-of-mama drama had a real propulsiveness. And 1968's "Love Child" for all intents and purposes *was* disco—souped-up with Gothic backup and a fast electroburble bassline pushing it ahead, into the '70s.

Pomp Up The Jam

So my problem with progressive-(so-called)-rock isn't any beef with the esteemed European academy *per se*—I *like* drama and grandeur and beauty and overblownness. My problem is with how classical music is *used* in prog-rock, and my eyelids turn just as heavy when rock uses funk or bluegrass or hip-hop or African drumming or jazz ("free" or otherwise) or literary references or scatology the same way (and these days it usually does—"classical-rock" is kind of a dead issue by now). Basically, I prefer vitality and accidents and confusion to "concepts" spoonfed from a silver platter—I can't stand pandering. Liking music "in theory" is what turns most rock critics into liars. I don't want music too fearful and full of itself to leave room open for trapdoors.

Yet while I've never cared much for prog-rock as a *genre*, I'm a sucker for fancy prog embellishments used as hook-flavoring in more boppy, less convoluted music. I love how the keyboards used by early '80s skinny-tie bands like the Tubes and Brains and Hounds poke out of their new wave metal-pomp with such gurgling Morse-Code-miniature extravagance. I like when prog sells out, shortening songs to match Top-40 attention spans, abbreviating crescendos into hooks, and topping it off with words approximating how real people talk. Give or take the linguistic part, this isn't far from where prog first *started*—think of mysterious relics like Procol Harum's "Conquistador" and "A Whiter Shade of Pale," Argent's "Hold Your Head Up," Spirit's "I Got a Line On You," and Sugarloaf's "Green-Eyed Lady," the first two of which can almost be considered post-Dylan piano blues, and the last three of which have splendiferously structured arrangements but riffs and undertows that make them rock hard anyway. And obviously first Cream (in "Tales of Brave Ulysses" and "White Room") then Led Zeppelin (in "Communication Breakdown" and "Immigrant Song" say) then a handful of '70s bands (most of whom you've probably never heard of: Babe Ruth, Crack the Sky, Gasolin', Golden Earring) had both a knack for turning Valkyrie rides into genuine throbbing force-of-nature rock'n'roll and a knack for beauty unmatched by, say, any '90s "industrial rock" acts (who none-theless tend to be better at pretty background music than the frightening dance music they *think* they're making). And we better not forget *Sgt. Pepper's*.

All sorts of '70s album-rockers used Beatleslike euphonies and polyphonies to keep their pomp light on its feet, if usu-ally too twinkletoed to sink in: Supertramp, ELO, Flash and the Pan, the Babys, Queen, Pilot, 10cc (who on their first couple albums managed to be quite rhythmic and funny as well—"Silly Love" even sounded like Cheap Trick before Cheap Trick did). The Sweet and Raspberries used fancified frills to make overpure pop less pure, and Blue Öyster Cult's 1976 *Agents of Fortune* was a gallant and triumphant attempt to meld catchy-sweet mood-music harmonies onto epic art-metal and make both seem smart; it didn't hurt that its most noble guitar lines, the ones in "Don't Fear the Reaper," came from the Byrds. Ireland's Thin Lizzy were primarily about big cordial riffs and soul-song (as opposed to blues-boogie or funk-dance) beats and vocals, but on *Jailbreak* (also 1976) they used itty bitty classical movements and wistful Celt-folk undercurrents, more for tunefulness than for showboating. And speaking of showboating, Van Halen didn't do any-where near as much as dumb virtuosity fans wanted Eddie Van Halen to, and early skirmishes like "Ain't Talkin' Bout Love" and "I'm the One" squeezed heavy Zepness into teen-pop platform shoes (an idea perhaps lifted from earlier Heart attacks like "Barracuda").

Quite a few '70s R&B acts even incorporated prog-rockish influences. Sly and the Family Stone's *Stand* had pompy little keyb and guitar spans, way back in 1969. Prince's "When You Were Mine" has a synth break that sounds like Styx going reggae, and his "Head" has a noodly keyboard explosion that could be Yes. The Brothers Johnson's 1977 hit "Strawberry Letter 23" is vaguely reggaefied LSD bubblegum that antici-pates mid-'80s Prince with hippy-dippy hallucinations about purple showers, not to mention a "Strawberry Fields"-like ti-tle and waterfalling filligrees *extremely* reminiscent of Yes. Barrabas's 1977 *Work Out* hides AORish ballads, a Moog, and high-flung Jethro Tull flute-flights inside its Latin disco.

Donna Summer's 1980 "Grand Illusion" gets its title from Styx and its vocal quacking from Rush. And Earth, Wind and Fire and the Jacksons were no doubt guilty of all of the above. Or at least they *wished* they were.

Roman Catholic Pagan Ritual Rock

Early in 1994, a monastery full of Spanish Friar Tucks entered the *Billboard* pop top ten (and the classical chart at number-one) with a CD of centuries-ancient church songs. *Chant*, by the Benedictine Monks of Santo Domingo De Silos, was a smash all over Europe with teenagers not born yet when most of it was recorded twenty years before, much less when most of the chants were first sung *1400* years before, during the 590–604 A.D. reign of Benedictine monastic-discipline reformer Pope Gregory I (not to be confused with Pope Gregory XIII, who didn't introduce the Gregorian calendar 'til 1582). Compared to the monotonous Ambrosian chants which had come before, Gregorian ones were thought to be quite gregarious, as liturgical music goes.

Chant was the '90s' second huge ecclesiastical pop smash— the first, a Gregorian/disco/orgasm jumble called "Sadeness" by the German studio group Enigma, was one of the best singles of 1991. (Enigma's second album, coincidentally, wound up in the top ten at the same *time* as the Benedictines, but instead of dead languages it had cannibals singing in pygmy or pig or something. Their debut album, meanwhile, remained on *Billboard*'s charts for years, apparently because everybody decided it was good to have sex to.) Marc Weidenbaum of *Tower Pulse* explained in 1991 that Gregorian chants had long been popular with college dope-smokers, since their avoidance of metronomic pulse makes them otherwordly, yet they sound like people talking. But I have a different excuse. One time back at Immaculate Heart of Mary elementary, Sister Mary Elephant made us raise hands about which hymns should be sung more, and which ones sung less, in our weekly get-togethers. Being a reactionary kid and digging Latin to the max, I naturally nominated "Ave Maria" for increased airplay. All that hippiefied folk-mass garbage, what with the bright felt fish cutouts scattered across the walls, not to mention nuns who wore street clothes that proved they didn't shave their heads after all, conflicted with my whole theological aesthetic—I mean, what good's religion if ain't *scary*, right?

Anyway, Enigma were actually far from the first pop act to take a stab at Gregorianism—more likely that'd be the Shangri-Las, who used yon dungeon moans in 1965's "Out in the Streets" and who certainly never struck *me* as potheads, even if one of 'em (Marge Ganser) did eventually die of a drug overdose. Their only real competition was the Yardbirds, who: (1) used morose Moorish chords and worried about "deep and dark despair" in "Heart Full of Soul"; (2) started pleading "when will it end, when will it end" in the middle of a Russian dance in "Over Under Sideways Down"; (3) stuck druids intoning the melody from "The Lion Sleeps Tonight" plus chains being dragged around and Chicken-Little poetry about the sky falling in "Still I'm Sad"; and (4) opened "Ever Since the World Began" with an evil ritual about laughing at the devil—the blueprint for Black Sabbath's whole career! (Or at least for Sabbath's own tzany Gregorian instrumental called "Supertzar," on 1975's eccentric *Sabotage*.)

The Yardbirds' high-mass and pessimism experiments were imitated by lots of frowny '60s guys, spawning a completely-ignored-until-now pagan-grief-rock subgenre, just about: Bee Gees ("Every Christian Lion-Hearted Man Will Show You"), John Fred and his Playboy Band ("AcHenall Riot"), Troggs ("When Will the Rain Come"), Turtles ("Grim Reaper of Love"), Grass Roots ("Wait a Million Years"). Also, the Electric Prunes put together an LP called *Mass in F Minor* which I've never heard, but people who have tell me I'm not missing much. Then in 1974, an Aussie nun named Sister Janet Mead ascended to number-four on the pop charts with an almost-acid-rock version of "The Lord's Prayer."

In nascent heavy metal terms, the real maestros of monkitude weren't the nightmaremongers in Sabbath so much as Uriah Heep, formed in England in 1969. Basically, these guys invented Goth-rock: a few times per year they'd work into a dense, not quite danceable but certainly energetic, roil of guitar/bass/keyboard rhythm, which they'd make super thick. Then a madrigal glee-club full of gargoyles would interject a gorgeous and gritless yet ghastly harmonized "aaaaaaaaaah!" or "ooooooo-aaaah!" like they were at the dentist's office and he just hit a raw nerve. (Wow, so maybe Uriah Heep's screeches are the root-canal roots of Mariah Carey's, too—their names even sound the same!) Uriah's words tended toward archaisms and sentence structure from medieval times, or earlier—toward the days when, as Erik Davis put it in the *Village Voice* once, "Goths-Vikings-Celts and other nomadic shit-kickers from Northern Central Europe turned metallurgy into art." Black Sabbath had a vaguely similar bent, but Heep were faster, and a bit more rhythmically creative.

Alice Cooper made Uriah's Latin-percussion-into-Latin-mass idea more explicitly double-Latin in his 1976 "Go To Hell." Queen's 1974 "In the Lap of the Gods" had Uriah-ornate caw-caws turning into a Bryan Ferry imitation; Donnie Iris (whose 1970 frat hit "The Rapper" with the Jaggerz was def by definition) used similar caw-caws in a bubblegum context in his 1981 AOR hit "Ah! Leah!" Aerosmith covered Shangri-Las and Yardbirds numbers, and their '70s ballads ("Dream On," "Seasons of Wither") had ice-blue strings climbing candlelight ivory towers toward anguished shrieking. Heep's (and Sabbath's) Behemoth downer-groove later had a bearing on depressive drones purveyed by Joy Division's gloom-punk offspring, most notably Sisters of Mercy, who Gregorianized okay in their 1987 club cut "This Corrosion."

Visiting the Metropolitan Cathedral in Mexico City's Zocolo Square in 1993 confirmed something I'd long suspected: namely, that the Catholic masses I was raised on were some pre-Christian pagan ritual in disguise. The cathedral was built on Aztec pyramid ruins, relics of which are still visible around the edges. The Aztecs used to display bones of unlucky enemy soldiers on the pyramid steps; in front of the church you run into a prehistoric crucifix fashioned from two logs, surrounded by four skulls. Born Catholic in a nation where Catholicism was frowned upon for most of this century, the *rock en Español* band Caifanes eat up this stuff: one of their song titles translates as "Ash Wednesday," and they load up their CD covers and videos with skeletons and crosses and heathen icons. Their definitive Adrian-Belew-produced 1992 *El Silencio* album opens with breakneck punk-metal reminiscent of Led Zep's "Communication Breakdown," then soars through cotton-candy high notes, electro-handclapped flamenco darkness, and catacomb cumbias over chattering timbales.

Caifanes' countrygoths La Castañeda are both harsher and more pretentious. Onstage they do kabuki-costumed performance art, and the cover of 1993's *Servicios generales II* depicts them as four monk-robed dorks without faces, doing a primitive dance on the steps of an art museum. But nimble low-droned guitar and synth orchestrations, Gregorian choral effects, and tribal-drummed salsa-boogaloo breakdowns make their guttural graveyard plod stately, saving it from numbnuts Nine Inch Nails frostbite. If Uriah Heep had ever thought to combine the Latin backbeat of "Look at Yourself" with the overdriven tempo of "Easy Livin'," they *might* have kicked in as ferociously as La Castañeda do in "Quenegro!" and "Nadaparami" and "Misteriosa," but I doubt it.

Regardless, Heep may still be the key to figuring out how come, when James Hetfield talks about "they" in Metallica's 1991 "The Unforgiven" (referring to some scary monsters or something, and the only reason I know about the song at all is 'cause the video with the little kid crawling through sewers then turning senile is a real knee-slapper), his forboding tone always reminds me of Cerrone's French 1978 sci-fi disco thriller "Supernature" for a few seconds. As does "Natural Science" by Rush from 1982, which also uses the "London Calling" Clash guitar riffs Cerrone invented in "Rocket In the Pocket" in 1978. And the strategic-defense-initiative clang of Celtic Frost's 1986 Swiss monster-metal instrumental "Tears in a Prophet's Dream" sounds similar to Cerrone's "Sweet Drums," and Frost even gave disco the old college try on 1987's *Into the Pandemonium*—somewhere lost in milleniums-old Nordic history, there's a common denominator.

The *Supernature* album cover has a dismembered heart lying on the floor, surrounded by mutant pigmen and dogmen with fangs; the title track is ecology armageddon like Sabbath's "Iron Man" or any random Voivod song, only disco, sung in church-trained soul-music voices: "Things are different today, darkness all around." Basically, laboratory creatures evolve, then take over the world; nature reaps its revenge on mankind. The music is whooshing symphonic synthesizer grandeur closing in on you, made creepier by howling wind effects, doubling and tripling and quadrupling and eventually culminating in disastrous killing denseness, then turning quiet and calm on the day after. It's as dark as anything Metallica or Voivod have ever done, *way* darker than the hack German sludge-pomp outfit Helloween's comparable DNA-deformity epic "Dr. Stein" (from 1988). But unlike any of these, "Supernature" is also *joyous*; the mutants taking over the planet are disco's nocturnal freaks. You could counter that mad-scientist punk numbers like the Dictators' "Science Gone Too Far" and X-Ray Spex's "Genetic Engineering" are joyous, too; but they're not really *dark*, even though X-Ray Spex's one starts with Hitler addressing the hordes—they're just *cute*.

Disco, though, can be dark and joyous *at the same time*—quite a trick. In 1979, Michael Jackson opened "Off the Wall" with cackling witches and "She's Out of My Life" (wherein he considers suicide) with extreme-unction Aerosmith keyboards. 1980's "Heartbreak Hotel" had Michael stumbling into his personal purgatory amid crashing windows and violent grunts from his big brothers. "Beat It," "Torture," "Dirty Diana," and "Give in to Me" use scary effects and death-ray grunge from the planet's most famous guitarists to turn hard rock into horror rock—"Beat It" opens with Eddie Van Halen sounding like he's banging some pre-Christendom mortuary bell, seven times. And "Thriller," full of creaky doors and baying wolves and footsteps down the hall, is apocalyptic alien-night-creature rock in the tradition of "Supernature" itself. It warns that anybody who refuses "the funk of 40,000 years" will rot in hell for eternity.

Most fright-disco is more obscure, of course. Tantra's 1980 Eurosingle "Top Shot" starts with the famous horror-movie melody that we used to sing "pray for the dead and the dead will pray for you" to when we were kids. (You know: "Dum. Dum. De-dum. Dum. De-dum. Dum-dum-dum-dum." The

"Marche Funebre" from Chopin's "Piano Sonata No. 2 in B Flat Minor," my wife says.) Then in comes some last-rites wah-wah, and these monotonally emotionless Eurotrash chants saying "don't really know what to do, I think I'll kill myself," surrounded by voice-and-string crescendos and a metal-riff bridge (which Falco later stole in "Rock Me Amadeus"). Mysterious Art's German-recorded/Dutch-re-mixed 1990 "The Omen" gets introduced by Alfred Hitch-cock calling it "music to be murdered by," then the same fu-neral notes as in the Tantra song introduce a witchy woman who refers to *The Exorcist* as if it was *Ghostbusters* or some-thing ("if there's a devil in your dreams, call the Omen"), which makes no sense to me because I went to Catholic school and after *I* watch *The Exorcist* I can't sleep! Lady's been spurned, see, so she's casting spells on you, summoning goblins. Her voice isn't "camp"—it's *bitter*. Music starts fast, comes to a dead stop, then starts again real slow and sleazy and speeds up quick, with cries of distress trying to curdle your blood, haunted-house thumps in the night, thunder, bells, papists belting out ancient hymns from their church pews. And that's just the "Vogue Mix"!

Then there's Santa Esmeralda's 1978 album, *Beauty*. These flamenco-loving Spaniards did a ballad called "Nothing Else Matters" thirteen years before Metallica, and by *Beauty* they were feeding blazing castanets into shadowy Romanticist death-disco. The five-part side-long title-track suite was a true doomsday doozy: starts with heavy breaths pulsating like heartbeats or pistons, then bolero guitars and welcome-you-to-the-main-event brass gear up, then a panicky falsetto say-ing "the holy sidewalks are now the highways and homes to the sinners and thieves." Male lead Jimmy Goings warns you to beware the eyes of the beholder (cryptic paranoia reiter-ated by Metallica in 1988 on . . . *And Justice For All*), and there's a Colosseum crowd cheering on a hangman, or maybe they're siding with the lion against the Christians. On the album cover Goings looks like Gomez Adams being cat-scratch-fevered by Morticia after she just said something French, and inside sometimes he works himself up to a hor-rendous Iron Maiden screech, but it *works*. He could be taunting the death of rock, or of Western Civilization: "It's only a fiction, but it's an age-old well-known sold-out show. Just take your chances, lay down your hopes on a vanishing lie." Gipsy guitars start tingling, then seraphic choirs join in.

Back to Cerrone for a minute: on the back of *Supernature* he thanks Michigan-born Stiff Records braid queen Lene Lovich, who shows up on other late '70s disco albums (Chi Chi Faveles's *Rock Solid*, for one); Lovich wound up winning new-wave fans a few years later with a cornball Balkan routine that in turn directly inspired slithering fungi like Berlin's Nina Hagen to turn Goth-rock into something approaching a salable genre, what with heretical album titles like *Nunsexmonkrock* and all. Cerrone also collaborated now and then with Alec R. Costandinos, a European producer famous for his 1979 Love and Kisses hit "Thank God It's Friday" and for exposing women's nipples on his two Love and Kisses album covers. Alec's 1979 "For Amusement Only" has gargantuan guitars, grim backup wails, amphetamine synths, and disjointed vocals that serve as yet more links between Eurodisco and Heep/Sabbath Goth-metal. Alec also scored an undanceable classical-disco version of *The Hunchback of Notre Dame*, using Santa-Esmeralda-type Spanish flavors and one character *named* Esmeralda. And Santa Esmeralda did a "Quasimodo Suite" on 1978's *The House of the Rising Sun*, and both Costandinos and Esmeralda worked with Don Ray. And Don Ray's loopy, sometimes sambafied, and briefly depressive 1978 *The Garden of Love* album was co-produced by Cerrone, and Don thanks Lene Lovich on it!

What all this is adding up to is that, basically, Enigma's "Sadeness" wasn't the isolated novelty occurrence its chart position made it seem like. By the '90s, *plenty* of dancefloors had hosted druidic rites. Donna Summer used massive cathedral gospel and catacombic choruses way back in "Now I Need You" in 1977. And Enigma producer Michael Cretu himself had worked some Romance-language religion in among the muffled vista-disco fog of released-only-in-Germany Sandra albums like 1988's *Into a Secret Land* and 1990's *Paintings in Yellow*, which had Led Zeppelin riffs and song titles like "The End" and "Hiroshima."

Dead Can Dance, Anglo-Irish art-dullards who didn't use electrodance rhythms yet nonetheless recorded 14th-century Italian *saltarellas* and 16th-century Catalan songs, have been cited as an important Enigma predecessor, but if you're gonna do that you might as well cite "old music" bringer-backers like Hesperion XX, available in your record store's classical section. Also, Siouxsie and the Banshees' initial 1976 gig consisted of a Beelzebub version of "The Lord's Prayer" with Sid Vicious drumming, and 1979's "Playground Twist" made use of Transylvanian melodies and bats-in-belfry churchbells. The noisy guitars more than likely hide dippy poetry about footsteps and staircases.

In 1987, the Pet Shop Boys put out their slippery fall-from-grace masterpiece "It's a Sin," complete with grieving sound effects from Brompton Oratory candleholder cleaners and Westminster Abbey pastors, plus classical shlockestrations, three verses of Catholic guilt, and a confession booth scene—not bad for a top ten hit! (R.E.M.'s "Losing My Religion" in 1991 was basically just "It's A Sin" with the rhythm and other good stuff all taken out, and even *that* wasn't bad.) "I've been lapsed since I was sixteen, but I don't think Catholics ever *really* lapse," Pet Shopper Neil Tennant told me once. "If they were dying, and somebody asked if they wanted to see a priest, they'd say yes."

New Order and Depeche Mode stuck coven-like clerical vocal congregations into their respective 1982 "Blue Monday" and 1987 "Pimpf" (which I guess is a song about a guy who bosses around pfrostitutes), and New England Anglodisco wannabes Book of Love likewise did some proto-Enigma catechism-class disco in the '80s, using sighing Vatican voices and windchime ones plus pipe organs and gongs and reams of violins in "Modigliani (Lost in your Eyes)" on their *Book of Love* album. (They also did a song called "Lost Souls" that droned like kindergarten Joy Division.)

Yet it's only been in Enigma's wake that I've noticed a worldwide *deluge* of Dark-Ages-pop tunes: From Spain (Mecano), Germany (KMFDM and Cetu Javu), Canada (One 2 One), Chile (Los Prisioneros), Italy (Eros Ramazzotti), Sweden ("Crucified" by Army of Lovers and "Happy Nation" by

Ace of Base—their *saddest*-sounding song, full of Moorish camel-calling vocal gloom and philosophy about how "a man will die but not his ideas"), the U.S. (Latin-freestyle tracks by Corina and Sandée). In 1995, Coolio's Gregorian hip-hop "Gangsta's Paradise" became the most popular rap song in the history of the universe; in 1996, Weird Al Yankovic's "Amish Paradise" sounded exactly the same as Coolio but with Pennsylvania Dutch accents and improved words rhyming "thine" with "tonight we're gonna party like it's 1699." I even read someplace that the early '90s were marked by a renaissance of certain Renaissance *clothing* fashions! Except they made them into miniskirts, so ex-Catholics like me wouldn't get nervous.

Tombstone Blues

Black Sabbath and Uriah Heep were the first wholly European-*sounding* hard rock bands. Unlike earlier Brits of the Yardbirds/Cream/Zep stripe, and unlike their comparably vociferous American '60s-metal predecessors (Iron Butterfly, Steppenwolf, Blue Cheer), if Sabbath or Heap had an ounce of Delta blues in their blood, they were either too inept or loaded with 'ludes to let it show. And what those two bands were to FM, Abba was to AM.

Forget Abba's hits and check out the big ballads filling space on their albums, and suddenly you're confronted with a *hausfrau* sitting alone watching soaps, waiting for the kids to come home, facing a sad menopause on a dark, barren afternoon. Yet even 1977's number-one "Dancing Queen" has a void-bound melody countering its happy words, making the "having the time of your life" stuff seem ominous, even cynical. 1979's "Voulez Vous" opens with near-metal guitars, then breaks into a German-lieder-gone-electrochacha rhythm under an odd melody that keeps slipping into sections of murky darkness and unintelligible babble, something about a "sense of lipstick potion hanging in the air." And 1975's "S.O.S." is the real "Love Will Tear Us Apart," an unguarded last-ditch cry for help. A desperately shouted symphony chorus cuts through wispy, nervous verses full of minor-key bistro-pianoed teardrops, interrupted by a riff that sounds like Led Zeppelin gone Muzak. A woman confides that something that once made her feel alive no longer exists—"I try to reach for you but you have closed your mind."

A 1993 *60 Minutes* story about the '80s/'90s Finnish tango craze pointed out that its songs were all pessimistic ones about nobody-will-love-me-anymore; a happy Finnish tango would make no more sense than a Finnish tango sung in Japanese. Abba are Swedish not Finnish, but let's not get picky, okay? They're also probably the only group in music history whose best album is a K-Tel compilation (*The Magic of Abba*, 1980). But they *invented* something—along with the girl-group, hard rock, countrypolitan, and ragtime they took to the ski lodge, Abba brought Continental mother tongues:

German cabaret, Spanish bullfight boleros, classical romanticism, Italian organ-grinder hooks. Add ballet, lullabies, polkas, oompahs, Irish jigs, and the rest, note-patterns centuries older than the blues, douse it all in edelweiss wine, and you've got more than mere synthesis—you've got rock'n'roll meeting its Waterloo. No wonder Europop never really broke our banks: it wasn't our language. It sold better in England, but where it really took off was Munich, Stockholm, Madrid, Paris, Milan, and beyond—onward to Bombay, Tel Aviv, Johannesburg, Tokyo, Mexico City, you name it.

Both Abba and Sabbath/Heep helped insure that rock dirges could sprout from roots far removed from the Mississippi—not just Druidic monks, but Gustav Mahler's turn-of-the-century neoromanticism and James Whale's 1931 movie *Frankenstein*. (You might even want to throw in Ornette Coleman saxophone sobs like "Sadness" and "Lonely Woman," or Beto Villa y su orquestra's 1948 death-norteño "Morir Sonado." Or St. James Infirmary.)

Problem is, I don't *know* much about all that non-blues stuff. I don't know much about the blues, either, except that Robert Johnson's songs were as glum as Greil Marcus claims in *Mystery Train* but also too damn *slow*; even though they all clock in around two and a half minutes, they all seem to last forever. (He didn't have a magnificent sense of rhythm or melody, either.)

So anyway, taking into account what little I do know, my nomination for the first true tomb-rock song goes to Tennessee Ernie Ford's early '50s "Dark as a Dungeon," originally a country hit for Merle Travis in 1947 but Ernie gave it rock'n'roll weight by bookending it with pumping hillbilly boogie like "Blackberry Boogie" and "Shotgun Boogie." There's not much music to it—just Ernie swishing his drawl around, plus a flute maybe.

He addresses all you "fine young fellers," ostensibly about working in a mine but it could just as well be about shooting up heroin: "It'll form as a habit and seep in your soul till the stream of your blood is as black as the coal," right morbid stuff. Goes on to talk about how dangerous it is down there in the hole, how there's no sun or rain and the demons of death sneak up behind you when some slate falls on your head and you get buried alive. At the end, Ernie says when he dies he wants his body to turn into fossil fuel so miners can dig his bones!

Ernie did other dreary ditties like "The River of No Return" and "Worried Mind," plus covers of American-history favorites ("Stack-O-Lee," "Davey Crockett," "Dixie") and lotsa pap-smeared swill. His hillbilly boogie hits helped invent rockabilly, and starting in November 1955 his most *famous* miner-blues, "Sixteen Tons," topped the pop charts for eight weeks. What I don't think anybody has noticed is that this white-hick blues was the most popular song in the country the week RCA signed a white blues hick named Elvis Presley—so in a sense maybe, Elvis was just riding on Long Tall Ernie's coattails; he played Silverchair to Ernie's Pearl Jam, sort of. And a couple months after "Sixteen Tons," beginning in March 1956 to be exact, Elvis did his *own* eight weeks at the top of the charts with "Heartbreak Hotel," a dirge about a place down at the the end of lonely street where men wearing black shed tears into the gloom and yearn to die.

Another herald of future hopelessness in 1956 was Allen Ginsberg's beat-up beatnik-beat-off poem *Howl*—"I have seen the best minds of my generation destroyed by madness." And there was *Tragic Songs of Life*, a concept album comprising Eeyore-like tunes Alabama-born country-sibling duo the Louvin Brothers had been brooding into Chattanooga's chasm of nothingness for peanut money since Independence Day 1941. The bloodiest cut, "Knoxville Girl," is one of those tales (one of which—I forget which—was covered by Holly Hunter in the 1987 movie *Raising Arizona*) where a boy and girl walk hand-in-hand down to the waterfront and later she's found dead there (like G.B. Grayson's '30s folk ballad "Ommie Wise," Bobbie Gentry's 1967 number-one "Ode to Billie Joe," Richard Marx's 1992 top-ten "Hazard," the Coon Creek Girls' "Pretty Polly," Everly Brothers' "Down in the Willow Garden," FSK's "Lonely River Rhine," and Your Mom Too's "Roger Williams in America," not to mention the movie *River's Edge* and the public-domain "Ballad of Ted Kennedy at Chappaquiddick").

Close quiet harmonies can sound sepulchral when they want to. In 1959, four Pittsburgh boys in the Tempos warned of "danger in the summer moon above" in "See You in September"; in 1961, four New Jersey girls in the Shirelles postulated in "Dedicated to the One I Love" that "the darkest hour is just before the dawn." A few months later, Olympia, Washington's two-boy/one-girl Fleetwoods cracked 93 seconds of the secretly sadistic "He's the Great Imposter" in half with the line "I stood and watched her fall, couldn't help her at all," then went on to predict tomorrow's misery—suburban dread at its squeaky-clean hack-up-your-mother utmost. Still, it took about ten years from *Tragic Songs* and "Heartbreak Hotel" for gloom/glum/glam/doom/dumb/damn to start turning itself into a fullblown bonafide rock *genre*.

I'd pinpoint 1966, circa not just the Yardbirds but also the Stones' "Paint It, Black" and the black leather gloves the L.A. garage rubes in Music Machine used to wear. (I could pick 1964 for the Zombies, but I won't because I don't think they got *really* haunting until "Time of the Season" in 1969.) Music Machine partook in a grungy moodiness that directly forecast Uriah Heep and Black Sabbath; in fact, Uriah's best (and fastest) song and only pop hit, "Easy Livin'," is a perfect rip of Music Machine's best song and only pop hit, "Talk Talk." And though misanthropy had of course run rampant through earlier Stones standards like "Satisfaction," "Get Off of My Cloud," and "19th Nervous Breakdown," "Paint It, Black" is the one where Mick shielded his eyes from girlie glare and tried to blot out the sun; it's the daddy of *Exile of Main Street*'s "Rocks Off," where sunshine bores the daylight out of him. The Stones were glam-rock before glam had a name—they wore psychedelic shirts, longish hair, striped gangster jackets, polkadot ties, flowered suitcoats—but sometimes the only color they wanted to see was black. Eventually they managed to turn black into a kind of shtick.

In "As Tears Go By" in 1966, Mick saw smiling faces but not for him, and was matter-of-fact about it; by *Let it Bleed* in 1969, his despair was presented as a Big Deal. Which isn't to say it didn't work—"Gimme Shelter" is like the wrath of God, or the sound of solid citizens waking up to air-raid sirens and wishing they'd tucked a hardhat under their pillow (blueprint for Dylan's "Shelter from the Storm," Springsteen's "Cover Me," Donna Summer's "Running for Cover," Taylor Dayne's "I'll Be Your Shelter," Cinderella's "Shelter Me," Candlebox's "Cover Me"); "Midnight Rambler" sneaks out of the alley to pugilize your steel door and throw Delta harmonicas through your plate-glass window. But unlike, say, the disappointment that haunts Monkee dreams in 1967's "I'm a Believer" or the gloom that keeps the Temptations locked in their rooms in 1968's "I Wish it Would Rain" or the sun blotted out in Bill Withers's 1971 "Ain't No Sunshine," *Let it Bleed*'s dark Stygian dirging was unequivocably supposed to be Art, or at least Important.

Let it Bleed's influence reverberated throughout rock music, even into R&B, blazing a trail for Sly Stone's stoned 1971 *There's a Riot Goin' On*, Curtis Mayfield's 1972 "Freddie's Dead," War's 1972 "Slippin' into Darkness." Yet the Rolling Stones weren't the first rock act to wear their dolor like a crown. Simon and Garfunkel and Janis Ian, for instance, were seminal freshman-lit-magazine mopes, patron saints of '80s college radio only with a better sense of rhythm; S&G first hit the charts addressing darkness their old friend in "The Sounds of Silence" in 1965, and by their chilly reunion "My Little Town" a decade later they were saying all the people back home were dead and all the rainbow's colors were black and Paul was itching like a trigger finger. Heroin addict Dion systematized his earlier pop gloom with the dinky funeral organs and lowing backwoods howling on his 1968 "Abraham, Martin and John"/"Daddy Rollin' (In Your Arms)" single. Jimi Hendrix did "I Don't Live Today" and "Manic Depression." And Lee Hazlewood tunes like "Some Velvet Morning" and "Sand" (both later covered by '80s art-noise bands) mixed Vegas cigarette-butt slush with phantom strings and poetry.

Even a baby could plot a timeline from "Paint It, Black" and Music Machine through to the Doors, who grumbled about killers on the road and sweet families dying, using somber tempos and mortuary keyboards and noirish vocals and Arab tonalities and meaningless lyrics and offhand lounge-unto-free-jazz crap and showbiz supper-club slime and obscene gestures and so forth. Jim Morrison's deep melo-drama is *thee* Gothdance mouth-sound prototype, and they covered Kurt Weill and Howlin' Wolf and pretended "all the children are insane." There's even been movies about it. But what the movies fail to comprehend is that Jim Morrison, Elvis Costello, and Prince are *all the same person*!

It's kinda obvious when you ponder it a little: their music all featured trashy organ parts played with two fingers at a time; Costello and Morrison, especially, tended to emphasize competent-to-catchy Farfisa rhythms where most rock acts would put basslines or even guitars. (Costello and maybe Morrison picked up their organ sense from ? and the Myste-rians; Prince inherited his via the Cars, though his "Shake" and "Cream" are more direct "96 Tears" clones.) The Doors ended their 1967 debut with "The End," Elvis Costello ended his 1977 debut with "Waiting for the End of the World." Prince's most famous album, 1984's *Purple Rain*, ends with its title track, which is about the end of the world (and which gets its title from a line in America's "Ventura Highway"!), and the album's most famous song, "When Doves Cry," deals with the same Oedipal folderol as "The End." (Prince also doodled about doomsday in "Ronnie Talk to Russia," "1999," "The Cross.") They all peaked real early in their careers—Morrison with his first LP, Costello with his second, Prince with his third. Morrison was a piddly narcis-sistic reduction of Dylan/Jagger nihilism in the same way Prince and Elvis C. were piddly narcissistic reductions of Johnny Rotten nihilism. And they were all primarily obsessed with trying to get laid.

The End (of this Sentence) is Nigh

Further fun examples of rock groups Waiting For the End of the World (or as Def Leppard put it, Armageddoning It):

Armageddon—ex-Yardbirds vocalist Keith Relf's crazed-but-lovely-guitared 1975 band, before he electrocuted himself.

Boney M—"We Kill the World (Don't Kill the World)," their last U.K. chart hit (1981), starts with a German accent fretting about atomic mushrooms, then seduces us with pleasing war sounds. Halfway through, a chorus of kids and adults comes in and imitates "We Are the World" (which didn't exist yet!).

Jimmy Castor Bunch—their bump newscast "Hallucinations" from 1974 says unemployment and murder are at record highs, the Dow Jones at a record low. Then a missile blows up the planet.

Change—best song called "The End" ever to end an album: "The End," *The Glow of Love*, 1980. A wordless six-minute Italodisco simulation of floating through space, with angels.

The Clash—"Armagideon Time," which spelling is either an attempt at a pun about hotel room bibles or a sign of illiteracy. (Their Slade influence showing again?—No, actually it's a cover of some old reggae obscurity.) The music is dirged-out dub.

Skeeter Davis—a country singer, supposedly, once married to *Nashville Now* TV talkshow geek Ralph Emery. But between the luxurious strings and hums and whistles in her sparse 1963 pop number-two "The End of the World," her flat sweet tone sounds almost like the Velvet Underground's Moe Tucker, four years before the Velvets recorded. If she's not loved anymore, Skeeter posits, the sun shouldn't shine and birds shouldn't chirp.

Bob Dylan—in 1963's "Talking World War III Blues" he has a bad dream, so he visits a shrink who says he's insane. Except the doctor had the same dream, and then everybody else does, but everybody else's dream has only *them* walking around after the war's over. "Ballad of a Thin Man" from

1965 (the one where something's happening but Mr. Jones can't figure out what it is) starts with portentous piano-note thunder and moves at a dirgelike pace with eerie whistling sounds to match the scriptural chorus. And when the one-eyed midget screams "You're a cow!," Dylan's aniticipating both the dream sequences in *Twin Peaks* and one-eyed midget Bushwick Bill of the Geto Boys.

Marvin Gaye—on *What's Going On*, he agonizes about dead young men, trigger-happy police, poisoned wind, mercuried fish, oily oceans, black skies, famine spreading, bills piling up, infant mortality, buried nuclear radiation. So have a nice day.

Robert Johnson—"If I Had Possession Over Judgment Day," 1936. Says he wouldn't let his woman pray. He sounds quite tense.

Lil Louis—there's a little flowchart on the back of this Chicago house iconoclast's 1989 debut album, *From the Mind of Lil Louis*. In the middle is the word "Trust," and from there, arrows marked "definitely," "maybe," "no," and "doesn't matter" point (respectively) to "Love," "Sex," "War," and "Hate." Each of these abstractions precedes a list that ends in the word "obsession," and a bigger arrow points from "Trust" to "In God." Lou thanks "all the ladies that have passed personally through my life." Inside, God makes an appearance in "Blackout," a booming biblical prophecy about the end of time: "Think about it: if the Lord built the world in six days, how long do you think it would take him to *demolish* it?" Lou asks if we know the Commandments, and he shouts a psalm at us. Two cuts later, in "French Kiss," one of the ladies who passed personally through Lou's life experiences multiorgasmic ecstasy for six minutes.

Meat Loaf—in their 1977 duet "Paradise by the Dashboard Light," Meat pledges eternal love to Ellen Foley if she'll have sex with him. She does, so now he's waiting for the end of time.

Public Enemy—"Countdown to Armageddon" (1988) starts with a black fraternity "step" routine, then claims we're late for the end of the world and need a late pass. (They're teasing.)

R.E.M.—"It's the End of the World as We Know It (and I Feel Fine)," 1987; one of their best, though not half as good as what it wishes it was: namely, Dylan's "Subterranean Homesick Blues," or the Hombres' "Let it Out (Let it All Hang Out)." Their doomsday starts with an earthquake, then they drop lots of names.

Sandra—second-best song called "The End" ever to end an album: "The End," *Paintings in Yellow*, 1990, actually part five of "The Journey," a seven-minute Eurodisco-unto-heavy-metal *Volksmarch* squeaked in a Teutonic Kate Bush hush and produced by Michael Cretu, who builds the music toward a melody he'd use again in Enigma's monastery-disco "Sadeness" a year later.

Sex Pistols—no future for you. (Modified by the Pet Shop Boys in "West End Girls": "Got no future, got no past, here today, built to last." Then the Spin Doctors in "Two Princes": "Got no future or family tree.") But a few years into his own future, as half of Afrika Bambaataa's Time Zone, Johnny Rotten embarrassed himself with a hokey rap called "World Destruction."

Shonen Knife—from these usually cheerful Japanese women, parts of 1991's "Shonen Knife" rap came as a surprise: first they say everybody's been waiting for their new album, then suddenly they switch toward the Greenhouse effect destroying "ozonic status." Third verse lists their favorite new wave bands; fourth equates atomic energy with the end of the century.

Sonny and Cher—"Love Don't Come," 1967. Bongolated Dylan-cum-Yarbirds-mimic Gregorian-folk-rap B-side about fate, chaos, hippies, Socrates, eulogies, anarchy, "everybody running bare not exactly knowing where or why or who." Cher asks love never to come again because she'll only lose it anyway. Truly ominous.

Steely Dan—sang about the economy collapsing in 1975's "Black Friday," California collapsing in 1972's "My Old School."

Voivod—in these Montreal sci-fi fans' 1988 fairy tale "Cosmic Drama," a hot asteroid races toward earth, ground shakes, space turns red, plants and animals get intoxicated, darkness falls, and a funny-accented robot intones "every-zeeng eez over."

Warrant—"April 2031," 1992. A fusion of David Bowie and Iron Maiden where people hug aluminum pillows and gaze at the manmade ring around the moon until the arms race annihilates mountains and seas. We're not even allowed to blame God for it.

Surprise Attack

Death, dope, guns, gloom, and acknowledgment that the world's a mess from musicmakers generally associated with kindnesss and gentleness (bubblemetal bands, Top 40 popsters, MOR smarm-mongers, disco acts, girl groups, etc.) almost always cut closer to the bone than similarly negative stuff coming from practitioners of more conventionally "hostile" genres (speedmetal, industrial, gangsta-rap, grunge, free jazz, etc.). Geoffrey O'Brien has suggested in the *Village Voice* that, "by adopting the form of a comic book, *Mad* [magazine] had the advantage of surprise, like a sniper firing from an unexpected position." Pop music can work the same sneak attack.

"Rage" genres turn rage into an easily digestible shtick, an impotence that might jar grandma or grandpa, but big deal. I've met people whose idea of a relaxing hobby is chronicling histories of serial murderers, and that's a musical genre of its own by now. Pigfuck/clodmuck assholes like G.G. Allin turn jacking off and rolling in glass and tossing shit on stage into a pro-forma geek Olympics; frat-hazing fanzines like *Forced Exposure* feature reasonably privileged and educated young white adults celebrating misogyny and perversion as express means of shocking the unshockable, railing at "lefty humanist fuckers" who wouldn't have any reason to buy the rag in the first place. In small defiant doses, this sort of irony might be effective at knocking complacent liberal scum off their high horses—I've done it myself, it's easy. But music (and writing) that's all fucked up and "fuck you" tends to be even more useless than tripe that admits to nothing but peace, love, and understanding.

Sometimes artists who you'd expect would think everything is hunky-dory put out a song that proves just how *wrong* you are. Like Faster Pussycat's "Shooting You Down," AC/DC's "Dirty Deeds Done Dirt Cheap," Guns N' Roses "Used to Love Her," Aaron Neville's "Over You," and everybody's "Hey Joe," Pete Wingfield's "Eighteen with a Bullet" (which went #18 with a bullet on 11/22/75) revolves around a husband's death-threat to his wife—only this time, the threat's disguised as a falsetto-funk doowop revival novelty about *Billboard*'s pop chart. Honky-tonk singer David Allen Coe performs the second ("Su-i-Side") side of 1978's *Human Emotions* as a suite, without spaces or pauses between songs, to build tension and momentum; he climaxes with "Suicide," where he fantasizes doing away with both his spouse and his self, splattering blood all over the wall. And Richard Marx's 1992 "Hazard" is a homicide tale by an AOR-shlock guy, coated in a creepy London fog of synthesizers and strings.

It can work the other way around, too. Part of what makes the doubt and remorse and bad dreams and death wishes in the Geto Boys' only great song so powerful is that such vulnerabilty emerges from such a violent sphere, from a band whose other songs are all graphic and gratuitous snuff movies. The Houston rappers themselves admitted as much in a record-label press release: "Willie D and Scarface feel the plot of 'Mind Playing Tricks on Me' thickens because these psychotic reactions are not limited to those with 'sick minds'; it also includes those with 'normal minds.'" So in the song they go to church every Sunday, and they worry their kid will wind up orphaned, and their noses bleed. One of them thinks his woman's out to get him, but when she leaves, he misses her and he's lonely. On the 12-inch sleeve, they don't look mad—just beaten up.

Sometime in the late '80s, a growly-voiced African gentleman named Senyaka put out a record called "Aids." Over jolly jungle polyrhythms, he kept chanting stuff like "AIDS! Has come! To *Keeell* You!!," then he actually dramatized keeling over. He said he was "dying a slow death," so he reminded me of a song *called* "Slow Death," fifteen minutes of self-consciously decadent electro-grunge recorded by the occasionally amusing Swedish Goth band Leather Nun in 1979 (which in turn reminds me of the draggy 1976 blues dirge "Tea For One" by Led Zeppelin, where Robert Plant kept moaning "I've got 24 hours . . ." over and over).

Today's gangsta-rappers just do what's expected of them, but it wasn't always that way. Early rap music imitated the world it was created in: celebratory house and street parties which suddenly erupted into 30/30 crossfire from gangsta-leaning "stick-up kids" walking around like Pretty Boy Floyd. Solid C, Bobby D, and Kool Drop's "Wack Rap," from 1979, opens with a few minutes of wacky lemon-to-a-lime/lime-to-a-lemon bragging from Bobby D and Kool Drop, over a lowdown bass-disco rumble. It's quite friendly. Then suddenly Solid C starts in: "I am the ass kicker, the titty picker," and so forth, into a story about playing craps late one night, and his cashflow's getting kinda low, so "next news, I was bustin' ass." The music gets deadly—all these background grunts, louder and louder, echoing like dub. But then the rappers return to making merry yes-yes-y'all slamdunk funk, like the assbusting never happened.

On pop radio, hip-hop violence can still sneak up on you—Bobby Brown's best single, 1988's "Every Little Step," has bouncy cliches interrupted by "anyone step in my way they get *slayed*"; Brotherhood Creed's 1992 "Helluva" raps falsetto-sweet about a girlfriend with good hair over a Young Rascals "Groovin' " sample, as summery and suburban as any rap's ever been, so unless you listen close you won't notice when Sean McDuffie pulls his pistol at the mall to defend said girl, who gets mad at him for it. Likewise, in Vanilla Ice's "Ice Ice Baby," when gunshots from Jay's gauge and Vanilla's nine ring out like a bell, they mug you from behind and steal all your bubblegum.

This kind of gunplay can be traced back to the scores of "Stagger Lee" yarns Greil Marcus documents in his book *Mystery Train*, and to other pre-blues curiosities like Alec Johnson's 1928 "Mysterious Coon" and May Irwin's 1907 "The Bully" (featuring a lady carving up mean guys with straight razors).

Likewise in rap's ancestry are the shootouts on '70s records by crazed Sergio-Leone-loving Rastas like Dr. Alimantado, Big Youth, and U-Roy. On the 1973 soundtrack to the movie *The Harder They Come*, the Slickers' "Johnny Too Bad" has its protagorist walking down the street with pistols and ratchets at his waist, and Desmond Dekker's "Shanty Town" has rudeboys looting and shooting while on probation from jail; Dekker also babbled nonsense about Bonnie and Clyde in his 1969 top-ten Jamaican bluebeat hit "Israelites." Prince

Buster had a U.K. hit three years earlier with "Al Capone," and later opened a surfable instrumental called "Texas Hold Up" with a gigantic volley of gunshots, exclaiming "AIN'T NOBODY MOVE!" midway through. Another late-'60s reggae singer even *named* himself Dennis Alcapone.

These reggae toasters were basically *comedians pretending to be cowboys*. So it should be no surprise that the archetypal gangsta-rap record, Trickeration's 1980 "Western Gangster Town," is the same sort of Clint Eastwood gunslinger fantasy. I don't know who Trickeration were; only that their "Rock Skate Roll Bounce" is rollerskate-funk about a guy named Willie who hates the country so he moves to the city. In "Western Gangster Town," the B-side, it's high noon at the swinging-door-and-jukebox saloon. Lead Trickerator Disco Rick offers a woman some cheebah, they go upstairs, she takes her clothes off, and it suddenly occurs to him he's in a whorehouse. When her 6'4'' boyfriend comes in packing heat, Rick puts his pistol up against his head, "and if he woulda made a move I woulda shot him dead." Rick hightails it outta town, but the party keeps on—his partner teaches us dancesteps and recommends Scott tissue for runny noses, then says he used to be in jail for stealing cars. Thick curdling disco doubles back on a hard Chicago blues guitar riff.

There were other cowpoke raps after "Western Gangster Town"—the Sugarhill Gang's racially insensitive "Apache"; Kool Moe Dee's "Wild Wild West"; Crucial Conflict's "Hay" (from 1996, and the first gangsta-rap hit ever from Al Capone's hometown Chicago); Jonzun Crew's "Space Cowboy" (which is also yodel-disco like Sly Stone's "Spaced Cowboy," Sequence's "Funk You Up," Edelweiss's Austrian "Bring Me Edelweiss," Francky Vincent's Antillean *zouk* "Anti-Mako," and maybe Pere Ubu's "Lonesome Cowboy Dave"). But Trickeration's violence-for-the-heck-of-it was simply an accepted part of the pre-gangsta-rap landscape; assuming anybody noticed it at all, nobody made a big stink about it one way or another. Probably they were all too busy dancing.

In Spoonie Gee's 1980 "Spoonin' Rap," Spoonie picks up a woman in a disco, takes her home, fornicates for three hours straight, finds out her man's in jail, and brags that if he runs into the guy he'll shoot to kill. Spoonie calls himself a baby maker, woman taker, smooth talker, midnight stalker, and (I swear) a jay walker. He raps about hot-butter-on-say-what-the-popcorn, then starts explaining how when you commit a crime and go to jail, some perv will start ogling your body and jerking off in the shower. (The Fat Boys' best song, "Jailhouse Rap," is a bubblegum version of the same situation—they break rocks with a big hammer.) Then suddenly Spoonie's jumping turnstiles in the subway, and a cop pulls his gun from his holster "but he did not shoot, so come on everybody let's Patty Duke." Yeah, let's dance to celebrate not getting *killed*! Spoonie lets you know how screwed up life is, but his music sounds so *jubilant*, he's just gotta be enjoying himself. He can't live with women, can't live without 'em—he doesn't want a woman with good taste, he wants a woman who tastes good. He's always talking about women *beating* him. His alluring adaptation of the Temptations' "My Girl" on his 1987 *The Godfather of Rap* album starts with him cooing about how "sweet" it would be if he could just break some gal's neck.

Oddly enough, not until Schoolly-D's 1986 debut *Some Where in the Land of No Rap*, released on his own label in Philadelphia, did outsiders seriously start bugging out about violent rap lyrics. Schoolly used to mug old ladies or study art or something in Parkside in Philly, and he'd made a single called "Gangster Boogie" in 1985; it basically sounded like a clone of Run-D.M.C.'s "It's Like That," just an ultraspare machine-gun electrodrum and voice echoing like they were recorded in a basement crawlspace, joking about selling nickel bags for $5.89. The album's beats were more like somebody banging a swingset with a monkey wrench, so people called it "scary." But even B-boy stances like "P.S.K. What Does it Mean?" (it means Parkside) and the great "Gucci Time" had a ditzy humor to them.

On 1987's *Saturday Night: The Album*, Schoolly D undercut his big bad Negro rep by putting himself in the most mundane situations (watching *Brady Bunch*) or just plain silly ones (like where his mom pulls a gun on him, because, well, "you know how mothers are"). Like Trickeration and Spoonie Gee used to (and blunted Latin linguists Cypress Hill would later on their first CD), Schoolly makes murder seem dangerous *and* fun.

The Beastie Boys picked up a thing or two from Schoolly D, at least on their 1986 blockbuster *Licensed to Ill,* where they brag about carrying .22 automatics and shooting AIDS victims but make it as rollicky as third-grade recess; they also play cowboys in "Paul Revere." But be that as it may, Salt 'N Pepa note on the back of *their* 1986 debut that "We get a lot of compliments on our show because we smile for one thing. MCs don't usually smile, they usually act angry." Which means hip-hop "hate" was already deadset on turning into a big hackneyed bore.

The record generally acknowledged as the "beginning" of wildin'-rap proper, N.W.A.'s 1988 "Gangsta, Gangsta," sounds to me more like the end of the line. It's the only driveby I've ever heard by them (or their spinoff icon Ice Cube) that doesn't seem strained. Sets the world record for the most "fuck"s per minute (a record they've no doubt broken since), but comes with a "radio edit" anyway. The 12-inch sleeve's got white people eating watermelon and shining N.W.A.'s shoes. Ice Cube rhymes "ruthless" with "toothless" and asks whether he looks like a motherfuckin' role model; in 1991, 16-year-old Eric Kinslow, purchasing a copy of N.W.A.'s *Niggaz4Life* in Louisville and queried about it by *Entertainment Weekly,* answered Cube's question: "I know a lot of white guys listen to it, because blacks are now role models for white guys." Novelty-Act With Attitude—the shit certainly got old fast, didn't it?

The Gladys Knight and the Pips Rule

A correlative of my surprise-attack-from-happy-music theorem is what I call my Gladys Knight and the Pips Rule: Rock'n'roll works best when it seems both good for you and bad for you, nutritious and unnutritious, at the same time. Since pop music is a leisure activity, but since even at leisure nobody likes to feel stupid, everybody who listens to pop music subscribes to this principle in some sense or another—think, for example, of "aerobic disco," which sounds like the most unhealthy music ever made, but which is actually fairly good for you, *especially* if you use it to slim down your thighs in thirty days.

But that's not quite what I have in mind. The reason I call it the Gladys Knight and the Pips Rule is because, in "Midnight Train to Georgia," which everybody I've ever met acknowledges as a great record, the frivolousness of the Pips doing their train-whistle ooo-wooos (especially if you're watching it on TV and they're gesturing and spinning around in unison at the same time) is what keeps Gladys's soul singing down-to-earth. Without the Pips, Gladys would be merely "intense"—not catchy enough, therefore boring, therefore not intense at all, really. Calling music "intense" or "emotional" or "soulful" is usually a euphemism for "it seems like something I'm supposed to like." It's fairly obvious that the Pips alone would be an ignorable proposition; my point is that Gladys alone would be just as ignorable. And, in fact, the problem with *most* soul music is that it's all-Gladys/no-Pips: e.g., '60s Aretha Franklin subscribed to the fallacy that by removing shlockish prettiness from music (Dionne Warwick's "I Say a Little Prayer," say) you improve it, when really you just make it more reverent.

In Public Enemy, obviously, Flavor Flav is the Pips to Chuck D's Gladys. But in her 1989 single "Friends," Jody Watley is the Pips to rapper Rakim's Gladys, and in "What Have I Done to Deserve This?," Dusty Springfield is the Pips to the Pet Shop Boys' Gladys—so the Pips part doesn't have to be *silly*, necessarily; it's a sweetener, a softening agent, something to counter the seriousness. Pipsness is the Deadhead sticker on the Cadillac of rock'n'roll (or maybe the Cadillac sticker on the Deadhead of rock'n'roll, how would I know?). A spoonful of sugar helps the medicine go down, in a most delightful way.

Softness makes hardness harder, and that's a paradox people have trouble dealing with; in fact, lots of people seem to think Pipsness cancels Gladysness out. They don't think you can have both, which can probably be blamed on teachers who made learning a chore by making kids sit still. When I was in the Army my wife worked as a drug counselor on the base, and one time some buck private wrote an appraisal of a class she taught, rating her as being "intelligent but friendly," as if most smart people are really mean. (More recently, my big-haired beautician buddy Jennifer was talking about implanting jewels into a customer's fingernails once, and my wife scoffed "That's so tacky," then Jennifer rebutted "it's tacky but *beautiful!*" So here's a verse I wrote: "I'm intelligent but I'm friendly/I'm tacky but I'm beautiful/I've got one hand in my pocket/And the other one's changing the channel on that damn Alanis Morissette song.")

Then again, since rock'n'roll *is* a leisure time activity, there are inevitably people who act like music should be all-Pips/no-Gladys. But that wouldn't work, either, since Gladysness is where music's tragedy comes from. As often as not, I *need* moroseness or violence in my disco. My sense of humor's fine, but the trash-aesthetic concept of forced insignificance (where ideas and passion and audacity are shrugged off as "pretentious") isn't fun—it's lazy. I have about as much use for Mojo Nixon/Rev. Horton Heat-type lampshade-wearing-booger-eating-hillbilly-partydog crap as I have for *Hee Haw*—you've seen one sniveling thespian patronizing boondock yokels, you've seen them all.

"Specialize in having fun," some Doors song went, but I really don't think "fun" is what that band's good songs (they had a few, you know) were about. "If all I've been is fun, then let me go, don't wanna be in your way," Gloria Estefan warbled in Miami Sound Machine's heartmeltingly perceptive and bloop-bloopingly gorgeous top-ten 1988 breakup-obses-sion ballad "Can't Stay Away from You." That goes double for this *book*, got it?

Which isn't to say I don't want selfsame book to be a wild party, too—I'm a schizophrenic kinda guy. Which no doubt makes it easier for me to identify with such exemplary Gla-dys-Knight-and-the-Pips Rule specimens as the ones below, forthwith:

—Their use of jugs and washboards keeps the Memphis Jug Band's '20s/'30s music from feeling stodgy like "real" blues.

—How *The Freewheelin' Bob Dylan* (1963) moves from the comical "Bob Dylan's Blues" to the armageddonoid "A Hard Rain's A Gonna Fall" serves the same-if-reciprocal purpose as how, on their 1990 *Journey Home* album, Florida folk-disco Vesuvius-climbers Will to Power jump directly from scoffing at new age spiritualism and endorsing the N.R.A. in "Koyaanisqatsi" into a cover of Heatwave's 1977 bubblebump hit "Boogie Nights."

—Betty Everett's 1964 "The Shoop Shoop Song (It's in His Kiss)" comically undermines the serious question "In his warm embrace?" with the answer "No, that's just his arm." (X's 1980 rewrite, "The World's a Mess: It's in My Kiss," wasn't so fun.)

—In "Ode to Billie Joe" (1967), the terror of Bobbie Gen-try's suicide yarn keeps being interrupted with asides like "pass the biscuits, please." Reminding us it's just *gossip*.

—The lowdown bassman voice in foreboding '70s Tempta-tions sociology lessons like "Ball of Confusion" and "Papa Was a Rolling Stone" inevitably made them rather silly too. As did lines like "only safe place to live is on an Indian res-ervation."

—Don McLean, "American Pie," 1971. Gladys-profundity into Pips-mundanity; two ways to use rock music: it can save your mortal soul, or you can learn how to dance to it real slow.

—In their number-one 1974 collaboration "Then Came You," the Spinners answer Dionne Warwick's plaintive "How did I live without ya" with a ridiculously conceited "I don't know, baby."

—In Teena Marie's 1981 "Revolution," she solemnly mourns the '60s having been blown away with a revolver, but lightens up with absurd lines about Pepperland toe-jam and telling her "bestest friend Mickey we're really in a sicky world"—same way as how *It Must Be Magic's* album cover and sleeve balance anti-racist poetry with a picture of toddler Teena on the toilet.

—Frank Kogan's 1984 four-track recording "Grenadine Blood" has you in his machine gun sights until a bum taps him on the shoulder and asks him to light a cigarette. Curses, foiled again.

—On the front cover of the Cover Girls' 1987 New York Latin pop "Inside Outside" 12-inch, they're wearing wholesome fluffy sweaters, ready for a ski weekend (red, green, and white: Christmas colors, or Italian flag ones); on the back, they've got on slinky skimpy black dresses and plenty of jewelry and hot pink lipstick. Outside side is Pips; inside side is Gladys.

—Brenda Fassie and Xuxa make African and Brazilian rhythms entertaining (not merely geographical) by reshaping them into extremely catchy post-Mickey Mouse Club twist-band disco songs. Xuxa mixes up fast circus salsa with the sad blond Abbapolkas of her old-country ancestors, and millions of non-blond kiddies watch her TV show every day, inevitably calling-and-responding in voices louder than Xuxa's own; that she used to be a softcore porn actress and Pele's girlfriend and is now the 37th-highest-paid entertainer (according to *Forbes*) and 94th-most-beautiful person (according to *People*) in the world doesn't hurt. But South African boomgirl Yvonne Chaka Chaka might go even further in "Umqomboti," turning chanted Afrobeats into a beer commercial.

—John Cougar Mellencamp's 1987 "Hot Dogs and Hamburgers" mixes up its Indians-got-a-bum-deal history lesson with jaunty nostalgia about trying to cop a feel in a car. And lots of John's other "political" songs are *saved* by tossed-off jokes tucked in.

Will To Power: is Bob Rosenberg a scary-looking guy, or what?

Stacey Q . . .

. . . and Pajama Party surf through Babylon into Nowhere.

Janis Ian (left), Heart, Nena: fantasy children, skimming mirror waves.

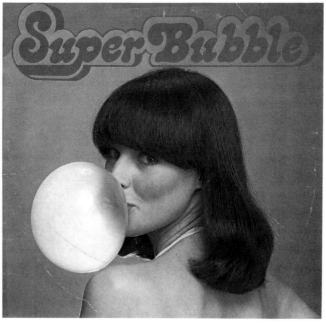

Debbie Gibson (above) and Fun Fun wait for their bubble to burst.

CHARLEY
PATTON

FOUNDER
OF THE
DELTA BLUES

Charley and Teena: schizoid rather than eclectic.

Thin Lizzy: how cool kids dressed for Dino's Bar and Grill, 1976.

Hip-hop's secret history: circa 1930, 1967, 1981, 1988.

Mutants from disco's dungeon laboratory—with no chest hair!

If Ace of Base's nation is so happy, how come they're not smiling?

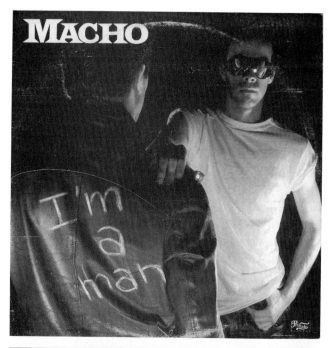

Sundry disco orifices open up and let '60s garage seeds come inside.

Sundry country orifices open up and let '70s disco seeds come inside.

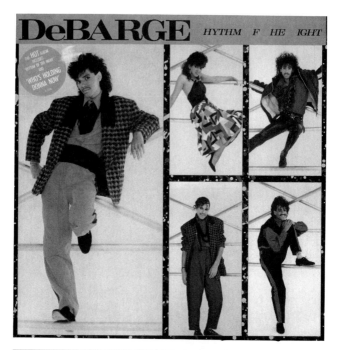

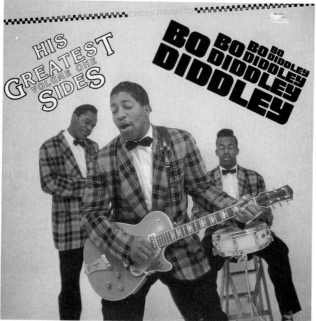

Eldra DeBarge and Bo Diddley: plaid to the (herring?) bone.

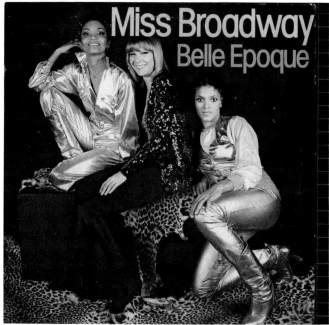

The Surfaris and Belle Époque find new uses for what Bo knew first.

Rufus Thomas as Satchel Paige; Oran "Juice" Jones as O.J. Simpson.

Joe Jacksonless shoes as Shoeless Joe Jackson; Babe Ruth as the
Elvis Presleys (and therefore the Babe Ruths) of Latin prog-metal.

Olga Tañón: can't imagine why Juan Gonzales left his wife, can you?

"This album is dedicated to our mothers"–Lordz of Brooklyn, 1995.

Louis Prima, Matys Bros.,
Joe Cuba, '60s frat rock:
"The Party was the one
thing we had in our lives
to grab onto."
—Lester Bangs, 1971.

Estamos Haciendo Algo Bien!
We Must Be Doing Something Right!
JOE CUBA SEXTET
NEW WAVE BAND

WE'RE PISSERS To Jan all My Love Joe Cuba

Xuxa (on set of her TV show) from Brazil, Los Fabulosos Cadillacs from Argentina: the wildest parties nowadays are below the border.

Soft and wet salsa-syncopating Miami pube fantasies Sweet Sensation.

If Jane Birkin had Liz Torres's nails, somebody would be bleeding.

DONNA SUMMER

Love To Love You Baby

JE T'AIME

Jane Birkin and Serge Gainsbourg

Beautiful Love

Johnny Rotten-then-Lydon: feral and paranoid, like Michael Jackson.

SYLVIA'S MOTHER
ACAPULCO GOLDIE
FREAKIN' AT THE FREAKER'S BALL +
MAKIN' IT NATURAL
PENICILLIN PENNY

COVER OF THE ROLLING STONE +
GET MY ROCKS-OFF +
CARRY ME, CARRIE +
QUEEN OF THE SILVER DOLLAR +
ROLAND THE ROADIE AND
GERTRUDE THE GROUPIE

Dr. Hook, Geto Boy Bushwick Bill, their pals, and their eyepatches.

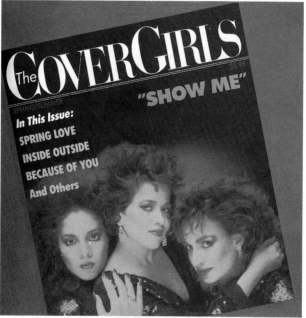

"Be My Baby" fans Rikki Rockett (bottom right on Poison album) and Angel Sabater (left on Cover Girls album) could pass for twin sisters.

Tiffany: greasy hair and greasy cleavage, this must be her destination.

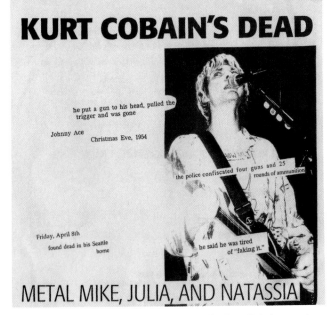

X-Ray Spex were proud to be "art-i-ficial"; Kurt Cobain wasn't.

We Can't Complain
But Sometimes We Still Do

Politics is a real good idea in music as long as it doesn't detract from anything else—that is, as long as it balances itself with sufficient pleasure, surprise, and energy. Which it hardly ever does, and that's the problem: most metal and rap acts seem to think protest can compensate for some *lack*, so they wind up stiffening their beat and uglifying their voices to make room for it. When "reality" is the entire package, it's bound to fall flat—Rage Against the Machine play clumsy, sexless pogo-funk crud, and, until they learn to sell out, "riot girl" (insert Dan-Quayle-style spelling) bands like Bikini Kill mostly play generic hardcore slowed down, with no hooks, no imagination, nothing but vocals that imitate people throwing up. Needless to say, they're lauded by tastemakers who can't tell good intentions from good music.

(Well, okay, I'm exaggerating a little. It's not like they could've gotten any worse than before, but Rage Against the Machine's 1996 "Bulls on Parade" did seem to add a certain Red-china-shop-trampling *push* to their rhythmic constipation. And when I saw the riot grrrl trio Sleater-Kinney that same year, they at least managed to front some swarming-if-stiff *Confusion is Sex* Sonic-Youth-type schmaltz with emphatic-if-incomprehensible Hole-type harangues that broke my heart once I heard their CD. And man, do they ever have a cute audience! Let's just say that, if I wasn't married, I have a feeling I'd be attending *lots* of riot grrrl shows at all-woman colleges.)

No record is an island, and just because we're dancing doesn't mean we have to stop thinking about the world we're dancing in—mind/body dualism is a crock. But it helps if the thinking arises from what's happening in the music instead of just seeming like it's stuck there to flatter erudite snobs. In cases where the music's close enough to OK that all it needs to make us pay attention is some interesting headlines to kvetch about, topicality can help for sure. For instance, Aerosmith's "Janie's Got a Gun" (child abuse), Neil Young's "Rockin' in the Free World" (garbage-pail kids), the Ramones' "Bonzo Goes to Bitburg" (Reagan visiting old Nazi graveyards), REO Speedwagon's "Golden Country" (racist zoning restrictions), maybe even "Jeremy" by Pearl Jam—for most of these famous hard-rockers, topicality seemed the only thing at those phases of their careers that could help them *get it up*, musicwise.

Protest has been an inescapable part of rock music at least since Charlie Poole and the North Carolina Ramblers' late '20s banjo ditty "White House Blues" (about Teddy Roosevelt replacing McKinley; later updated by Tom T. Hall as "Watergate Blues" in 1973) and such '30s depression marvels as Hezekiah Jenkins's "The Panic Is On" and Lil McClintock's Atlanta anti-repossession ode "Furniture Man." Songs like these intertwined social comment with clownish singing and situations; likewise, Woody Guthrie's politicking worked best when used as a punchline to end his shaggy-dog stories—for instance, a line about how salmon run every four years, just like presidential candidates.

Pigmeat Markham was working in this tradition when he tossed lines about Ho Chi Minh running for president into his big proto-rap hit, 1968's "Here Comes the Judge." And '60s and '70s folk (Bob Dylan), funk (Jimmy Castor), and reggae (Tapper Zukie) proto-rappers fused comment and comedy as a matter of course. Rap-music-proper's initial social-consciousness moves (Brother D with Collective Effort's "How We Gonna Make the Black Nation Rise," South Bronx's "The Big Throwdown," Grandmaster Flash's anti-repossession-and-other-stuff "The Message," all '81–'82) were interesting *as* moves, if only because they all arose out of a context where editorial opinions were still unexpected.

But even *those* raps were a step back. They were turning a wisdom that was already *in* rap into Big News, and thereby necessarily cheapening it. "The Message" was originally a verse in Flash and the Furious Five's 1979 party epic, "Super-rappin'," with Melle Mel's ghetto-to-jailhouse-noose horror story just stuck in there in the middle, amidst all the joyous boasts about Mercedes, young lay-dees, and wanting to be rich. "The Message"'s message was immeasurably more effective in its "Superrappin" version, when its rhythm was looser and faster, more disco.

By the time rap turned into Arrested Development, I couldn't figure out if the group was auditioning for *Sounder* or if they were just extras from some old John Cougar video (and they even brought the shack with them!) I'm all for revolutionary sentiments: It was *neat* when my wife's librarian union went on strike and she prepared for it by hiding reference books to make life hard for scab supervisors. But to me, that cartoon on the front of the first Gang of Four album about a cowboy befriending an Indian so "now he can exploit him" always seemed kinda *funny*.

As often as not, anti-protest songs wind up sounding smarter than protest songs—i.e., Three Dog Night's "Easy to Be Hard," which says people who care about social injustice can also be real meanies. Mott the Hoople's "All the Young Dudes" (anti-"revolution stuff"), Ten Years After's "I'd Love to Change the World" (which says we can't), and Buffalo Springfield's "For What It's Worth" (where picket signs proclaim "Hurray for our side") fit here, too. And anti-environment rock can also be cool: The Dictators' "Master Race Rock," where they brag about causing an oil spill, or the Who's "Going Mobile," where they brag about air pollution from their car. (Certain bleeding hearts might consider Jim Morrison ecologically incorrect as well, but "When the music's over turn out the lights" is actually really good advice if you want to save on your electric bill.)

"Gestures of rebellion have long since lost their meaning and have become instead gestures of conformity," Christopher Lasch wrote in *The New Radicalism in America*, over thirty years ago. Schoolmarm-hyped grrrl grrroups like Bikini Kill and Babes in Toyland ain't never gonna smash no phallocentricity as long as they sound exactly like every other ignorable gang of punk hacks who've ever tried too hard to sound hard. They should learn to live by the protest dogma postulated by D.H. Lawrence inside the gatefold of an old Mott the Hoople album—namely, that the only good reason to overthrow applecarts is for the *fun* of it.

There's a Riot Goin' On (in my Pants)

One of the few things that does save revolution music from boredom is *Spanish guitars*. Spain's proximity to Western Europe and Northern Africa gives it simultaneous access to both gushing melodies and rocking polyrhythms, so flamenco has the unique ability to sound mournful and alive at the same time. Hence naturally I'm a big fan of such Eurotrash history chapters as Abba's "Fernando" (people cross the Rio Grande shouting for liberty but don't get it), Mecano's "1917" (an instrumental apparently in honor of World War I or maybe Pancho Villa), Brotherhood of Man's "Angelo" (enemies in love commit suicide), and Laura Branigan's "Spanish Eddie" (where Ed dies and "insanity prevails" while Dylan's "Desolation Row" blares from the radio).

Frank Farian must have spent plenty of spare time reading library books, too, because he has Boney M do: "El Lute" ("no one gave you a chance in Spain those days," so El Lute escapes then his nation changes); "Jimmy" (young men take up arms past Marrakesh and Casablanca to defend Muhammad's honor); "Consuela Biaz" (a woman bathes a soldier's wounds in San Domingo then they dance to "the throb of flamingo guitars," strummed by pink birds maybe); and "Chica Da Silva" (an improved version of Jorge Ben's Brazilian "Xixa Da Silva" about a seductive woman spy who dies for the cause). Which might make the Kingston Trio's "Remember the Alamo" proto-Boney, and the Pet Shop Boys' "Tonight is Forever" and "I'm Not Scared" over-obtuse attempts at post-Boney Catalan memoirs. (And their "Domino Dancing" could refer to revolution in Central America if you connect its salsa bent with the mythical Cold War "domino effect," which could also align it with the Clash's "Spanish Bombs" and the parts on *Sandinista!* about Washington bullets in Santiago Stadium and Managua. And even if your average Nicaraguan felt her life as threatened by Sandinistas as by contras, which is highly likely, it's still not hard to *comprende* why the Clash are such a popular influence on '90s

Latin American *rock en Español* bands: Tijuana No cover "Spanish Bombs," Los Fabulosos Cadillacs do "Revolution Rock," and Attaque 77 do "I Fought the Law." Clash alumni even make actual guest appearances on the Cadillacs' 1995 *Rey Azucar*, and said Argentine combo's videos mix Catholic saints, on-stage assassinations, and death-squad bullets spilling blood onto jailhouse floors into a veritable mambo-metal fiesta.)

In 1986, the New York City Opera supposedly staged a horrible 50th-Anniversary-of-the-Spanish-Civil-War version of *Carmen*, while Dutch starched-funk politicians the Ex definitely put out a horrible four-song, three-language, double-seven-inch EP called *1936: The Spanish Revolution*. The Ex had entitled an earlier single "War is Over (Weapons for El Salvador)." They housed *1936* in 144 pages of pictures from the Amsterdam Institute of Social History, depicting anarchists rioting in Barcelona's streets, building tanks, and burning down monasteries . . . Okay, I admit it—I fell for it at the time. I was young and naive, and falling for it seemed like the responsible thing to do.

Refried Dreams

In 1973, a British art-metal band called Babe Ruth released a song called "The Mexican" that opened with Spanish guitars, then turned into the Doors' "Riders on the Storm" then Ennio Morricone's Sergio-Leone-movie theme "For A Few Dollars More" over an absolutely realized Latin disco rhythm two years before disco existed. The song concerned a soldier named Chico Fernandez dreaming of Santa Anna with his gun by his side, as a war raged around him. Fronted by sexily-tough-voiced hippie Jennie Haan, Babe Ruth's LPs also contained scarifying folk-gone-heavy remakes (Jesse Winchester's "Black Dog"), gay-bar dance hits ("Elusive"), immensely hard/fast-rocking missing links between Janis Joplin and Suzi Quatro ("Jack O'Lantern"), more Morricone ("A Fistful of Dollars"), and extended suites that used Spanish and Caribbean the way colder prog-rock bands used classical ("Amar Caballero").

"The Mexican" was not a certified hit, but it became a secret cult favorite in discos, covered by the German acts Bombers (who hired Haan as a singer) and Disco Circus, then rapped over by Funky Four Plus One and (at least onstage) Soul Sonic Force, then taken onto the dance charts in 1986 as the B-side of Jellybean Benitez's top-20 Madonna-penned Tom Tom Club imitation "Sidewalk Talk." In 1987, Latin freestyler Noel had a club hit with "Silent Morning," reportedly initially about a bullfighter and called "Sad Morning" (a phrase repeated again and again in "The Mexican" 's chorus). Then in 1989, post-acid-house/proto-rave mixmathematician Todd Terry, under the pseudonym Orange Lemon, put out a "Dreams of Santa Anna"/"The Texican" 12-inch comprising two "Mexican"-inspired instrumentals.

Tex-Mex border (*conjunto/norteño/ranchero/mariachi/corrido*) rhythms have always constituted a valiant rock heritage, used (frequently in low-calorie form) by Ritchie Valens, Buddy Holly, Chris Montez ("Let's Dance"), the Champs ("Tequila"), Marty Robbins ("El Paso"), Jay and the Americans ("Come a Little Bit Closer"), Sam the Sham ("Wooly Bully"), ? and the Mysterians ("96 Tears"), the Sir Douglas Quintet ("Mendocino"), Freddie Fender ("Wasted Days and Wasted Nights"), and lots of East L.A. frat bands back when a bouncing beat was a necessity taken for granted. Roy Orbison turned cool *ranchero* dressing morbid; Neil Diamond's early hits had all the venom and Rio Grande mud of garage-band 45s of the same period, and he even presented himself as a snotty punk on the cover of his kick-ass 1966 *The Feel of Neil* album, but for some reason adults liked him more than kids.

The Drifters were big on mambo castanets and what producer Mike Stoller claimed were South American *baion* rhythms; he says they had to rent lots of imported instruments to pull it off. Sam Cooke had the self-explanatory "Everybody Likes to Cha-Cha" and other West-Indianized hits like "Wonderful World." The Kingston Trio attempted calypsos, flamencos, and mariachis (not to mention Zulu chants, Hawaiian ukeleles, Appalachian banjos, and Irish pub sloshes). Bo Diddley made the Cuban *clavé* his own, but also had piano rhumbas like "Crackin' Up" and "Say Man." Bobby Freeman's "Do You Want to Dance" had Cubanesque drums; the Tempos' "See You in September" was Latinized doowop.

Chuck Berry did calypsos ("Havana Moon"), cha-chas ("Too Pooped to Pop"), and comely bossa-nova-tango-type things ("Drifting Heart," which he says sold 17 copies). But in "Rock & Roll Music" he says he doesn't *want* to hear mambos or tangos or (sic) congos, even though as he sings it he slips into a Latin rhythm (just like he incorporated jazz rhythms but said anti-modern-jazz stuff, and sang ballads but said "if it's a slow song we'll omit it" in "Little Queenie," and recorded "Rockin' at the the Philharmonic" two years after "Roll Over Beethoven"). And his "Anthony Boy" sounds like a polka but maybe it's really Italian since Anthony's an Italian name (which might make sense since Joe Dolce's "Shaddap You Face" from 1980 sounds like polka but is obviously Italian too—a tarantella, maybe?). And "You Never Can Tell" has French words and a guy named Pierre in it, so maybe its characters got married in New Orleans.

New Orleans had always implied rock'n'roll as an intrinsic element in its bloodflow, ever since back when France and

Spain were shuffling it back and forth before the Louisiana purchase. Which led to all these African voodoo practitioners and American Indians and Creoles and Cajuns (like that guy in the potato-chip commercial) comingling their disparate gene pools and setting up shop on Bourbon Street. Which led to Mardi Gras parades and Dixieland improvisations and barrelhouse piano players picking up syncopations which somehow filtered up via the Gulf of Mexico and which *already* had plenty of Spanish-and-African miscegenation going on. So for instance Professor Longhair did rhumbas ("Her Mind is Gone" in 1949), and sometimes employed a steel drummer.

Jamaicans tasted the flavors flowing down from New Orleans (especially Fats Domino's) and played the beat backwards because their radio reception was fuzzy, which resulted in bluebeat, rocksteady, ska, poppatop, and reggae, which from what I can tell are more or less the same as each other but get slower every time the name changes; bluebeat bands supposedly skipped a beat every two measures, which might make sense if I knew what measures are. Ska was a conscious rhythmic simplification: in "Jamaican Ska" by the Ska Kings, they say "not everybody can do the cha-cha, not everybody can do the twist, but everybody can do the ska." Yet Richard Berry's "Louie Louie" is said to be both an ancestor of reggae *and* a cross between Chuck Berry's "Havana Moon" and some cha-cha number by Ricky Rillera and the Rhythm Rockers (of which Richard Berry was a member). (You could throw Louis Jordan's 1947 calypso "Run Joe" in there too, I think.) Richard Berry sang "Louie Louie" in a fake island patois, then in 1963 Portland's Kingsmen took it to number two using a jokey sort of Frito Bandito accent. The Kingsmen version led directly to "All Day and All of the Night" by the Kinks and "Wild Thing" by the Troggs, which led directly to heavy metal.

Around the turn of the '60s there were hints that tropical rhythms might unseat rock'n'roll (oh I mean whitebread pop) as America's preferred music. Martin Denny went to number four in 1959 with a faux-Hawaiian birdcall-and-bamboo instrumental called "Quiet Village" and scored big with his proto-new-age *Exotica* album, the success of which has been attributed to the nation's then-burgeoning fascination with things primitive, such as Tiki motels and Tahitian villages in California and the jungle habitats in Walt Disney's Magic Kingdom. Harry Belafonte had a handful of pop-calypso hits, the biggest being "Banana Boat (Day-O)" in 1957; Millie Small ("My Boy Lollipop"), Chubby Checker ("Limbo Rock"), and Jimmy Soul ("If You Wanna Be Happy") also scored with island music, all between 1962 and 1964. Stan Getz and Astrud Gilbero hit number four in 1964 with Brazilian composer Antonio Carlos Jobim's lush samba-and-jazz-fusing bossa nova "The Girl from Ipanema." Like Martin Denny, and for that matter like Kyu Sakamoto's 1963 Japanese-pop number-one "Sukiyaki," "Ipanema" basically sold ethnic exotica as easy-listening mood-setting music. None of these fads wound up having any long-lasting effect, of course (the "lounge revival" of the mid-'90s was a boring media hoax), though bossa nova did manage to briefly mingle with soft rock in tunes like Janis Ian's "At Seventeen," Simon and Garfunkel's "So Long Frank Lloyd Wright," and Sade's "The Sweetest Taboo." (Frank Sinatra, Tony Bennett, and Elvis Presley made bossa moves, too. Frank even tried singing calypso—"The Coffee Song" in 1960.)

Caribbean rhythms were more prevalent in subsequent '60s and early '70s rock than most people remember. The Marvellettes' 1961 chart-topper "Please Mr. Postman" had Gladys Horton singing a funny calypso parody that went "delivah delettah, desoonah debettah"; later Jamaican or Trinidadian skanks showed up in the Beatles' "Ob-La-Di, Ob-La-Da," the Kinks' "Lola," Bobby Bloom's "Montego Bay," Nilsson's "Coconut," Stephen Bishop's "On and On," Johnny Nash's "Hold Me Tight" and "Stir it Up," the Sweet's "Papa Joe," and a zillion more hits once the reggae hype started. Dionne Warwick used light Latin lilts in "Walk on By," "You'll Never Go to Heaven," "Message to Michael" (or maybe that one's jazz), and especially "Do You Know the Way to San Jose?" The Shangri-Las and Young Rascals did some Drifters-style Cuban-instrument borrowing. Additional attempts at Afro-Latin percussionizing found their way into "Magic Bus" by the Who, "Carrie Anne" by the Hollies, "Sherry" by the Four Seasons, "Hush" by Deep Purple, "Do It Again" by Steely Dan, "Me and Julio Down by the Schoolyard" by Paul Simon, "Midnight at the Oasis" by Maria Muldaur, "Black and White" by Three Dog Night, and (most unrestrainedly) "I'm a Man" by the Spencer Davis Group.

By the '70s, such partially Latin combos as Santana, War, Mandrill, and the Jimmy Castor Bunch were working timbales into funk and hard rock on a regular basis. Singer-songwriters like Billy Joel ("Los Angelinos," "Big Shot," "Don't Ask Me Why") made Latin moves for variety's sake. And even such country hicks as Jimmy Buffett and David Allen Coe and the Bellamy Brothers mixed in tropical congas and maracas (too loose for calypso or reggae, more like "soca" I guess: they liked sun, ganja, and laziness). But too many of the more urbane '70s ethnomusic fans were working the same album-rock "open-mindedness" terrain that occasioned hippies to burn out to Ravi Shankar mantras, and in many ways they're responsible for paving the way for such '80s twits as David Byrne and Peter Gabriel and Sting. Like Paul Simon, whose less showy ethnic parroting through 1980's "Late in the Evening" was more or less tolerable but who turned into The Enemy once he put out *Graceland* in 1985, these creeps reduced "worldbeat" usage into just another pretentious shtick.

Captain Beefheart (in "Tropical Hot Dog Night") and V-Effect (somewhere) actually took some "intriguing" shots at marrying salsa to avant-garde noise; too bad the singers sucked eggs. By the late '80s, you'd get too many records like Arto Lindsay and the Ambitious Lovers' *Greed*, where the only vaguely affecting moments were brief little foreign-language fragments where you couldn't make out the words. Brazilian-born Arto stirred willed innocence, skewed sarcasm, and mixed-metaphor puns into some bent-over top-button-buttoned art-salsa, and suckers called it "erotic." But compared with a Latin dance 12-inch like Sweet Sensation's "Take it While it's Hot," *Greed* came off laborious and frigid—disco acts still used Third World rhythms *as* rhythms, not just safari curios to display in a trophy case.

With shnooks like Lindsay and Byrne constantly trying to elevate dance music by draining its life out, it's no wonder so many rock fans are turned off by the whole idea of a xenomanic "worldbeat" movement and all the noble-savage canonization it implies. Industry ethonmusicology boosters haven't helped much, either: blame high ticket prices or cosmopolitan condescension or the Ugly American guilt complex, but there's something dilettantishly nose-in-the-air about the context in which foreign music is appreciated. For one thing, the stuff plugged as classic almost always winds up being folkloric if not outright pompous—if Brazilian bores Rubén Blades and Caetano Veloso came from the United States, they'd be dismissed as the frigid art-rock fish they are. Brazilian *Tropicalismo* is supposed to be "a cultural movement based on the concept of anthropology," which essentially means it employs clinical bricolage clichés and limits its use of English words to structuralist poetry nonsense.

Highbrow geography snobs can't hear the Gipsy Kings' godhead rhythm section because it rocks too hard to be folk music. They don't want to know about the amazing disco coming out of South Africa (Yvonne Chaka Chaka) or Brazil (Xuxa) or Puerto Rico (Lisa M), music millions of real people actually dance to and live with and *buy*. Instead we're told to settle for tepidness, parchedness, new age. Specialty labels like Shanachie and Earthworks and Realworld act like any music with hooks or energy is sinful. So the novelty wears off fast—in the end, most eager cultural-relativist prognosticators seem to care less about the music than about some dubious agenda: we are the world, it's a small world after all, we've got the whole world in our hands. Pretty asinine when the only U.S. city where "worldbeat" has made any real headway is New York, the one place whose population acts as if the rest of the country doesn't exist.   .

Two Big Horns and a Wooly Jaw

The 1975 Montreal compilation *Magic Bimbo* has a bunch of different versions of "El Bimbo" by Bimbo Jet and "La Bamba" by Ritchie Valens on it which suggest that said 1975 disco hit and said 1959 Chicano rock'n'roll hit are exactly the same song, as is "December 1963 (Oh What a Night)" by the Four Seasons. And if you believe Lester Bangs, "La Bamba" begat every punk rock song ever, from "Louie Louie" to "Blitzkrieg Bop" (and I suppose on to "Smells Like Teen Spirit"). So basically, THE ROOTS OF DISCO AND THE ROOTS OF GARAGE ROCK (especially the '60s kind) WERE EXACTLY THE SAME ROOTS! Supposedly the "bomba" was a traditional Puerto Rican rhythm brought into up-to-date danceability by vocalist Ismael Rivera and percussionist Rafael Cortijo in the late '50s. But on *Magic Bimbo*, none of the Bamba or Bimbo songs are credited to anyone with a Latin surname.

Disco, like rock'n'roll itself, would be inconceivable without old Caribbean cruise-ship counterrhythms: sambas, mambos, cha-chas, charangas, rico suaves, chimi changas. Disco and '60s garage rock are the most Hispanic-dominated genres in U.S. rock chart history; both started out as grass-roots fast-dance musics on independent labels, and both provided forums where complete nobodies could screw around any way they wanted and get a great record out of it, then vanish back into oblivion. If that's a bit too theoretical for you, here's a few *specifics* to consider:

—On her 1983 *No La De Da* EP, Claudja Barry covers the Yardbirds' "For Your Love," letting synths play the sombrero-bongo parts; Wayne Kramer, formerely of the MC5, plays guitar. And Boney M cover the Yardbirds' *mbaqanga* dirge "Still I'm Sad," and the Yardbirds' "Hot House of Omagarashid" was proto-disco, too: basically, it turned Bo Diddley beats into space music.

—"Soul Cha Cha" by Van McCoy (who also did "The Hustle") and "A Piece of the Rock" by Sir Monte Rock III (who also went by the name "Disco Tex") have all kinds of Sam the Sham "Aye yi yi yi yi eye!" picador-poking-bull-with-lance interjections.

—The Real Roxanne's "Roxanne's On a Roll" opens with the "uno dos tres quatro" from "Wooly Bully" (which Sam the Sham maybe stole from "Tic, Tic, Tic," by the Kingston Trio).

—Gino Soccio's 1980 *S-Beat* LP has "Tequila" guitar parts.

—"Boogie Oogie Oogie" by A Taste of Honey is pretty much the same song as Brenton Wood's 1967 Latin beach hit "The Oogum Boogum Song," an even drunker fraternity romp than "Louie Louie."

—On her self-titled 1980 EP, Amy Bolton uses white-trash garage riffs and trash organ (and words about sex with her sister and mom a few months before Prince put out *Dirty Mind*) in a disco context. She also covers "Talk Talk" by the Music Machine.

—Organ hooks out of "96 Tears" by ? and the Mysterians are used in "Disco Shirley" by Shirley and Company. (Frank Kogan believes ? might've learned to plink his Farfisa from soul monologuist Joe Tex, which explains why they call it "Tex-Mex").

—John Cale tinkles "96 Tears"–type organ notes in the Velvet Underground's "White Light/White Heat" and at the end of "I'm Waiting for the Man." And "Sister Ray" swings moderately and repetitively for seventeen minutes, building gradually into dense beauty and noise and easy-to-misunderstand words about men wearing ladies' clothes, making it proto-disco in a sense, or at least proto-art-disco; in fact, John Wilcock's liner notes inside *The Velvet Underground and Nico* claim "art has come to the discotheque." Proof—how Bionic Boogie chant "sweet Jane, sweet sweet Jane" all through their 1978 dance track "Chains."

—Purebred Native American band Redbone worked proto-disco strings and post-toga-party backup into the family-platter gator-steak clatter of their early '70s hits "The Witch Queen of New Orleans" and "Come and Get Your Love." P.J. Proby, whose 1967 hit "Niki Hokey" was written by Redbone's Pat Vegas, Eurodiscofied "Witch Queen" in the early '80s. And in 1995, a hit German house music cover of

"Come and Get Your Love" by Real McCoy cleverly pigeon-holed Redbone's Latinized swamp hoodoo as a bridge between "Hang on Sloopy" by the McCoys and "The Hustle" by Van McCoy!

—Turn-of-the-'70s minstrel-rock acts initiated the disco idea that square white groovesters could pretend to be funky black guys by singing oily and macho like Tom Jones. "One Fine Morning," a big 1971 hit by the Toronto band Lighthouse, stuck post-boogie/proto-house piano solos and a metal guitar climax on top of big-band brass and maracas. Looking Glass, Three Dog Night, the Guess Who, and the Ides of March figure here as well.

—The Commodores' 1974 instrumental hit "Machine Gun" sounds like a funk update of some early '60s surf-guitar wipeout.

—Other famous garage-into-disco links: Jugband vet Norman Greenbaum's polyrhythmic fuzzbox Jesus-freak rock in 1970's "Spirit in the Sky"; Uriah Heep using Latin percussion in "Look at Yourself" in 1971 then pasting "Shaft" chukka-chukka under acid-metal in "Sweet Lorraine" in 1972; Golden Earring putting a boomy techno-tribal break under horned grunge in "Radar Love" in 1974. Probably Grand Funk's "We're an American Band" (1973) and Rick Derringer's "Rock and Roll Hoochie Koo" (1974), too.

—The gay disco popularity of the Spencer Davis Group's 1967 top-ten "I'm a Man" makes perfect sense, given that it has the most devastating extended Latin-American congabeats in guitar-rock history, and given Steve Winwood's hypermasculine Iron John lyric about messy apartments and whiskery chins and country music and playing to win and hearts of stone and no time for lovin', which rhythm and prose make both the Village People's "Macho Man" and Right Said Fred's "I'm Too Sexy" sound timidly heterosexual in comparison. An Italian act called Macho, led by Mauro Malavasi and Jacques Fred Petrus who went on later to produce the group Change, did a butch-and-sleazy 17:45 version in 1978. Cerrone (as Kongas) covered "Gimme Some Lovin'" (as "Africanism") instead—but with noticeably less chest hair.

—Will To Power's chart-topping 1988 merger of "Free Bird" and "Baby I Love Your Way" into "Free Baby" is a disco analogue to Detroit garage-R&B king Mitch Ryder's merger of "Jenny, Jenny" and "C.C. Rider" into "Jenny Take a Ride!" in 1966. (Mitch later had more hit medleys, then covered Prince and sang about sodomy.)

What Bo Knows

What all this is probably adding up to is that rock'n'roll bands should be allowed to choose from among three kinds of drums—timbales, congas, and tom-toms. (Okay, maybe bongos too: like the Yardbirds in "For Your Love" and Steven Adler on Guns N' Roses' *Appetite for Destruction*.) I have trouble telling which species is which just on mere hearing, but I *can* tell the difference between this category of drums and others, and to my ears this category always makes the music *move* more.

I even have a soft spot for Burundi rhythms, for example the ones used in Gary Glitter's 1972 hit "Rock And Roll Part 2"—sort of a doubled, lightened adaptation of the Bo Diddley beat, which Bo somehow developed out of the knit-three-pearl-two rhythm pattern called *clavé*, first developed on wooden clacking instruments in Cuba and allegedly a common denominator of all Latin and Caribbean grooves: mambos, rhumbas, sambas, calypsos. Other people say Bo's beat is really the *hambone* beat; i.e., "shave and a haircut, *two bits!*" Probably they're right, too.

Rhino Records' 1992 *Bo Diddley Beats* compilation traces the beat back, through Gene Krupa's 1940 "Tonight (Perfida)" and a '30s fieldworker blues chant called "Chevrolet," to the *Kpanlogo* beat: invented by drummers in what is now Ghana, West Africa, over a thousand years ago. A guy named King Cotton claims in his liner notes that Africans would pound on a couple drums and lots of percussion at funeral wakes, improvising the beat into a jam, so men could strut and women shimmy private parts lewdly to it. Eventually, long after *Kpanlogo* merged with something Spanish into *clavé*, Bo electrified it via rectangular guitar, and put Jerome Green's maracas on top. (And his beat has since been re-incorporated into African music, for instance in Moussa Doumbia's extremely squawky "Yé Yé Moussa.")

The beat kind of goes "Boom-ChuckaChuckaChucka-Chucka-Boom Boom." On top, in Bo's own version anyway, there's a nasal, raunchy voice, boastful and making fun of you like in rap, and more guitar, noisy like in heavy metal.

"Who Do You Love," where Bo tries to impress some lady by telling her his necktie's a snake and he walks on concertina wire and builds chimneys from people's skulls, is nihilist overstatement like in punk rock.

In 1957, according to wealthy rock critic Dave Marsh, Mickey and Sylvia came up with a more "polished" version of Bo's beat, though to me "Love is Strange" sounds more like a calypso; a year later, jump-joint bandleader Johnny Otis adapted Bo's basics into "Willie and the Hand Jive," a top-ten hit about jacking off. Elvis Presley's 1961 "(Marie's the Name) His Latest Flame" has a beat that's sort of post-Diddley/proto-Burundi, and the blatantly Bo-like "Not Fade Away" was the closest Buddy Holly ever came to making a hard rock record, so the Stones covered it. Freddie Cannon's "Buzz Buzz a Diddle It" incorporated Diddley into both its syncopation and (sort of) its title.

The most masterful turn-of-the-'60s rhythm kings were surf bands—the incomparably wild tom-toms in the Surfaris' 1963 "Wipe Out" were banged out on seventh-grade desktops throughout the land for years thereafter. Preston Epps' 1959 "Bongo Rock," Sandy Nelson's 1961 "Let There Be Drums," and Jorgen Ingmann's Danish 1961 "Apache" were all covered later by the Dutchmen or whatever they were in the Incredible Bongo Band, whom old-school hip-hop deejays used to scratch every chance they got.

But it was the Strangeloves (who were actually three Brill Building employees who once wrote the Angels' "My Boyfriend's Back," one of whom went on to produce the Go-Gos and Blondie) who may well have invented Burundi *per se*—in 1965's "I Want Candy" (later remade by Burundi concept band Bow Wow Wow), they used a tympani-and-drumslam mixture they claimed to have swiped from New Zealand Maori and Australian aborigone barbarians. Similarly, singer Joe Elliott has explained to me that the Burundi beat recurring intermittently throughout Def Leppard's 1989 hit "Rocket," which I always assumed came from "Rock and Roll Part 2," was actually sampled instead from a genuine African field recording by Burundi Black (alias the Royal Ingoma Drums of Burundi). He says you'd only know if you played them side by side, but it's *different* from Gary Glitter's beat, somehow. So maybe the Strangeloves actually stole it from these Burundi Black guys, too. Or maybe the other way around—you tell me.

In 1969, Iggy and the Stooges took oil-drummish Bo Diddley polyrhythms and fuzzed and stretched them toward purgatory ("1969," "I Wanna Be Your Dog"); it's possible they stole the idea from the Byrds' 1968 "Tribal Gathering." Many later hard rock bands (UFO, Van Halen, Mudhoney) tried to pick up on this innovation, albiet with diminished success. Better was how, in the early '70s, tom-tommed rhythms were applied to any number of trash-pop and glam-rock hits: "Radar Love" by Golden Earring, "Na Na Hey Hey Kiss Him Goodbye" by Steam, assorted tunes by the Sweet, Mud, Suzi Quatro. Not to mention "He's Gonna Step On You Again" by bearded Brit John Kongos—Kongos's last name is almost "congas," and in the '80s his hit became a bigger hit for Manchester dance frauds Happy Mondays. Lake Erie beach band Pere Ubu's 1978 "Life Stinks" was the art-rock "Wipe Out," then in 1980 Adam and the Ants revived Burundi as "Antmusic."

Oddly, though, the most rock'n'roll drum rumbling of recent times has actually turned up on *disco* records. In her 1975 top-20 one-shot "Up in a Puff of Smoke," a British singer named Polly Brown used carbon-copy "Rock and Roll Part 2" Burundi rolls, and did a decent Diana Ross imitation to boot; in 1978, Eurodisco unknowns Belle Epoque had high-register girl-screeches and symphonic airiness giving way to a guy who kept shouting "Haaaay, Miss Broadway" (the title) over unabashed Bo-hambone beats. And Bohannon's post-Diddley 1975 "Disco Stomp" sounds exactly the same as Hello's 197? post-Diddley-glam "New York Groove," covered into a top 20 U.S. glam/disco crossover by Ace Frehley of Kiss in 1978 (and both songs sound not unlike the theme music from the popular '90s kids' cartoon *Doug*, on U.S. cable TV's Nickelodeon Network, about a twelve-year-old boy and his problems and his girlfriend Patty Mayonaise who sounds even more like Peppermint Patty than Liz Phair does, but with a Southern drawl).

In fact, give or take Slade's Celtic-and-electro-informed 1984 "Run Runaway," the clearest precedent for Def Leppard's Burundi abuse in "Rocket" is a disco song, not a rock one. The title track of Boney M's 1978 *Nightflight to Venus* connected blatantly to fellow German discophiles Silver Convention's concurrent "Mission to Venus," and Burundi-beating helped segue the cut directly into Boney's unforgettable worldwide-except-America (sort of like soccer, Frank Kogan points out) balalaika-disco smash (and "Russian love machine" rah-rah cheer), "Rasputin." But mainly, "Nightflight to Venus" was "Rocket," a decade ahead of schedule. A vocodered cyborg voice greets us for the journey: "Ladies and gentlemen, welcome aboard the spaceship Boney M for our first passenger flight..." Then comes countdown and liftoff, then faster-and-faster Gary Glitter drums amid techno synths, flamenco brass, "hey! hey! hey!" gang chants.

(Which "hey! hey! hey!"s—often pronounced "oi! oi! oi!" instead—obviously deserve their own chapter in this book, given their frequent rowdy recurrence throughout the history of '30s stage musicals, Jamaican ska, garage rock, glam, disco, heavy metal, skinhead punk, north Indian bhangra, and World Cup soccer matches, not to mention how they invariably sound eager to pump their bloody fist into your kisser. But hey hey hey, I've gotta save *something* for the sequel, don't I?)

Beats for Bleacher Bums

In a column Dave Molinari contributed in 1991 to *The Hockey News*, he calls Gary Glitter "arguably the most influential man in hockey." He says Gary's "Rock and Roll Part 2" is usually referred to in icing-the-puck circles as "The Hey Song," and that it's received far more airplay in sports arenas than it ever received on the radio even when it was a hit, and that North Stars fans made 1138 requests to hear it during the 1991 playoffs alone. ("Or, by my calculations," Molinari computes, "1138 times for every different word in the lyrics.") He claims Gary Glitter's only real competition, very *distantly* in second place, is "Na Na Hey Hey Kiss Him Goodbye" by Steam. (Joni Mitchell's "Raised on Robbery," about trying to pick up a barfly who's got money riding on the Maple Leafs, doesn't even rank.)

Anyway, my big sports problem lately is that I think I have attention-deficit disorder, just like all those little kids who can't keep their mind on one thing until their parents buy them K'Nex blocks instead of Legos or Lincoln Logs. So when the baseball strike happened in 1994, I really didn't mind—baseball games last too long these days (just like CDs) anyway, thanks to batter's box fillerbustering and TV commercials. While I'd much rather listen to music than read about it at this juncture, I'd much rather read about baseball than watch it.

As for football, in high school my brothers and I used to bet on ten games per weekend on Mafia-type betting cards, and I probably went to more Detroit Lions than Detroit Tigers games growing up, since my stepdad got season tickets through the Elks Club. But I've never really *cared* about the sport.

On the other hand, I would still much rather watch football than basketball or hockey, which just seem to me like unstructured messes where plays have no beginning or ending and everybody's always bumping into each other and you have trouble telling who's who because everything's going too fast. At least in football, the progress from one end of the field to the other is gradual enough that your head's not jerking back and forth and you can always pinpoint where the action is. But football's still not as good as baseball, since the people hide under too much equipment and don't look like people.

All of which explains why, even though I went to journalism school to be a sportswriter, I wound up being a rock critic instead. Also, not to be morbid or anything, but the only NHL hockey (Red Wings, to be specific) game I ever attended in my entire life ended about nine hours before my dad died.

Still, if you want rock for jocks, I'm happy to oblige: depending on who you ask, the rhythm of World Cup soccer fans Def Leppard's "Pour Some Sugar on Me" sounds either like Queen's "We Will Rock You" (which I'll get to later) or "I Love Rock N' Roll" by Joan Jett (who dedicates albums to the Baltimore Orioles). "Pour Some Sugar On Me"'s beat was in turn stolen in Warrant's 1990 "Cherry Pie," which had lines about baseball in it, and Warrant covered "We Will Rock You" on the *Gladiators* soundtrack! Otherwise, baseball-rock is mostly all obvious Berry/Springsteen/Fogerty stuff, or it's available on Rhino's 1989 *Baseball's Greatest Hits* (the high point of which is Dave Frishberg's *Baseball Encyclopedia* tone poem "Van Lingle Mungo").

Except Rhino forgot Meat Loaf's use of Phil Rizzuto in "Paradise by the Dasboard Light," and Cookie Brown and the L.A. Fans's 1995 "Hideo Nomo Song" (which sounds like "Day-O" by Harry Belafonte), and Warren Zevon's "Ballad of Bill Lee" (and "Ain't That Pretty At All," where he hurls himself Jimmy-Piersall-like against the walls of the Louvre). And how Bob Dylan sings about Willie Mays and Catfish Hunter (and how I always think the diplomat in "Like a Rolling Stone" is gonna carry on his shoulder a baseball bat, but it turns out to be a Siamese cat). And how on *Go Girl Crazy!* the Dictators called themselves rookies with good pairs of hands, and how in "Hey Ladies" the Beastie Boys have more hits than Sadaharu Oh (the Babe Ruth of the Japanese League). And how Madonna's "Vogue" (unlike Simon and Garfunkel's "Mrs. Robinson" or John Fogerty's "Centerfield") is the only Dimaggio Rock song where the singer might be talking about Vince or Dom instead of Joe, since she omits his first name. And how Charlie Pride played for the L.A. Angels, and the Marcels' "Blue Moon" was about John Odom.

T-Bone Burnett sang once that "baseball players aren't so square, they got beards and stringy hair," a phenomenon initiated in the '70s by Joe Pepitone and Ken Harrelson and eventually perfected by John Kruk. Texas slugger Juan Gonzalez denied accusations by his wife in 1994 that he left her for mucho-cleavaged salsa diva Olga Tañon. And when lots of *Billboard* records broke in 1992, like how Kris Kross rocketed to number-one faster than any new act in decades and Boyz II Men's "End of the Road" stayed at the top of the charts longer than "Don't Be Cruel/Hound Dog" and Billy Ray Cyrus eclipsed Vanilla Ice's rookie hitting streak, cynical oldtimers blamed it all on Astroturf, night games, expansion teams, and the 162-game season.

"Madison Time" by the Ray Bryant Combo, on the other hand, is *basketball* music, since it mentions Wilt Chamberlain. "Papa Hobo" by Paul Simon refers to the Pistons, and John Fred of "Judy in Disguise (With Glasses)" fame used to shoot hoops at Louisiana State, plus his dad played baseball for the Tigers. (I don't know if the *Residents* had anything to do with sports—give or take the Eskimo variety, like walrus-curling maybe—but I want to suggest here that the mysterious identity of the Residents may well *be* John Fred and his Playboy Band, since they both came from Shreveport and made fun of the Beatles.)

The best early rap groups (which as far as I'm concerned means the best rap groups ever)—namely the Furious Five and Funky Four Plus One—had five bodies, like a basketball team. (Well, actually, the Furious Five had *six* bodies total if you count turntable-spinner Grandmaster Flash, but they had five *voices*.) Said squads traded off lines like Curly Neal and Meadowlark Lemon passing behind their backs—with extroverted showmanship that was equal parts clownish trickery and agile grace. In 1980, both "Freedom" by the Furious Five and "Zulu Nation Throwdown" by the Soul Sonic Force compared rapping to dribbling free throws or whatever it is that basketball players do. (And in 1970 the Globetrotters even made a proto-rap album.)

As for *boxing* rock, I already explored it in my heavy metal record guide *Stairway to Hell* (page 90—buy a copy), but I inadvertently left out "Hurricane" by Bob Dylan (about Hurricane Carter), not to mention videos for Cracker's "Low," House of Pain's "On Point," Banda Pachuco's "Te quiero a ti," and John Cougar Mellencamp's "Authority Song."

Queen's hip-hop-inspired "Another One Bites the Dust," onetime Detroit Lions fight song, is football rock *à la* Mel and Tim's "Backfield in Motion," or Steely Dan's "Deacon Blues" (which calls Alabama the Crimson Tide), or Hootie and the Blowfish's "Only Wanna Be With You" (the only song ever about being a fan of both the Miami Dolphins—are dolphins blowfish?—and some Bob Dylan song where somebody shoots a man named Grey then goes to Italy and inherits a million bucks).

Everything TLC does belongs to football, now that Left Eye burned down some Atlanta Falcoln guy's house. And my favorite O.J. Simpson tribute ever was Oran "Juice" Jones' spookily prophetic 1986 top-ten soul single, "The Rain": "I saw you and him walking in the rain. You were holding hands and I'll never be the same . . . My first impulse was to run up on you and do a Rambo . . . What was you trying to prove? This was the Juice!"

When the marching band refused to budge for the pigskinners in "American Pie," Don McLean was arguing the primacy of music *over* football. And Queen's "We are the Champions" is only good if you win the pennant (and probably not even then). "We Will Rock You" by Queen is obviously the *real* queen of sports songs—thanks to its words, but also its beat, a sort of a wallflower version of Bo Diddley by way of John Lennon's "Give Peace a Chance" which goes something like "Stomp-stomp-clap, Stomp-stomp-clap, Stomp-stomp-clap," only distorted, with lotsa mud on its face a big disgrace kickin' its can all over the place. Yet it's simple enough to be pounded out by hands and feet of blotto bleacher bums, with doggerel on top about dirty brats on the street (what all those bleacher bums probably were when they first heard it) noisily growing into manhood.

Kissing cousins to "We Will Rock You" 's beat that ought to be used at sports events but for some reason *aren't* include Plato's-form clapbeats introduced in the Bay City Rollers' number-one 1975 "Saturday Night" ("Clap! Clap! Clapclapclap! Clapclapclap! Clap!"); Rose Royce's number-one 1976 "Car Wash" ("Clap! Clap! ClapCl'Clap ClapClap!"); the Village People's number-three 1979 "In the Navy" (Clap-clap-clap, Clap-clap-clap, Clap-clap-clapclap-cl'clapclapclap!"); and above all Tony Basil's number-one 1982 "Mickey" ("Clap stomp clapclapclap, Clap stomp clapclapclap, Clap stomp clapclapclap!") "Mickey," it should be noted, utilizes a vamp derived in part from the Knack's "My Sharona," and it's also one of the best examples of cheerleader-rock. (The Jackson Five's "Going Back to Indiana," Jimmy Buffett's "Cheeseburger in Paradise," and Weezer's "Buddy Holly" likewise all feature mid-song chants resembling cheers being led. And Gillette's 1994 debut album *On the Attack* was oppressive like a cheerleader boxing your lights out, especially if your dick was too short.) "Mickey," incidentally, was recorded by a middle-aged woman who once worked on music TV shows (*Shindig, Hullabaloo*) and movies (*Easy Rider, The TAMI Show.*) It also elliptically refers to anal sex, but I guess that's not a real sport so never mind.

Anyway, back in baseball land, both the Fine Young Cannibals and Boston did homages to Lot's wife called "Don't Look Back," and Bob Dylan gave a movie he made that title, but the person who said "don't look back, they might be gaining on you" wasn't a rock band at all but rather Satchel Paige, who won 2000-or-so Negro League games before joining the Cleveland Indians in 1948, at 42 years old. He last pitched major league ball for Kansas City in 1965, when he was 59. But despite countless refusals-to-hang-up-spikes by over-the-hill has-beens (like you know, P.J. Harvey) in recent times, rock's only true Satchel-equivalent ever would be Rufus Thomas, an old vaudeville entertainer who didn't debut hitwise until "Walking the Dog" when he was 46 in 1963; he scored three more hits in his mid-50s, then rapped on a

Jon Spencer Blues Explosion album in 1996, when he was 79. Pigmeat Markham, who first hit at 62 in 1968 then never again, and Louis Armstrong, who last hit humously at 62 in 1964 then post-hu at 86 in 1988, deserve honorable mentions.

And though the '70s British proto-*rock en Español* prog-funk band Babe Ruth was sort of a missing link between spaghetti westerns and disco, the only rock'n'roller comparable to the *real* Babe would be Elvis Presley, who was Bambino-worthily gigantic in terms of popularity, among other gigantitudes. (Greil Marcus should write an essay about it). But Elvis (along with Neil Sedaka, Cliff Richard, Frank Sinatra, Rolling Stones, Ray Charles, Beatles, Paul Anka, Michael Jackson sort of) can also be considered an equivalent of Ted Williams, Early Wynn, Warren Spahn, and Minnie Minoso, since they all scored hits in four different decades. And rock drummers are more or less the same as baseball catchers, since they both stand in the same place in relation to everybody else, plus they're generally fat and ugly. And Ricky Ricardo's mambo classic "Bob Alou" was a sonic predecessor of Matty, Jesus, and Felipe Alou (and now Felipe's kid Moises too, who has at least as many vowels in his name as his dad). And Joe Jackson is the Shoeless Joe Jackson of rock—he even left his shoes on the cover of his *Look Sharp* album!

Finally, now that famous folk-metal revivalists Pearl Jam (once called Mookie Blaylock) have fought Ticketmaster prices (which I guess is supposed to make me "respect" them, though I still don't *plan* to respect them until they write a song whose lyrics make sense), maybe it's time for Eddie Vedder's barroom-brawl partner and pitching whiz (and part-time leader of the fake grunge band Stick Figure!) Black Jack McDowell to start fighting to keep ticket prices for *baseball games* down. I got it: if the prices don't fall, all the baseball players could just *refuse to play!* How come nobody else ever thought of that?

Party-in-the-Background Rock

You hear shouting and handclaps and feet shuffling around and bowl games blaring from the TV and cups being refilled and traffic coming up the driveway and body parts being pinched and guests playing pin-the-tail-on-the-donkey and blowing out candles and repeating gossip and punching each other in the nose and freebasing and forgetting punchlines and otherwise trying to impress each other with their astute wit—no song I've ever heard *with* party noises recorded in the background would sound better *without* them. They make the sound more full, the motion more multidirectionally alive, everything more *free*.

It's impossible to say who first came up with the idea (probably somebody actually *at* a party with loud music on in the background!), but I vote for polka bands. Novices in search of wildly accordioned songs with funny words and lots of pierogi-accented hooting and hollering should track down Frankie Yankovic and his Yanks' late '60s *Greatest Hits* and the Matys Bros' 1963 beer barrel bash *Who Stole the Keeshka?* —both of which claim some *dupa* named Yasha returned the keeshka to the butcher shop, so my Polish-American wife and I have developed what we call the "single Yasha theory." (K-Tel's 1971 *25 Polka Greats* sampler is more uneven, but it has some great band names, like Six Fat Dutchmen and Whoopee John's Wilfahrt Orchestra for instance.)

Salsas (maybe mambos and cha-chas too) probably featured as much audible partying as polkas did. (Johnnie Bomba even did a "Bomba Polka" in the '50s, though that might just be 'cause it was his name. It doesn't sound very much like the "La Bamba Mambo" Hector Pellot's combo does on Epic Records' 10-inch '50s *Dance the Mambo* compilation.) Louis Prima and Huey "Piano" Smith were ahead of the party-noises pack as well. Louis's 1957 jazz-woogie instrumental "The Shiek of Araby" has a pattycatting and babbling and tarantelling wedding reception going on. And intentionally or not, all the out-of-tune and out-of-synch Mardi Gras Vaudeville "ha ha ha"s and "goobah goobah goobah"s in Huey and the Clowns' 1958 "Don't You Just Know It" suggest their whole *life* (much of it spent in women's clothes) was a party.

Then again, the El Dorados' kitchen-sink Chicago doowop "At My Front Door" (a.k.a. "Crazy Little Mama") included a short party break in 1955, so maybe *that's* where to start; it was begged or borrowed or stolen by the Drifters in "At the Club" in 1965, which from its Latin percussion on up sounds like a '60s-garage-rock precursor (or maybe the other way around—mostly it resembles the McCoys' "Hang on Sloopy," which actually topped the charts two months *before* "At the Club" peaked).

In Claudine Clark's 1962 "Party Lights," she can hear the party going on across the street and so can you; Janis Ian's 1967 "Younger Generation Blues" could be Claudine five years later, rapping like Bob Dylan and extrapolating his riffs and anticipating "Shaft" rhythms, but still whining about her parents (who won't let her smoke) and still letting us hear the party. Dylan made his own party-noise rock with "Rainy Day Women #12 and 35" in 1965, trying to sound stoned, but R&B unknowns Gene and Wendell bashed more blotto in "The Roach" in 1963 or so.

You can almost always detect stomping Hispanic teenagers having a "hey hey hey" party in mid-'60s Latin bugalu music by guys like Joe Cuba, Ray Barretto, Jimmy Castor, and Johnny Rios. Cuba's furious "El Pito (I'll Never Go Back to Georgia)" (a rewrite of "Montega" by Dizzy Gillespie sez jazz know-it-all Richard C. Walls) shows up in both a Ru-Paul convenience store scene in Spike Lee's *Crooklyn* and on Cuba's own *We Must Be Doing Something Right!* album, my thrift-store-purchased copy of which has "To Jan All My Love Joe Cuba" scrawled in ink on its cover, but I don't know if it's his real autograph or not. If it is, Joe had a screwy sense of humor, because also on the cover somebody has followed the words "Joe Cuba Sextet" with the inked words "New Wave Band," and beneath the band picture where all six guys look dapper in turquoise smoking jackets and scarves and holding long cigarette holders, the same person has inked in "We're Pissers." Anybody else, I'd say no way, but Joe's music makes me think that really could be his writing on there.

Equally rambunctious '60s keggers-in-background inhabited greaser-band rousers like "Farmer John" by East L.A.'s Premiers, "Double Shot of My Baby's Love" by South Carolina's Swingin' Medallions, and "Latin Latin Lupe Lu" by Detroit's Mitch Ryder and the Wheels. Then for Slade's 1972 *Slade Alive* album, the British group stuck microphones in the audience "to add to the atmosphere," and Noddy Holder told them that "all the drunken louts can shout anything ya like." So the fans are constantly slapping each other on the back and doing these chants like "go, go, go, go, go, go, go . . . ," like they're part of the band.

Mainly, though, the impending age of sedate and Valiumized post-hippie radio abruptly shifted the '70s party solar plexus to black rock like the Ohio Players' "Love Rollercoaster" (remote conversation from the other end of the amusement park), Marvin Gaye's "What's Goin' On" (its start—the rare instance of a background blowout in a *mellow and unhappy* song), and War's "Southern Part of Texas" and "Why Can't We be Friends." These last two are especially intriguing: given War's proud low-rider heritage and their offhand Sam the Sham "hooey!" and "ungh!" *muchacho* ejaculations, not to mention that on their first hit (1970's "Spill the Wine") they served as the backing band for aging Animal Eric Burdon, War can be thought of as an extension of '60s garage punk as much as a herald of funk to come.

Early disco, back when it still meant actual bands playing instruments, was frought with all sorts of background parties: the tipsiest festivities I know of showed up in Crystal Grass's 1975 "I Wanna Thank You For the Music." There were some slack years toward the end of the '70s, but then hip-hop brought the concept back like a full-force gale. Sugarhill and Enjoy Records seemed to have a couple readymade background party tracks they'd use again and again, interchangeably and indiscriminately on just about every record they put out between 1979 and 1982.

In Treacherous Three's "Put the Boogie in Your Body," the party is almost the whole record; Grandmaster Flash and the Furious Five's "Birthday Party" has joking around that sounds a *lot* like a Chicano frat-rock band. Other labels followed suit (Paul Winley with Afrika Bambaataa's "Zulu Nation Throwdown," Brunswick with South Bronx's "The Big Throwdown," Mercury with Kurtis Blow's "The Breaks"), as did the best of the remaining self-contained funk bands (Slave, Unlimited Touch, Positive Force, Trouble Funk). But before long (by 1983) it was over.

If you listened close, you *might* hear surfers hanging ten behind a manipulative (albeit not quite hateable) turd like the Fat Boys' 1987 "Wipe Out" collaboration with the Beach Boys (their best hit in 21 years!). And in 1988 some rap unknowns known as Taking Your Business made equally blatant connections to '60s frat splat in "Just Got Laid"—informed by *Animal House*, Spike Lee's *School Daze*, and Johnny Kemp's "Just Got Paid," it had saxophone honks and hazing-week backup barks disintegrating into a pasture of bleating sheep. Jazzy Jeff and the Fresh Prince's "Summertime," one of 1991's best singles, had picnickers playing on swings and firing up steaks over hot coals, making the record feel almost *humid*; "Tequila," one of 1992's best, had Latin rappers A.L.T. and the Lost Civilization dishing double-shot-of-their-señorita's-love booze puns over one of the most invincible horn riffs known to Pee Wee Herman. On the B-side, called "Refried Beans," they toss a *frijole* party.

As for guitar rock in the post-disco era, well, let's just say it tried desperately to keep up but couldn't. Kudos to Warren Zevon's "I'll Sleep When I'm Dead" (which improved on Dylan's "Rainy Day Women" everybody-stoned crowd concept), the Eagles' slimy "The Greek Don't Want No Freaks," the Clash's "Should I Stay Or Should I Go" (trumped-up jumping-bean Mexicans allegedly ripped off some Kingsmen live album), Midnight Oil's "This Dead Heart" (aborigone-on-the-outback chatter within a song unwittingly quoted by Eagle crony Jerry Brown when he put his hat in the ring for the 1992 presidential race—so it's *political*-party-in-the-background music!), Girlschool's raucously sexy "Danger Sign" and "Tiger Feet," Bryan Adams's "Ain't Gonna Cry" (which also adds Dumpsters to his ever-riotous gang vocals), the Kings' "Partyitis" (Toronto new-wavers going bonkers over Led Zeppelin riffs), Joe Dolce's Australian Italo-polka "Shaddap You Face," Hoodoo Gurus' "Get High" (another every-body-must-get-stoned update), Garth Brooks's "Friends in Low Places" (drunk-and-disorderly honky-tonk-wrecking yee-haws), Kix's "Cool Kids," and Quarterflash's "Welcome to the City" (though the latter two are more sidewalk than rec-room). "Woody and Dutch on the Slow Train to Peking" by Rickie Lee Jones has a block party on it too, but it stinks, so I won't mention it. (Whoops.)

In 1987, the most famous lady on earth raised the stakes: Madonna's perfectly titled "Where's The Party" on her *You Can Dance* album ties together Latin rock, salsa disco, *and* old-school rap, loses control like the singer says she wants to, and makes it all look like an accident. Ska-and-cumbia-happy guitar bands from Quebec (Dédé Traké), France (Elmer Foodbeat, Mano Negra), and Mexico (Bötellita de Jerez, Cafe Tacuba) have begun doing something similar in recent years with surprising regularity. As have Mexico's dozen-member glitzily-cowpoke-costumed sax-swinging doubletimed-polka *banda* ensembles (such as Banda Bahia, who put out a CD where they ricocheted through renditions of "My Way," "Ghostbusters," "Mambo No. 8" by Perez Prado, "El Mata-dor" by Los Fabulosos Cadillacs, *and* "Speedy Gonzalez" by Pat Boone!).

Likewise, hot-pantsed Brazilian TV-host Xuxa's best tracks have always been the fast semitropical ones where dense ay-oh-ay-oh!/olé-olé! repartee with her prepubescent "shorties" helps you visualize the color and chaos of her *Xou da Xuxa* show; i.e., three or four layers of action all the time, audi-ence members clapping and yelling behind waving Peruvian flags behind *chicos* and *chicas* finding out who can stuff more balloons down their trousers. Until some gringos come up with craziness to match such piñata-bashing feats of ingenu-ity, whiteboy rock is destined to remain a party second-po-tato, a bridesmaid. A mere wallflower.

All By Myself

Roseanne Barr has said that she and Tom Arnold used to throw eggs at partying neighbors when their noise kept Roseanne's kids awake at night. I can relate: on New Year's Eve 1991 I stayed home and went to bed early, as anybody with respect for planetary alignment and his own safety and disrespect for the whims of the herd would, but the dickweeds across the hall had co-yuppies over and played too much bad Peter Gabriel and babbled and drank loudly deep into the night, keeping *my* kids awake. So at O-Hangover-Thirty Military Time, we did the sensible nuclear family thing—we dug out the Stooges' *Raw Power* and all our toy drums and tambourines and Chinese-made Batman spark pistols, and we tuned the telly in to *Mighty Mouse*, and we got REVENGE.

In "Get Off of My Cloud," Mick Jagger grumbles about a neighbor's 3 A.M. party driving him crazy, demanding, "Don't hang around, hey, *two's* a crowd." Solitude might be the perfect rock'n'roll condition: Lester Bangs and the Delinquents "I'm in Love with my Walls"; Sex Pistols "No Feelings" ("... for anybody else except for myself"); Kinks "Got My Feet on the Ground" ("I don't need nobody else"); Dead Boys "Sonic Reducer" (Stiv Bators has his electronic dream so he doesn't need a mom or dad or human race); Neil Diamond "Solitary Man" and "I Am I Said"; the Platters "The Great Pretender" ("adrift in a world of my own"); New York Dolls "Private World"; John Cougar Mellencamp "Rumbleseat" (can't call up girls 'cause he's scared of the phone and he combs his hair with a belt); the Fall "No Bulbs" (Mark E. Smith can't find a belt 'cause his apartment's a mess—maybe Mellencamp took it!); Martha and the Vandellas "In My Lonely Room"; Beach Boys "In My Room"; Gilbert O'Sullivan "Alone Again Naturally." (Of course there's also *anti*-hermit rock, like Simon and Garfunkel's I-assume-ironic "I am a Rock" and Warren Zevon's ditto "Splendid Isolation," where he makes fun of "Michael Jackson in Disneyland." It might be the hokiest, most stupidly self-righteous genre known to mankind: you could also call it "Nyah-Nyah I Have More Friends Than You Rock").

No point in chronicling the whole history of masturbation rock; it's been done way too many times already by everybody else (except my college friend Steve who said he only tried it once but didn't like it so he quit), most comprehensively in Dave Marsh's "Onan's Greatest Hits" chapter in Greil Marcus's 1979 desert-island-disc-essay anthology *Stranded,* and no amount of Divinyls touching themselves or Green Day pudwanking losing its fun since then is gonna change that. My personal favorite is "Solitaire" by Laura Branigan just because it's more vicious than anybody would expect (and I'd be happy to play cards with her anytime if she's still looking for a partner); loneliest and most obsessed about obsessing is "Overkill" by Men at Work ("alone between the sheets only brings exasperation"); best rewrite of the Who's "Pictures of Lily" is Kix's "The Itch," where they staple a full-size blowup above their bed and get two walletsize too. ("The Itch" and the Isley Brothers' 1969 line "itch your thing do whatcha wanna do" were anticipated by *Bugs Bunny* cartoon scorer Carl Stalling's "To Itch His Own.")

The closest real-life equivalent of *Onan's Greatest Hits* is *Super Star Collection,* a double-album 1978 compilation that suggests a mad genius hard (in more ways than one) at work somewhere in the K-Tel archives. The music is mostly very simpy, with lots of strings, but included among various other shades of slime and swish we find: (1) "Imaginary Lover" by Atlanta Rhythm Section, one of the mushiest uses of blues chords ever, where Jergen's-lubricated rednecks serenade midnight fantasies "always there when you need satisfaction guaranteed," then end with suggestive breathing. (2) "Undercover Angel" by Alan O'Day, about "a dream that makes sweet love." (3) "I Like Dreamin' " by Kenny Nolan, featuring "paradise 'til the morning light." (4) "Blinded by the Light," written by Bruce Springsteen but performed by Manfred Mann, who refer to an adolescent pumping "his weight into his hat." (5) Hot's "Angel in your Arms," which says said angel is "phony," like maybe it's an inflatable toy. And (6) "Lonely Boy" by Andrew Gold, which doesn't get specific but you can read between the lines, can't you? My only complaint is that they left out Leo Sayer's 1977 number-one "When I Need You," where he tells a long-distance pal that all he needs to do to be with her is hold out his hand, "and all that I so wanna give you, babe, is only a heartbeat away." Kinda graphic, no?

What all these songs demonstrate is that "community" is far from a musical necessity. Right, most great music's *made* with help from other people, not by the individual geniuses of yore, and listening to your car radio can connect you to the big out-there. But when do you *play* that radio louder—when you've got passengers to talk to, or when it's just you and the steering wheel? Punk rock meant the most in its initial solipsistic tear-your-world-to-pieces stage; when it started providing a comforting sense of belonging for likeminded losers, it became just another dumb genre. Music fans know their truest (some would say "guiltiest") tastes are those records they play when nobody else can hear them, not ones used to seduce dates or out-blast tone-deaf assholes in the next dorm. I always got my worst grades on "group projects"; "collaborating with others" was never my strong point. But it didn't matter much—now I'm happily married with three kids. The acned teen whose only friend is the disc jockey or the record store clerk at least has a friend, right? And singing about being alone *is* a way of relating to other people. And listening to music is a social act in and of itself, unless you're the one who made the music.

Sorry, dude—didn't mean to get *sociological* or anything.

House of Ill Repute

I went to discos once or twice my plebe year in college (1978–79) to see what it was like. I'm not much into wearing fancy clothes, so I felt out of place. Disco Sucks was a war (we'd been attacked), and I enlisted—maybe I'm part of the reason the stuff didn't kill off guitar rock like it should've. By the late '80s, the neatest thing about how rancid underground white rock had become was that I no longer felt guilty about not going out to see bands, since there weren't any. I started figuring disco people must get something out of music that rock people don't, because no way could they have it any *worse*.

Maybe it was just that the music was so foreign to me that I actually found myself wondering what they were gonna do next, but all I know is that, as a jaded rock guy, I was nothing less than humbled by the sheer variety of finery, flash, sass, and spirit on the twelve discs of open-ended, unpolished, stretched-beyond-common-sense and lewd-beyond-your-wettest-dreams modern disco that comprised BCM Germany's 1987 *The History of the House Sound of Chicago* box set. When I first heard Chicago s house music while fighting I-94 traffic past Comiskey Park and the Sears Tower in the summer of '86, and especially a month or two later when the obligatory hype knocked three singles onto the Limey top ten, I passed it off as a hoax. But eventually I decided that if this music makes me identify with people who've got nothing whatsoever in common with me, how bad can it be?

From what I could gather, house was pretty much the province of dilettante-duded-up dipshits stoned on Contra cocaine, rubbing big shoulders under mirror balls. Instead of solid label-and-release date info, Stuart Cosgrove's unctuous liner mumbo-jumbo to *The History* . . . has much gossip about "decadence," and how the music's "designed to take dancers to new highs." Yeah, well, narcissism used to disgust me, and now I try to be amused. And usually house music's "taboos" made me laugh: the sleazo pickup artist in T-Connection's R&B-hard "At Midnight" tells me to look into his eyes for possibilities, 'cause "when the sun goes down, my fantasies run wild." Boy, I can't wait. Over handclaps and Caribbean cans in Raz's "Amour Puerto Riqueno," an effeminate male voice talks about hot spicy Spanish lust, then everybody starts begging "I want more, is there any left for me?," then guys start moaning—how can anybody take this tripe seriously?

Well, I guess we can conclude all this fantastical bedhop business was at least partly a compensation for AIDS-era lack of preconjugal interaction, right? Mere conjecture, y'understand, seeing as how I've never been to Paradise Garage, the legendary New York disco (open 1976 to 1987) where all this non-interaction is supposed to have initially asserted itself. But legend has it that Frankie Knuckles has been there, and that when said disc jockey transferred west to the Hog-Butcher-of-the-World's Warehouse Club (whence house derived its name) in the mid-'80s, he was working to recreate the eccentric barrage that the Garage had long supported: subcultural chant-skank that stuck zillions of silicon BPMs under Delta wails and old-school-rap clatter, thus straddling the chasms betwixt gospel grit, Tinseltown schmaltz, and post-Sly-Stone superfreak thump. The idea was to come up with dance music that fought back against megacorp-regulated rhythm-retrenchment, homogenized positivism, and gloss gimmicks. And too often, house was a step back from its German and Italian Eurodisco forebears. But once in a while, it worked.

Early house music was a quick-changing, room-disrupting idea glut, a tossed salad with most every song rooted in a world party that spanned from Munich to Miami to the Bronx. It had funk's plantation dirt on its hands, but it still felt like disco. So when it was bad, there was a lack of tautness that made it feel flabby as a flounder. But when it was good, when nothing was hiding and the don't-leave-me-this-way went all out, house showed off an abandon that oozed out of your speakers like boiled Log Cabin syrup until your floor got all gooey.

As much as the most monofunctional '70s disco, house suffered from a dearth of first-class heart-tugging/revving song-writing—there's tons of attraction/repulsion and better-not-fuck-with-me, and even some jackshit-lazy "social concern," but not much moral force. Yet house was a one-shot/song-not-the-singer/everybody-is-a-star world. And usually, at least in early days, its disposably expedient avoidance of pseudo-substance was just as important as its brain-bypassing beat; in something like Tyree Cooper's obsessively paranoiac "I Fear the Night," we're talking a raw ingenuity entirely devoid of artifice—Tyree's a man, fresh from his church choir, but his falsetto's got this chilling accidental-punk ineptness that reminds me of the Shangri-Las in "I Can Never Go Home Anymore," Moe Tucker in the Velvet Underground's "After Hours," Ana Raincoat in the Raincoats' Brit skiffle-punk "Only Loved at Night," Susie Timmons in The Scene is Now's New York poindexter-punk "Finding Someone." There's a world of difference between ingenuousness like this and the babyfaced Buying Into The Big Lie you get from thumbsuckers who grew up on Jonathan Richman.

House music had as much shock-of-the-new as rap ever did: car-crash percussion breaks, voices in unheard-of keys, ant-farm-maze keyboard improvisations in John Rocca's "I Want to be Real," snares manhandled by billy clubs then torn to pieces and mourned by munchkins in Arrogance's "Crazy." It balanced styles in ways that made Prince and George Clinton seem as clumsy as any prog-rock oaf, and it had an inborn ability to defy expectations that post-Public-Enemy rap could only dream about. A nonchalant mosaic like T-Coy's "Cariño" could progress from *Star Wars* galaxy-swooshes through little salsa-piano arpeggios to some colossally polyrhythmic vibes and congas, and with detours so subtle you barely knew your nerve-endings were being re-routed. Sometimes all you'd hear was some spaz pointlessly fiddling with the RPM control, so sometimes "wacky" house tracks do the same thing Susan Sontag once wrote about the movie *All About Eve*—they "try so hard to be campy that they're continually losing the beat." In Monfou's "Shut Up" some twit yells the title umpteen times like he's mad at his kids, and it's not funny at all, just dumb. But when used for hooks (and not just as gratuitous time-filler not too far from your typical arena guitar solo), studio sound-sculpturing could be big fun—the j-j-jumps in the trash-organ-matrixed hit "Do it Properly" by Two Puerto Ricans, a Black Man, and a Dominican, for instance.

In its (tossed) salad days, house music piled everything but the outhouse sink on a technologically modifed R&B beat, and though the drum-sound wasn't as nuts-cracking as in rap, the music had an expansiveness that counteracted (most) hip-hop's restrictivness: one level up from the Eurodisco pulsations, there's rhythmic turmoil from cause-and-effect tribal timbales or Billy Squier Zepbeats or ping-pong balls from heaven or the revolution-on-the-West-Bank undulations of staccato basslines folding back on themselves. And up top you'd get Donna Summer toot-beeps, doowop harmonies, blues-riffed guitar parts. House architect Marshall Jefferson, in cuts like "Move Your Body" and "Ride the Rhythm," lays down fleet-fingered jukejoint pinetop in the half-century-old Chicago tradition of '30s piano cats Meade Lux Lewis and Albert Ammons; Sampson Moore's "House Beat Box" is a rough-hewn instrumental that combines manly boogie-woogie with Duane-Eddy-ish rockabilly twang and Fat Boy Tarzan burps. And everywhere, there's the lowdown fervor of preachers casting hot-buttered-soul exhortations down from their pulpits.

Unfortunately, these deep brownbear-bass voices belting out love-mystery manifestoes shared certain affinities with the overbearingly unrelaxed throats that clogged up more mainstream charts—it's not for nothing that noted "diva" Jocelyn Brown did a Michael Bolton duet. The Puerto Rican, Black Man, or Dominican who booms out "Do It Properly"'s chorus for some reason reminds me of a young Paul Rodgers (and by the time the trio changed their name to C & C Music Factory and commenced to dominate the 1991 pop hitlist, they'd hired a rapper named Freedom Williams who sounded like an even *more* bloated bully). No surprise, either, to learn that economy-sized Daryl Pandy, whose exaggerations in Farley Funk's overpublicized "Love Can't Turn Around" are as fatuous as he is fat, learned his trade in opera class. This volcanic gutbusting pinpointed where house was heading—basically, towards the same putrid "retro-nuevo" gentility that's greased

Urban Contemporary Radio into rancid oblivion off and on ever since disco first kicked the bucket. Other typical mid-'80s travesties were On the House's semi-laid-back coked-up-pimp offensiveness in "Pleasure Control," Steven Dante's Al-Jarreau-worthy Blackface to the Future zippedee-doo-dah in "The Real Thing," J.M. Silk's sepia Sinatra bit in "Shadows of Your Love," and Kelly Charles's torchish "fine taste" crap in "You're Good for Me." In the context of wilder stuff, they didn't sound horrible, I suppose: in a way, it's neat that they were allowed to exist. Problem is, they were The Future.

Within a couple years, the major labels picked up house, and such soul-roots revivalists as Ten City and Lisa Stansfield (followed by Crystal Waters, Rozalla, Ce Ce Peniston, and Robin S.) prospered with it; likewise, when rap-twerp Marky Mark wanted house respectability, he hired an aging soul-disco shouter named Loleatta Holloway. The resulting records forfeited most of what once made the genre interesting: the starship-troop quasar/laser dizziness, the mini-orchestral take-you-for-a-ride travelogues, the giddy girlies, the Spanglish multipercussing. By the mid'90s, Krishnas in search of spiritual fulfillment had long drained house music of its chillingness, cheesiness, warmth, and wit.

Its name changed to "rave" and "jungle" and "trip-hop" and "ambient" and "drum and bass" and "acid jazz"—if you can't come up with exciting new sounds, exciting new words are apparently the next best thing. House production techniques wound up co-opted by every branch of pop R&B and art-punk. And in rap's case, for instance, the "hip-house" hybrid pretty much rolled over and played dead after its first couple circa-1988 singles: the Jungle Brothers' uncharacteristically unstilted grass-hut hit "I'll House You," and Cookie Crew's absolutely undissable "Rock Da House," where four women with Cockney accents slammed down a deliciously dexterous and curtly worded post-toasty speedo soliloquy as a whole pachyderm's worth of black and white ivory got rammed through your skull. After that, hip-house showed isolated flashes of life (from the Wee Papa Girls, Technotronic, Snap, the KLF, even Vanilla Ice), and in 1995 a four-man Chicago production team called 20 Fingers (why not *40* Fingers?) actually managed to concoct a bunch of hilarious house-like novelties about penises and cavemen. But the terrific thing about *early* house (not unlike '60s punk, or early '70s glitter, or late '70s disco, or early '80s rap) is that flashes had nothing to do with it—the whole damn *pan* was on fire.

Orgasmusic

The way Denise Motto recites the acronymed title of her late '80s house obscurity "IMNXTC," it might as well be her license plate number—dance music's pornwise pleasuredome patter sure can get annoying when you can tell they're *faking* it. But back in 1975, Donna Summer brought disco to mainstream America with a radical single called "Love to Love You Baby," the most famous and extended use of human orgasmal panting as a musical instrument in history. The album version had foreplay helping basslines build tension for just under 17 minutes, and the 45 version rose to number two on the charts and was rumored to have been put to tape while Donna was, um, *otherwise occupied.* Alternating honkytonk with ambient early-morning haze and murmured twang with downhome funk wah-wah, the *Love to Love You Baby* album entirely belies conventional wisdom that Donna suddenly became "eclectic" later in her career (on 1979's *Bad Girls*, say). On her next set, *A Love Trilogy* in 1976, she turns all hot and bothered and starts sighing "now that I've got you I want you to come . . . come . . . come . . . come . . . into my arms" over Chopin and Barry Manilow piano music. But she also names the finale "Come With Me" and doesn't do anything naughty in it!

The erotic abandon of fucking-sound-effect records (not to be confused with fucking *sound effect* records, which I'll get to seven chapters from now) often embarrasses me by making me feel like a peeping tom. And though the use of such coital mutterings as disco instruments is far more common than their guitar-rock use, the latter is more common than you'd guess.

Here are a few rock instances that cum to mind: John Fred and his Playboy Band "Judy in Disguise (with Glasses)" (brief panting in the middle); the Troggs "Come Now" (sweet French nothings); the Bob Seger System "Heavy Music" ("deepuh! deepuh! woagh! woagh!"); Daddy Dewdrop "Chick-a-Boom (Don't Ya Jes Love It)" (kitschy pistonlike ooo-haaah's); Led Zeppelin "Whole Lotta Love" (male grunting as noise); T. Rex "Jeepster" ("uh! uh! uh! oh!" ending gasps);

Meat Loaf "Paradise by the Dashboard Light" (coitus-inter-ruptus); Guns N' Roses "Rocket Queen" (whisper-to-moan-to-screech as rhythmic/dramatic boost); Santa Sabina "Mirrota" (steamy 1992 Mexican vampire-Goth chick inching her gar-goyle gargles toward a headboard-banging thrust-lust opera). I also recall overhearing a couple buttheads back in high school talking about something by Aphrodite's Child in this light. (They were Greek, and made an album called *666* in 1972. Their leader, Vangelis Papathanassiou, had a number-one instrumental with his "Chariots of Fire" theme ten years later.)

As for disco, Donna's not exactly the person who intro-duced pornography to it—in fact, it'd be more accurate to say that this sort of sexual explicitness was implicit in the music disco *evolved* out of, from Isaac Hayes purring and pouring wine and taking his girlfriend to the brink in "I Love You That's All" on 1973's *Joy*, to a studio-looped Yoko-Ono exhaling hard through her snoozy early '70s trance "The Path," to Jane Birkin *avec* Serge Gainsbourg doing what comes naturally to French movie stars in their blushless 1966 Antonioni-flick classic "Je T'Aime . . . Moi Non Plus." (Which latter was covered by sapphodiscophiles Saint Tropez on their *Je T'aime* album and Donna Summer herself on the *Thank God It's Friday* soundtrack. Possibly a formative influ-ence on Faster Pussycat singer Taime Downe as well, who knows?)

Gospel ecstasy often hinted at spilling over into the libidi-nous variety too, of course, as the Staple Singers make clear by exclaiming "mercy!" a lot in their 1972 number-one "I'll Take You There" (thus modifying the meaning of the "there" they'll take you to). The Chakachas' 1972 top-ten one-shot "Jungle Fever" has a Belgian girl panting "Nah! Nah! Nah!" amidst betwixt-Santana-and-disco Caribbean polyrhythms; the mixture was later copied by Van McCoy in "Soul Cha Cha" and Silver Convention in "No No Joe." Marvin Gaye's 1973 *Let's Get it On* credits Madeline and Fred Ross for "those sex voices on intro to 'You Sure Love to Ball.'" Sylvia's 1973 number-three "Pillow Talk" has attempts to catch breath be-tween lines at first, but then toward the end she starts "oh-mi*godd*"ing. B.T. Express's 1974 number-two "Do It ('Til You're Satisfied)" has people doing it 'til they're satisfied in the middle. All of which begat Diana Ross's dizzily drugged number-one "Love Hangover" in 1976, "Mission to Venus" (rhymes with penis!) by Silver Convention in 1978, Seduction's unique orgasm/noise/long-worded-philosophic-poetry experiment "Seduction's Theme" in 1989 (featuring the voice of future MTV veejay Idalis Leon), many lesser peepshows.

Kate Bush's 1985 "Running Up That Hill" climaxes with ecstatic untranscribables after plenty of concerned partner-urging. Lil Louis's Chicago house "French Kiss," which almost went Top 40 in 1989, has seven minutes of magnifying and accelerating deep-throat moans stuck inside ten minutes of amphetamized Kraftwerk hypnopulsations that eventually completely drop out then slowly come back, imitating expanding and contracting mattress springs. The "Violent U.S. Mix" of Enigma's 1991 Gregorian disco smash "Sadeness" has session intercoursers commencing at the beginning of the fornication session and moving from hushed humming to outright obsceneness sometimes but other times we accidentally open the door when it's just starting to get really exciting. Samantha Fox's 1991 "(Hurt Me! Hurt Me!) But the Pants Stay On" is (like Salt 'N Pepa's "Push It" and Debbie Gibson's "Shake Your Love") supposed to be about dancing rather than sex, but Sam simulates lewdness anyway.

Sweet Sensation's 1988 "Take it While it's Hot" is a pert perc-happy Miami pube fantasy with soft and wet hot pink Hispanic hormones busting out all over and pleading "the door is open wide so woncha come inside" as the spicy salsa syncopation gets all sweaty soaking stinking slimy damp with back'n'forth rocking and tumbling in and out motion, coagulating toward onanistically viable vibrations. Pajama Party's 1989 "Yo No Sé" has stuttering Miami-Latin freestyle beats at least as immodest, plus all kinds of odd rhythmic flourishes, and basically concerns the Catholic girl from Billy Joel's "Only the Good Die Young" experiencing multiple climaxes on the dancefloor but not realizing that's what's happening: "When you do what you do to me I don't know what is going on." Or whether it's right or wrong either, natch.

(Incidentally, I'd rather hear generic Latin freestyle than generic soul-diva house music any day, and I wouldn't even swear the reason is entirely aesthetic: part of it's that I'm usually just more attracted to Hispanic than to black women —hey, sue me, we all have our preferences. And actually, all things being equal, I'm more attracted to Hispanic than to *white* women, too.)

The all-Limey-woman Raincoats' 1980 post-punk feminist "In Love" parodies orgy-disco to prudish but charming effect. "Popcorn Boy," by the Raincoats' U.K. Rough Trade labelmates Essential Logic, has vocal cracks and snaps turning into la-la-la's and possible beatnik sex. In the Flying Lizards' 1984 single "Sex Machine"/"Machine Sex," the music literally acts like machines making whoopee, with monotonal Brit-proper accents and awkward piston sounds. Parallels can be drawn to the fanciful and simultaneously female and male internal-combustion "sex cylinder" Marcel Duchamp included in his humorous 1912 dada masterwork *The Bride Stripped Bare By Her Bachelors, Even*: "The Bride . . . furthers her complete nudity by adding to the first focus of sparks (electrical stripping) the second focus of sparks of the desire-magneto." (Huh?)

At the end of Francky Vincent's *zouk* tune "Piña Colada," Antillean babes start going "oh yeah! eye-yi-yi-aaah-ungh," then faster and louder, "okkey-ohkeyohkey-oui-oui!-oui!-oui!," while all the while "Doctor Porn" (as Francky calls himself) does all sorts of leering-old-man seduction stuff. (The notes to Virgin Records' 1988 *Hurricane Zouk* compilation refer to him as "a cheeky looking chappie who refuses to be photographed with less than two women around him.") And though "In the Closet" off *Dangerous* has Madonna or some facsimile writhing in throes of cat-scratch fever (and though I shudder to think who might make *Michael* writhe in real life), the sex in Michael Jackson songs comes from his very own lips—all those demented whoops, cries, wheezes, yelps, chikichikas, shammows, and ditdit doos.

If I Ran the Zoo

Michael Jackson's man-in-the-mirror mutilation and morphology (as symbolized by the men and women changing into each other in his "Black or White" video) were the ultimate taboo-trouncing glam rock mindfuck. So it's no mistake that queen bitch David Bowie, from his "fights under neon and sleeps in a capsule" in "Jean Genie" to his oxygen tank and silicone hump and mannequin with kill appeal in "Diamond Dogs," foretold so many of Wacko Jacko's tabloid/MTV antics back in the '70s.

But in some ways Michael is more like Johnny Rotten—an incomparably feral and paranoid performer disgusted by his own animal desires. Michael's "It's too high to get over, too low to get under" in "Wanna Be Startin' Somethin'" could be Johnny trying to figure out how to get to the hate on other side of the Berlin Wall in "Holidays in the Sun." Michael sings about "Human Nature," but in "Wanna Be Startin' Somethin'" he likens people to vegetables. He loves E.T. and owns a zoo—who knows what kingdom of living things he belongs to? The Sex Pistols stole New York Dolls "Human Being" riffs in "Anarchy in the U.K." (where Johnny says he's "no dog's body"), and in "God Save the Queen" Johnny denied *royalty* was human. In his nasty fetus-liberation editorial "Bodies," he turned into the Elephant Man: "I'm not an animal an animal I ain't no animal."

Lou Reed, the MC5, Axl Rose, Chuck D, Trent Reznor, and Olivia-Newton John ("let's get ani-muh, ene-ma, let's get into animals") have all compared themselves to "animals" in lyrics or album titles. "Animal" was also the name of both the large-codpieced frontgrunt of oi! legends the Anti-Nowhere League and the hippie-freak drummer in the *Muppet Show* band. "Animal" by Def Leppard (1987) was the best video ever with a rhinoceros in it (as opposed to "The House at Pooneil Corners" by Jefferson Airplane, which was the best *song* ever with a rhinoceros); "Animal" by Cleveland industrial slimers Prick (1995) was the best video ever with a pygmy hippopotamus. Greil Marcus wrote in *Stranded* that the first time he heard of a band called the Animals, he laughed. Then he heard their music, and shut up.

The Elephant Man is the most deformedly steppenwolfish outcast I can imagine. David Bowie played him on stage; Michael Jackson (rock's most prominent hermit/freak/intentional amputee ever) supposedly tried to buy his body. Rickety-soaring nuclear-synthesizer-and-atonal-guitar-squawk Boston scientist-punk outfit the Girls recorded an "Elephant Man" song as the B-side of their 1979 debut single on Pere Ubu's old Hearthan label. And at the beginning of "Psychiatric," on Mylene Farmer's top-10-in-France 1991 *L'autre...*, the Elephant Man (probably sampled from David Lynch's 1980 movie) insists he's a human, not an animal, after which Mylene softly confides to us that she's losing her mind, like it happens every day. The music is ornate ivory runs under layers of clanking mechanical melodies ready to disintegrate into air. Catholic churchbell keyboards mimic the opening of Bon Jovi's "Livin' on a Prayer," then evolve into hip-hop heaven.

Despite All the Amputations

Philip Kulp, the only college roommate I ever got along with, had lost half his leg in a motorcycle accident, but his fleshtoned false one looked real enough to keep strangers from gawking at him. He'd tell drunk University of Detroit Iranian exchange students he was God, then prove it by taking off his leg. They never accused us of being undercover C.I.A. again!

Conversely, Def Leppard drummer Rick Allen lost his left arm on the last night of 1984, when he smashed his black Corvette into a wall of stone. Before long he became a role model for physically handicapped kids, who started wheelchairing to Def Leppard shows in droves. But Rick was not the first amputee in the history of rock, and he won't be the last. His direct predecessor was of course Moulty, who drummed for the momentarily famous mid-'60s Boston band the Barbarians; Moulty had a left arm, but no hand—he'd lost it in an accident *before* he learned to bang skins, replacing it with a hook. He even told his sad tale in an outcasts' anthem called "Moulty." Before him, there was instrumental and session drummer Sandy Nelson (of "Let There Be Drums" and "Teen Beat" fame), whose right leg said a partial *sayonara* during a 1963 bike accident. And supposedly there was a band called Los X-5, big in Mexico for a while, and *their* drummer had *no* legs. Official 8 × 10 glossies often showed him prone across a railroad track, reenacting his original mishap.

Do eyes count? If so, there's plenty of famous cyclopses, Sammy Davis Jr. among them, not to mention Ray Sawyer of Dr. Hook and the Medicine Show. (Ray *was* Dr. Hook, albeit one-eyed instead of one-handed, and the only other good thing about the album with "Sylvia's Mother" on it was how on the LP cover Ray discussed how his pirate eyepatch frightened people.) And how about this eye-opening 1991 Rap-a-Lot Records dispatch: "Bushwick Bill, the four-foot-six rapper who fronts the Geto Boys, lost his right eye after being shot in the face by his 17-year-old girlfriend, Nicole Randleston, which (sic) is pregnant with Bushwick's child. Bushwick

(Richard Shaw) on Friday May 10th threatened her three-month-old son, hurled a vacuum cleaner at her, and then handed her a loaded cocked .22 caliber Derringer and insisted that he wanted to die; Bushwick is alwright (sic) and underwent surgery on May 15th to remove his damaged eye, which was replaced with a glass eye." Later, Bushwick documented the incident in "Ever So Clear," a highly humorous music video.

(Concerned young people often complain about how few women place in the *Village Voice* Pazz & Jop rock critics' poll, but one-eyed midgets generally fare *much* worse than women. In two decades, only one single by a band with a one-eyed-midget has ever appeared in the poll results—the Geto Boys' "Mind Playing Tricks on Me." A few Bob Dylan albums have placed, though, and he *sang* about a one-eyed midget once, in "Ballad of a Thin Man.")

Who else? Link Wray, the guitarist who invented heavy metal, had only one lung. Black Sabbath's Tony Iommi, the guitarist who first made heavy metal *heavy*, did so by ingeniously first shortening the fingers on his guitar hand in a factory accident. And speaking of Sabbath, how about all those bats whose heads Ozzy Osbourne bit off, causing them to fly around like chickens with their heads cut off? And Gene Vincent, Teddy Pendergrass, and Ian Dury were crippled thanks to a motorcycle crash, a Rolls Royce crash, and polio, respectively, but if you count them you gotta count blind guys, and there's no time for that, sorry. (Myself, I have anosmia, which is the inability to smell, which is unfortunately not the same as the inability to stink. And I've never even applied for a handicapped parking space!) For true dislocation of bodily organs there's always *baseball*. Mike Downey of the *L.A. Times* asks in *Cult Baseball Players* "which baseball players have physical deformities?" "Answer: No Neck Williams, Three-Finger Brown, and Sixto Lezcano." (This was before the Angels drafted one-hand Olympics hurler Jim Abbott.)

Oldest rock'n'rollish song *about* appendage abduction came from medicine-show veteran Al Bernard and his Goofus Five, bridging the historical gap between blackface minstrely and

Western swing with "Hesitation Blues" in Year of our Lord 1927: "Russia is a mean old place, they chop off your head and throw it in your face." Nine years later, Robert Johnson sang "32-20 Blues," one of his musical comedy numbers, pledging to "take my 32-20 and cut her half in two." Beautiful lass Marlo Venus (alias Venus de Milo I bet) loses both arms in a wrestling match in Chuck Berry's 1956 "Brown-Eyed Handsome Man." Before the '50s ended, rockabilly psychotic Hasil Adkins, making 45s for some buddies in his Virgina shack, yawped at least *three* songs about chopping off women's heads and hanging them on his wall; he usually even scheduled time for the dismemberment (say, "half past ten"), and in the best one he helpfully pointed out that his date would never be able to eat any more hot dogs.

MORE HEADS: Julie Andrews threatens "All I want is 'enry 'iggins' 'ead" in *My Fair Lady*; Izzy of Guns N' Roses finds one in a trashcan in "Double Talkin' Jive" in 1991; Johnny Wakelin and the Kinshasa Band praise a shuffling boxer jabbing noggins off necks in "Black Superman—Muhammad Ali," a 1975 novelty hit. MORE ARMS: "Bop-doo-wop, baby I'd chop off my right arm for your love," Southern soul star Z.Z. Hill, 1981. LEGS: 1991's "Got No Legs? Don't Come Running To Me" is the jolliest song U.K. oi!/grindcore-fusion jokers Lawnmower Death ever did, who cares. HANDS: Gator bites one off in Jerry Reed's 1971 swamp hit "Amos Moses," and a mom hunts for one in the snow in Yoko Ono's 1969 "Don't Worry Kyoko." EYES: Angry Samoans poke-poke-poke 'em out in "Lights Out," 1982; Alice Cooper asks us to remove his in "I Never Cry," 1976. EARS: Dad cuts off part of a boy named Sue's in Johnny Cash's beloved 1969 rap ditty, and when A'me Lorain says "I don't have any ifs" in her 1990 one-shot "Whole Wide World," it sounds more like "I don't have any ears."

In "Akhbar, Ahram, Akha Saah," an accordion-and-trumpet-based *shaabi* (backstreet-tavern protest blues) dirge on 1990's *Yalla: Hitlist Egypt* compilation, Shaaban Abdul Raheem (who usually irons shirts for a living in the Shobra ghetto) warbles words which translate thusly: "With a big knife she created a massacre. She took the body and put it in plastic bags, and scattered it in many places." Reportedly this was a major fad among Egyptian women teed off at their stupid husbands in 1989!

In 1989's "Fatal Attraction," lady rapper Roxanne Shante castrates a gent and puts her prize in a pickle jar for safe keeping. There's a store in Germany called Dyckhoff, pictured on the cover of Glasses' staticky mid-'80s Italosalsa 12-inch "Dancing in the Street"; in the Fall's 1981 "Lie Dream of a Casino Soul," Mark E. Smith rants "no nerves left Monday morning, I think I'll cut my dyckhoff-ah." ("Dyckhoff" is how he spells it on the cover of *Hip Priest and Kamerads*.) When the Bee Gees say they love somebody "backwards and forwards with my heart hangin' out" in their 1979 number-one hit "Love You Inside Out," it's no different from Iggy Pop begging "to feel your hand and lose my heart in the burnin' sand" in the Stooges' 1969 "I Wanna Be Your Dog." Metallica's jaunty 1988 Dial MTV smash "One" was about a soldier getting arms and legs blown off. And last but not leashed, there's the Velvet Underground: "Despite all the amputations, you could listen to the rock'n'roll station, and it was all right." So maybe Lou Reed saw Def Leppard coming.

Your Mom Dresses You Funny

One-armed-drummer band the Barbarians' biggest hit was the great "Are You a Boy or Are You a Girl," which went to number 55 in 1965, addressed to a guy with long blond hair who swam "like a female monkey." A common complaint in the wake of the Beatles, no doubt. But then again, Charles Lamer has theorized in *Maximum Rock & Roll* that most '60s garage-rock angst resulted from frustration over no-jeans-or-T-shirt high school dress codes, and from boys in Beatle shags being *beaten up* by greaser gangs. Moptop cuts were really popular in the genre, especially among the Shadows of Knight and Blues Magoos. Bangs falling into your face were quite the craze at first; then as hippiedom appeared, shoulder length locks parted in the middle took over.

Lamer figures that garage-rock musicians dressed to please female fans, who liked their boys wearing lacey shirts of bright colors, pointy-toed high-heel boots, and extremely flared pants and/or black stovepipe jeans. Said girl fans supposedly returned the favor by wearing miniskirts and mod corduroy hats and ironing their long hair, which in turn supposedly led jealous high school boys to wish the girls paid attention to them instead! Sounds pretty far-fetched (girls dress to impress other *girls*, my wife points out), but maybe not in all cases, and maybe one such boy (after a stint in glitter band Sweeney Todd!) grew up to be Bryan Adams, whose 1985 "The Kids Wanna Rock" equates weird haircuts with wasting your life away (and who in 1996 finally got a weird haircut himself!). And maybe some British equivalents turned into Dire Straits, who stodgily scoffed at trumpet-haters wearing "brown baggies and platform soles" in their 1979 blues-revival-revival-in-and-of-itself "Sultans of Swing," then went on to insult earringed MTV transvestites in "Money for Nothing." (And in "Sweet Emotion," Aerosmith made fun of "wearing other things that nobody wears," hence making me quite self-conscious as a teenager. And in "Rapper's Delight," the Sugarhill Gang said Superman's blue pantyhose make him look like a "fairy.")

But Charles Lamer might be oversimplifying. For example, the photos I've seen suggest that lots of '60s garage bands (even future loinclothers Ted Nugent and the Amboy Dukes!) wore suits and ties so they'd be able to play Saturday night dances. In fact, I'd say that garage-rock apparel can pretty much be subdivided into the same sorts of categories that you can classify all hard-rock wardrobes. To wit: School Clothes Rock—Angus Young of AC/DC (prep-school in his case), Buzzcocks, the "goofy" half of Cheap Trick, Nazareth (especially the guy in the sweater). Play Clothes Rock—the rest of AC/DC, Bad Religion, Kix, Loverboy, Lynyrd Skynyrd, Nirvana, pre-leather Steppenwolf. And other hard-rockers (Girls Against Boys, Jonathon Fireater, Jon Spencer Blues Explosion, Urge Overkill, Afghan Whigs, even Joan Jett sometimes!) dress snazzy like they're going out on Saturday night to meet some girls, and still others wear Halloween costumes. And oi! bands wore work clothes, even though most of them were on the dole. (Also, some members in all clothes-subgenres prefer not to wear *shirts*.)

Then there's Scott Ian of Anthrax, who claimed in 1986 that "because we have no image and because we go onstage in our jeans and T-shirts, people relate to us better." But, as Bret Michaels of Poison pointed out back when his band was still knee-deep in pink lipstick, "no image is an image too." In fact, it even has a name—Barry Hennsler, lead singer of Michigan grunge bands the Necros and Big Chief (who himself looks short and squat and scarlet-topped not unlike Mick Hucknall of Simply Red but without Mick's astronomy jewelry and fancy nightgowns) has referred to dressing-down thuswise (with the pantyhose left at home with Lil Sis and the smokebombs and Mr. Wizard set with the kid bro) as "the Metallica look." Which look (eventually abandoned by Metallica themselves in 1996 when they sold out to short-haired Smashing Pumpkins/Sponge glitter) reinforces the populist myth that hard rockers aren't jetsetters or design-school theorists, just grimy-haired streetkids in ripped pants.

Said just-like-you-and-me costume was apparently invented by the Ramones (who tossed in leather jackets) in 1976, then transferred into metal circles by Def Leppard in 1980; in Def

Leppard's case it was nowhere near as extreme, of course, but for sure they came off as regular boys on their album covers. Maybe it's just that their crossdresswear–purchased largely at Top Shop and Chelsea Girl, Joe Elliott told *Star Hits*–seemed more "normally male" than Judas Priest's leatherboy studs. "If you want to buy some gear for onstage that looks a bit different from what your audience is wearing, you're not going to get it at Burton's the tailor's," Elliott said. The Clash, who equated wearing Burton's suits with selling out the punk ethos in "White Man in Hammersmith Palais," might not agree.

Should rock stars try to look like plain folks or not? Tiffany says yes: "Madonna (when she was new) came out with a different look, but it was something anyone could do by going to your local K-Mart or thrift store. All you had to do was buy some bows for your hair, things like that. It was something kids could afford. I think I've got the same kind of look." But Poison had other ideas: "We were living in the streets and trying to act like we weren't dirty," Bret Michaels told *Rolling Stone*. "We were the kids without the money trying to look like we were glamorous. We wanted to be the jewel in the rough."

Mostly, rock'n'rollers just try to look *cool*. "The only reasons I put my hair up is because Izzy had these pictures of Hanoi Rocks and they were cool," Axl Rose said, back when fanzines still misspelled his name A-x-e-l, "and because we hung out with this guy who studied *Vogue* magazine hairstyles and was really into doing hair." When Disco Tex, a part-time hairdresser himself, says on his first album that "nobody cares how you wear your hair, darling," he's probably being *sarcastic*. Prince is lying through his black bikini briefs and new-wave rudeboy coif in "Uptown" when he says where he comes from "our clothes, our hair, we don't care." And I don't believe Charles Wright and the Watts 103rd Street Rhythm Band for a second when they argue (in "Express Yourself") that "it's not what ya look like when ya doin' what ya doin'," much less Martha and the Vandellas (in "Dancing in the Street") when they plead, "It doesn't matter what you wear, just as long as you are there." Of *course* it matters—it's a mating ritual, right?

"The music and fashion worlds have always lived together in a harmonious relationship," Judy B. Hutson writes in her liner notes to the Cover Girls' 1987 Latin girl-group debut album. The album cover tells us Caroline Jackson is the "girl next door," Angel Sabater is "the cool one," and Sunshine Wright "is referred to as the 'Brickhouse' of the group." Frank Kogan has pointed out that "the first Poison album starts with the same drum beat that starts 'That Boy of Mine' by the Cover Girls (their worst song), which is the first drum beat in Martin Scorsese's *Mean Streets*, which is the beat that starts 'Be My Baby,' " thus suggesting that '80s glam-metal and '80s girl-disco were both rooted in the same 1963 Ronettes oldie. But you could make an identical "Be My Baby" drumbeat claim for the Bellamy Brothers' "For All the Wrong Reasons," Yardbirds' "Still I'm Sad," Four Seasons' "Rag Doll," Jesus and Mary Chain's "Just Like Honey," Billy Joel's "Say Goodbye to Hollywood," '70s U.K. punks the Boys' "Brickfield Nights," and Asia's "Heat of the Moment." And in "Take Me Home Tonight" by Eddie Money, Ronnie Spector actually *sings* part of "Be My Baby," so the only *real* conclusion you can draw is that everybody's rooted everywhere!

Still, Judy Hutson is right about that music-and-fashion-in-harmony stuff. "Look at the Rock and Roll Hall of Fame. About thirty percent of them had a guitar," record exec Michael Ayeroff told *Rolling Stone* at the end of the '80s, defending MTV-era pop. "The rest of them were voices, or they moved, or they had a look, or they had a hairstyle. Elvis couldn't play guitar for shit. You know, it was just like a shirt on him." The Byrds complained way back in 1967 that all you needed to become a rock'n'roll star was the right hair and tight pants.

And John Lydon complained in 1980 that people only saw him for his hair color (red) and the clothes he wore (torn), but to suggest that clothes and hair have nothing to do with rock'n'roll is to suggest that rock'n'roll has nothing to do with the real world, where clothes and hair *do* matter. They certainly matter in Detroit, where shootings and muggings of public school students have long adapted to victims' observance of shifting fashion trends, from Max Julian coats in 1982–83 to Fila gym shoes in 1985, from Troop jackets and gold dukie ropes in 1988 to Triple F.A.T. Goosedown coats and top-of-the-line Nikes in 1989. (By 1995, I think everybody was *dead!*)

Keeping up with trends is hard work. "I cut my hair when I learned that it was in," Alice Cooper sings in his doowoppish "Teenage Lament '74," my favorite song by him, about how hard it is to be fifteen years old. "I looked like a rooster." In "Every Picture Tells a Story," Rod Stewart (who usually looks like a rooster on *purpose*) combs his hair a thousand ways but comes out looking the same; in "Life During Wartime," Talking Head David Byrne (who invented new wave's brief "no sideburns" look) changes his hairstyle so many times he can't remember what he looks like. But other hair songs are just concerned with good grooming—Kix's Steve Whiteman getting his part just right so he can go out to a nightclub in "Walking Away," say, or Kenny Rogers setting out to win over Dolly Parton "with a fine-toothed comb" in their chart-topping 1983 "Islands in the Stream."

Other singers are *complacent* about grooming, deferring to other priorities: in "Rumbleseat," John Mellencamp says he'd *like* to own some stylish clothes but they cost too much, and in "Pink Houses" he decides that greasy hair and a greasy smile must be his destination. Which might be what Tiffany decided too, judging from her picture on her 1991 Pro Set Inc. Super Star Music Card (No. 96), where her head's sideways and her greasy red hair's *all over the place.* They only gave her one card, but they gave Debbie Gibson five. And when I reviewed the complete set in *Request* magazine and pointed this out, a girl in Quebec thought I was making light of *Debbie's* hair, so she wrote me a nasty letter about it: "Shit (like your article) looks greasy, real greasy. But Debbie Gibson's hair doesn't. I know 'cause I have hundreds of pictures of her. And I wash myself twice a day *and* wash my hair every day. No schmooze . . . Va Te Faire Foutre, Chuck!

Translation: Fuck You, Chuck!" People tend to take it person-ally when you insult their heroes' hair.

Prototype Debbie Gibsons the Chiffons (in "One Fine Day," 1963) have a crush on "that handsome boy over there, the one with the wavy hair"; prototype Tiffanys the Shangri-Las (in "Give Him a Great Big Kiss," 1965) like wavy hair too, but it's gotta be *thick,* and there's other requirements: shades, high-button shoes, light-feathered pants, dirty finger-nails, "always lookin' like he's got the blues." Fairly apt de-scription of fellow glitter godparent Bob Dylan on the cover of *Highway 61 Revisited* if you ask me, and that came out in 1965 too!

In a 1966 *Playboy* interview, Dylan explained that he grew his hair long so the hair inside his head wouldn't be taking up so much space, thus leaving more room for brains. "Who are they to judge us, simply 'cause our hair is long?," Marvin Gaye queried in 1971, presaging the defiant pro-glam/proto-Rancid sentiments of Cinderella's Tom Keifer, who asks "Who's to care if I grow my hair to the sky?" in 1988's "Gypsy Road." (Same year Rachel Sweet dreamt that *her* hair was "ten feet high" in "Hairspray," theme song from John Waters' movie about early '60s "hairhopper culture.") Ian Hunter grows his 'fro just to scare his teacher in Mott the Hoople's 1972 "One of the Boys" (and in "All the Young Dudes" he praises a boy "who dresses like a queen but he can kick like a mule," but I still think the *Detroit News* should use "All the Young Dudes Carry the News" as a slogan to re-cruit new delivery boys. Ian used to be a newspaperman, and in Mott concerts he covered "American Pie," which discusses paper routes. So he'd appreciate the joke.)

Having long hair could get you picked on, or worse—"Hair-waves" by Mars, on the 1978 *No New York* no-wave compila-tion, humorously approximates the sound of a half-electro-cuted hippie's hair frying to a crisp as he stumbles around in the dark trying to find help. Sonny Bono gets hassled for his hair in "Laugh At Me" (1965—a direct forerunner of Smiths-type sorry-for-yourself rock). The sign in the Five-Man Electrical Band's 1971 (and Tesla's 1991) "Signs" bans long-haired freaky people from applying for jobs. Merle Haggard bragged in 1970 that Muskogee Okies "don't let their hair grow long and shaggy like those hippies out in San Francisco do" (and they prefer manly leather boots to Roman sandals). And Jerry Reed made fun of "boys who look like Cher" then demanded more beehives and belly-rubbing music in "I'm Just a Redneck (in a Rock and Roll Bar)."

Which made Charlie Daniels and especially David Allen Coe rebels with more than one cause: in chubby Charlie's 1974 "Longhaired Country Boy," which actually works more as proto-Axl leave-this-lazy-libertarian-alone rock, Charlie's hair is a badge, though not so much a source of conflict as his reefer. But in Coe's 1975 "Longhaired Redneck," the "bikers stare at cowboys who are laughing at the hippies who are prayin' they'll get out of here alive." It's mods against rockers (or Sharks against Jets, as in *West Side Story*) all over again. (Or, as the Clash explained it in "Last Gang in Town" in 1978, punks against rockolas against crops against stiffs against spikes against quiffs against old soul rebels against ska punks against rockabilly rebels against skinheads against zydeco kids. "Do the Dog" by the Specials and "Come Out and Play" by the Offspring were later variations on the same theme.) Hecklers make fun of Mr. Coe's earring in "Longhaired Redneck," but on the cover of 1978's *Human Emotions*, he sports said bauble along with skull tattoos, frizzy Afro, studded bike jacket, Harley Davidson cap, sunglasses, beard stubble, a humongous belt buckle with his name on it, and a gold Star of David pendant. He looks *scary*.

The Cowsills' eclectically composed hit theme from the 1969 shlock musical "Hair" has them letting their tangles, mangles, and spaghetti grow so birds, bees and fleas can nest in there. But Sly Stone knew prejudice was a two-way street; he'd seen "the long hair who doesn't like the short hair for being such a rich one." And sure enough, *Bay Area Music*'s letters pages bristled in early 1991 with epistle upon epistle arguing about proper heavy metal hair-length. A woman named Delilah (!) complained that cleancut guys cause all the violence at metal shows (give or take ones by Slayer), and that you can't judge other metal fans against haircuts of metal fans fighting for freedom in Desert Storm in the Gulf because the military makes *them* cut their hair (so they don't really count, see?). Another woman wrote in that her husband was a long-haired engineer whose dad recently received leukemia treatment from a long-haired doctor. She argues that closet headbangers with professional careers should "show a little backbone–grow it out!" And apparently this wasn't the *only* hair controversy raging out West at the time, judging from a *BAM* beauty shop ad reading as follows: "THE 'WAR ON EXTENSIONS' CONTINUES . . . GROW YOUR OWN LIKE VIXEN: THE BEST REAL HAIR IN 'ROCK AND ROLL.' "

Girl You Know It's True

I used to think that rock was only good inasmuch as it told "The Truth" (you know—like Vixen's 'real hair') but now I'm not even sure what truth I was referring to. Songs that move us or jar us are generally the ones where we convince ourselves the singer's emotion isn't being faked. But it's a trick: "If you wanna know how I really feel," ironically monikered porn-turned-disco-star Andrea True wisecracks in her 1976 top-five "More, More, More," "get the cameras rolling."

The world is a stage. Once we were watching the movie *Goonies* and somebody got their tongue chopped off, and my son Linus (who was five at the time) asked whether the moviemakers used a "fake real tongue" or a "real fake one." He wanted to know if we were supposed to *think* it looked real—I'm not fibbing. In Def Leppard's 1983 "Action! Not Words," Joe Elliott confesses he wants to star in a movie and just needs a video camera to pull it off; he turns into Andrea True, says "let the camera roll" 'cause he wants to get sexy. People behind him chant "top gun!" or "hot blood!" or "hot tub!"; he answers "bump and grind!" He says his co-star is gonna have wine and caviar. But I predict she'll eat collard greens instead, lie about it, then brag about the bunk she's dishing—just like Teena Marie did with fake filet mignon in 1981's "Square Biz."

It's not hard at all to imagine situations where lying-when-you-shoulda-been-truthing is more compelling than telling-it-like-it-is. Music that tries hard to be "honest" inevitably comes out phony: once you've saddled up to that microphone in that studio or on that stage, you're doing something unnatural; you're *performing*. You're not on your back porch in Mississippi serenading your dead dog anymore. And it's immaterial whether I'm convinced you're expressing truth about your own life, because where your music makes things happen isn't in your world, anyway—to understand your music, I don't need to understand *your* world; I need to understand mine.

Vanilla Ice's lies (that he was a ghetto bastard, that he wrote words he didn't, etc.) made him *more* interesting. Back in 1990–91, I got a real kick out of watching him—here was a microphone commando who *didn't* drain his corpus of energy by trying to be a cartoon (maybe because he already *was* one), what a revelation! There was a rubelike Elvis quality to his confidence, or his arrogance. That "Ice Ice Baby" line about "got my ragtop down so my hair can blow" was his best lie ever: glued down the way he had it, Ice's coiffure was at a standstill!

And what about Milli Vanilli? Some complained because said Krauts danced better than they sang, and old people everywhere whined when Rob Pilatus claimed his duo was better than Bob Dylan in *Time* magazine, but as Phil Dellio has pointed out in the fanzine *Throat Culture*, nobody bothered to check and see if Rob was right. Dellio did, and he painstakingly computed that Vanilli are at least *four times* as good, mainly because twice as many Dylan albums are worse than Vanilli's question-beggingly titled *Girl You Know It's True* than are better. (Bob himself has said that, within the Gates of Eden, truth doesn't exist and "what is real and what is not" doesn't matter.) *A&R Report*, a newsletter put out by ex-members of the old Indiana science-grunge combo MX-80 Sound, has predicted that, by the year 2000, the Vanilli controversy will only seem quaint. Once audio-animatronics and virtual reality work their way into homes enabling made-to-order superstars and seeming reincarnation of beloved corpses, nobody will *need* to lipsync anymore.

Lead blowhard Chuck D of Public Enemy once confided to *Spin* that lying is just fine with him. John Leland, the same muckraker who unearthed the Vanilli "scandal," argued that manipulating the truth is the mark of a politician; Chuck answered, "you tell me another way to tell the truth to black people if they don't want to hear the truth straight out." Bottom line is, speaking with a forked (fake real or real fake) tongue is a time-honored rock tradition. That's what the plastic spoons and imitation leather boots in the Who's "Substitute" were about.

"I could never be honest and to you I've always lied," Mouse and the Traps snap in their '60s counterfeit-Dylan hit "Public Execution," an impossible sentiment, since if they're *really* lying they're telling the truth and therefore *not* lying. (But when John Lennon made *his* "Subterranean Homesick Blues" Xerox, he called it "Gimme Some Truth"!) Michael Jackson frets in "Billie Jean" that "lie becomes the truth." And in their 1977 AOR hit "Barracuda," Heart suggest that "if the real thing don't do the trick, you better make up something quick."

Guns N' Roses labeled their second album, the one where Axl Rose complains about "niggers" and "faggots" in his passway, *Lies*; on *Use Your Illusion I*, though, Axl criticizes somebody who's "getting farther from the realness of truth" (almost as redundant as U.K. oi! boys Chron Gen referring to "the real reality" in their 1981 single "Reality"). The best early rap records were all exaggerated yarns bearing false witness about being stronger than Superman, but Run-D.M.C. brag in their rap-metal watershed "Rock Box" that "we always tell the truth and we never slip the lies in," and their protégé L.L. Cool J does "That's a Lie," likening rappers who brag about cars and money to Pinnochio. When Scarsdale college-geek ironists Too Much Joy covered "That's a Lie" in 1988, they misspoke that they taught L.L. the words, and also that they played the harmonica solo all by themselves.

The seminal British sax-punk band X-Ray Spex open their 1978 *Germ-Free Adolescents* with a track called "Art-i-ficial"; on the album cover, the band is pictured as test-tube babies with bright-colored non-matching socks. Another song on the album is entitled "I Am a Poseur." And in "The World Turned Dayglo," they drive polypropylene cars and eat rubber hamburger buns and watch synthetic leaves fall from trees made of rayon.

But sometime in the '80s, probably when it stopped being "new wave" and started being "alternative," post-punk guitar music switched from being proud of its artificiality to being as obsessed with authenticity as any barefoot granola-gobbling hippies ever were. Kurt Cobain grew up as part of a subculture that puts a premium on stupid integrity, and he was eventually embraced by sanctimonious rock critics who put a premium on stupid integrity. Naturally, he didn't want to disappoint them.

Cobain's "I wish I was like you, easily amused" sarcasm in "All Apologies" reminded me of fanzine jerks who used to whine about my writing being nothing more than trivial pursuits, but it also reminded me that alternative rock fans are easily amused by retarded shtick. Refusal to be easily amused is a badge of honor, like refusing to sell out. So is the title of "All Apologies," at least if you hear it wrong: "What else can I be? Oligopolies." But Nirvana sacrificed nothing by working for David Geffen, and it wasn't oligopolies that killed Kurt Cobain. It was integrity. (That and a bullet through his skull.)

Here's how big a jerk I am: after Cobain emerged from his barbituate-and-champagne coma a few weeks before he died, I wrote a couple letters joking that maybe his bandmates should increase the dosage next time. His Intense New-Age Sincerity in Nirvana's acoustic "All Apologies" video convinced me he was getting ready to move in with Sting, and I'd seen him on MTV going on about how great it was that the Beatles could progress from "I Want to Hold Your Hand" to *Sgt. Pepper's* (how great it was that they sunk from rock'n'roll into pompous mush in other words), and Kurt was hoping Nirvana could do something similar. (I heard the news today oh boy about a lucky man who made the grade. He blew his mind out in an attic or somewhere, I forget. The lyric sheet's so hard to find, what are the words oh never mind.) A few years earlier, Mike Saunders of the Angry Samoans had joked to me that if Lou Reed had shot himself after *White Light/White Heat,* there'd now be way fewer lousy Lou Reed albums on the shelves. Who knew any fool would actually *do* it?

And that's how I initially thought of Cobain—as a fool, a shmuck. My own dad was a manic-depressive who hung himself when I was thirteen, four years after my mom died of uterine cancer. So mostly I identified with Cobain's *kid,* Frances Bean. But what I wasn't brave enough to admit at first was how much I also identified with Kurt himself, and not just because I was a young dad in charge of baby bottles at the time and because I'd had my own painful stomach traumas, either. Curt's family had a history of suicide, and so does mine: my dad's manic depression was a chemical imbalance passed through generations to him, and I've always known in the back of my mind that it could someday be inherited by me—I've had a grandfather and a sibling try to kill themselves as well, and I spend way too much of my own free time fretting myself into ulcerous states over stuff I have no control over. If that side of me doesn't often show up in my writing, it's mainly because on days when I'm nervous and gloomy, I *avoid* writing, because writing (playing "Chuck Eddy" as opposed to just "Charlie," who the people who know my true personality know me as) only makes me *more* downcast.

So those are the tears of a clown when there's no one around. In twelfth grade, 1977, I tried to end it all by swallowing Lysol. I chickened out and told my stepparents about it, got yelled at for my trouble, and haven't looked back since. I can't imagine anything similar happening in the foreseeable future, but I also realize I've still got plenty of muck clogging up my psyche that I someday need to dredge out; when it comes to dealing with insurmountable problems, my dad wasn't exactly the best role model. I'm not stupid enough to deny the effect of what was doubtlessly one of the defining events of my life.

The first time I heard of Leonard Cohen was when I noticed a poetry book by him on my father's shelf a few days after the funeral. Maybe part of my aversion to Nirvana, and maybe even to dark depressing sounds in general (and their glib chicness in "alternative" circles) is owed in part to me shielding myself from emotions I'd rather not think about. Sometimes, listening to Nirvana basically *creeps me out*. They hit too close to home. Like Cobain's widow Courtney Love warbled with weird circular logic in "Doll Parts," "I think it so true I am beyond fake." And I admit it's not just Kurt's biography that gives his music that quality: there's something eternally sad in his *voice*.

But that only means he's sincere and he means it and he's not acting, even when he's just reciting his usual meaningless gobbledygook—it doesn't make me want to *hear* him, and it doesn't convince me that his depression is in any way especially entertaining. On the other hand, I love "Smells Like Teen Spirit" and "Sliver," and a handful of Nirvana's other tracks move me, too—Kurt Cobain was obviously blessed with a talent for pretty melodies and gnarly guitar parts if not comprehensible lyrics, so it's not like I avoid his outfit's output on *principle*.

And despite everything I've just confessed, I still don't think my problems with the poor guy are all in my head. Nirvana popularized the hokey "here comes the part of the song where we have a tantrum" school of '90s rock that's played a major role in hiding Courtney's powerful voice ever since, and they were pioneers of the ubiquitious "you can tell this song is serious because we're playing it really slow" school as well. Sometimes they sound merely bland, and even when they creep me out, they tend to creep me out in a boring way, like a funeral parlor. And I've been bored in more funeral parlors than you'll ever know.

Technometal

People have been worrying that technology might render music inauthentic and cold ever since Thomas Edison invented the phonograph in 1878, or maybe since John Shore invented the tuning fork in 1709. The highly accelerated pace of change since 1980 or so has ensured that more people would complain and resist than ever. "The rise of computer technology makes it easy to romanticize rock's past, as if a sound that emanates from Synclavier or a Yamaha DX7 inherently has less integrity than one from a Fender Strat," Don McLeese wrote in *Rolling Stone* at the end of the '80s. So hair-metalers Tesla proclaim "NO MACHINES" (probably meaning "no synthesizers") on their album covers, and get rid of plugged-in guitars entirely on one record, yet their first album is called *Mechanical Resonance*, and their second is *The Great Radio Controversy*. They're even named after Nikola Tesla, the guy who patented the alternating-current motor!

Rock'n'roll and heavy metal were byproducts of technological change in the first place—of the industrial revolution, and the increasing availability and affordability of machines you could make noise with: electric guitars, amplifiers, wah-wah pedals, fuzzboxes, Mellotrons, vocoders, quadrophonic sound. And metal, especially, has always been very proud of this distinction. It wanted to sound anything *but* human.

"Watch out honey, 'cause I'm using technology," Iggy Pop warns in the Stooges' "Search and Destroy." AC/DC praise high voltage and fall in love with a fast machine who keeps her motor clean; Axl Rose calls himself "a mean machine drinking gasoline." Black Sabbath scream about electric funerals, the MC5 about human-being lawnmowers, the Who about pinball wizards who "become part of the machine." Vom want to electrocute your cock; Sonic Youth want you to hot-wire their heart. The Maryland band Kix (who insist they're mechanically inept when it comes to *really* fixing cars) ask you to overjuice their circuits in an electric chair: "Give me an offer that I can't refuse—blow my fuse."

For fifteen years, Kix were the greatest rock'n'roll band in the world.

Tough chicks:
Shangri-Las '66,
Flirts '85,
Girlschool '81,
Vixen '88.

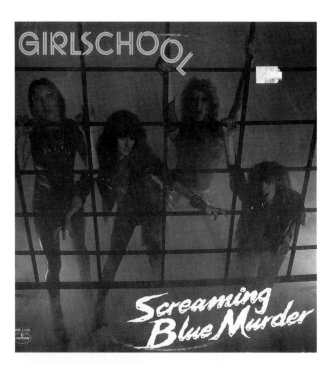

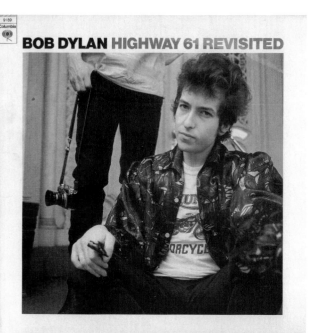

Tough guys:
Bob '65,
Neil '66,
Slade '72,
David Allan Coe '7[

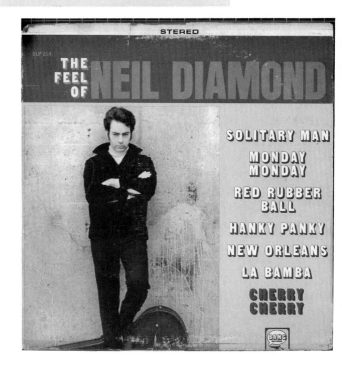

Offspring: the fellow in sunglasses has a Ph.D. in molecular biology.

Einstürzende Neubauten mourn the loss of their pet jackhammer.

Automotive Rock from Germany; Washing Machine Rock from Surinam (via Holland). I wonder if Trafassi are wearing pants.

I can never remember how to spell Afrika Bambaataa's name.

Accidental
evolution of
the jetboy
look: 1973,
1979, 1983,
1988.

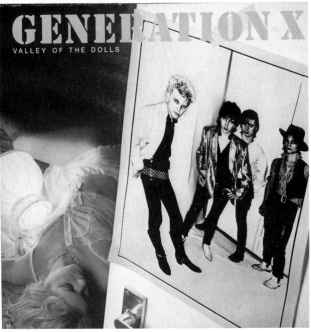

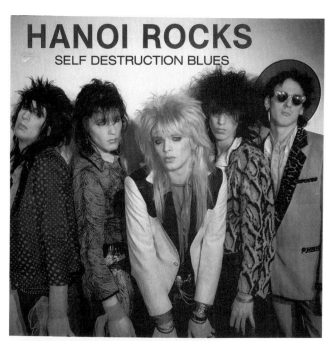

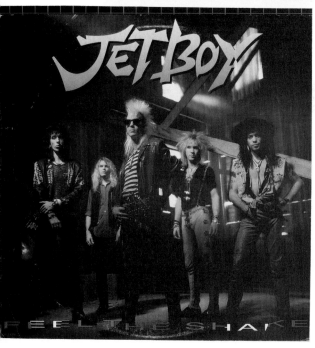

Doob-reggae poets explore the latest treatments for glaucoma.

"My Name is Tim; I'm a lesser-known character."—Rancid, 1994.

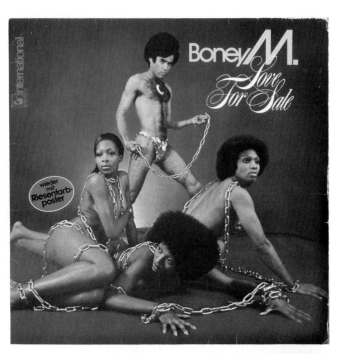

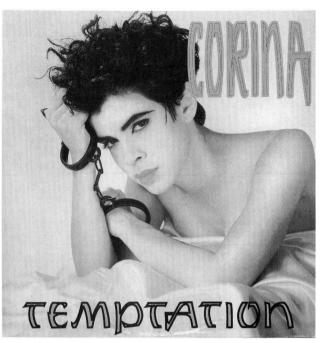

"The shackles I am wearing on the cover of this record do not in anyway represent bondage (not in the way some of us might think anyway)."–Corina, liner notes to her 1991 "Temptation" single.

Friday night and the Strip is hot: Wildside (top) and Bang Tango.

Motörhead named an album after Jane Fonda's 1968 *Barbarella* Orgasmatron (putting it in the Barbarella rock category with Archaeopteryx's "Barbarella," Boney M's "Barbarella Fortune Teller," Kraut-disco weirdo Sven Väth's 16 Bit/Off spinoff act Barbarella, and Duran Duran, who named themselves after the movie's villain), so it should come as no surprise that most vibrator rock is on metal's cusp. The Beach Boys picked up excitations from good vibrations emitted by the antennas of a rare psychedelic noise instrument called a Theremin, and Stacey Q's loudest guitars are in "Hard Machine," about giving up a boyfriend for a device that'll "rock you 'til you drop . . .'cause it don't ever stop." Which harks back to the notes to Suzi Quatro (another S.Q.!)'s 1974 debut LP: "Imagine yourself strapped to one of those vibrating exercise machines that makes you shake uncontrollably like a bowl of Jello, flesh aquiver. Now, imagine that a demon inside the machine has accelerated the belt, and you can't slow it down, let alone stop it." Michaelo Williams's *Velvet Underground & Nico* notes had earlier described the Velvets as "an assemblage that actually vibrates with menace, cynicism, and perversion." So it makes perfect sense that in 1977 the Velvets' "Here She Comes Now" was namedropped in "Sweet Sweet Heart" by British proto-Green-Day punk-poseurs the Vibrators.

Jefferson Airplane's 1967 "Plastic Fantastic Lover" used its garage-band snarls and wah-wah guitars as a frame within which Grace Slick introduced techno-obsession to hard rock, glorifying data control, neon, IBM, and trapezoid thermometers. Years later, Laurie Anderson had a corny bit where the teenage girl she sat down next to on an airplane only talked about boys in terms of switching, networking, digital modes, and circuitry.

Canada's Voivod turn the radars and switches of what they call "killing technology" into celibate wow-man sci-fi about computers taking control and kids traded for robots. As part of a much larger techno-entertainment boom encompassing everything from the spreading outreach of cable networks to rumors of bionics and artificial reality, the Microsoft onslaught was impossible to keep up with, and ominous in a way. That's what all those *Terminator* and *Robocop* movies were about. "Ban Lo Performance Drivers, Not Hi Performance Cars," a popular '80s bumper sticker in bombed-out *Robocop* homebase Detroit read. If you weren't up with the newest gadgetry, you were *obsolete*.

On the other hand, back when I was in the Army, lots of people used to insist that standard transmission is obviously better than automatic because it gives you more "control" of your car. But I've never learned to drive a standard and never will, because my automatic gives me all the control I'll ever need. As Richard Meltzer likewise pointed out about attempted reversion to extinct musical roots in *The Aesthetics of Rock* in the late '60s, "a renaissance may be a euphemism for kicking a dead horse." The embrace of long-gone musical traditions is just a last-gasp grasp for standard-transmission standards that make no sense whatsoever in an automatic-transmission world.

ObLiGaToRy NOISE!! InTeRlUdE

Okay, here's the rationalization: what with all these crazy machines and all, noise is simply part of "our" environment, so it's no wonder "our" music mimics it. It's the *usual* scheme of things, harmony's just an escape, yeah yeah yeah. Rock noise serves as a metaphor for urban living (police sirens, gunshots, streetdrills, subway trains, sewer hiss, gnawing rats, skidding tires, wailing victims' moms), World War III, snuff fantasies, insanity, carnage, carrion, helter skelter, the whole screaming industrial breakdown. It makes life more "bearable," they say.

How you know noise when you hear it: sounds that don't belong together collide with each other, you can't hum along, there's "disorder." It's a frightening senselessly violent edgy paranoiac booming mutated disruptive manic experimental confrontational horrible harrowing sadistic random big-ass viciously sculpted hard harsh headspin of hate, that sort of thing—distorted feedback, tape-deck and computer-sampler collage juxtaposition (samplers are said to be the first instrument whose "basic principle" is noise, but hey, what about bagpipes?), unusual keys and timbres and pitches (you know, like Luis Tiant's hesitation windup), vocal howls, wrong notes, sound effects, atonality, guitars imitating machines, impromptu improvisation, rakes and plungers, drones. *Lots* of drones.

Disorder's a real easy thing to plan. "How do you plan an accident? That's what we're all about," Sonic Youth nitwit Thurston Moore admits. Elvis Presley ("Milkcow Blues Boogie"), Stan Freberg ("I've Got You Under My Skin"), Bob Dylan ("Bob Dylan's 115th Dream"), the Clash ("Wrong 'Em Boyo"), and George Strait ("The Chair": "can I drink you a buy?") have put "mistakes" in their songs then corrected themselves but left the original mistakes in, at which time they weren't mistakes anymore. Joe Elliott has credited strange spans of Def Leppard's *Hysteria* to any number of factors—"studio wanking off, putting stuff through an echo machine or slowing it down like 200 times"—but adds that "some of it was just mistakes we decided to leave in." (That's one of the main principles of dub reggae, too. Tapper Zukie's "Simpleton Badness" has synthesizer errors that disrupt the proceedings like free-jazz sax or no-wave guitar, or maybe they're the uncle of hip-hop record-scratching, which they resemble only I'm pretty sure they're scratchier.)

Anyway, noise might be defined as any sound that jars you, that happens when you don't expect it. But one problem with "noise-rock" (Sonic Youth, Ministry, Test Dept., Tricky, Public Enemy, Slayer) is that you *do* expect it, so the noise doesn't generally work very well, though a few of those groups have been known to stumble onto moments that aren't completely wretched. (They'd stumble onto more if they had better singers.) Public Enemy's second-best song (after "Sophisticated Bitch," which is real sexist with loud guitars) is called "Bring the Noise"; Chuck D says they use noise "to agitate, make the jam noticeable"—so when a car passes by, you'll know it's pumping P.E. right away. So noise "serves as a uniform," Chuck has told *Spin* magazine. "We wear it sometimes, and sometimes we don't."

But noise works best when it's *not* a uniform, when it's just a byproduct of whatever else is happening in the music. In rock'n'roll, this happened most often back before "noise-rock" made noise an end in itself. You can go back to blues vocal mumbling, to early holes-in-the-speakers/aluminum-foil-in-the-amps feedback accidents by Link Wray and Ike Turner, to the drums in Louis Prima's jump-jazz "Sing Sing Sing" (a humongous precursor of John Bonham's big boom in Led Zeppelin). By 1959–61, feedback solos were working their way into pop hits like the Regents' "Barbara Ann" (noisy sax too), the Del-Vetts' "Last Time Around," and Dave "Baby" Cortez's "Happy Organ."

Prisoners broke rocks with hammers in Sam Cooke's 1960 "Chain Gang," and chisels clinked and clanked and chipped away at fossil-fuel deposits in Lee Dorsey's 1960 "Working in the Coalmine" (though such proto-industrial clank percussion actually dates back to Dann Quinn's stormy 1902 Irish-American gangboss tavern tune, "Drill Ye Terriers Drill," which also featured dynamite explosions!). Phil Spector's *A Christmas Gift for You* compilation used all sorts of clatter, especially in the Ronettes tracks; Frankie Ford's knife-in-the-back boogie "Sea Cruise" had boat-docking tintinnabulation and foghorns; the Electric Prunes' "Get Me to the World on Time" had horrendous vocal hum and bent fuzztones all through. In 1965, the Who's record company supposedly returned their "My Generation" recording to them, assuming Pete Townshend's guitar-smashup feedback was just an oversight on the band's part. But by the time the Byrds' "2-4-2 Foxtrot (the Lear Jet Song)" and the Beatles' "Tomorrow Never Knows" made psychedelic drug music inevitable in 1966 or so, cacophony was well on its way to becoming an accepted rock "norm" in and of itself—especially in heavy metal, where barely anything was ever taken for granted *except* loud noise.

Which invariably rhymed with "*boys*"—this is extremely important. Thus did Slade rhyme "Cum on Feel the Noize" with "girls rock your boys." And thus did Mott the Hoople claim in "One of the Boys" that they don't say much but they make a big noise. And thus did Def Leppard, in "It Don't Matter" on their debut album, call themselves "boys with heads full of noise." (Their noisiest moment may well be the endnotes to "Billy's Got a Gun" on *Pyromania*—sounds like supply carts being wheeled across an officeroom floor by robots with peg legs, then goes into some time signatures played backwards, all after somebody shouts "bang! bang!" And said sequence of post-"bang!" events repeats itself twenty or thirty times before the stylus gets rejected.)

Some people say noise bands aren't really musicians. Other people say they're self-indulgent elitists too hip for their own good, inaccessible hypocrites who care about social decay but not social rebirth, self-conscious windbags who pretend horror-movie clichés mean something, put-on artists who can't rock or swing. Sometimes people who say these things are full of shit, but usually I agree with them more than the ones who think noise forces you to "deal with" something, that it's an antidote to sentimentalism and studio gloss and mystification and mindless apathetic consumerism and audiophile fastidiousness and all sorts of other "constraints" (as if noise rock isn't just as constrained), and that that's a real big deal because rock thrives on controversy or risks being "mere entertainment."

This idea that noise is good for you, it's hardly new. In *Let Us Now Praise Famous Men* in 1939, James Agee recommends that you procure a copy of Beethoven's Seventh Symphony or Schubert's C-Major Symphony, crank the volume all the way up to ten, press your ear against the speaker, and try not to breathe: "If it hurts you, be glad of it. Is what you hear pretty? Or beautiful? Or legal? Or acceptable in polite or any other society?" Quick, somebody give this guy an *Artforum* column!

Well, personally, I think Schubert sucks. And I'd say the best noise bands are ones who know how to be *musical*—ones who can combine dissonance with harmony and a beat, who have a sense of humor, who use hooks so their noise isn't completely formless and so it'll stick in your head. (This is what Naughty By Nature meant by "harm me with harmony" in their 1991 rap hit "O.P.P.") Very few people are capable of such a trick, and if they are, noise is probably their least relevant trait anyway.

Supposedly noise-rock bands in the '80s wanted to combine "conscious" art-music noise with "unselfconscious" rock'n'roll noise, but rap and dance people in the first part of the decade had better ideas: scratching styluses across old vinyl (as in 1981's "The Adventures of Grandmaster Flash on the Wheels of Steel"), or demonstrating bad manners with their vocal chords and larynxes (as in the Fat Boys' 1984 "Human Beat Box"). Or simulating the sound of mirrorballs smashing (as in C-Bank's 1985 "One More Shot"), or just sticking a big cosmic imploding grrrrrrrr in there (as in Dimples D.'s 1983 "Sucker D.J.'s").

In avant-rock circles, attempts at noise disruption were so old-hat they no longer disrupted: to quote Tom Carson, writing about "post-whatever" rock in the *Village Voice* in 1988, "the very ideas of offensiveness, disturbance, and challenge have grown corny." Eventually the same thing happened in dance music. R&B had relied on applied science, more on rhythm and less on blues, ever since soul became disco in the early '70s (if not since T-Bone Walker plugged in his six-string in the '30s), but starting around 1987 a barrage began to emerge from Chicago that completely tried to obliterate song and sense with machines.

Phuture's "We Are the Phuture"/"Slam!"/"Spank-Spank" EP was background music that refused to stay in the background, arrogant laser-zooms thickening into a dark, viscous gel as skeletal kickdrums pushed through wormholes grinding conflicting gears against each other. Somebody named it acid house, in honor of Phuture's "Acid Tracks." Soon it turned into "techno." And within a couple years, before the '80s even ended for Chrissakes, techno settled on just sitting there and looking like that line in Clint Eastwood's *Heartbreak Ridge*—"ugly as a piece of modern art." When noise becomes a genre, it's on its deathbed.

Fucking Sound Effect Records

I occasionally write for a fanzine called *Why Music Sucks* that my friend (and yours by now) Frank Kogan puts out. Every issue, Frank sends a few people a blindfold test tape with 25 or 30 songs on it, and he doesn't tell them the songs' titles or who's performing, but he asks them to rate and write about the tunes anyhow. On the tape he sent me in July 1995, I decided that every track was at least tolerable except one, which I more or less hated. I had no idea who it was by, but it was so awful that I had no doubt that Frank intentionally put it on the tape for that very reason, just to see how everybody would react to such lousy dogshit. I actually didn't mind its first minute or so (vaguely reminded me of "Sentimental Journey" by Pere Ubu), but then I started writing stuff like this: "I don't like the way the guy's whispering; sounds 'ominous' not because he's a scary person (what I bet he wants me to think) but because it's a highly disturbing omen that the song's about to suck. And sure enough, he's loading up his gun (you can hear him fiddling with its chamber) and he's gonna shoot himself. What is this, a fucking *sound effect* record?" The song just kept going on and on, forever, and it just kept getting worse.

I decided Frank must've borrowed it from his roommate Elizabeth's pile of old Swans albums. So I kept writing: " 'Label me insane,' oh is that right, lady? Oh god, fuck this shit." Anyway, a couple months later over the phone, Frank explained to me it was by Brit "trip-hop" artiste Tricky, which made my day since Tricky's *Maxinquaye* CD was clearly well on its way to finishing second behind P.J. Harvey in all the 1995 rock critics' emperor's-new-clothes polls. It's still the only Tricky track I've heard, and I don't intend to find out how typical it is.

Believe it or not, not too long ago, sound effects used to be *fun*. In bilingual circles they were called "*audio verité*" or "*musique concrète*" and frequently credited as the invention of Eric Satie (turn-of-the-century piano satirist) or Spike Jones ('40s/'50s classical parodist) or a whole bunch of mid-century Frenchmen named Pierre (Boulez, Schaeffer, Henry) or Lee

Perry (dub-reggae instigator who shot pistols, smashed glass, made infants weep, and broadcast BBC news on his records starting in '60s) or the Beatles (for whatever it was they did on *Revolver* and *Sgt. Pepper's*). Or the 1963 *Stereo Spectacular Demonstration and Sound Effects* hi-fi LP, maybe. (Movies have 'em too, I'm told. I have kids, so it's hard for me to find time to see any.)

Herewith theretofore you may observe a catalogue of a few which have occurred throughout history (sometimes real, sometimes staged, usually I have no idea), alphabetically ordered:

ARROWS: Sam Cooke "Cupid."

BABIES CRYING: Obed Ngobeni "Miyela U Ngarli (Don't Cry)" (all through it. The translation says otherwise, but to me this is a South African Shanagaan Jive—whatever that is—*lullaby*, with Obed rocking little Obed Jr. to sleep); Regina "Baby Love."

BEER BOTTLES: Replacements "Treatment Bound."

BOMBS DETONATING: Big Black (they use Army field-training exercise mortars on *Atomizer* somewhere); Jimmy Castor Bunch "Hallucinations"; Guns N' Roses "Civil War"; Love "7 and 7 Is" (atom bomb test-blast in Nevada desert).

BOWLING BALLS ROLLING DOWN BOWLING LANES AND SCORING A STRIKE: Devotions "Rip Van Winkle"; Prism "N-N-N-No!"

BURPS: Iggy and the Stooges "Raw Power"; Soul Survivors (somewhere on their 1967 album once owned by my brother Louie).

CAMERA CLICKING: Duran Duran "Girls on Film."

CANTINA GLASSES BEING CLANKED THEN TEQUILA SHOTS BEING GULPED: Grupo Exterminador "Las Novias Del Traficante" (Mexican cowhands from the Rio Grande whose name kills bugs deader than Black Flag and who wear clothes seemingly designed from window curtains and whose 1996 border-polkas-vamped-into-Caribbean-funk-novelties disc *Dedicado A Mis Novias* also audibly features guns executing banditos, cocks fighting, and caballeros plotting mayhem while riding horses—you can even hear the hooves!).

CAR IGNITION: Kraftwerk "Autobahn"; Vanessa Paradis "Joe Le Taxi"; Pearl Harbor and the Explosions "Drivin' "; Roxy Music "Love is the Drug"; Sham 69 "Angels with Dirty Faces" (from a *stolen* car, apparently, seeing how a barely teenaged Irish lad named Angel Lopez was found driving my missing '83 Chevy Capris in 1990, and then five years later a young policeman also named Angel Lopez tried to pick up my friend Jennifer at a Automatic-Teller machine. He said he was her guardian angel!).

CASH REGISTERS: Pink Floyd "Money."

CLOCKS TICKING: Indochine "La machine a rattraper le temps"; Paper Lace "The Night Chicago Died" ("a time bomb for an entire generation," sez Phil Dellio); Will To Power "Clock on the Wall."

COWS MOOING: The Ramrods "(Ghost) Riders in the Sky" (a 1961 instrumental which also contains eerie proto-Spaghetti-Western "oooowooooheeeooo"s and "giddyaps"). Both Weird Al Yankovic's "Smells Like Nirvana" and the Beatles' "Good Morning, Good Morning" feature *various* animals of the farmist persuasion.

CROWDS OF FAKE PEOPLE CHEERING ON A NON-LIVE RECORD: Boston "Rock and Roll Band"; the Byrds "So You Want to Be A Rock 'N' Roll Star"; Captain and Tenille "Love Will Keep Us Together"; Chic "Chic Cheer" and Def Leppard "Stagefright" (but not Chic "Stagefright"); Guns N' Roses "Get in the Ring"; Michael Jackson "Dirty Diana"; Elton John "Benny and the Jets"; Jordy "Jordy Rave Show"; Mel and Tim "Backfield in Motion"; Pulp "Sorted For E's & Wizz."

CRICKETS CHIRPING: Mbuti Pygmies of the Ituri Rainforest "In the Rainforest Approaching a Forest Camp" (a.k.a. "Birds and Crickets: Bark-Cloth Hammering with the Voices of Young Boys in the Background," whew! Field-recorded in the '50s, echoes like dub reggae two decades early); Tyree Cooper "I Fear the Night" (a paranoid house music whisper also featuring the low drone of those incinerator things behind the back doors of restaurants, and ringing phones killing the silence); Warrant "In the Sticks."

DOGS BARKING: Beatles "Being for the Benefit of Mr. Kite"; Elton John "Social Disease"; Los Prisioneros (the Cars/Clash of Chile!) "El Baile de los Que Sobran"; Pet Shop Boys "Suburbia."

DOORS SLAMMING: Lovin' Spoonful "Summer in the City"; Temptations "Psychedelic Shack"; Joe Walsh "Life's Been Good." (Audible *absence* of doorslam: Bruce Springsteen "Thunder Road.")

DUCKS QUACKING: Rick Dees and his Cast of Idiots "Disco Duck"; La Neuva Fattoria "Disco Pollo"; Strawberry Alarm Clock "The Birdman of Alkatrash" (B-side of "Incense and Peppermints").

EIGHTBALL IN THE SIDE POCKET: Lordz of Brooklyn "Brooklyn Pride."

ELECTROCARDIOGRAMS OR WHATEVER THOSE HOSPITAL MACHINES ARE CALLED: Guns N' Roses "Coma" (also has emergency-room crosstalk, as in Velvet Underground's "Lady Godiva's Operation" and some song on *Flat Out* by Buck Dharma of Blue Öyster Cult).

FARTS: Somewhere on Girlschool's *Nightmare at Maple Cross*.

GARBAGE DUMPSTER: Bryan Adams "Ain't Gonna Cry."

GLASS SHATTERING: C-Bank "One More Shot" (actually works as *percussion*, ditto in Trinere's "How Can We Be Wrong" and Jenny Burton's "Remember What You Like"); Joy Division "I Remember Nothing" (their tribute to Sgt. Schultz of *Hogan's Heroes*, I think); Sheila E. "The Glamorous Life"; Stan Freberg "The Banana Boat Song (Day-O)" (Harry-Belafonte-like calypso singer breaks window so he can get back into the recording studio to record the loud vocal parts, after recording the quiet vocal parts from a room down the hall); Grandmaster Flash and the Furious Five "The Message" (after "broken glass, everywhere . . ."); Michael Jackson (all over *Dangerous*, and in the original unabridged version of his "Black or White" video, where he smashes windshields with a tire iron, throws a garbage can through a window Spike-Lee-style, and lets Macaulay Culkin turn up his amps and blow out the windows of his parents' house); Pere Ubu "Sentimental Journey"; Pet Shop Boys "West End Girls"; UK

Subs "Stranglehold"; Velvet Underground "European Son" (sort of a joke, since it follows the noisiest little guitar explosion rock fans had heard up to 1967); Kim Wilde "Water on Glass." But not in "(I Love the Sound of) Breaking Glass" by Nick Lowe!

GOOSESTEPPING NAZI FEET: Angry Samoans "They Saved Hitler's Cock"; Mel Brooks "The Hitler Rap"; Mekanïk Destrüctïw̄ Komandöh "Berlin"; KMFDM "Liebeslied"; Sex Pistols "Holidays in the Sun."

HORROR MOVIE/HAUNTED HOUSE MISCELLANEA: Michael Jackson "Thriller"; Jacksons "Heartbreak Hotel"; Mars "Puerto Rican Ghost"; Pere Ubu "Dub Housing"; Pere Ubu "Thriller!" (hmmm . . .).

HOUSEFLIES: Kix (at tail end of their *Hot Wire* album).

ICE CREAM IN A CUP WITH A WOODEN SPOON: Listed (along with "two Pioneer stereos") in the credits to A'Me Lorain and the Family Affair's *Starring In . . . Standing in a Monkey Sea* album.

JACKHAMMERS: Einstürzende Neubauten "Kangolicht" (but they "stopped using the jackhammer when it was stolen by Copenhagen squatters in 1988 who finally restored it to its original use," though Kraut-shlock aficionados claim Neubauten themselves stole the idea from Neu!'s early-'70s debut album in the first place); Lovin' Spoonful "Summer in the City"; Slaughter "Up All Night."

KIDS RUNNING DOWN STAIRS, PUTTING TACKS ON TEACHER'S CHAIR, TYING KNOTS IN SUSIE'S HAIR: Britny Fox "Girlschool"; Pink Floyd "Another Brick in the Wall"; Van Halen "Hot For Teacher."

LIONS ROARING: Jethro Tull "Bungle in the Jungle"; Edgar Varèse "Hyperprism" (from 1924—he simulated the sound by using "a tub with a hole in the bottom through which a player pulls a rope." And in "Ionisation" in 1931 he used two sirens, sleigh bells, and a dessicated Cuban gourd. What a showoff.)

MOTORCYCLES REVVING UP AND/OR CRASHING: Billy Joel "Movin' Out (Anthony's Song)"; Meat Loaf "Bat out of Hell"; Mötley Crüe "Girls Girls Girls"; Shangri-Las "Leader of the Pack."

PIGS OINKING: Lots of reggae-toasting records. (Frogs too.)

POLICE BULLHORNS: Michael Jackson "Smooth Criminal"; R. Dean Taylor "Indiana Wants Me" (the cop is shouting "Give yourself up!" Cars would pull over when the song came on the radio because drivers thought it was real, and directed at them!)

RAZORBLADES ON A MIRROR: Einstürzende Neubauten "Yü Gung" (elsewhere, these Teutonic goofs enjoy employing devices such as "airducts arranged like dominoes" and "water dripping off hot stoves." And as Dieter of *Sprockets* used to say on TV, their bamboo whips never fail to pull down my pants and taunt me!).

SEAGULLS: Beach Boys *Pet Sounds*; Enigma (Side Two of their *MCMXC A.D.* album—the too-damn-quotable Frank Kogan says it'd be better if they'd gotten seagulls to imitate guitars instead of the other way around); Don Henley "Boys of Summer"; Jeanne Mas "Le contrechamp"; Pere Ubu "Sentimental Journey"; Otis Redding "Sitting on the Dock of the Bay"; Shangri-Las "Remember (Walking in the Sand)"; Temptations "I Wish it Would Rain."

SHOTGUNS: AC/DC "For Those About to Rock (We Salute You)" (21-gun salute); Dr. Alimantado "I Killed the Barber"; Bob Dylan "Like a Rolling Stone" (really a drum); Georgie Fame "The Ballad of Bonnie and Clyde"; Kool Moe Dee "Wild Wild West"; Mott the Hoople "Crash Street Kids" (more like machine guns); New York Dolls "It's Too Late" (produced by Shadow Morton of Shangri-Las fame); N.W.A. "Gangsta Gangsta" (and so many ghetto-mofo driveby-raps after this one that sampler-era hip-hop holds the dubious distinction of being the first music to make sound effects *boring*—I left the zillion raps I don't give a shit about off this list); Ohio Players "Love Rollercoaster" (an actual homicide, according to legend!); Yoko Ono "No No No" (four shots and a scream, after her husband died); Prince "Gotta Broken Heart Again" (suicide—after he says "there ain't nothin' left to say"); Prince Buster "Texas Holdup"; Junior Walker "Shotgun."

SNORES: Devotions "Rip Van Winkle" again.

STUFF BEING SET ON FIRE: Def Leppard "Rock of Ages" (on *Pyromania*, get it?); Einstürzende Neubauten "abfackeln!"

TELEPHONES RINGING: Beastie Boys "Cookie Puss"; Blondie "Hanging on the Telephone"; Cheap Trick "She's Tight"; Yoko Ono "Telephone Piece"; Sugarloaf "Don't Call Us, We'll Call You" (best song ever about sending demo tapes to record labels).

THREE KNOCKS ON THE CEILING, TWICE ON THE PIPES: Tony Orlando and Dawn "Knock Three Times."

THUNDER AND RAIN: Garth Brooks "The Thunder Rolls"; the Doors "Riders on the Storm"; Guns N' Roses "November Rain"; Oran "Juice" Jones "The Rain"; Shonen Knife "Devil House"; Wings "Uncle Albert/Admiral Halsey." (And several "quiet storm" soul-to-make-out-to records *literally* feature quiet storms.)

TIDE: Otis Redding "Sitting on the Dock of the Bay."

TOILETS FLUSHING: Cerrone "Rocket in the Pocket"; Joe Cuba Sextet "Si Me Paro"; the Fiends (I forget); Indeep "Last Night a D.J. Saved My Life"; Lord Tracy (I forget); Yoko Ono "Toilet Piece"; Run-D.M.C. "Wake Up" (peeing *and* flushing!); TLC "Sexy-Interlude" (oops—that's *also* got a telephone).

TRAFFIC-JAM HORNS, CAR-SKIDS, POLICE "SYE-REENS", etc.: Junior Brown "Highway Patrol"; Cactus Brothers "Highway Patrol"; the Clash "White Riot"; D.J. Jazzy Jeff and the Fresh Prince "Parents Just Don't Understand"; Michael Jackson "Speed Demon"; L.L. Cool J. "I'm Bad"; Lovin' Spoonful "Summer in the City"; L'Trimm "Cars With the Boom"; Slaughter "Up All Night"; Soul Survivors "Expressway to your Heart"; 13th Floor Elevators "Fire Engine"; Vixen "Hard 16"; Wildside "Hang on Lucy." (And if your stereo's on and you hear a police siren or fire engine out your window, sometimes you gotta turn the volume down to see if the sound was indeed in the song; conversely, sometimes phone-ring sound effects trick you into answering your *real* phone. Some music may well be made with such environmental factors in mind!)

TYPEWRITERS: Madonna "Words."

WAR MOVIE NOISES: Def Leppard "Die Hard the Hunter"; Jefferson Airplane "Lather" (tanks and overheard soldiers); Metallica "One" (*M*A*S*H* copters); Public Image Ltd. "Careering."

WEATHER REPORTS: Pere Ubu "(Pa) Ubu Dance Party."

WIND: David Allen Coe (too often); Kix "Atomic Bombs" (were "7 and 7 Is"-type bombs too expensive?); Specials "Ghosttown."

WINDSHIELD WIPERS: Temptations "I Wish It Would Rain" (sounds like they're *stuck*, good thing it's not raining yet). Also, I can't recall if you can actually *hear* windshield wipers in Eddie Rabbit's 1980 number-one single "I Love a Rainy Night" (and I'm not about to check), but I *do* remember he does a snazzy little rap *about* windshield wipers, and it sounds exactly like Bob Dylan doing "Subterranean Homesick Blues," more or less.

WOLVES HOWLING: Deep Purple "Hush."

ZIPPERS UNZIPPING: Mitsou "Dismoi, Dismoi (Last Tango Mix.)" And until you rip it, of course, the album cover to the Rolling Stones' *Sticky Fingers*. (Music packaging you can *listen* to!)

Onomatopoeia Rock

A more subtle form of sound effects can be found in the tax-onomical phylum known as onomatopoeia rock (and what a lot of vowels are in *that* word, no?); that is, all music which works by means of imitating the natural sound of the items or actions addressed in a song's lyrics. Frequently this can be accomplished via the use of clever auditory punning. For example, in Kriss Kross's irrepressible 1992 chart-topping tyke-rap "Jump," the pre-puberty voices jump to a higher pitch whenever they say the title, and especially when they squeak "how high? *real* high!"

Which is exactly the opposite of how Garth Brooks's voice goes real low whenever he says "I got friends in low places," or how Warren Zevon's does the same when he says "I think I'm sinking down" in his 1977 "Carmelita." Likewise in '77, the Waitresses' "Slide" was about a dance-step but had slide guitar.

The Ruts' 1980 "In a Rut," released right around the time punk was getting into *its* rut, has a part where they repeat the title line then "gotta get out of it out of it out of it" enough times to simulate the sound of said rut itself. (But note Ram Jam, "Keep Your Hands on the Wheel," 1977: "There's such a fine line between a rut and a groove.") In Will To Power's 1988 "Say It's Gonna Rain," the word "rain" starts sprinkling then pouring like raindrops. John Anderson's 1982 "Swingin'," about porch-swing smooching, swings as freely as any '80s country hit, while Seven Mary Three's 1996 bandwagon-grunge Buzz-Binner "Cumbersome" ranks with the most cumbersome rock hits ever.

In 1978's "Roll with the Changes," REO Speedwagon's piano notes *literally* roll with the time changes. Jefferson Airplane's "White Rabbit" rhythm marches like knights on a chess board, and they just had some kind of mushrooms. And whenever Joe LeSté says the word "vamp" in Bang Tango's 1991 "Dressed-Up Vamp," about either a transvestite (I say) or a vampire (he says), his voice *does* a little vamp—i.e., as my *dictionary* says, it improvises accompaniment by striking a different chord.

(And what about songs that sound like the performers *look*, like how rap songs by Chubb Rock and Heavy D always seem to *wobble*, as does "Whole Lotta Loving" by Fats Domino, appropriate given the singers' unignorable overness in the weight department? And J. Geils's "Centerfold" has a gangly swagger like Peter Wolf, and Sabrina's songs sound quite buxom and busty for Italodisco.)

Then there's immersion rock—songs about getting soaking wet that seem to be recorded beneath the sea, or that bounce up and down, above and below the H_2O surface: Donna Summer's bubble-entendral 1977 "Theme from the Deep (Down Deep Inside)," the Sex Pistols' drone-drowned 1977 "Submission," Implog's stoned-to-the-gills 1980 "Holland Tunnel Dive," Arthur Russell's oceanically burbling 1986 "Let's Go Swimming," the end of the Floaters' 1977 proto-Color-Me-Badd "Float On" (where somebody seems to toss an inner tube into a pool's deep end), the "takin' a dive" echoes in Electric Light Orchestra's 1976 "Livin' Thing." (And let's not forget that legendary 1960s dance step, the Swim.)

Yet another ever-popular branch on the Onomatopoeia Rock family tree is heartbeat rock: the obsessive electrobeats in Vivien Vee's 1987 "Heartbeat"; the obsessive bassline in Taana Gardner's 1981 "Heartbeat"; Van Morrison telling us that his heart goes "boom! boom! boom!" in 1972's "Jackie Wilson Said"; Dion saying in his 1962 dirge "Little Diane" that without Diane he'd die and that he feels it in his heart so why doesn't she stop it (after which she stops the *beat*, thus *murdering* him, oops!). Most influential of all are the repetitive bubblegum heartbeat-punctuations that unintentionally paved the way for disco—in "I Think We're Alone Now" (revived as sort-of-disco in 1987 by Tiffany), a heartbeat comes in whenever Tommy James says "the beating of our hearts is the only sound" (and the music tumbles to the ground when the teen puppy-lovers do, and it gets quiet when Tom says no one seems to be around). And in the Defranco Family's 1973 "Heartbeat (It's A Lovebeat)," the line "listen to my heart sound, listen to my heart pound" precedes a big Caribbean-like garbage-can-timbale interlude bolstered by drug-cultured effects. (Happens three times.)

In 1969 John Lennon and Yoko Ono recorded "Baby's Heartbeat," using a *real* heartbeat in utero as an instrument. It goes "whooooshwhooooshwhoooosh" for five minutes. You can buy "mommy's heartbeat" teddy bears that sound exactly the same to relax your younguns, but they really eat up batteries, so don't waste your money. (Pediatricians argue that many lullabies—"Rockabye Baby," "Are You Sleeping Brother John," "Twinkle Twinkle Little Star"—*already* have rhythms based on genuine human heartbeats.)

Finally, the cold, unceasingly telegraphed lines in British artpunk originators Wire's 1978 "Heartbeat" are an attempt to demystify the heart back into mere circulatory organhood devoid of emotional function, as are the song's lyrics. Wire liked onomatopoeias a lot—"Fragile" was their prettiest track, locating some delicate creepy quiet energy punk forgot, and numbers like "I Am the Fly," "Being Sucked in Again," and "Dot Dash" buzzed, engulfed, and stuttered like their titles suggest.

Yet for the most part (just like the Cars wanting to sound calibrated, machine-tooled, streamlined, and turtle-wax-sleek like real cars), what Wire meant to resemble was a wire itself—spindly, utilitarian, factory-constructed, and shocking if you mess with it. To this end, Martha and the Vandellas' "Live Wire" sounds more like a live wire than Mötley Crüe's or Die Kreuzen's "Live Wire"s do, though one could easily draw parallels between how Martha Reeves electrocutes you with her screeches and how Die Kreuzen's Dan Kubinski attempts to do the same.

Train Rock

Kraftwerk's "Trans Europe Express," a definitive Teutonelectronic chant-trance that was actually a huge hit with urban African-American street kids in 1977, isn't just *about* a train, it *sounds* like one, in true onomatopoetic tradition: an unyeilding automatic chug. There's a chance with chants that reciting them might induce a trance, and "trance" sounds like "trans," but the "trans" in Kraftwerk's title doesn't mean "trains," it means "across"—neat, huh? And train-sounding train songs are the roots of car-sounding car songs, which are the roots of airplane-sounding airplane songs, which are the roots of rocket-sounding rocket songs. In fact, a direct line runs from the deadpan, subliminally accented asides about running into "Eeegy Pop" and "Day-veed Boe-wee" in Offenbach or Dusseldorf in "Trans Europe Express" to similar glam namedrops in "Rocket" by Def Leppard a decade later. And "T.E.E." means quite a bit to me *personally*, because the only time I ever rode a train anywhere on a regular basis was while in the Army in Germany, from Bad Kreuznach to Mainz early in the morning, then back at night, and to record stores in Frankfurt on Saturdays.

Michael Freedberg suggested at least the first plank of my train-to-rocket theory in a 1980 *Boston Phoenix* piece called "Doin' the Loco-motion: A Rock 'n' Roll Memoir." He traced blues-based trains from 1928 ("The Railroad Piece," a harmonica instrumental) through 1946 (jump-blueser Louis Jordan's "rhythm of the clickety-clack" in "Choo Choo Ch'Boogie") through 1977 ("Trans Europe Express" itself.) Sounds like a lot, and it was—he mentions a boxcar's worth of blues stuff I doubt I'll ever want to hear. But believe it or not, he barely drove the first spike. This schedule should take you from coast to coast:

T. Lawrence Siebert and Eddie Newton "Casey Jones," 1908. That's when they published it, in *Railroad Man's Magazine*—"Greatest Comedy Hit in Years: The Only Comedy Railroad Song," its sheet music brags. Yeah, real funny: the engineer gets killed! Siebert and Newton were white; a black Mississippi train-cleaner named Wallace Saunders probably wrote it, according to Paul Oliver in *Songsters and Saints: Vocal Traditions on Race Records*. Most of the people who sang it were white, too.

Reverend A.W. Nix "Black Diamond Express to Hell," 1927. A sermon recorded by a black Baptist Alabama minister who played piano, and the origin of Chuck Berry's "Downbound Train," Blue Öyster Cult's "Hot Rails to Hell," and gloom rock. Shoveling coal in hell-hole mines taught Nix how to mix ominous metaphors.

Jimmie Rodgers "Waitin' for a Train," sometime in the '30s. Doesn't really have a train rhythm, but does have this one-time Mobile and Ohio Railroad brakeman's (and blackface medicine-show minstrel's) lonesome engine whistles at the start, so you can see grimy smoke in the distance almost. Dang good yodels, too!

Mariachi Vargas "El Tren," 1937. A border-crossing *son*, from the first mariachi band with trumpets and an acoustic bass.

Glen Miller "Chatanooga Choo Choo," 1941. White guys trying to figure out Louis Jordan's clickety-clack of five years later.

Leadbelly "Rock Island Line," 1948. Thanks to the fast slaps he keeps delivering to his guitar body, deliberately imitating the sound of a train's metal wheels cracking against lumber railroad ties, one of the most rhythmic songs in his *Last Sessions* box set. (Only competition: "Black Betty," where he does the same thing, but sounds like he's banging on a door.)

Hank Williams "I Heard That Lonesome Whistle," 1951. Midway point on track between "Waitin' for a Train" and "Mystery Train."

Elvis Presley "Mystery Train," 1955. A chain-jangling death train, and the root of Greil Marcus's book *Mystery Train* to boot. But more important, the root of Bananarama's 1991 "Long Train Running," which fashions Doobie Brother words and gipsy-flamenco guitars into what may well wind up the scariest death-train of *its* decade: Miss Lucy's seen wandering by the tracks with no home or family anymore, and they won't be coming back.

Johnny Burnette and the Rock 'n' Roll Trio "Train Kept A-Rollin'," 1956. As the Yardbirds proved again in the '60s then Aerosmith in the '70s, this song is locomotive-breath as the hottest body-rock (not to mention the loudest and heaviest music of the '50s): oral-harp action as steaming tongues and lips, rhythmic momentum as torsos slapping against each other.

Stan Freberg "Rock Island Line," 1956. Makes fun of the barnyard-animal story-opening in the version by skiffle king Lonnie Donnegan, who went top ten with it that year (the biggest skiffle hit in U.S. history, until Lonnie followed it up with "Does Your Chewing Gum Lose its Flavor"). The producer tells the singer to "get the train rhythm going, never mind the sheep."

Louis Prima "Whistle Stop," 1957. About living near Petticoat Junction: whistles all day long, all through the song.

Chuck Berry "Johnny B. Goode," 1958. His 1955 "Downbound Train" has a more obvious choo-choo undertow, but this one defines the aesthetic: "The engineer would see him sitting in the shade, strumming with the rhythm that the driver made."

The Coasters "That is Rock & Roll," 1959. We might think we hear a freight train, they tell us, but it's actually a hillbilly banging piano notes out there among the railroad ties.

Kingston Trio "M.T.A.," 1959. A rocking folk (as opposed to "folk-rock") protest about escalating subway rates in Boston, it starts slow then speeds to high velocity, but stays funnier than the Trio's dark "Mystery Train"-like "Fast Freight" all down the rail line. Subways are underground trains, of course, and whenever bands from cities with tube systems talk about trains, that's what they're referring to: think of "Subway Train" by the New York Dolls (who actually first played in Cooper Union Station of the IRT), or "The Train" by the Roches, or "Tales from the Rails" by '90s Mafia-rappers Lordz of Brooklyn, or the part in "The Message" where Grandmaster Flash and the Furious Five rap about girls being shoved in the path of oncoming headlights.

James Brown "Night Train," 1962. A sluggishly moving old hornridden hulk of a thing, with the conductor calling out names of cities in the south (Miami, Florida! Atlanta, Georgia! Raleigh, North Carolina!), then Washington, Virginia, Philadelphia, Boston, New Orleans—must be the "scenic route."

Little Eva "The Loco-Motion," 1962. In which a babysitter employed by Carole King tells you to move around "like a railway train, now." She sounds like the little engine that could.

Shangri-Las "The Train from Kansas City," 1965. Given its eerie proto-Eurodisco keyboard-and-bass pulse, a real precursor of "Trans Europe Express." A girl awaits a visit from her ex, whose heart she has to break. She's dreading it, because she knows his visit might cause her to break her current boyfriend's heart instead. The beat keeps trying to turn back, but can't.

Nancy Sinatra and Lee Hazlewood "Jackson," 1967. Doesn't say how they're gonna get there (where they plan to wreck their marriage, which oughta make Frank Sinatra happy), but for the last minute they've got a mechanistic train-like voice going "Jack-son, Jack-son, Jack-son." So I suppose they went by rail.

Desmond Dekker "Rude Boy Train," 1968. Ska 45, less trancey but way more fun than Cool Sticky's 1967 "Train to Soulsville" (though not than "Train to Skaville," done by Boney M in 1981).

Brook Benton "Rainy Night in Georgia," 1970: "The distant moans of a train seem to play a sad refrain." *Very* rainy-night.

Yoko Ono "Mind Train," 1971. She squawks gibberish that sounds like "Johnny Rotten Johnny Rotten" and "don't stop don't stop," predicting both punk and rap for 17 minutes. But the incessant idiot-savant warped-blues-repetition-unto-eternity mirrors what the German group Can was doing at the same time—I'd bet a few *deutschmark*s Kraftwerk took note of this one.

Cher "Train of Thought," 1974. Her hardest-rocking hit, at least guitar-wise, and it magnifies the title's pun with a rhythm halfway between a whistling train and Bob Dylan's streams of consciousness. Cher compares herself to a train, then goes insane. Talks about her man talking about other women his sleep, slips into a trance: "Gotta get off gotta get off . . ."

Silver Convention "Love in a Sleeper," 1978. "Trans Europe Express" with a libido, and nifty skidding violin interplay.

Giorgio Morodor *Midnight Express*, 1979. The train song as drug-movie soundtrack, though the flick that really reflects disco's railroad concerns is *Strangers on a Train*, from 1951, for its title and for Danny Peary's rave in *Guide for the Film Fanatic*: "Hitchcock creates excitement by building suspense, stopping short and starting over, only to reach the climax when no one is prepared." Not a bad description of Eurodisco at all.

Telex "Moskow Diskow," 1979. The bubblegum "Trans Europe Express," or "We're an American Band" for "super chic" European boys with synthesizers. Filled with vocodored wooh-woohs and toot-toots, this cutiepie tune by Belgium's first and best "newbeat" combo regularly convinced hallucinitaing Chicago house revelers that a big caboose was *really about to run them over.*

DNA "Lionel," 1979. The only known example of model-train rock. You can actually hear this little N-gauge scooting around its circular track real speedy, trilling when it gets to a crossing, and when it hits a tunnel its lights go on. Initiated a trend, perhaps best realized by Pavement in their 1990 song "Forklift," where artpunk bands mimicked pieces of machinery.

The Clash "Train in Vain," 1980. Lyrically trainless, but Mick Jones said they named it such for its train rhythm. Which I don't hear, though in "Clash City Rockers" two years earlier, they *had* cited "tube train accelerators" as a sonic influence.

Swell Maps "Bridge/Ghost Train," 1981. Rumbles and rambles through the fog for eight minutes, pretty darn long for a British punk band. More successful is their 1986 "Rundown Tube," where they really do clang and sputter and honk like one. (Both train tracks can be found on their 1991 compilation *Train Out of It.*)

Fun Fun "Happy Station," 1983. Tracks intersecting, bringing in friends from all over Italy. Wheezing trains pull to a rusty little stop, people disboard, and two happy girls smile at them.

Three Johns "Do Not Cross the Line," 1985. Starts with a snatch of Hank Williams, ends with a snatch of Jimmie Rodgers. In between, there's hoots the lyric sheet spells "woo ooo ooo," plus a smog-wheezing churn that reminded me of the Gang of Four's worrywart "Outside the Trains Don't Run On Time" until I realized it rocks harder, almost like the Yardbirds (though much less sexy). The Limey sarcasm concerns a coalminer riding south from Leeds with feet in his face and his seat occupied and luggage tumbling from racks, only to find out in the end he's on strike.

S-Express "Theme From S-Express"/"The Trip," 1988. You're riding a Class 120 Bobo alone at night from Milan to Munich, and everything's flying past your window: puppy dogs, ping-pong balls, trumpets, clarinets, dopefiends, babelicious *frauleins*, kilometers of hilly geography, yam-cramming performance moron Karen Finley (real briefly, fortunately) telling you to suck her off. The relentlessness of the maximalist electronics, more corny than campy but usually neither, puts it over. It's fast.

Tribantura "Lack of Sense," 1988: "Trans Europe Express" redone by guys with whiney adenoids and surname umlauts as a *Sprockety* racket Jean-Paul Sartre would appreciate. Riding at quarter-to-two has become a tiresome facade, so Frank Rückert gives up all hope: "Own zee unzerground train, nuzzeeng at all."

Guns N' Roses "Locomotive," 1991. They try to fabricate a refrigerator-car rhythm with boogie bass and rhythm guitar. But at least until Slash's dazed mantric end-strumming, their train sounds too lumbering, black, old, and coughy—in 1991, an anachronism. Not like their previous "Nightrain" (which has more funk in it than the James Brown grunt of the same name), though in both songs you can tell Axl just needs to get away.

The KLF "Last Train to Transcentral," 1991. The Monkees' "Last Train to Clarksville," updated as "Trans Europe Express."

Quad City DJs "C'Mon And Ride It (The Train)," 1996. Florida booty auteurs fond of little-train-that-could "I think I can" affirmations carry the electronic planet-jamming on late '80s choo-choo-rap samplers like Pandisc Records' *Miami Bass Express* back to the plantation station of T.C.I. Section Crew's '20s blues choo-choo rap "Track Linin"; that is, back to the lowdown locomotive deep-South whorehouse woogie that hip-hop was born as.

Underworld "Born Slippy," 1996. For at least the first four of its ten slippy minutes, the most train-tranced track on the *Trainspotting* soundtrack, closest thing to a "rave" compilation I've ever liked if only because its concrete non-rave songs (by Iggy Pop, Lou Reed, Pulp, Sleeper covering Blondie, maybe even New Order who don't bug me so much when they talk about eye colors) offset its ravier inner-space snoozing. The movie had very little to do with trains (and, contrary to hypee, didn't make heroin use seem very attractive either). But by the time Underworld succumb to the sterile style of revolving-elevator-door emptiness that Kraftwerk made inevitable, they've already sneakily sucked me into their maelstrom by convincing me I can't live without some cute tomboy who's just smiled at me.

Equestrian and Pedestrian Rock

Okay, we'll get to the car-like car songs in a minute. But people had to get from point A to point B even *before* there were trains, and there still exist certain songs with rhythms that might be considered residue of that period: (1) Bicycle Rock: Most obviously Queen's 1978 concept single "Fat Bottomed Girls"/"Bicycle Race" and Melanie's squeaky 1971 "Brand New Key." But also Kraftwerk's 1983 "Tour de France" (where old "Trans Europe Express"/"Autobahn" fans started yelling "enough already!") and Orbit's lusty 1997 "Bicycle Song" and Tomorrow's 1967 Brit-invasion "My White Bicycle," which features future Pink Fairie Twink and future Yesman Steve Howe, not to mention a clangalanging bike bell just like Melanie's song. And Nino Rota's music for Fellini's 1963 $8\frac{1}{2}$ employs a bicycle rhythm, as demonstrated in *Pee Wee's Big Adventure*. (2) Boatride Rock: Frankie Ford's foghorned "Sea Cruise," Lee Dorsey's splashy "Riverboat"—both from New Orleans, oddly enough. (3) Sleigh Rock: The Ronettes' "Sleigh Ride," pulled through the snow by dappled gray mares with bells on. (4) Washing Machine Rock: The Electric Eels' Ohio punk "Agitated," Pretenders' Ohio new wave "Watching the Clothes," Five Royales' dirty doowop "Laundromat Blues," and especially "Wasmasjien" by Trafassi, five Surinam *zouk*ers recording in Holland c. 1983, bare-chested on the 45 sleeve while their shirts pre-soak and while they pick up hot spin-cycling Surinam women.

Slightly more common (and no doubt influenced by countless TV westerns) is Equestrian Rock—the Ramrods' 1961 open-prairie "(Ghost) Riders in the Sky," Prince Buster's trotting mid-'60s rudeboy toast "Texas Holdup," America's clippity-clopping 1972 "A Horse with No Name," the Osmonds' whinnying 1972 "Crazy Horses," Aerosmith's 1977 Osmonds Xerox "Back in the Saddle," Poison's 1988 Aerosmith Xerox "Back to the Rocking Horse."

Lee Dorsey gave Equestrian Rock its first *obscene* twist in 1965's "Ride Your Pony," where he used pre-Chic bass-scratches to boost the bumpy drums' barebacked New Orleans gallop. Numerous disco artists picked up on this idea years later, and made the metaphor naughtier—Disco Tex and his Sex-O-Lettes in "Ride a Wild Horse" ("saddle up, get down to the source"), Blake Baxter in "Ride 'Em Boy," Hot Posse in "Ride It," Jamie Principle in "Baby Wants to Ride (X-Rated)." And, most famously, seminal Danish synth duo Laid Back with their 1984 top-30 cocaine-not-heroin commercial "White Horse." When dancers do the lambada, they literally ride each others' thighs like a rocking horse.

Still, Equestrian Rock probably isn't as important as Pedestrian Rock, dating back at least as far as Leadbelly's highly influential 1930s invention, the walking bassline. When I call it "pedestrian," I'm not making a value judgment:

Robert Johnson "Walking Blues," 1936. Dawdles like he's got no particular place to go and nothing left to lose.

Ernest Tubb "Walking the Floor Over You," 1941. Feels like the hospital-hall pacing husbands do outside delivery room doors. But Ernie says *his* wife is just *mad*. And she's on her way home.

Johnny Cash "I Walk the Line," 1956. Eyes wide open, keenly vigilant, even paranoid. Not like some drunk who a cop is *forcing* to walk the line. But guess what? I've still never liked it much.

The Diamonds "The Stroll," 1958. Hit song as metaphor for (line?) dance as metaphor for walking her home hand in hand.

Santo & Johnny "Sleep Walk," 1959. Keeps bumping into walls.

Eddie Cochran "C'Mon Everybody," 1959. Bare-feet-slapping-on-the-floor rhythm. (Also, a direct ancestor of the party invitations in Bryan Adams's 1992 "There Will Never Be Another Tonight," but you know what they say—it's not a real party until something *breaks*. Nothing breaks at Bryan's party.)

Fats Domino "Walking to New Orleans," 1960. Fats employs a metronomic beat that sounds like tired but determined-to-get-there footsteps (and they're absolutely drenched in strings, not hardly what you'd expect from such a big guy). But his 1957 "I'm Walkin' " is more confident: a sharp, dignified swagger.

Ventures "Walk Don't Run," 1960. But walking *fast* is okay.

Rufus Thomas "Walking the Dog," 1963. My daughter Coco memorized almost all of these words (in 1996!) *before* she ever heard the song, while jumping rope. I also have a feeling it's where Aerosmith (who covered it) first learned to walk this way.

Four Seasons "Walk Like a Man," 1963. Struts like a rooster, head held high, with excellent posture. The voices take steps: "Walk! Walk! Walk! Walk!" But when obese bad-movie transvestite Divine covered it as Eurodisco in the mid-'80s, the harsh bite in his/her bark brought out a psychotic vengeance that Frankie Valli had barely hinted at. Divine makes it *cruel*, like "Pushin' Too Hard" by the Seeds. "No woman's worth crawling on the earth": a dad who's apparently learned the hard way (from Mom?) teaches his first-born that being a man means not letting yourself not be pussy-whipped. Somehow, I doubt Divine ever had that problem.

Nancy Sinatra "These Boots are Made for Walkin'," 1966. About being the sort of woman Papa Valli warned Frankie about.

Velvet Underground "I'm Waiting for the Man," 1967. Lou Reed ventures to the black side of the tracks to spend $26 on dope, then climbs three flights of brownstone stairs, then walks home, as does the music. The Deviants' "I'm Coming Home," from a year later, features a creepy ascent halfway between Lou's one here and the one in the Rolling Stones' 1966 "Goin' Home." But what General Johnson climbs in the Chairmen of the Board's 1970 "Give Me Just a Little More Time" and Lou Gramm climbs in Foreigner's 1984 "I Want to Know What Love Is" is much taller—a *mountain*.

Tommy James "Draggin' the Line," 1971. Supposedly about snorting cocaine, but the beat drags its feet like the title.

Bohannon "The Bohannon Walk," 1975. Not as slow as his 1972 "The Pimp Walk." (Slower than 1975's "Disco Stomp," his best cut maybe, but that's a *train* song—you can tell because he calls out names of cities, like James Brown in "Night Train.")

Disco Tex and his Sex-O-Lettes "Strollin'," 1976. About *doing* the stroll, just like Led Zeppelin's "Whole Lotta Love." But the whistles and adenoidal tones sound more like Axl Rose!

Aerosmith "Walk This Way," 1977. I would, but I don't think I have the hips for it. (I think I stole that line from Groucho.)

Pere Ubu "Sentimental Journey," 1978. A drunk man, not old, walks along a River Cuyahoga pier, picking up bottles, smashing them against the dock, kicking them, knocking over garbage cans, lighting up a joint or blowing his nose. A storm starts, cools the air some. The man starts babbling. Seagulls squawk over the water, the tide rolls in, the wind blows in his face, it's turning real cold, blustery. "Table and chair and TV and books and lamp all the stuff, it's home, it's a rug, it's a rug, it's a window, I don't, yeh-ech pleh, hungh puh, hungh puh, I'll go home, I'll go home . . ." Then he starts breaking stuff again. Some of it sounds like he's turning pool tables over and the balls are tumbling down, but how could he do that? Everybody knows there's no pool tables outside by the river.

Bellamy Brothers "Get into Reggae Cowboy," 1980. Shuffle-them-boots-on-the-street (between Nashville and Kingston) rhythm.

Minor Threat "Out of Step (With the World)," 1982. Awkward, and when Ian MacKaye frets "I can't keep up, I can't keep up, I can't keep up!," his band falls all over each other trying.

Kate Bush "Running Up that Hill," 1985. Allegedly an erotic metaphor, and on the 12-inch cover she seems topless, plus I detect some indecipherable phenomes of pleasure after the "c'mon c'mon baby, c'mon c'mon angel" part. But Sister Kate's not the type to raise much of a sweat, so it's hard to say. Decent art-rock appropriation of Italodisco something-or-other, and the hill climbed *does* peak with a climax—a classical one, almost.

Operation Ivy "One of These Days," 1989. San Francisco ska punks, Rancid in their larval stage actually, start by bellowing "These Boots are Made For Walkin'," boots their favored apparel (apparently) for kicking teeth in. They surf into a reggae break then walk all over you, scared geeks obviously acting hardassed as a defense mechanism. In the CD's next track the vice-principal busts a kid just for *trying* to walk—out of school, I suppose.

Kix "Cold Chills," 1991. Your friends all take off early, so you have to walk home alone, late, through a scary part of town. You peer back over your shoulder the whole way; and somehow, this Maryland party-glam band who so rarely do non-upbeat songs mirror your shaky nerves with their tempo. You hear footsteps, oh no . . .

OMC "On the Run," 1996. Having battled his way through the streetgangs of South Auckland, subliminally inspired by the voice and rhythm and title of Trinidadian Billy Ocean's 1984 number-one hit "Caribbean Queen (No More Love on the Run)," half-Islander/half-Maori Pauly Fuemana and his Otara Millionaires Club concoct a unique Polynesian polyglot of marathon-chugging disco propulsion, hard-twanged surf guitars, and dark fugitive truths: no more sunrise or sanity or family, so Pauly asks himself a hundred times why he fucked up, even hopes for a heart attack, but demonic voices inside his head remind him "if you do the crime you must then do the time." He keeps running anyway; in New Zealand, there's always hope that the edge of the world can't be too far off. Or at least the edge of the song: on his album, Pauly jogs straight from this one into "How Bizarre," an automotive concoction about hopping a '69 Chevy to the circus. Driven by garage-organ/soulchick-chorus/Tijuana-brass hooks whose easy infectious warmth convinced doubters that '90s radio had just been a bad dream, it topped pop charts everywhere from Toronto to Tasmania.

Automotive Rock

Okay, this one's almost too easy. The first rock'n'roll fans were grease monkeys who flunked out of everything except shop class (a.k.a. "industrial arts"), and they liked to rebuild carburetors and steal hubcaps (and I'm pretty sure they all looked like Fonzie). Garage bands practiced in buildings where cars lived, not people. The first real rock'n'roll song was Jackie Brenston's "Rocket 88," recorded with Ike Turner on guitar through a speaker stuffed with paper after the amplifier fell off the back of a truck; the noisy jump-blues topped the R&B chart in 1951, and it was about a fast car. So were all of the Beach Boys' songs, except ones that were about surfing, and all of Bruce Springsteen's songs, until he got too old to drive.

Rock'n'roll was music for car radios, that's obvious. Rock'n'rollers died in cars (T. Rex frontfruit Marc Bolan), or got crippled (Jan Berry, fulfilling "Dead Man's Curve"'s prophecy), or lost their arms (Def Leppard drummer Rick Allen). Some music (fast rap music and hard rock) sounds much *better* in a car (where you can blast it at innocent passersby, maybe) than at home. Other records (ballads and house music) are useful at home but make considerably less sense on the road. When rockers stopped caring about cars, rappers took over—Chuck D says the car tape deck accelerated the advancement of hip-hop, which supposedly used to be made for home and club stereos (even though early rappers always talked about driving their "def O.J.'s" without ever explaining what "O.J."'s are). But nowadays, Chuck says, rap's not music you can relax in your living room to; it requires "activity," a "ride." (Excuses, excuses—how come he doesn't just come out and *admit* hip-hop's dead-ass boring now unless you've got a bass fetish, Jeep, and crackpipe?) Record executives have even drawn analogies between the music industry's growing complexity and the increasing availabity of power brakes!

Well, anyway, what I'm most concerned with, again, is the *onamatopoeia* factor—car songs that *sound* like cars, which narrows the category some. Though not as much as you might hope:

Chuck Berry "Maybellene," 1955. Chuck's "V-8 Fode" races a Cadillac doing 94, motorvates over a hill, and rainwater under its hood does its engine good. But I don't believe him for a second when he says Maybellene is some chick in a Coup de Ville—I think it's his *car* that won't be true, that goes back doing the things it used to do. Just like my old '84 Horizon. Which is spooky, seeing how one time when I was driving said lemon, Chuck's "No Particular Place to Go" came over the oldies station with its stop-at-the-stop-signs-until-you-reach-the-open-road tempo changes, and my safety belt wouldn't budge at the exact moment Chuck said *his* wouldn't. Never happened before or since.

Fats Domino "I'm Gonna Be A Wheel Someday," 1959. Has a guitar riff going round and round, maybe anticipating the day Fats won't have to walk everywhere like in all his other songs.

Bo Diddley "Road Runner," 1960. A car tune based on a cartoon about a bird and a coyote, complete with "beep! beep!"s.

Dave Dudley "Six Days on the Road," 1962. Initiated C&W's truck-driver subgenre with semi-rockabilly percussion that approximated the sound of 16 worn tires bumping in and out of chuckholes, commandeered by a caffeine-and-speed insomniac.

Jimi Hendrix "Crosstown Traffic," 1968. Ninety MPH, through traffic jams, to the other side of town. Which is 95 MPH slower than Joe Walsh's Maserati in "Life's Been Good," but Jimmy Castor scolded his hero Jimi in 1977's "Mind Power" anyway: "moving ninety miles an hour but you're using all your power, too bad."

Vanity Fare "Hitchin' a Ride," 1970. Cars-and-trucks-flying-by whoosh-effects, with unexpected pickups once in a while.

Commander Cody and his Lost Planet Airmen "Hot Rod Lincoln," 1972. Creaking brakes and a rattle under her hood, but when a Cadillac honks at her, she leaves said Caddy in the dust.

Deep Purple "Highway Star," 1972. Chuck Berry's car rhythms rolled over by Beethoven's tradition: big, brisk, and European.

Eagles "Already Gone," 1974. Sounded *real* good in May 1986, driving away from Fort Knox after my final day in the Army.

Bachman-Turner Overdrive "Let it Ride," 1974, and "Roll on Down the Highway," 1975. Chuck Berry with four-wheel drive.

War "Low Rider," 1975. Chuck Berry with a green card, fuzzy dice in the rearview mirror, and spicy mariachi music blasting out the eight-track deck of his chopped-down 1957 Chevy.

Sammy Johns "Chevy Van," 1975. Laid-back parked-in-an-apple-orchard if-the-van's-arockin'-don't-come-a-knockin' rhythm.

Kraftwerk "Autobahn," 1975. A stupefying 23 minutes down Hitler's world wonder. I've driven there, so I can vouch for this song's accuracy: fun fun fun 'til daddy takes your VW away.

Meat Loaf "Bat out of Hell," 1977. Not automotive exactly, but just as much horsepower—a "motorcycle guitar" romp through Dante's Inferno, with Evel Knievel ramp jumps over long vacant Piggly Wiggly lots, then up through heaven's gates, and back down into the fire, across 500 miles of desert straightaway, and into the night. The last notes are the Tokens' "The Lion Sleeps Tonight," whispered. Like if Springsteen wasn't chicken.

Jackson Browne "Running on Empty," 1978. The most successful revival of the "Six Days on the Road" rhythm ever: *only* makes sense in a car, with the road rushing under your wheels, and where the title can be more than just a cheap baby-boom metaphor.

DNA "5:30," 1981. One minute and five seconds of glottal Esperanto-cum-Portuguese blues-yawp splatter and bass-rumbling, extremely cluttered and hurried: rush hour in New York City.

Ricky Skaggs "Highway 40 Blues," 1982. Same rhythm as "Running on Empty," except bluegrasser Ricky says he's wearing holes in his shoes. So maybe he borrowed Fred Flint-stone's car.

Kix "Layin' Rubber," 1985. A stop-and-start drag through a hick town in Maryland, one foot on each pedal: "Yes! No! Stop Go!," over and over, fast-slow-fast. I hope nobody gets hurt.

L.L. Cool J "The Boomin' System," 1990. Downing Heine-ken and cranking the volume knob with one motive in mind: "Because I want attention when I'm driving by." (Axl would understand.) L.L. rolls a fat blunt to pass around, like Neil Young in "Roll Another Number." But though he promises his jam won't be getting any airplay, its 12-inch single comes with two "radio versions"!

Sir Mix-a-Lot "My Hooptie," 1990. "The Boomin' System" in a total junker, littering Seattle's streets with rusty parts.

Will To Power "Journey Home," 1990. Title track of what might end up my favorite album of the '90s, seemingly based on "Cruisin' With the Deuce," off Quarterflash's first album, one of my favorites of the '80s (about primal scream therapy during solitary night driving: "you can shout out your fear, NOBODY CARES WHO YOU ARE"). In "Journey Home," Bob Rosenberg says he's got to keep his motor running, but not only can you feel the machine's momentum (in the rhythm), you can also feel stormclouds settling in (in the voices). The words detail the final leg of a car trip you're sick of. A woman tells him there's "no turnin' back, time's a wastin' "; Rosenberg shifts them gears.

Tom Cochrane "Life is a Highway," 1991. Harmonica boogie with percussive clanks so incongruous I'm always sur-prised when the blues-talking starts. Tom's fellow Canadian Alanis Morissette trills its title (or at least that's how it sounds to me: "life is a high-ee-way") in the prettiest parts of her big 1996 hit "Ironic." Which explains why she was driv-ing a car in the video.

Presidents of the United States of America "Mach 5," 1996. Tailor-made for gas pedals, by three gangly Seattle geeks with receding hairlines, a sixth-grade fanbase, and an off-kilter plop from five (three guitar plus two bass) strings.

Rocket Rock

Jackie Brenston's (aforementioned) "Rocket 88" was the first rocket'n'roll song, obviously, even though it's about a car. Other important stuff: the word "rocket" sounds like "rock it!," as in Queen's "Rock It (Prime Jive)" from 1980, and as in the Jets' 1988 candyfunk smash "Rocket 2 U" (by a big family whose parents come from the South Pacific nation of Tonga). Or as in the part in 1988's "Your Mama Don't Dance" where Bret Michaels of Poison tells his drummer Rikki Rockett to "rock it, Rockett!" (On the album cover, they put Rikki in a kind of futuristic setting, with lots of TV screens playing astronomy movies behind him and a little R2D2 and laser-gun-lady by his side.) Also as in the 1977 Ramones album *Rocket to Russia*, and as in Cleveland post-'60s-punk/proto-'70s-punk legends Rocket from the Tombs. And Herbie Hancock's 1983 "Rockit" (where he came to terms with rocket-song electronics) too.

Rockets are phallic symbols, or they can be—has to do with how they're shaped and how they erupt. (This would seem to be the case in Kiss's 1978 "Rocket Ride"; maybe also in how Whitney Houston followed up her 1991 hit "All The Man I Need," about some well-endowed hunk filling her up with more love than she'd ever seen, with "The Star Spangled Banner," about "rocket's red glare, bombs bursting in air.") If you haven't figured it out already, what we're dealing with is a shifting sense of what vehicle might bring adventure/freedom/mystery, from trains from the '20s through mid-'40s to rockets through whenever there's enough money to restart the space program and we get bored by it again. Apollo 11 putting men on the moon on July 16, 1969 no doubt set *something* in gear; in 1973, thanks to guitaring futurism buff Paul Kantner, Jefferson Airplane devolved into Jefferson Starship, and you can call that a turning point as well. *Star Wars* (1977) and *E.T.* (1983) didn't hurt (nor *Star Trek*, *Lost in Space*, or above all the vastly more compelling *My Favorite Martian*). But we need to start much earlier.

The earliest space-rock songs were of two varieties—moonstruck makeout moodzak about the moon, and novelty ditties about little green men. In the first category we find the many versions of Rodgers and Hart's "Blue Moon" (Elvis Presley, the Marcels, etc.), which had actually been more u-biquitous in 1935, when *three* different renditions went top ten. (Elvis also did "Blue Moon of Kentucky," not exactly necking music, but a more fun record.) Add the doowop group the Moonglows, plus the Capris' Wop doowop hit "There's A Moon out Tonight," plus the Heartbeats "A Thousand Miles Away" if you interpret it as a thousand miles straight up (as the Stones and Boney M sort of eventually did in "2000 Light Years from Home" and "10,000 Light Years"). Henry Mancini's non-doowop 1961 lounge instrumental "Moon River" green-cheesily made you feel you were floating on one. Then in the mid-'60s, future Genesis producer Jonathon King swooned through "Everyone's Gone to the Moon" and Frank Sinatra crooned both his famous Count Basie/Quincy Jones collaboration "Fly Me to the Moon" and his all-moon-tune concept LP *Moonlight Sinatra.*

The martian novelty songs were crazier, of course. In the '50s, interplanetary wackiness provided an excellent context for being sonically innovative without making "sonic innovation" your explicit game plan. (So gimmicks which later qualified as "art" were initially just presented as "jokes"!) Inspired by Sputnik, pasta-rock whizz Louis Prima sang in 1957's "Beep! Beep!" about his baby "fooling around with a satellite," boosting himself with screwy honking effects garnered through primitive overdub techniques. Sheb Wooley's "Purple People Eater" (which spent six weeks at number one in 1958) and the Ran-Dells' 1963 "Martian Hop" had singers electronically speeding their voices to resemble extraterrestrial chipmunks (a technique eventually borrowed by Brownsville Station in "Martian Boogie," Newcleus in "Jam On It," Stacy Lattisaw in "Attack of the Name Game," and George Clinton way too fucking often).

Buchanan and Goodman's 1956 "The Flying Saucer" initiated the idea that you can create a record by stealing parts of other records, thereby setting the stage not only for "EXP" by Jimi Hendrix (via bogus *War of the Worlds*-style newscaster hysteria), but for every recording which has ever employed a sampler. The Tornadoes' 1962 instrumental "Telstar" was not only the first single by a British rock band to top the American charts, but probably the first hit record anywhere to pass off blastoffs and engine kabooms as "music"—that is, it was the first one to fully qualify as rocket-rock *per se*. Then in 1963 the Marketts took the universe to the beach with their raunch-guitar-and-dink-organ "Out of Limits," based on the theme to TV's *Outer Limits*.

New wave bands in the '70s and '80s would eventually revive rock'n'roll's early martian novelties (and such concurrent sci-fi B-movie horrors as *Plan 9 from Outer Space*) as nudge-wink campiness (think of the B-52s' "Planet Claire," Graham Parker's "Waiting for the UFOs," the Angry Samoans' "Not of this Earth"—Creedence Clearwater Revival probably started the trend with "It Came Out of the Sky," if not Billy Lee Riley with his wild-but-so-what 1957 rockabilly "Flying Saucers Rock'n'Roll.") But in the scheme of the '60s drug schmaltz that came to be known as "space-rock," "Telstar" was probably more influential. And actually, "Telstar" did have some precedents of a sort—the soundtrack to the 1950 sci-fi groundbreaker *Rocketship X-M* put to use a new-fangled Russian thingamajig called a Theremin where you monkey with tone and pitch by waving your hands above a pair of antennas, and later '50s flicks like *Destination Moon* and *Forbidden Planet* had scores featuring primeval synths and tape loops. Such '70s and '80s moon units as Pink Floyd, Hawkwind, Amon Düül, and Von Lmo eventually milked similar milky-way procedures to death.

The first space-rock *band* was almost unarguably the Byrds, who did songs like "Mr. Spaceman" (about a visitor who leaves flies in your beer and smears your toothpaste) and "5D" (about dimensional limitations) and "Space Odyssey" around the same mid-'60s time zone that they were doing "Eight Miles High" and "2-4-2 Fox Trot (The Lear Jet Song")." (As far as *airplane* rock is concerned, the Byrds' only competition came from Mark Lindsay, who sang "The Great Airplane Strike" for Portland garage gods Paul Revere and the Raiders in 1966, then developed an aerodynamically gossamer brand of quiet-to-loud soaring in his solo "Silver Bird" and in "Observation from Flight 285," which he loaned to his worthy Seattle quasi-folkie discovery Merilee Rush.) The Electric Prunes' 1967 "Get Me to the World on Time" was a crass Seattle school-snot Byrds ripoff that naturally improved on the Byrds' concept: after opening with a Gothic proto-industrial technodrone, singer James Lowe wails that the disaster he's heading for increases his heart rate (and he sounds unbelievably excited about it, like his imminent death is a great reason to have a party!). Then you hear rockets (supposedly actually autoharps) taking off. Then he says he'd run away if his feet weren't stuck, then he starts spinning like a top higher and higher into space, and his adrenalin won't let him stop. All probably just 'cause he was nervous on account of some bully (or some girl he had a crush on) who just walked into the room!

Needless to say, space-rock could only go downhill from there—Lester Bangs put forth the only possible intelligent reaction to Pink Floyd: "Big deal, so go see Buck Rogers!" *Kick Out the Jams*, the 1969 debut album by Detroit boogie-jazz terrorists the MC5, had both "Rocket Reducer No. 62 (Rama Lama Fa Fa)" (a glop-sloppy rocker with Little Richard squeals and a dying engine) and "Starship," composed by a jazz-piano joker named Sun Ra who thought he was born on Saturn. "Starship" starts with some hesitation (it's one of the first rocket-rock songs with a countdown in it), then has the music "leaving the solar system." It might be better if it didn't have so much "anarchic" guitar goo. Eventually the guitars calm down and float around a bit—there's a nice quiet part, but mostly it's even more aimless and half-formed-with-its-testicles-hanging-out-all-over than the rest of the MC5's cloddish blackface. They tell of "a land where the sun shines every day," but they're too manly and theatrical and afraid of melody to conjure such a place.

Early-'70s metal bands learned some tricks, though. Deep Purple's "Space Truckin' " was as energized as it was cold, and Hawkwind's "Psychedelic Warlords (Disappear in Smoke)" used bass and synth to push its arms buildup toward an air-to-ground missile of feedback barrage. Black Sabbath's "Into the Void" was an okay post-garage grunger about machinery flying through the astral plane at the end of time; their "Supernaut" was even better, with Ozzy Osbourne howling indecipherably about how he wanted to reach out and touch the sky over a sprung, densely propulsive rhythm that could almost pass as a metal mambo.

Come the late '80s, spacegunky rumble-combos like Voivod and Bloodstar would look back to Sabbath as an astronomical ultimo. (Though in "Angel Rat," where someone tells them to "try to catch the eclipse," Voivod—being Canucks and all—seem more indebted to Carly Simon going "up to Nova Scotia to see the total eclipse of the sun" in "You're So Vain." Mama always told me *not* to look into the sights of the sun. Oh but mama, that's where the fun is. Every now and then I fall apart. It's a total eclipse of the heart . . . Turn around, bright eyes!)

Bloodstar's 1991 "Hyperspace"/"Exterminator 666 Does Not Answer" 10-inch rode celestial repetition-metal distortion atop hypnotic repetition-disco pulses, like Giorgio Morodor producing Hawkwind at a Swiss watch factory, with sad cosmonauts snoring next door. Bands like Bloodstar tried hard to invoke the secret warp worlds Charles Berlitz describes in *The Bermuda Triangle*: "areas where the laws of gravity and normal magnetic attraction no longer function in ways with which we are familiar."

Black Sabbath and their armageddonoid disciples tied into a tradition that associates space-travel with doomsday. I believe this tradition was invented by my mother, a devout papist who was convinced during Apollo 11 that the astronauts were opening up Pandora's box by trying to take a shortcut to heaven. Or maybe some Catholic church teaching equated risking getting burned up by the sun with risking hellfire; all I'm sure of is I got nightmares after looking at the astronaut pictures in my Cub Scout manual. My mom passed away a year later, so I don't remember much, being only nine at the time. But oddly, the most popular record in the country the week Neil Armstrong became the first human to walk on the moon was also the first record I positively remember being obsessed enough as a kid to buy a copy of: "In the Year 2525" by Nebraska singing duo Zager and Evans. It was dark corny psychedelic-influenced sci-fi shlock about the downfall of mankind and the end of the world.

Sabbath's "Into the Void" connected rocketships to pollution and woe; that was 1971, same year as "Inner City Blues" by Marvin Gaye ("rockets, moonshots, spend it on the havenots"), same year as the MC5's "Gotta Keep Movin'" ("rockets on the moon, they wonder why the kids are growin' up too soon"), one year after the Temptations' "Ball of Confusion" ("shooting rockets to the moon, kids growing up too soon"). (Kinda obvious who plagiariazed who *there*, huh?) Meanwhile, the Temptations' 1968 "Cloud Nine" was Motown's answer to "Eight Miles High," only more so: "a million miles from reality." And Dennis Coffey and the Detroit Guitar Band's 1971 "Scorpio" was a groundbreaking constellation-funk instrumental (roots of the Floaters' "Float On" and any number of early rap singles, where everyone in the group told you his zodiac sign). "Scorpio" rose to number six; later, Coffey's inevitable followup, "Taurus," stalled at eighteen.

In "Freddie's Dead" in 1972, Curtis Mayfield complained that people can deal with rockets, but not reality. (Prince revived the argument fifteen years later in "Sign O' The Times," blowing spaceships to smithereens in the wake of the Challenger tragedy—it was pretty lame.) But not everybody equated the cosmos with chaos. The road to space-disco may well have been paved by the Supremes, whose 1967 number-two "Reflections" had a rocket blasting off, then astronomical blips and bleeps all through—Diana Ross sings about looking through the mirror of her mind, but sounds more like she's looking through the porthole of a spaceship; the percussion is intoxicating, an assembly line of electronic maracas and classical drop-ins.

In 1970, *Creem* magazine dubbed as "space-soul" the sound of Parliament-Funkadelic, who did not-abridged-enough "thangs" called "Unfunky Ufo" and "Mothership Connection" and were even known to land their ship on stage. Another space-disco forebear came from Brit studio jockeys Apollo 100, who hit in 1972 with "Joy," basically Bach's "Jesu, Joy of Man's Desiring" with an updated beat. Suicide's 1977

"Rocket USA" was the space-age synth-sequel to "Trans Europe Express" and "Autobahn" Kraftwerk never got around to making, albiet with Manhattan overseriousness replacing deadpan *Deutschland* nutsiness. (Sigue Sigue Sputnik's "Love Missile F1-11," a huge hit in England in 1986, was sort of a half-wit "Rocket USA"—hence, an improvement, since it beat having no wit at all.) And in 1978, the German label Arcade put out a charming rocket-pop concept album called *Hit Rocket: 20 Super Hits*, featuring Sweet's "Stairway to the Stars," "Magic Fly" by Space, and "Star Wars Theme" by Nova (not as amusing as Bill Murray's *Saturday Night Live* version, which had words).

Slick's 1979 "Space Bass" was seven minutes of flatulent Eurodisco philharmonics and techno-tribal beats, plus wisdom from a freefalling girl's voice about how "time ain't no faster than the funky speed of sound." Which theorem was perhaps best illustrated on the front cover of Sheila and B. Devotion's 1980 *Spacer* album, which depicts an Italian woman parachuting past pteradactyls, and on the back, where she and her all-black band wear astronaut suits. Inside, her nervous little accent floats effortlessly between asteroids of Nile Rodgers guitar chaos, pledging eternal love to her "star chaser" boyfriend, contacting ground control with phonetic-alphabet technospeak out of Bowie's "TVC15," racing toward the same doom and disaster the Electric Prunes enjoyed so much in in "Get Me To the World on Time."

After initially exploring space in their wonderful and Burundiful 1978 "Nightflight to Venus," German reggae-disco goofballs Boney M turned positively otherworldly on *Ten Thousand Light Years* in 1984. "Exodus" depicts a ride on "Noah's Ark in the year 2001," escaping our ugly dying planet for a better world. "Future World"'s drugtrip disco takes us to the same utopia, 10,000 light years away. Boney M could get away with such moody airheadedness because their artless electroglitz had both sweet prayerful beauty and nonstop hooks. Also, because no one took them seriously, though they were maybe the biggest group in the non-English-speaking world, from South Africa to Thailand, and beyond: in 1992, Frank Kogan was watching cable and saw a

Japanese group segue Boney's "Hooray! Hooray! (It's a Holi-Holiday)" into Lobo and Herman's Hermits oldies; later that year, Peter Manuel's notes to Indian soundtrack composer Vijaya Anand's not-Boney-influenced-enough *Dance Raja Dance* observed how, on the streets of Bombay and New Delhi, "pirate Boney M cassettes share space with medieval folk ballads."

Afrika Bambaataa and Soul Sonic Force scored in 1982 with "Planet Rock," briefly inspiring such wacky astrobeatbox breakdances as "Space Cowboy" by Jonzun Crew, "Jam On It" by Newcleus, and "Scorpio" by Grandmaster Flash (the last of which featured bedspring Prophet-synth noise anticipating late-'80s Chicago acid-house records like Phuture's time-traveling-Klingon-recited meteor-shower-and-laser-gun mantra "Phuture Will Survive"). "Planet Rock" itself was all electrosputter, built from Pac-Man beats on not-quite-learned-yet Roland-and-Fairlight-brand studio gadgets. Evil robot-froggy voices leap in, real random-like, and at the end, a spacecraft takes off.

In 1987, Guns N' Roses let loose "Rocket Queen," whose beat came courageously close to disco—Ann Marlowe reported in *L.A. Weekly* that more than a few African-American session musicians hailed drummer Steven Adler's fondness for 16th notes, missing-in-action rockwise since disco scared rock guys away from dancebeats in the mid-'70s. The rhythm section shifts into an unbeatable funk break halfway through; Axl Rose could easily rap over it, but instead a girl climbs toward the heights of intercoursal passion, like so many disco dollies before her. She could be the rocket queen, but Axl doesn't talk about her, really. So I think the queen is him— "Axl's voice flies Sylvester-high," disco expert Michael Freedberg writes. "I think he thinks it's *hard*. In fact it's *soft. Thin. Chiffon.* But it's vast." Guns N' Roses come closer to conquering disco emotional terrain (and punk emotional terrain, which might be the same thing) than any other metal-identified rock band ever. "Standing on your own, it's such a lonely place for you to be," Axl cries, then he lets his voice lose control to scatting: his own orgasm.

Michael Jackson's "Another Part of Me," likewise from 1987, has a title not far from what Michael's fellow paranoid Axl claimed in "Don't Damn Me": "It's all a part of me." The rhythm has some violent, skidding changes—listening to it is like watching Michael dance. And the words are a message from alien intelligence, aligning heavenly bodies, sending out truth and love: "This is our planet, you're one of us." But the past decade has mainly seen space-disco and rocket-rock increasingly forfeit any verve they once had—listless English hypes like Adamski, the Orb, Spaceman 3, and Stereolab (the latter of whom can admittedly be quite pretty) make a big deal of inserting Pink Floyd's and Hawkwind's psychedelic ooze into groove music, as if disco hadn't been taking said "fusion" for granted forever.

Jet Boys in Outer Space

In 1983, German one-hit-wonder Peter Schilling had his one hit, a slice of rocket-rock etherea called "Major Tom (Coming Home)." In a *Boston Phoenix* review, disco critic Michael Freedberg made the obvious connection—to David Bowie, whose astronaut Major Tom was born in 1969's "Space Oddity," then addicted to heroin in 1980's "Ashes to Ashes." "But Schilling's jetboy messages and jetdance sound effects have more to do with Eurodisco," Freedberg wrote; Peter "simply realized Bowie's lonely-loverboy design as Eurodisco enthusiasts understand it."

Five years later, Def Leppard had a hit with their strange dub-echoed track "Rocket." Space-shuttle transmissions opened it up, then Gary Glitter's "Rock and Roll Part Two" beat came in, orbited by a concentric riff. This is the music Suede and Smashing Pumpkins and Radiohead (all of whom are better than they deserve to be) think they're making now (though Foreigner's 1977 "Starrider" actually came closer to pulling it off). A male voice in "Rocket" sets the scene like a Reuters correspondent on assignment in a Munich disco, telegraphing his observations about the light, the city, the street, the people, the time of night, the magic, the craziness. Then he catalogues what he hears: "Jet flash: Rocket Man, Sgt. Pepper in the band. Ziggy, Benny, and the Jets," then later, "G.G., Killer Queen. Dizzy Lizzy, Major Tom . . ." He tells us he's our satellite love.

Def Leppard had already done a song called "Satellite" in 1980—it was almost as good as the song called "Satellite" Vancouver bubbleproggers Prism did the same year (just like Lep's "No No No" was almost as good as Prism's "N-N-N-No!," and Lep's "Armageddon It" was almost as good as Prism's "Armageddon." Basically, Prism made late-'80s-Lep-sounding records when Lep were still sounding like early-'80s Lep, and maybe what inspired them to do so was Vancouver's underdocumented late-'70s/early-'80s new-wave disco-metal glam-survival scene starring Loverboy, Streetheart, and Sweeney Todd alumni Nick Gilder and Bryan Adams. Saga in Toronto and Aldo Nova in Montreal may well have been

distantly connected with it, too—Nova even had an astronomical last name!) The Def Leppard "Satellite" had fussy
space-drool zooming, a '70s quadrophonic headphone gim-
mick fast losing favor. Guitars and bass spun out repetitive
outer-limits loops like disco synths, or like the Sputnik cir-
cling the earth in 1957, kicking off the space age.

On *The Rise and Fall of Ziggy Stardust and the Spiders from
Mars* in 1972, Bowie had sung like an alien adrift, "like a
leper [or Leppard?] messiah," a starman waiting to meet us.
The album's deep production, otherwordly melodies, lyrical
fixation on unhuman machines (TVs, radars, electric eyes),
and flourishes of strings and guitar and incidental noise
forecast how disco would feel. His earlier "Space Oddity" was
about losing contact with reality, with ground control, in a
tin can high above the world. In '80s Germany, not only Peter Schilling but also Boney M (in "Exodus") and future
Enigma Gregorian-sex symbol Sandra (in "Celebrate the
Sky") peered down at Major Tom's earth in their lyrics (and
in their sound too), and saw it was blue.

Elton John's "Rocket Man," alluded to in "Rocket" just like
"Space Oddity," also came out in 1972; it was his first real
good hit single. (The Louisville AOR station I was sharing
lunchhour with played it the day the Challenger burned up:
how tasteful!) Elton's astronaut was a guy we could empa-
thize with, missing his wife, realizing you can't raise kids on
Mars, admitting science is Greek to him; it's just his job. "I'm
not the man they think I am at home"—at home he stays in
the closet, guarding a secret. "It's lonely here in outer
space."

"Rocket" refers to Elton's "Bennie and the Jets" as well—
named for an *imaginary* group, like the Spiders from Mars or
Sgt. Pepper's Lonely Hearts Club Band. But they wore electric boots and mohair suits anyway, and girls in my eighth-
grade gym class sat by the wall repeating "bennie and the
jetsssssss," dragging the hiss like nicotine, making themselves
seem menacing and old enough to try high school things
when I was still spooked by floor hockey. Grownups even de-
nounced Elton's trumped-up rebellion: kids fighting parents
out in the street, oh no!

"Jet flash!," Joe Elliott exclaims in "Rocket"—an urgent dispatch from our nightclub reporter in Munich. Or maybe Def Leppard's jet is meant to be flown by the jetboy the New York Dolls introduced in "Jet Boy" in 1973—same year as Bennie, year before Roxy Music quitter Brian Eno's *Here Come the Warm Jets* and Paul McCartney and Wings' yummy and ridiculous "Jet," three years before the debut of Runaways leather lolita Joan Jett, same general era as Bimbo Jet's wacky post-"Shaft"/proto-disco mambo shuffle instrumental "El Bimbo" (or maybe El Bimbo's wacky post-"Shaft"/proto-disco mambo-shuffle instrumental "Bimbo Jet," how would I know?), where some guy keeps chanting "beem-boe, beem-boe" (code for not being very heterosexual, I'm told).

The Dolls' jetboy could "fly up in the sky higher than anybody." But Johnny Thunders's fuzz-punk guitar and David Johansen's fizz-punk grammar go so off-kilter that I can never figure out what happens to Jet Boy next—only that the kid is "preoccupied," that he's got nothing to hide, that where he lives no one cares. David Johansen stutters into oblivion: "He was all endangered zone where we're having fun," sounds like. Makes almost as little sense as the Sgt. Major's daughter in "Jet" (though the Wings song does contain at least *one* familiar sentiment: "The only lonely place was on the moon").

Yet "Jet Boy" apparently meant quite a lot to *some* people—the '80s L.A. glam-sleaze band Jetboy, for instance. (Best tracks on their 1988 debut *Feel the Shake*, in case you've been wondering: "Locked in a Cage," "Talkin'," "Bad Disease.") And in 1978, British new waver Elton Motello had a dance hit with a song called "Jet Boy Jet Girl" (later covered by punk hacks the Damned, censored so it gives hell instead of head by oi! hacks Chron Gen, and sanitized into "Bad Boy Bad Girl" by '80s island-deesco beemboes Two Man Sound). Motello swiped the punk Beach Boys beat from his Belgian pal Plastic Bertrand's then-current "Ça plane pour moi" (a 1993 remake of which is Sonic Youth's funniest recording ever). But Motello turned Bertrand's happy-go-lucky foreign words slimy, chortling and snickering about some fifteen-year-old male concubine he enjoys punching, the sight of blood being a major turn-on and all. He threatens to turn his jetboy into a jetgirl. Whenever he sees the kid with some-one opposite-gendered, Motello yells out "HE GAVE ME HEAD!"

In his 1980 album track "When All the Boys Are English," Motello confessed "I don't want to be straight again/A jetboy has to play the game." In "Jet Boy Jet Girl," he'd referred to grabbing and kissing his boyfriend "on a ballroom blitz," al-luding to a classic 1975 Sweet song (which the Damned *also* covered). "Ballroom Blitz" was my favorite song my freshman year in high school because it had more energy and efferves-cence than anything else on the radio, and I don't think my tastes have changed much since. The rest of the Sweet's *Deso-lation Boulevard* had timbales, tubular bells, gongs, and syn-thesizers that split the difference between the Who and Eurodisco; "Fox on the Run" began with a UFO touchdown snatched unaltered from the Ran-Dells' 1963 sci-fi novelty "Martian Hop," and robots in "I Wanna Be Committed" called themselves "spaceage cowboys" (I betcha weren't ready for that). (Gratuitous Steve Miller allusion, sorry.) In "AC/DC," the Sweet's girlfriend might have really been a boy ("wanna see her dingaling"), or a lesbian. Or maybe just a jetgirl who does jetboys like they're jetgirls.

A Brief History of Dub-Metal

Somewhere in the middle of "Rocket," Def Leppard's Joe El-liott tells us he's taking us to the "center of the dawn" on a collision course. But this isn't hardguy cock-rock muscle mu-sic—it's light, *feminine* almost. There's a strange montage that melts into a dub section, then backwards vocals sampled from a different song on the same *Hysteria* album. The vo-cals work as individual piano notes, as a synthesizer, as ex-tending devices—Joe told me that the track was three minutes long when he left the studio once, eight minutes when he came back. Instruments drop in and out, count-down commences, then liftoff.

A pop-metal song is hardly where you'd expect to find dub music, so I wonder where it came from. Was producer (and future Shania Twain husband) Mutt Lange a closet reggae fan? And if so, *why*? Most dub (which deserves to be pro-nounced "doob" but isn't) floats way too flimsily and shape-lessly toward the twilight zone for my ground-grounded ears. The dub albums that lasted longest in my collection before I got rid of them were Lee "Scratch" Perry and Dub Syndi-cate's *Time Boom and de Devil Dead*, Suns of Arqa's *Vol. 5* (a major inspiration for acid house, legend has it), and a couple Adrian Sherwood anthologies, and I still haven't determined if "trip-hop" is the new imaginary genre that bores me stiff exactly like Sherwood wound up boring me, or if "jungle" is. I listened to the Augustus Pablo records I used to own even less; ditto for Burning Spear's allegedly surfish *Garvey's Ghost*. Dr. Alimantado's *The Best Dressed Chicken in Town* and Tapper Zukie's *Man Ah Warrior* I *do* kind of like, but I con-sider them toasting records—more reliant on songs, beats, and voices than technology. (See, at first "dub" just meant DJs talking over reggae, but eventually it came to mean the seemingly random removal and return of vocal parts and non-bass-and-drum instruments until the music became a mere rhythmic special-effect shadow of its original self. Prince Buster suggested the sound with the title of his '60s Jamaican "Ghost Dance," which had burps in it but no black-outs yet.)

Certain art bands I've "appreciated" at tonedeaf stages in my rock-critic career have used dub one way or another: the Mekons, Membranes, E.S.G., Ruts, Mark Stewart. Also, from the louder-guitar side of the fence, Young Gods, Bad Brains, Celtic Frost, Butthole Surfers, Faith No More, Blind Idiot God, Pankow, A.R. Kane, KMFDM. Not to mention opera-sludge drudges Armoured Saint, who for the first eight seconds of their 1984 Metal Blade debut EP played basslines that sounded exactly like "Albatross" by Public Image Ltd. Essential Logic ("Bod's Message"), Einstürzende Neubauten ("Yü Gung"), the Fall ("Marquis Cha Cha"), Killing Joke ("Change"), Chain Gang (*Mondo Manhattan*), the Clash (side six of *Sandinista!*), and the Slits (*The Peel Sessions*) had somewhat more memorable moments. Given their months' worth of psychedelic-effect drumbeat-delay, the Chambers Brothers' "Time Has Come Today," Black Sabbath's "FX," Led Zeppelin's "Whole Lotta Love," and Funkadelic's *Funkadelic* album are *pre-dub* dub-metal, maybe.

Circa the end of the '70s, *Village Voice* critic Robert Christgau brainstormed that dub and heavy metal "share certain affinities," though he never explained *which* affinities. My guesses: noise, slowness, apocalypse, marijuana use, cumbersome basslines. Patti Smith tapped both genres on her early albums, even rewriting Prince Buster's "Ghost Dance." And Public Image Ltd. wound up offering further connections on 1980's *Metal Box*, making random clatter and disco-obsessive bass-and-drum murk radiant by tying Johnny Rotten's immortal sneer to the most gorgeous art-rock melodies of all time. Pere Ubu did okay, too, especially in "(Pa) Ubu Dance Party" on the aptly named *Dub Housing*—post-surfboard garage-rock filtered through Lee Perry's and Dr. Caligari's respective houses of mirrors. (Dr. Caligari being an evil magician in some silent German horror movie from 1919 I slept through once, referenced in another Ubu song on the same album—I'm just *showing off*, okay?)

Be that as it may, none of this stuff is anything Def Leppard would be likely to have heard, and even if they did, it's doubtful they took note of it. The dub use in "Rocket" seems closer to how *dance* acts used it throughout the '80s: that is,

as an incidental remix-style-hook additive. The trend probably dates back to late-'70s/early-'80s acts on the reg-
gae/disco cusp (Boney M, Eddy Grant, Linx, Grace Jones,
Goombay Dance Band, Hot Chocolate, Stevie Wonder); one
of the wildest examples was USA-European Connection's
1978 "Come Into My Heart," which also had some wicked
jazz piano. On the other hand, there *were* isolated instances
of dub-like echo popping up on AOR songs around the same
time—in the Stones' "Emotional Rescue," Loverboy's "It
Don't Matter," Queen's "Another One Bites the Dust," Kix's
"Walking Away," and Rush's "Overture" to *2112* (as in 300
years after 1812, as in Tchaikovsky doing rocket-rock, dude!),
plus a whole precinct's worth of tracks by the Police.

We're getting warmer, but I doubt we're quite at "Rocket"'s
dub root yet. Frankly, echo was happening in rock music
long before pot-smokers invented dub; maybe even before
they invented *rock*—in the early '50s, Johnnie Bomba's Orchestra recorded an "Echo Polka" which became the theme
music for the favorite radio-hour of my wife's Indiana *bushi*
(Polish for "grandma"). Then in 1956, Stan Freberg's version
of "Heartbreak Hotel," which actually hit number 76 on the
charts, parodied Elvis Presley's reverberation-use and credited Mammoth Cave for it.

By the '70s, Gary Glitter (called "G.G." in "Rocket") was
frequently using dubbish blackouts to trail guitar notes, mir-
roring his parentheses in titles like "Do You Wanna Touch
Me (Oh Yeah)" and "Didn't Know I Loved You ('Til I Saw
You Rock And Roll)." Gary's fellow glamsters the Sweet had
a few dub breakdowns too. And even more important might
be stage actor David Essex's chart-scaling 1974 hit "Rock
On," which I remember kids singing on the bus on the way
to Our Lady of Refuge, and the title of which Def Leppard
themselves quote in "Rock of Ages." "Rock On" was a feast
of heart-murmur electronics, disco-ready strings, and Jimmy
Dean hair tonic, atop a techno-Latin bump. Essex shouts
"dee-jay!" like Neneh Cherry would in "Buffalo Stance" in
1989 and "hey kids summertime blues" like R.E.M. would in
"Drive" in 1992. (And Def Leppard's "Hysteria" has the same

guitar melody as "Drive" by *the Cars*, what a small world!) In the end, echo swallows David Essex's song whole.

I don't think Essex and Glitter were necessarily reggae fans, but I do think that glam and reggae shared a common root—reggae was invented when Jamaicans played Fats Domino's beat backwards because their radio reception was fuzzy, and Frank Kogan has suggested that certain Slade songs (especially "Take Me Back 'Ome" and the Mardi Gras transvestite romp "Gudbuy T'Jane," sounds like to me) used a New-Orleans-influenced rhythm ("how the beat dances around eighth-notes, not quarter-notes," whatever that means.) Slade also used handclaps as polyrhythm, and covered a song by Crescent City R&B duo Shirley & Lee once.

What's even more interesting is that England's skinhead culture, from which Slade (then the almost-bald "Ambrose Slade") arose, was obsessed with such pre-reggae forms as ska and rocksteady way back to the mid-'60s. Skins wore black work boots, suspenders, and real short hair in reaction against the brightly clad Carnaby Street mod scene, and if it's weird to think of a culture as flamboyant and open to difference as glam evolving out of a culture as drab and closed to the same as skinheads, well, it wasn't any direct progression. Still: by 1977 the Clash were stealing laddish/loutish Slade/Glitter soccer-shout choruses (just like World Cup fans Leppard would in "Rock Brigade" and "Rock of Ages"), and from there they somehow started covering Eddy Grant reggae songs. And they namedrop not just cool Jah operators Dillinger, Leroy Smart, and Delroy Wilson in "White Man in Hammersmith Palais," but also "old Bowie" and Gary Glitter himself in "Clash City Rockers." My theory is that Glitter might have introduced both Def Leppard *and* the Clash to dub reggae.

And the Clash aren't even the best example. The most glam-influenced by far of the early British punk bands was Generation X, who grew up on exactly the same '70s rock Def Leppard did—Joe Elliott told me the only thing that made his band "metal" and Billy Idol's band "punk" was that Lep knew how to play (though I bet they really just had bigger amps). The 1978 debut album *Generation X* featured glam-style tribal drums, and the band wore glam eye makeup—check the cover of 1979's *Valley of the Dolls*, produced by glitter icon Ian Hunter. The power ballad "Friday's Angels" was Mott/Dolls-type empathy for sweet killer queens in drag with their faces painted—not punks, *glitter* boys. Generation X liked reggae, too. They were the first punk band to record a echoplexed version of one of their songs, namely the "Wild Youth" doppelganger "Wild Dub."

And Billy Idol and Joe Elliott and Joe Strummer weren't the only fresh-faced British schoolkids listening to Gary Glitter in 1972. Adam Ant and Bow Wow Wow ripped off Glitter's sound wholesale, and in the 1976 song "Little Lover" by AC/DC (some of whom were born in Scotland not Australia), Bon Scott slavered "You had my picture on your bedroom wall next to Gary Glitter." Pete Shelley's affection for "Rock and Roll Part 2" never surfaced in his late-'70s band the Buzzcocks, but he came out of the closet with his New Romantic Burundi stomp "Homo Sapien" in 1981. The A-side was the alternative-lifestyle answer to Chuck Berry's brownskin metaphor "Brown Eyed Handsome Man"; the B-side, natch, was a dub mix. Slade and Gary Glitter had made the ultimate fist-pumping boys-together music, and by which parts of their bodies boys *got* together was the boys' own choice.

So let's take one last leering glimpse at those ballroom-blitzing Jet Boys. "1981 in Britain," Simon Frith wrote in *New York Rocker* early that year, "has so far meant a boys' club revival. The Blitz Kids found their first stalking ground in gay discos, on narcissistic male-only dance floors." Meanwhile across town, oi! lads were putting suspenders back on and shaving their scalps, beating up gays and Pakistanis and West Indian blacks, and shouting the shouts Slade had passed down to them through the Clash. Both movements were for boys, both had similar roots, both were used to escape Margaret Thatcher's dole Hell.

In April, riots started in Brixton, a part of London where unemployed blacks threw all-night reggae parties. Looting and burning were extensive by July, and such cueballed combos as 4 Skins and Punjabis fanned the flames. The number-one single in England was an artsy anti-fascist dirge with melodic ideas from German cabarets and Persian Gulf casbahs, though its graveyard mood had been anticipated by both Lionel Belasco's 1936 calypso instrumental "Depression-pasillo" and the Wailers' 1972 reggae weeper "Concrete Jungle." It was holepunched with dub, which the band's Caucasian members might've learned from Gary Glitter. Its B-side was the sing-songy singalong "Friday Night Saturday Morning," the title possibly a reference to Alan Sillitoe's novel *Saturday Night and Sunday Morning*, the *On the Road* of Britain's beatnik-era Angry Young Man counterculture. But on the A-side, called "Ghost Town," the singer moaned about young people fighting each other and danceclubs closing down. The group was the Specials, the mixed-race frontrunners in England's short-lived post-punk ska revival. The record's sleeve pictured two skeletons sitting down, one at a grand piano.

It's hard *not* to be inspired by music like that, and outside England, the inspiration never stopped detonating. In the '90s, it's been a major trend for outfits in Romance-language locations (Los Rodriguez and Um Pah Pah from Spain, Indochine and Mano Negra from France, La Derecha from Colombia, Desorden Publico from Venezuela, Chico Science and his band Nação Zumbi—whose "Côco Dub" is what "jungle music" *should* be: Fela Kuti riding a satellite into space—from Brazil) to make reggae and dub rock hard. The Clash and Jamaican toaster Big Youth help out on CDs by Argentina's Los Fabulosos Cadillacs, who regularly bounce Mariachi-chatter reggae into skinhead moshpit pogos—"V Centenario" is an unfettered hybrid of punky Specials-style ska with "America" from *West Side Story*. "Mi rumba tarumba" by Spain's Seguridad Social kicks its Latin (rhumba I guess) syncopation the way the Clash might've if they'd attempted *Sandinista!*'s worldbeat jackoff in 1977 instead of 1981. And Mexico's Maldita Vecindad y Los Hijos Del 5° Patio turn world rhythms—not just reggae, but also *norteño*, Algerian rai, calypso, polka, South African guitars—into jump rock the way early-'80s British two-tone bands like the Specials (who were faster and catchier *before* "Ghost Town") used to with ska (and like the Pogues for a few months in 1985 with Irish jigs).

In 1995, four good-natured California ballroom-blitzers with ridiculous glam-dyed Mohawks made the best Specials album ever and best Clash album in sixteen years (since 1979's U.S. version of *The Clash*, which I've always preferred to 1977's U.K. one, but then I'm a new waver not a punk). Coincidentally enough, Rancid's previous album *Let's Go* had been the best *oi!* album ever, which by definition means it was about ten times as fun as the best hardcore album ever (there's a difference—even blatant Rancid wannabees like Bouncing Souls and Suicide Machines bring more hardiness to the party than most of the mythic zit-tantrums puked up in '80s Los Angeles). Where the Clash had forfeited the speedy urgency they were born with by the time they expanded their sonic boundaries on 1980's *London Calling*, Rancid's gutturally slurred tube-station tour-diary shouts on 1995's . . . *And Out Come the Wolves*, finally given room to breathe amid all the punk-drunk claustrophobia, communicated a warmly plainspoken empathy and battering-ram tunefulness that never let up. Nobody since Guns N' Roses on *Appetite For Destruction* had written rock songs so rocking or so specific, and no Americans had ever mined so much effortless power out of Jamaican rhythms.

On the Run

Cars and trains and rockets are all used either to get *to* somewhere or get *away from* somewhere, and the screwy thing about rock'n'roll is that the only time the aimless sonuvabitch ever lets you accomplish the first of these objectives is by trying first to accomplish the second. That is, this music isn't really concerned with *arriving*, just with *going*. Escaping has been an inescapable goal of rock'n'roll ever since the glory days of Sojourner-Truth-or-whoever and her underground railroad.

About the only time its protagonists seem to care much about where they end up is in rock's longstanding post-Stephen-Foster-doing-"My Old Country Home" tradition of "going back to find a simpler place and time"-type roots-as-moral-imperative lyrics: Gladys Knight and the Pips' "Midnight Train to Georgia," Lionel Richie's "Stuck on You" and "Sail On" (the former *also* involving leaving on a midnight train, the latter done with the Commodores, and both significantly rural-sounding), the Beatles' "Get Back" (where they significantly quote Chuck Berry's car-escape ditty "You Can't Catch Me"), the Judds' "John Deere Tractor" (a letter from sick-of-New-York-perfume newlywed Wynona to Naomi back where the bluegrass grows), Dionne Warwick's "Do You Know the Way to San Jose?", John Denver's "Take Me Home Country Roads," pot-smoking bebop hillbilly Smokey Wood's 1937 "Carry Me Back To Virginny" (where he pretends to be a "darkie" who misses laboring "so hard for old massah"— hey, *I* didn't write it!).

Chuck Berry sang about returning back-where-he-started–from both in "Back in the U.S.A." and "Havana Moon," paving the way for the Beatles' and Richard Berry's later respective yearnings for the Soviet Union and Jamaica in "Back in the U.S.S.R." and "Louie Louie." But though Chuck wasn't immune to nostalgia (see also "The Things I Used To Do," "Childhood Sweetheart," "Time Was"), mainly he hail-hailed rock'n'roll as something that could deliver him *from* the days of old.

A rule: where you're *not* is always better than where you *are*. It's sort of like how '50s Situationist International founder Guy Debord "detourned" his Paris street maps to suggest a "random" ballet through the avenues—those Sits were really big on "drift," Greil Marcus says—except rock is even *more* random about it. No doubt realizing that it's impossible to be completely autonomous since we're inevitably controlled by our genes and environs, the best rock music doesn't even worry about a streetmap in the first place, except maybe one that'll make money. Otherwise, it lets the chips fall where they may.

Don't believe me? Consider the profusion of fate rock (or predetermination rock), as opposed to free-will rock. In the "fate" category you get Van Halen ("roll with the punches to get to what's real"), B.J. Thomas ("I'm never gonna stop the rain by complainin'"), the Supremes ("there ain't nothin' I can do about it"). Plus crapshoot crap from the Rolling Stones ("roll with the tumbling dice"), Yoko Ono ("I'm paying the price for throwing the dice in the air"), Lloyd Price ("Stagger Lee," where Billy Lyon pays the price for *literally* throwing the dice in the air), Jim Croce ("Bad Bad Leroy Brown," the baby-boom "Stagger Lee"), Jerry Reed ("When You're Hot You're Hot," the redneck-minstrel "Stagger Lee," except this time Stagger spends welfare bucks on a Cadillac). Bob Seger brags he "learned to spin fortune wheels and throw dice when I was just 13" in "Ramblin' Gamblin' Man" and complains that "you always won every time you placed a bet" in "Still the Same." And cardgame rock definitely fits as fate in most cases—for instance, the Bobby Brown line "don't know where my cards may fall." Steamroller-lipped diva Taylor Dayne's best album is called *Can't Fight Fate*; the title track, written by the universally despised Dianne Warren, theorizes that "you can run but you can't run away."

Free will anthems include two songs *called* "Free Will," both by ruggedly libertarian high-pitched Canadians: Rush ("if you choose not to decide you still have made a choice") and Prism. Plus Michael Jackson's *Free Willy* movie theme "Will You Be There," plus a bunch called either "(It's) My Life" or "(It's) Your Life" (by Sylvester, Loverboy, the Animals, Billy Joel, Corina, Will To Power, Konk, Smokie). For quantity, and for the overall *thought* they've given the issue, the fatemongers win hands down. Grandmaster Flash and the Furious Five have a song called "Freedom"; it tells you to "do the freak dance, become a victim of circumstance." So to them, "freedom" 's just another word for becoming a victim of circumstance!

Anyway, rock'n'roll is too *paranoid* to feel free. '60s gloom-punks the Music Machine worried in "Talk Talk" about "what everybody has against me," and Axl Rose sings "Out Ta Get Me," and Chuck D thinks his phone is tapped (probably by rock critics and urban-contemporary disc jockeys!). In "Mind Playing Tricks on Me," rap's Geto Boys can't sleep at night because of bodies being burned and can't drive because the guy they shot last week might be shining his headlights. And then there's Michael Jackson. He checks into "Heartbreak Hotel" in 1980, people act like they know him, "this is *scaring* me," he winces, turning back into a little kid. "Every smile's a trial thought in beguile to hurt me," he says. "Hope is dead." In "Beat It" boys kick him and beat him then tell him it's fair; in "Billie Jean" a girl's on his tail 'cause the rabbit done died; in "Speed Demon" there's cops in his rear view mirror as he's headed for the border like Thelma and Louise; in "Dirty Diana" an evil temptress locks him up and loses the key; in "Smooth Criminal" a hoodlum smashes through a window on the Sabbath day leaving bloodstains on the carpet; in "Somebody's Watching Me" (which Motown magnate Berry Gordy's son Rockwell barely missed going number-one with in 1983 and which Michael sings backup on and I bet wrote most of the words and melody of), he has no privacy because nobody'll leave him alone. If all that ain't enough to make you grab your crotch and demolish car windshields with a tire iron, what is?

So rockers stay on the run. They are transients, ne'er-do-wells, fugitives, steady rollin' ramblin' gamblin' back door men on the lost highway, blowing down the dirt trail like the Dust Bowl dust, checking into fleabag motels under assumed names. They've always sung about road life and interstate love affairs, and always will. Woody Guthrie did it, and Hank

Williams all the time. The Drifters didn't do it much, but they called themselves Drifters anyway. (Not unlike the Rolling Stones.)

"I'm a trouble shooter, movin' down the line," Marvin Gaye boasts in "Trouble Man" in 1972, reinventing the blues as orchestrated R&B soundtrack shlock; in 1980's "Searching," the group Change go further, turning blues into Italodisco but keeping the walking basslines and downtrodden harmonicas, still singing about making a home wherever they find a light on. "I'd like to settle down but they won't let me," Merle Haggard drawls. "He who travels fastest goes alone." His gipsy road can't take him home. Don't look back Merle, they might be gaining on you.

And what do you need before you can escape? You need a *trap*, of course, and you need to be inside it. Trap-rock has its own history, dating back to Robert Johnson in "Crossroads" in 1936, standing at a dirt intersection with his thumb out, but nobody stopping to pick him up; same story decades later in "The Message," where the Furious Five try to get away from the ghetto but can't get far because their car's been repossessed by Prudential. Likewise the Animals in "We Gotta Get Out Of This Place," Martha and the Vandellas in "Nowhere to Run," Gene Pitney in "Town Without Pity" ("we're like tigers in a cage"), Claudine Clark in "Party Lights" (stuck in her room while there's a party across the street), Alice Cooper in "Ballad of Dwight Fry" (where a little sanitarium voice goes "I gotta get outta here I gotta get outta here I gotta get outta here").

Early '60s girl trio the Cookies (in "Chains") and frequent Oprah Winfrey guest Michael Bolton (in "Steel Bars") even imagine traps they don't *want* to escape from. In "D.O.A." (named after Vancouver's leading hardcore band!), Vancouver's Loverboy dismiss the U.S.A. because "all they got down there is liberty." In "What Have I Done to Deserve This?," spurned Pet Shop Boys wonder how they'll get through, now that they can do what they want to forever. (My buddy Tina confessed to me once that she often plays dominants-versus-submissives trivial pursuit in American On-Line's named-for-*The Story of "O"* Le Chateau computer chat room. I forgot to ask her whether the dominants ever let the submissives win.) "If only I could scold you I'd forget how it feels to be free," a confused Debbie Gibson reasons in "Only in My Dreams." The chains and handcuffs Corina, Boney M, and Isaac Hayes bind themselves with on select record covers might work as metaphors for similarly desirable traps. As, perhaps, does the entire subschool of masochism rock: the Crystals' "He Hit Me (and it Felt Like a Kiss)," Samantha Fox's "(Hurt Me! Hurt Me!) But the Pants Stay On," John Cougar's "Hurts So Good," Faster Pussycat's "Where There's A Whip There's a Way," Devo's "Whip It," Velvet Underground's "Venus in Furs," Madonna's "Hanky Panky," X-Ray Spex's "Oh Bondage Up Yours!," the Andrews Sisters' "Beat Me Daddy Eight To the Bar." And above all, "Bad Boy" by Ray Parker Jr.: "Spank me, whoop me . . . break out the leather, baby!"

Inherent in escape is fear (of what you're running from—or maybe you're just bored by it, or maybe you did something wrong), but also courage (to start a new life). These are the seeds of bohemianism (escape from structured suburbs to structured seediness, heh heh), but also the seeds of suburbanism itself ("white flight," remember?) Escape one trap, you'll wind up in another soon enough. And the rockets jet-boys sing about are like drugs, or suicide. (See also Flaming Lips: "I want my own planet, 'cause this one here is a drag." Or Steely Dan: "Any world that I'm welcome to is better than the one I come from.")

Usually it's not quite as drastic as all that, of course. Rock's *real* escape-route roots dwell more in the time-honored American tradition of Running Away From Home, like Tom Sawyer, even Dorothy in *The Wizard of Oz*. The daddy of all runaway-rock songs is Dion's 1960 "Lonely Teenager, " about an absolute wimp ("I know I'll be alright if I stay out of sight") who's been surviving on the backstreets for a year. Next came Del Shannon's "Runaway," about being in love with one (just like lots of '80s pop-metal tunes!) but also a rain-soaked and misery-strewn dirge that's at least as much a real-life-suicide harbinger as anything Joy Division or Nirvana ever did—Del shot himself in 1990.

Next, in 1965, the *mother* of them all: "I Can Never Go Home Anymore," where the Shangri-Las create a title from the last line of Gene Pitney's 1963 runaway-husband beer-drainer "Twenty Four Hours From Tulsa," paint their faces with Hallmark Card classical melodrama, and remember back when mom used to tuck them in bed. They left because Ma wouldn't leave 'em alone, because every day was the same, because a boy came along. ("And that's called 'glad.'") But though these street-smart hussies ask their audience if their story sounds familiar, they also scream "Mama!!" from the abyss. It's a warning to kids that it's *hell* out there in the world—a veritable *moral lesson*.

Maybe the Shangri-Las were worried that they'd infected some impressionable young minds with "Give Us Your Blessings" earlier that year—a song where a boy and girl decide to elope. "Give Us Your Blessings" starts with a weird raga chant: "Mary run run run, Jimmy run run run, Mary run run run, Jimmy run run run." The Supremes had done a song called "Run Run Run" in 1964, and before that the Coasters had their "Stagger Lee"-like racial allegory "Run Red Run" and Chuck Berry had "Run Rudolph Run," about a reindeer. Two years *after* "Give Us Your Blessings," the Velvet Underground did a *new* song called "Run Run Run," which begat the "run Joey, Joey run run" hook in the 1968 bubblegum hit "Quick Joey Small" by the Kasenatz-Katz Singing Orchestral Circus. Which begat Jo Jo Gunne's grungy fugitive boogie stomp "Run Run Run" in 1972, which begat David Geddes's godawfully absurd "Run Joey Run," number-four chartwise in 1975. Starts with entombed Shangri-Las-type mourning, so go ahead and write it off as parody: a dad tries to shoot his daughter's boyfriend, but he kills the girl by mistake. Honest!

But I digress. The Temptations' "Runaway Child (Running Wild)" hit the stores in 1969, predating "Papa Was A Rolling Stone" by making Junior roll instead. This was in the Tempts' corny dress-like-hipsters stage, when they wore Fedoras and yellow bellbottoms. They sang about a kid running away 'cause Mom punishes him for playing hookey, and now he's scrambling "through the city, going nowhere fast." (You remember Nowhere, don't you?) Like they said (about white flight!) in "Ball of Confusion" the next year: "Run, run, run but you sho can't hide." Or Sly Stone, "Runnin' Away," 1971, in a squeak that could've come from squeaky-clean girl-group girls scolding a lost unwashed pal: "Look at you foolin' you . . . You're wearing out your shoes."

The first rock band to consistently look at runaways as heroines, I think, was the New York Dolls. David Johansen sang about Babylon girls without a past, growing up fast, and his bad girls and mystery girls and jetboys and girlboys making it with Frankenstein were all the same sort of trash, almost all throwaways; at the end of "Lonely Planet Boy," he quotes "Runaway" by Del Shannon. He established a new way to do things, and you can find it everywhere there's a mascara brush handy since: Mott the Hoople's "Whizz Kid" ("a New York City beat" with a punk dad and drunk mom), the Pink Fairies' "Street Urchin," David Bowie's "Rebel Rebel" and maybe "Jean Genie," Elton John's "Dirty Little Girl," Iggy's "Billy is a Runaway."

The cherries topping this '70s sundae belonged to Joan Jett and the Runaways themselves, who played the strays all the transvestite bands longed to take home—not being able to stay at home or school in "Cherry Bomb," gawking at freezing homeless guys in "Is It Day or Night," stealing cars and breaking hearts and taking pills and finally winding up in a "rundown teenage jail" in the ludicrous street opera "Dead End Justice."

Prole deities Slade and AC/DC gave badgirl rock a lovable twist in shouts like their respective "Standin' on the Corner" and "Whole Lotta Rosie," where they male-comraderied with potbellied white-trash tramps of the alleyways as if said dames were just some of the boys. (Unlike, say, Pete Townshend in "The Kids Are Alright," who says if she ain't one of the boys he don't wanna hang out with her.) Slade (whose later "Run Runaway" wasn't about runaways in any way I can figure out, by the way) just wanted somebody for skweeeeezing, somebody big enough to keep 'em warm in winter, a "sure shottin' shimmy shootin' hi falutin' rootin' tootin' lady, yeah." Bon Scott and Noddy Holder must surely be applauded by all feminists for rejecting accepted Western standards of female attractiveness.

Ditto for Michael Martin Murphy, whose object of desire in his 1975 top-five "Wildfire" happens to be a runaway *horse*. Said stallion may well have inspired John Lydon to neigh "run ahhh-way run ahhh-way" through "Albatross" by Public Image Ltd (which ended with a Roy Orbison "Only the Lonely" quote). That was in 1980, the same year another would-be corporation, Lipps Inc., went number-one with "Funkytown," which illustrated packing for a new home with a telegraphed chant that went "gotta move on . . . gotta move on . . . gotta move on." UK electrotweeters Bronski Beat crossed PiL's "run away" chant with Gino Soccio's swirly 1978 Montreal disco "The Runaway" in 1984's "Smalltown Boy," about a gay kid fleeing *his* hick burg. But in John Mellencamp's comparably titled 1985 "Small Town," Coug "married an L.A. doll and brought her to this small town," reversing a major motif.

See, the *real* trend in the '80s, as anybody hooked up to cable at the time ought to realize, was how Nerf-metal acts (mostly Los Angeles ones) carried on the N.Y. Dolls tradition, mainly by having small town dolls move *to* L.A.: Poison ("Fallen Angel," "Bad to be Good"), Precious Metal ("Emily"), Vixen (the Shangri-Las update "Hard 16"), Tesla ("Little Suzi"), Ratt ("Dance"), Girlschool ("Nowhere to Run," "Running Wild," "Running for Cover"), Pat Benatar ("Invincible," from the runaway movie *Legend of Billie Jean*), Aerosmith ("Janie's Got a Gun," about a teenage girl sexually abused by her asshole father: "run away, run away from the pain"). Mostly these were totally exploitive, which mostly made them fun. Faster Pussycat littered "Smash Alley" with "lipstick, junkies, and runaways," not to mention an exquisite "Batman" riff. Britny Fox's 1988 "Girlschool," one of '80s MTV's hardest-rocking hits, revives an old Dolls character: "Bad Girl, smokin' in school," breaking rules and popping ludes. Warrant's funkish and pretty "Down Boys," from the same year, is proto-bohemian—Dion's lonely teen sits at home, whining "I wanna go where the down boys go," so he's obviously not a down boy himself, at least not yet; he just worships the wild street kids who head out at a million miles an hour. The synth lines come from the Police, via "The Spirit of Radio," a Rush song which mimics the Velvet Underground's "Sweet Jane." And Warrant's guitarist plays "Sweet Jane" chords.

Weird, because if anything "Sweet Jane" was the Velvets' anti-wildchild number, the one where Lou Reed complained about evil mothers who thought everything was dirt and life was just to die. (Or maybe he was being ironic, but I'll give him the benefit of the doubt.) And that's a tradition itself, of course, anti-decadent cynicism stretching from Dylan's "Desolation Row" (with its girl for whom death was romantic and whose "sin was lifelessness") to the Dolls' "Looking For a Kiss" (where all the kids are shooting up and "so obsessed with gloom") to Frank Kogan's 1982 "Stars Vomit Coffee Shop" ("the stars let it go to hell as they express their inner self"). (Kogan also believes the escape song Kurt Cobain always wanted to write was "Get Away" by Flipper, whose T-shirt Kurt wore on *Saturday Night Live*: "Her life is all fucked up/She says she's gotta get away.")

One of the toughest sermons ever about the dark side of leaving home came in 1985 from rapper Spoonie Gee. (And unless you count U-Roy's reggae-toasted 1975 "Runaway Girl," where are all the *other* runaway-rap classics? I can't think of any. Maybe in a genre that takes growing up on the street for granted such thoughts are unthinkable. But what about rappers from *suburbia*?) Spoonie's "Street Girl" starts out on the wrong foot, arguing that all such women are alike, except for their names. And Spoonie's known all of 'em, and they're always begging for a "hit." The music is hard James Brown funk with creaky nuclear blips (synth noise like on Pere Ubu's early singles), and when Spoonie blames one such woman for turning a good man into a fugitive, the funk gets blacker, echoing into a dublike hole.

Street Girl spurned this guy, see, but somehow he convinces her to visit him anyhow. She lays down, he starts thinking crazy, and instead of taking her clothes off he puts two bullets through her body. But then Spoonie suddenly switches his third-person narrative to first, saying he carried a rose to her grave, praying she'd been granted salvation from eternal hellfire. (I believe we call that "blaming the victim.") She "played the game one too many"—just like in *Looking for Mr. Goodbar*.

Spoonie says his Street Girl likes bright lights and has never worked nine to five—she sounds like one of the women Donna Summer sang about on her two great double albums, *Once Upon a Time* in 1977 and *Bad Girls* in 1979. On *Once Upon A Time*, one song's called "Working the Midnight Shift"; on the front of *Bad Girls*, Donna's posed next to a street light. The first album outlines where street people (many of whom wound up as disco people) come from. Donna refers to a girl with dead dreams and no mom or dad who care enough about her to pay attention to what's bugging her, and nobody else at home to turn to. In "Bad Girls" on the album of the same name, girls like this one wind up in Hollywood, trying to be a star; the same thing happens in "Sunset People." They come from all over the country.

It's a Riot on Sunset Strip, a real exciting one: "Friday night and the Strip is hot." People try to make their fast living last, but they're all heading "Faster and Faster to Nowhere." And a "fast train to nowhere" is what Lester Bangs called *heavy metal*, and it's what Axl Rose sings about in "Nightrain." I mean, think about it—*Appetite for Destruction* and "One in a Million" are Donna Summer revisited. They're about kids leaving homes in middle America for the Strip, where maybe they'll be discovered, but all they find is a party jungle. In the version of "Faster and Faster" on 1978's *Live and More*, a voice yells "help me get outta here, I need helllllp!" like Alice Cooper in "Ballad of Dwight Fry" (an apparent inspiration for "One in a Million"'s melody) as Donna warns us to steer clear of the evil that makes kids scream in remote alleys at night. In "Bad Girls," Donna tells a streetwalker that the two of them are both the same except for the names they use (just like in the Spoonie Gee song), but she could just as well be addressing Axl—their ballads both kick in and rock out with lush acoustic guitars and pianos, they both put sex moans above hard dance beats, they both imitate Janis Joplin's wail (listen to Donna's "My Baby

Understands"), they both wound up as homophobes: Axl in "One in a Million," Donna when she was born again and spoke of AIDS as God's revenge on the first audience she ever had.

"If you flaunt it you can make them want it," Donna says. "All that glitter can turn into gold." And she's not talking to Hollywood mascara-metal bands and their groupies exactly, but she *could* be—"Sunset People" mentions "rock'n'roll every night" by name, and places it at the Rainbow and the Whiskey. Donna's Sunset people are the "streetlight people" the ghost of Sam Cooke screeches through Steve Perry's teeth about in Journey's underrated 1981 "Don't Stop Believin'," where over a barroom piano and disco synthesizer and power-ballad guitar orchestrated into symphonic gorgeousness, a smalltown girl and city boy take "the midnight train to anywhere." Which is to say they take Axl's fast night train to Donna's fast nowhere, away from the lonely places they came from. They meet together in a seedy bar, learn to work hard, confront the strange faces of slimeballs on the boulevard trying to get dirty kicks. And to some extent, of course, Guns N' Roses, along with all those other Hollywood metal bands, *were* the throwaway kids Donna and Journey sang about, or they were their little brothers, or even their kids. That's how those bands met, how they came to be.

When gun-toting gay teen Ricky on the 1994 TV series *My So-Called Life* got thrown out of his house by his dad and wound up in the street, it was almost the same as what happened to a different Ricky in Skid Row's 1990 "18 and Life" video (which novelist Mary Gaitskill described as homoerotic): a boy booted out by his dad accidentally shoots his best buddy while drinking tequila, thereby messing up the rest of his so-called life.

The instrumental B-side of the Champs' eternal 1958 "Tequila" was "Train to Nowhere." And in "Nonstop to Nowhere," one of the saddest and most propulsive rock singles of 1992, Taime Downe of Faster Pussycat says he's "on the late train, got a first class ticket" to you-know-where; it's five hours past midnight, and he can't sleep. So it ought to be obvious by now that railroad-escape songs are impossible to hate, though that still didn't prevent me from getting sick of Soul Asylum's Tom-Petty-melodied woe-is-me whine "Runaway Train" in 1993 when MTV was playing it every time I switched the goddamned set on. Donna and Axl and Journey and Faster Pussycat gave me an idea of what kids might run away from, and when they might do it, and where they might be heading, and what dangerous things might happen when they get there, and what might make the adventure exciting anyway. Soul Asylum somehow forgot about all that stuff.

"Friday night and the stakes are high," Sunset Strip hairband holdovers Wildside sang in "Hang on Lucy," best track on their 1992 debut *Under the Influence*—again, like Donna Summer singing "Friday night and the Strip is hot." A different Donna, Long Island sociologist Donna Gaines, stressed in her 1991 tome *Teenage Wasteland: Suburbia's Dead End Kids* that in the '80s "homeless runaway and throwaway youth enjoyed (?!) employment in America's sexploitation industries—pornography and prostitution"; appropriately, "Hang on Lucy"'s nasty defensive swing houses empathy (I'm not being sarcastic) for a sixteen-year-old "retail slut" who'll work the streets 'til she burns in hell.

Like rhythm guitarist Izzy Stradlin' told an interviewer when GN'R were still unknowns: "L.A. is where you end up." You might leave home with manifest destiny on your mind, like the Village People (and later the Pet Shop Boys) in "Go West" or Green Day in "Westbound Sign" or Everclear in "Santa Monica," then wind up hungry and hating yourself, like Albert Hammond in "It Never Rains in Southern California" or Rancid in "Journey to the End of the East Bay": "This ain't no Mecca man, this place is fucked." Or you might be Dionne Warwick in "Do You Know the Way to San Jose?," where LA is just a "great big freeway" where would-be stars pump gas. Or Bob Seger in "Hollywood Nights," a Midwestern boy on his own—just like Indiana Axl. (Or Alice Cooper, who actually moved *east*, from Phoenix to Detroit, but in "Caught in a Dream" he's Axl sixteen years early, running from success with a pistol at his back, thumbing for rides in luxury cars, equating smiling with insanity. And "Desperado" has Axl in it too: "You're a notch and I'm a legend." Or as Donna Summer put it: "I made a spectacle of myself and it seems like the world needs me.") (And "Welcome to the Jungle" also equals the Eagles' "welcome to the Hotel California," duh.)

Greg Sandow has pointed out in the *Village Voice* that Guns N' Roses weren't technically a Sunset Strip band, and that made a difference. "Poison (older brothers of every band on the Strip) sings about a world where your parents really do lead straight-arrow lives. And that means there could really be an escape," he writes. "But Guns N' Roses (the older brothers of the underground) might tell you that your parents' world is a mess: think of 'My Michelle,' about a girl whose father is in the porno biz and whose mother does drugs. And the world you escape to is also a mess." Disease for dollars, sort of.

And to escape from disease, you need medicine. "Coma" on 1991's *Use Your Illusion I*, a great song for the first 45 seconds or so until it turns into airheaded "experimental" shit, has Axl floating away into the blackness of eternal night, crossing Alice's "Ballad of Dwight Fry" welcome-home-sanitarium joke with any number of musical chemistry classes that try to scare you at the same time they lure you in, making pharmaceuticals and whatnot simultaneously attractive and repulsive. GnR's "Mr. Brownstone" and "Nightrain" had already done the same thing in a less detached way, but "Coma" connects more to the heritage: to the smack Lou Reed uses to nullify his mind of all those politician meanies in the Velvets' "Heroin," for instance.

There are other drugs-are-life-and-death-at-the-same-time escape odes. For instance, Phuture's Chicago acid-house "Your Only Friend," from 1987, where over violently randomized synth shuffles this rumbling drill-sergeant voice (reaching way far back to the Memphis Jug Band's "take a whiff of me" in their 1930 "Cocaine Habit Blues") says he's cocaine and he can make you feel fine then make you kill for him then make you die. And Sly and the Family Stone's "Luv n' Haight" ("feel so good, don't wanna move"), Marvin Gaye's "Flying High (in the Friendly Sky)," the Temptations' "Cloud

Nine," Grandmaster Flash's "White Lines (Don't Don't Do It)," the Village People's "Ups and Downs," Jefferson Airplane's "White Rabbit." All of psychedelica, maybe. (Hell, all of honky-tonk, too: 40-proof bottles of tear-stopper.)

Nerf-metal kings Def Leppard fell off the wagon into this tradition in the very first track on their very first album— "Wasted" on *On Through the Night*. It's a funny song whether it means to be or not (certainly funnier than the dumbass Black Flag song of the same name, though not half as "way-ayay-sted" as the Donna Summer one)—wobbling drunk and stout with powerchords and microphone hooks, literally about obliterating yourself through whiskey and rye, but sounding a lot truer to teen ethos when Joe Elliott confesses that he's wasting his *time*; i.e., he's just *lazy*. And he's not only squandering time, he's wasting *money* (why waste a chance for a pun?). Joe's going crazy out of his head, and suddenly blurts out that he wishes he was dead! Then sunbeam harmonies clear the air as if it's a whole new song, and Joe asks us nicely to help him through.

Another major laziness-rock landmark (from before indie bar-rock hacks like Dinosaur Jr. and Superchunk turned singing about being lazy and sleeping-in a lot precious by making their *music* sound lazy and asleep a lot) is, again, Axl's "One in a Million" ("some say I'm lazy, ooo-weee, others say that's just me"). Which harks back to John Lennon's "Watching the Wheels" ("people say I'm lazy, dreamin' my life away") and Charlie Daniels's "Longhaired Country Boy" ("people say I'm no good, crazy as a loon" just 'cause he drinks and smokes dope all day) and the Sex Pistols' "Seventeen" ("I'm a lazy sod, I'm a lazy Sid") and Jimmy Buffett's "Margaritaville" ("Some people claim there's a woman to blame but I know it's my own damn fault") and John Mellencamp's "Crumblin' Down" ("Some people say I'm lazy, uneducated, my opinion means nothin' "). *Especially* to Mellencamp, since both he and Axl are Hoosier "small town white boy" *Cool Hand Luke* fans who brag about dancing good!

(Lazy roots: Tom T. Hall's early-'70s capital-punishment yarn "Turn it On, Turn it On, Turn it On," which invents the word "slacker"; Buster Carter and Preston Young's comical old-timey '20s "A Lazy Farmer Boy"; and the Mississippi Shieks, formed in the '30s, according to notes to their reissue CD *Stop and Listen*, when lazy farmboy Lonnie Chatmon "got tired of smellin' mule farts" so he took up square-dance fiddles instead.)

Anyway, Axl yearns to return to the green grass of Paradise City, or he wonders in "Sweet Child O' Mine" "where do we go now, where do we go now?," like the only thing certain is that we have to *go*. So as "One in a Million" starts, he escapes on a Greyhound. And at that moment he's Robert Johnson in "Me and the Devil Blues," saying his old evil spirit will catch a Greyhound bus and ride. Or he's Chuck Berry boarding a Greyhound through the "Promised Land" in 1964, leaving Norfolk, Virginny with California on his mind. Or he's the Allman Brothers in "Ramblin' Man," "born in the backseat of a Greyhound bus, rolling down Highway 41." But more than anybody (soundwise *and* plotwise), he's Rod Stewart in 1976's "The Killing of Georgie," where a smalltown boy boards a Greyhound to the big city only to get fag-bashed to death. Axl twisted the storyline around a bit, but mostly he just chose to emphasize a different character. (X's 1980 rant "Los Angeles," where a girl leaves L.A. after learning to hate all the rich people, gays, Mexicans, and "every nigger and jew," figures largely into the equation as well.)

Axl Rose is a manic-depressive, so maybe it's natural that he can't stay in one place long. His music reflects a tug-of-war between contradictory impulses, constantly and schizophrenically switching gears (verse structure, mood, point of view) mid-song—from smack-addict anger to junior-high-crush sweetness, from soul bass lines and church pianos to whistle solos and reckless asides like "I never learn" and "sha-na-na-na-na-na knees" and "you're gonna di-i-ie!!" His pre-*Appetite* Janis Joplin imitation, "Move to the City," was about an unemployed sixteen-year-old girl who fights her parents, then steals their credit card and returns to "where it all began" (Axl's always been fond of those Uterus of Eden metaphors), but all she finds there is junkies and johns and "one big pain." As for Axl, he feels like a fish out of water down here on the farm. But ain't it fun when you're always on the run, and you've broken up everything you've ever begun?

Underground Rock

In "Patience," Axl Rose doesn't like "being stuck in the ground," but in "Used to Love Her," he offs his girl and puts her there anyway. Just like the one in "My Michelle": "She used to love her heroin, but now she's underground." Or like the spelunkers in San Francisco's Cacophony Society, whose nocturnal hobby involves using flashlights to explore below-sea-level excrement disposal systems. They wear boots and pants like they're expecting a flood, not to mention several rats and maybe a couple Ninja Turtles. They mostly listen to Underground Rock:

"Dark as a Dungeon" and "Sixteen Tons," Tennessee Ernie Ford. About shoveling coal to pay the mortgage on your soul.

"Don't Sleep in the Subway," Petula Clark. A big 1967 hit, and maybe a brave argument against the other kind of "underground rock"—"You don't realize that it's all compromise."

"A Horse With No Name," America. "Ocean is a desert with its life underground and a perfect disguise above." Profound!

"I Wish I Was a Mole in the Ground," Bascom Lamar Lunsford. 1928 folksinger tunnels through mountains, climbs hills hauling forty dollar bills, warns of railroad men drinking blood like wine (just like Dylan does on *Blonde on Blonde*).

"Me and My Wine," Def Leppard. 1981 B-side whereon railroad men defy Petula Clark: say they woke up shitfaced, in the subway.

"New York Mining Disaster 1941," Bee Gees. A husband buried alive under petroleum-deposited rubble calls out for his wife.

"Outdoor Miner," Wire. Obscure 1978 U.K. novelty sequel to the Moles' obscure 1968 U.K. novelty song "We Are the Moles."

"Over You," Aaron Neville. The title has a double meaning: Aaron used to love her but he had to kill her, he had to put her six feet under. Which makes no sense, since in New Orleans corpses are buried *above* ground so they don't float in a swamp!

"Sewercide," Electric Eels. I used to blame these mid-'70s Cleveland punks for helping invent '80s indie "good guitar sound" (read: everything else sucks) rock: lopsided-to-forced rhythms, mewling lisper with a shtick. But when I finally started feeling how tense they pushed, I learned to love the mewl's stubbornness.

"Sisterhood of Africa," Midi Maxi & Efti. Wherein a girl from Eritrea (assisted by two girlfriends) recalls growing up, hiding "down to the underground" from machine guns every morning.

"Subterranean Homesick Blues," Bob Dylan. I think he got its kooky title from that "better jump down the manhole" line.

Underground, Electric Prunes. '60s Seattle grunge, peaking with the underground-enough-titled Yardbirds ripoff "Hideaway."

"Underground," Sparks. Better than Men At Work or Ben Folds Five cuts of the same name: an invitation to an exploration, high hooks squeaked atop proto-punk-disco beats "on a basement day."

"Warrior in Woolworths" and "Let's Submerge," X-Ray Spex. First "rebel of the underground" Poly Styrene literally meets her pals in the Stockwell Tube; next, they sniff out "moulton larver sulpher vapours" in a bottomless pit. As Blue Öyster Cult once put it: "the heat from below can burn your eyes out."

"Working in a Coalmine," Lee Dorsey (or Devo). Industrial, at least in the sense that the people you hear excavating iron and coke and chromium steel in the background of "Allentown" by Billy Joel are industrial.

Hey Wait, I Got a New Complaint

Jim Bouton, pitcher for the 1979 Seattle Pilots and author of *Ball Four* (which I first read when I was ten), deserves a good deal of blame for inspiring me to be a writer: "I said to myself listen, they'll read the book—everybody in baseball will read the book—and they'll have a good laugh. Maybe they'll make a few policy changes to correct the evils I discussed (in recognition of my insightful brilliance) and accept the book as mature adults should. I thought that. I really did."

I used to believe that about my writing too, but I'm not so naive anymore. If anything, this book will probably just get me in more trouble. Nowadays rock criticism tries its damnedest not to raise a ruckus, tries not to be funny or surprising or to hurt anybody's feelings. It's not supposed to be messy like the world; it's supposed to be respectable like a grad-school symposium, or the goddam Rock of Gibraltar. A great party idea has backslid somehow into a somber institution that I can't imagine luring in any adolescent with half an I.Q.

Social-tranquilizer cult acts like My Bloody Valentine codify old Byrds and Velvet Underground moves into sexless obviousness, call it "mystic," and are embraced by critics who are in turn inspired to write with a lethargy that mimics the music; nobody ever cranks out reviews saying "these My Bloody Valentine songs kick butt, but these turds over here totally bite the oceanic big one." The generation of critics who grew up on college radio never learned how to get pissed off, how to make fun of their idols, how to *complain*. All those polite little whispery Sonic Youth and R.E.M. monotone-drone voices taught them not to be rude, so they wound up too wishy-washy to risk being called (as I was once, in a letter to the *Village Voice*) the Mayor of Asshole City. They don't know what they're missing.

Conflict is part of how I relate to my environment, so conflict is part of the reason I got into this game. I fell into rock criticism by accident: I was doing hard-news and sports-hack

reporting for my college newspaper in Missouri and a suburban weekly in Michigan, and I noticed other staffers review-
ing records. Being an arrogant jerk, I figured I could do it
just as well as them even though I owned notably fewer LPs
than your average college student (only four-or-so when I
graduated high school—one each by Heart, Jethro Tull, and
David Bowie, plus a cheapo Chuck Berry best-of on Gusto
Records).

Yet I got way more feedback to my music criticism than to
any other writing I'd done (threats on my life over the
phone for REO Speedwagon concert reviews, cool!), so I'd
obviously found my niche. I started using my writing to connect to the world, in the same sense that controlling less shy
people's turntables at parties was a way to force them to
mingle with me without working too hard. In 1983, an annual critics poll ballot I submitted to the *Village Voice*, in
which I complained for 11 pages about the state of rock criticism at the *Voice* and elsewhere, led to my being invited to
start writing there even though I was still a U.S. Army lieu-
tenant living in Germany.

"I just turned 23 a month or so ago, and I only started to
listen to music 'seriously' in 1979, and I haven't seen a real
rock'n'roll revolution yet, and I want a *There's a Riot Goin'
On* or a New York Dolls or a Johnny Rotten so bad I could
shit," I ranted. "But I'm not going to get one. What I'll probably get is World War III, and then we'll start all over again,
and if I'm lucky and I cut down on my salt intake I might
live to see Prehistoric Ring Shouts II when I'm an old old
man."

In 1993, another annual critics poll ballot I mailed to the
Voice, again complaining about the state of rock criticism, led
to my being told my writing career there was over. (Which
it was, for a couple years at least.) I guess New Yorkers
must've developed thinner skins over that decade. Since
then, especially after figuring out I've got the lowest reading-
speed-to-writing-speed ratio in human history, I resolved to
avoid looking at rock criticism as much as possible. So
maybe I'm a little out of touch, but I still don't understand
any forum that acts like the supposed "dominant discourse

of the day" prevents pop hits from working non-corporate-sanctioned miracles in people's lives. And I don't get how "culture" can mean anything *but* those lives.

Greil Marcus, one of the most respected (and best) rock critics ever, argued in *Esquire* in 1992 that rock has to either absorb the events of the world at large, and somehow bear a promise of unsettling that world, or else be doomed to a mere banal balancesheet existence. But when a Poison video unsettles *his* world by flaunting a kind of arrogant contempt that makes him sick, Greil doesn't embrace Poison; he opts instead for Nirvana, who reassure him that the spirit of "Blue Suede Shoes" might still be viable. He's contradicting himself, opting for what goes down easy. Which wouldn't be one bit objectionable if he didn't put rock back on his weather-beaten *Mystery Train* pedestal and submit that what he likes about Nirvana is that they supposedly provide anything *but* entertainment. Nirvana give their slice of the market the (Greil's words) "hopelessness and mistrust" dimwits tell us "Generation X" thrives on. But for us non-X-ers, "Smells Like Teen Spirit" was like "Ice Ice Baby" in 1990 or "Achy Breaky Heart" in 1992—a surprise crossover, a fun bopping novelty tune. And "Teen Spirit" made teenagers want to break free, like any decent pop-metal hit.

I don't think what passes as the cutting edge these days is especially sharp or pointed (even though it calls itself Nine Inch Nails sometimes). Cutting edges tend to be redundant, and today's seems even more so than usual. But then again, I'm admittedly prejudiced: for most of my life I've suspiciously assumed that cutting-edge types (hippies, burnouts, vegetarians, Thespians, lesbians, protesters, poets, punks, public radio fans, hackers, slackers, ravers, whatever) are all just secret conformists wearing cookie-cut costumes, trying to be "different" all in the same way as each other. Over the years, though, I've started to realize that the avant-garde (which category includes even me on some days) is scared just like everybody else out there. My writing now and then gets accused of being homophobic, but that's horseshit; I'm really biphobic, which means I'm scared of *everybody*. Yet it's not inconceivable that a few freaks hiding in the woodwork might be as intimidated by me as I am by them.

Sometimes cutting edges can work in non-cutting-edge ways, just by being sweet or screwy. Nirvana and *Pulp Fiction* were okay, and once I started paying attention to the singing and guitars, I realized Jefferson Airplane were hardly the just-more-braindead-hippies I'd always taken them for. Which might make Courtney Love the Grace Slick of the '90s: women singing downbeat complaint shlock aren't inherently stupider than ones singing pretty love shlock. Liz Phair's most famous song "Fuck and Run" has the same plot as Ace of Base's most famous song "All That She Wants" (they're both about getting laid then dumping the dork), and (conversely) Hole's best song "Violet"—"They get what they want then they never want it again"—has more or less the same lyrics as Selena's best song "I Could Fall in Love"—"If I take that chance right now, tomorrow will you want me still?" (The Shirelles called it "Will You Love Me Tomorrow"; Lisa Lisa called it "I Wonder If I Take You Home").

Maybe you think I'm joking; maybe you think this whole book is a put-on. To be honest, I'm not even sure myself anymore. Since the ideas contained herein tend to be presented as "Fucking Around" instead of as "Journalism" or "Aesthetic Discourse," people who think it's impossible to think and fuck around at the same time will doubtlessly pretend my ideas never existed. Some people will wish an editor chopped out all the freebies and surprises and riddles and sandbox play and extraneous asides unrelated to the Devastatingly Important Issue at Hand. But I think those loose ends are what gives my writing its push and depth; they're what makes it worth reading more than once.

I present a context in this book in which I can make fun of haircuts and namedrop television shows and remember what high school was like and discuss baseball and proclaim a political statement or two and pass it all off as "music history," because those are all valid ways we deal with the world in which history happens. What you wind up with is a big tossed salad—Don Rickles stuff, platitudes masquerading as "in-depth insights," insights masquerading as jokes, absurd puns, snooty references to serious works of art or current events I've been brainwashed into thinking I'm supposed to care about, maybe even a few lazy typographical and factual errors. It's probably best read on the toilet (which is where I wrote a lot of it—I'm an intense young man with too much intestinal fortitude in his intestines).

My favorite thing anybody said about my first book *Stairway to Hell* was three words in a short review in *Circus* magazine: "pretentious and hilarious." I took that as a compliment, because my problem with too much other music criticism I've come across in the '90s isn't so much that it's pretentious (which only means it aims high after all) as that it forgets the hilarious part. I hope this book doesn't. And I hope my pretentions have energy to them too, and I hope that energy ties my hodgepodge together.

Gratuitous Discography Rationalized by Flimsy Math/Rock Link!

Rock'n'roll is a game of numbers, of *Billboard* charts and sales figures and countdowns and Top Ten lists. The sticker on the cover of Def Leppard's *Hysteria* proclaimed "12 songs, 63 minutes," and it sold 10 million copies. Music is math even *without* the business aspect—eighth notes, hemidemi-semiquavers, two-steps, eights-to-the-bar. Disco deejays rate music by beats-per-minute (house tempo is around 120, Belgian rave 127–130), which is cool because it's *objective*, sort of like timing Nolan Ryan's fastball. And rhythm all boils down to fractions like 4/4 and 3/4 and 17/8, depending on what continent you're from.

Supposedly the Police used some real unusual meter-type fractions, but personally, people who discuss music in terms of fractions make me nervous. It's so *clinical.* In *Gödel, Escher, Bach,* Pulitzer prizewinner Douglas Hofstadter talks about how music and calculas both have "strange loops" where, "moving upwards (or downwards) through the levels of some hierarchical system, we unexpectedly find ourself right back where we started," big fun if you're a graph-paper geek. Me, I did pretty good in math percentile-wise up through my SAT's, but fraction-type musicology still reminds me too much of Olympic ice-rink judges holding up decimal-point ratings, cheating worldclass skate-punk Tonya Harding out of her hard-earned gold medal.

On the other hand, my youngest sister Emily teaches high school math, and in 1991 in Oakland she taught her classes a statistics lesson by having them register their favorite musical acts and genres, along with the first words that came to their head when certain performers were mentioned. (She was sort of acting in the tradition of the legendary '70s Saturday morning cartoon *Multiplication Rock*, which featured one times-table for each musical genre—the catchiest one being "Three is a Magic Number"). Emily's ninth graders mostly liked Mariah Carey, Naughty By Nature, MC Hammer, and Metallica; the older kids mostly hated rap, preferring Van Halen. Lots of kids said their favorite music was "mod" or "mawd" (like R.E.M. or Jesus Jones). Most had never heard of John Mellencamp; when they did, they generally dismissed him as a "retard from the '50s" or an "old hick" or "probably dead." One student called R.E.M. "all right fags"; another one said Guns N' Roses "suck blue whales (the largest mammal)." Most of the freshmen liked N.W.A. "a little," quite a few rejected Def Leppard as "out of date," and the overwhelming majority (36 out of 42 in one class) labeled Madonna a "slut." The most math-conscious pupil figured R.E.M. have "one or two good songs" (and I agree with him 100 percent).

Rock songs have lots of counting in them. The Ramones have their famous "one-two-three-fawh" countoffs; Sam the Sham and the Pharoahs in "Wooly Bully" go "*uno-dos-tres-cuatro*"; Shonen Knife in "Tortoise Brand Pot Cleaner's Theme" repeatedly count to "shi" in Japanese. Kraftwerk's proto-techno "Numbers" features counting in a whole *bunch* of different languages. In "When I Grow Up," the Beach Boys count year-by-year to adulthood in the background. In Yes's classical-rock classic "Long Distance Runaround," Jon Anderson can't remember if he and a friend really counted to 100 while high on drugs once.

Other musicians have *favorite* numbers. The notes to David Allen Coe's 1979 *Spectrum VII* say "This is my 7th album for CBS and it has 7 musicians on it. There's a song called 'Seven Mile Bridge' that is 7 minutes 7 seconds long, recorded on the 7th day of the month. Perhaps now my luck will change." Juju monarch King Sunny Adé says his number is 365; reggae forefathers Toots and the Maytals' number is 5446. The Marvelletes' is Beechwood 4-5789, you can call them up and have a date any old time. By contrast, Bob Seger just "*feels* like a number," but doesn't say which one. He's always looked a bit like 391 to me, but he's got a number called "2 + 2 = ?." So maybe his number's 4.

The 2 + 2 equation can also be found in "Bom Bom" by Jimmy Castor, along with 1 + 1 and 4 + 4; "Roberta" by the Animals has 1 + 1 and 2 + 1. The lovely but overloved '60s band Love did both "7 and 7 Is" and "Number Fourteen," but "Add It Up" by Violent Femmes has no addition in it at all, oddly. "Two Divided By Zero" by the Pet Shop Boys is impossible; if they'd named it "Square Root of Negative Two" instead it'd merely be *imaginary*. (There's a difference, though I won't claim I understand why.)

In his 1981 hit "Never Too Much," soul voice Luther Vandross hyperbolizes that "a million days in your arms is never too much," which taking leap years into account translates to something like 2,738 years and 320 days—older than anybody in my immediate family! Between September 10 and October 3, 1993, my younger son Sherman was two years old, my daughter Coco was twice Sherman's age, my older son Linus was twice Coco's age, and my wife Martina and I were both twice-twice Linus' age. Then Martina had to mess everything up by turning 33. (But Linus still turned three-squared years old on the three-cubed day of the third month of 1994!) Algebra rock: Laurie Anderson "Let X = X," Jimi Hendrix "If Six was Nine." (And for that matter why not George Jones's "Her Name Is . . . ," the Beastie Boys' "Cookie Puss," Boney M's "Bang Bang Lulu," Richard Hell's "Blank Generation," and any old used record with lots of pops and skips in the vinyl, where blank spaces can signify words left out?)

Sam Cooke admits to being algebra-, trigonometry-, and slide-rule-illiterate in 1960's "Wonderful World." And Debbie Gibson appears to be stuttering nonsensical excuses for not doing her geometry homework when she tells her teacher she can't offer him proof "and that is the that is the that is the truth" over amazing beat-calculus in "Shake Your Love." But the arty U.K. punks in Wire *loved* math—they had songs called "A Question of Degree," "12xU," and "Map Ref. 41°N 93°W," plus another that went "think of a number, divide it by two." Their record sleeves were full of latitudinal-longitudinal right angles and perfect circles meticulously drawn with T-squares and compasses on a drafting table. Also, physics music would overlap with math music on a Venn diagram—Miami disco trio Company B on Ohm's Law in 1989's "Gotta Dance" ("dance to the balance of no resistance"); Frank Sinatra on atomic particles in 1955's "Love and Marriage" ("try to separate them, it's an illusion"). I'm sure all the Bundys on Fox-TV's *Married With Children* would agree: math and rock go together like a horse and carriage.

Which is as good a reason as any for me to end this book with a self-indulgent albiet intricately tabulated and calibrated discography of all the albums that I think would constitute a respectable home library of 20th-century popular music, wouldn't you say? If not, tough—it'll have to do, and here's where the math comes in: I'm listing the fifteen best (or okay, my fifteen "favorite"—same thing!) albums to emerge every year during the '70s, '80s, and (inasmuch as they're over and done) '90s.

Before 1970, albums hadn't quite developed the appearance of surpassing singles as the industry's most marketable unit of mass consumption, so I was more selective for that era because I don't own as many albums from back then to choose from. Which isn't to say I think LPs were *worse* then; frankly, your average '60s singles-band knew way more about making a playable album than your average '90s album-band. Hardly anybody sticks to the perfect old LP length of ten songs in thirty-to-forty minutes anymore, and I get the idea the only reason CDs have so much music on them these days is that there's *room* for it. Lots of great old LPs were just a few great singles plus good cover-song filler!

And even in the '90s (which when you consider how people actually live their lives aren't nearly as different from previous decades as self-justifying cultural prognosticators pretend), music is still introduced to people, and people still develop their most passionate connection with, individual *songs*. Most "tenor of the '90s" criticism is an utter farce—one point I've proven in this book is that it's completely deceitful, or at best ill-informed, for "Generation X" critics with grad-school literary-theory vocabularies too big for their britches to pretend that "irony" or "mongrelism" or "contrariness" or "discomfort with boundaries" is something only humans born after 1965 were wise or with-it enough to invent. The "grunge/alternative revolution" was just another "New Improved!" stamped by sales nimrods on hard rock's cereal box, and we're no more "post"-rock than we were in 1980, or 1966. Most people I know find out about new Better Than Ezra or TLC or Shania Twain songs they like the same way people have *always* found out about new songs—from radio and TV and the dancefloor. I'm not convinced anything has changed, except in the minds of pompous crybabies who need a headline and have nothing to say about the real world.

Yet despite all that, I still limited myself to ten albums a year for every year from 1966 through 1969, then ten more for each of the following periods: 1964-and-1965-combined, 1960-through-1963, 1950-through-1959. If it sounds a bit unbalanced, let's just say I knew which albums I wanted to sneak onto your shopping list, and the quantities fell into place accordingly.

A few caveats, before you blow a gasket: I didn't feel like aggravating my ulcer by being anal-compulsively literal about release dates. '60s albums frequently didn't list them, and even on later albums, listed dates aren't always trustworthy—just because music was copywritten in a certain year doesn't mean it was for sale then. It's impossible to figure out the year lots of obscure records, especially imports, came out, so in many cases I just made an educated estimate, and here and there I might be off by a year or two. "Cusp" records that fell into stores when Christmas shopping season was winding down, and hence were mere trees-falling-in-the-forest-with-nobody-hearing-them until January, were often assigned to whichever year needed the most *help*. The hardest years for me to come up with fifteen great albums—hence, probably, the lamest rock years ever—were 1993 and 1994; the hardest lists for me to whittle *down* to 15 were 1979 and 1980—which, maybe not coincidentally, were the years I first seriously started paying attention to music. (An early-'90s study conducted by business schools at Rutgers and Columbia, incidentally, concluded that grownups tend to give the highest approval ratings to music that hit the top 10 when they were 23.5 years old. Men's taste in women's clothes and personal-appearance trends were almost exactly the same.)

Anyway, back to my lists: Greatest-Hits albums of recent music by still-active artists (and all reissues of '80s and '90s music, and a few repackagings of older music never before available in album form) were assigned to the years in which they were released. But for additional historical perspective, to fill gaps, and as a nod to the annoyingly overprolific but frequently useful CD-era old-music-reavailability boom, I'm also including lists of twenty-each *reissues* of music originally recorded primarily in the '70s, '60s, '50s, and pre-'50s-epoch—I avoided boxed sets, which are almost invariably useless since if you're enough of a fanatic to endure that much crap by anybody you probably already own all of it in the first place, in favor of less bloated reissues comprising songs I'd actually want to hear rather than simply own. (Obviously, many of these sets still overlap decades, so some randomness and coin-flipping were involved—Dion scored most of his hits in the '60s, but he still *seems* '50s. I also decided to cheat by counting separate volumes I like from multi-volume sets, even when only available for purchase separately, as sections of the same "record").

I didn't feel like yanking any more hair out of my head than necessary, so I listed records alphabetically within their individual years instead of in order of preference. Yet I did relisten to almost every album I own while doing my final roster-recheck, so if you can't find some hallowed classic tallied here, it doesn't mean I've overlooked it; it means everybody else is *overrating* it—these lists are comprehensive, ma'am. On the other hand, I don't plan to stop making discoveries in flea-market dollar-bins; there are still lots of surprises I've never heard. Catch up with me midway through the 21st Century, and I might swear the most exciting music of the second half of the 20th wasn't rock'n'roll at all, but some post-mambo combo of Latin rhythms. But until then these recommendations will suffice. If I had a hammer and chisel, I might even carve them in stone.

Discography

1996: Banda Bahia *Ghostbusters* (Unico); Gillette *Shake Your Money Maker* (Zoo/SOS); Great Society *Born to be Burned* (Sundazed); Local H *As Good As Dead* (Island); Mo-Do *Was ist Das?* (ZYX Germany); MX-80 *Big Hits/Hard Attack* (Atavistic); Nomads *Raw & Rare* (Estrus); OMC *How Bizarre* (Huh! New Zealand); Pointed Sticks *Part of the Noise* (Zulu Canada); Ruth Ruth *Laughing Gallery* (American); Sleater-Kinney *Call the Doctor* (Chainsaw); Sublime *Sublime* (Gasoline Alley/MCA); Weezer *Pinkerton* (DGC); Various *Trainspotting* (Capitol); Various *Youth Gone Wild: Heavy Metal Hits of the 80s, Vols. 1 and 3* (Rhino).

1995: Aterciopelados *El Dorado* (BMG Latin); Laura Branigan *The Best of Branigan* (Atlantic); Mariah Carey *Daydream* (Columbia); Desorden Publico *Canto popular de la vida y muerte* (SDI); Everclear *Sparkle and Fade* (Capitol); Lordz of Brooklyn *All in the Family* (American); Los Del Mar featuring Wil Veloz *Macarena* (Lime/Quality Canada); Rancid *And Out Come the Wolves* (Epitaph); Rednex *Sex & Violins* (Battery); Chico Science & Nação Zumbi *Da Lama ao caos* (SDI); The Scene is Now *The Oily Years (1983–1993)* (Bar None); Selena *Dreaming of You* (EMI); Supergrass *I Should Coco* (Capitol); Tapps *Greatest Hits* (Thump); Various *Playa Dance '95 Compilation* (BMG Latin).

1994: Ace of Base *The Sign* (Arista); Aterciopelados *Con el corazon en la mano* (RCA Latin); Beck *Loser* (DGC EP); Garth Brooks *The Hits* (Liberty); Gillette *On The Attack* (Zoo/SOS); Green Day *Dookie* (Reprise); Hole *Live Through This* (DGC); Kix *$how Bu$ine$$* (CMC); La Derecha *La Derecha* (RCA Latin); Peter Laughner & Friends *Take the Guitar Player For a Ride* (Tim Kerr); Los Fabulosos Cadillacs *Vasos vacios* (Sony Latin); Mano Negra *Casa Babylon* (BMG France); Rancid *Let's Go* (Epitaph); Santa Sabina *Simbolos* (RCA Latin); Um Pah Pah *Bordell* (BMG Spain).

1993: Cafe Tacuba *Cafe Tacuba* (WEA Latina); Caifanes *Caifanes: Edicion especial* (RCA Latin); Fobia *Leche* (BMG Latin); Guns N' Roses *The Spaghetti Incident?* (Geffen); Indochine *Un Jour dans notre vie* (BMG France); Jordy *Pochette surprise (Sur-*

prise Package) (Columbia); La Castañeda *Servicios generales II* (BMG Latin); K.T. Oslin *Greatest Hits: Songs From an Aging Sex Bomb* (RCA); Tom Petty & the Heartbreakers *Greatest Hits* (MCA); Liz Phair *Exile in Guyville* (Matador); Santa Sabina *Santa Sabina* (BMG Latin); Suede *Suede* (Columbia); Urge Overkill *Saturation* (Geffen); Urge Overkill *The Urge Overkill Story . . . Stay Tuned 1988–1991* (Touch & Go promo EP); Xuxa *Xuxa 3* (Globo).

1992: Caifanes *El Silencio* (RCA Latin); Mariah Carey *MTV Unplugged* (Columbia EP); Dédé Traké *Dédé Traké* (Select Quebec); East Beat *East Beat 4* (Tzwu Chyi Singapore cassette); Fobia *Mundo feliz* (Ariola Latin); P.J. Harvey *Dry* (Island); Indochine *The Birthday Album* (BMG France); Les Negresses Vertes *Famille nombreuse* (Delabel France); Loco Mia *Taiyo* (Sony Discos); Los Prisioneros *Grandes exitos* (Capitol/EMI Latin); Lisa M *Flavor of the Latin* (Sony Discos); Maldita Vecindad Y Los Hijos Del 5° Patio *El Circo* (Ariola Latin); Midi Maxi & Efti *Midi Maxi & Efti* (Columbia); Ramones *Mondo Bizarro* (Radioactive); Xuxa *Xuxa 2* (Globo).

1991: Bang Tango *Dancin' On Coals* (MCA); Mariah Carey *Emotions* (Columbia); Corina *Corina* (Cutting); Cypress Hill *Cypress Hill* (Ruffhouse/Columbia); The Electric Eels *God Says Fuck You* (Homestead); Amy Grant *Heart in Motion* (A&M); Michael Jackson *Dangerous* (Epic); Kix *Hot Wire* (Eastwest); L'Trimm *Groovy* (Atlantic); Mano Negra *Amerika perdida* (Virgin France); Niagara *Religion* (Traffic Quebec); Noir Desir *Du ciment les plaines* (Barclay France); Sandée *Only Time Will Tell* (Fever); Shonen Knife *Pretty Little Baka Guy + Live in Japan* (Rockville); Voivod *Angel Rat* (Mechanic).

1990: Mariah Carey *Mariah Carey* (Columbia); Yvonne Chaka Chaka *Thank You Mr. D.J.* (AIT World South Africa); East Beat *The Best of East Beat* (Tzwu Chyi Singapore cassette); East Beat *East Beat 3* (Tzwu Chyi Singapore cassette); Electric Angels *Electric Angels* (Atlantic); Maldita Vecindad Y Los Hijos Del 5° Patio *Maldita vecindad y los hijos del 5° patio* (Ariola Mexico); Love/Hate *Black Out in the Red Room* (Columbia); Madonna *The Immaculate Collection* (Sire); Shonen Knife *Shonen Knife* (Gasatanka); Liz Torres *The Queen is in the*

House (Jive); Warrant *Cherry Pie* (Columbia); Will To Power *Journey Home* (Epic); Xuxa *Xuxa* (Globo); Various *Electric Salsa* (Baja); Various *Newbeat Edit 1* (ZYX Germany).

1989: Company B *Gotta Dance* (Atlantic); Taylor Dayne *Can't Fight Fate* (Arista); Gloria Estefan and Miami Sound Machine *Hits* (Epic promo); Faster Pussycat *Wake Me When It's Over* (Elektra); Les Negresses Verdes *Mlah* (Virgin); Lord Tracy *Deaf Gods of Babylon* (Uni); L'Trimm *Drop That Bottom* (Atlantic); Pajama Party *Up All Night* (Atlantic); Stacey Q *Nights Like This* (Atlantic); Pull My Daisy *Pull My Daisy* (unlabeled Switzerland cassette EP); The Real Roxanne *The Real Roxanne* (Select); Seduction *Nothing Matters Without Love* (A&M); Skid Row *Skid Row* (Atlantic); Warrant *Dirty Rotten Filthy Stinking Rich* (Columbia); Will To Power *Will To Power* (Epic).

1988: Bananarama *The Greatest Hits Collection* (London); Cinderella *Long Cold Winter* (Mercury); Death of Samantha *Where the Women Wear the Glory and the Men Wear the Pants* (Homestead); Flipper *Sex Bomb Baby!* (Subterranean); Spoonie Gee *The Godfather of Rap* (Tuff City); Guns N' Roses *GN'R Lies* (Geffen); The Holy Cows *We Never Heard of You Either* (Herb Jackson); Joan Jett and the Blackhearts *Up Your Alley* (Epic); Journey *Greatest Hits* (Columbia); Kix *Blow My Fuse* (Atlantic); Teena Marie *Naked to the World* (Epic); Poison *Open Up and Say . . . Ahh!* (Enigma/Capitol); Stacey Q *Hard Machine* (Atlantic); 16 Bit *Inaxycvgtgb* (BMG Germany); Various *Hurricane Zouk* (Virgin).

1987: Angry Samoans *Inside My Brain* (PVC); The Cover Girls *Show Me* (Fever); Def Leppard *Hysteria* (Mercury); Exposé *Exposure* (Arista); Faster Pussycat *Faster Pussycat* (Elektra); Debbie Gibson *Out of the Blue* (Atlantic); Guns N' Roses *Appetite For Destruction* (Geffen); Michael Jackson *Bad* (Epic); The Leather Nun *Force of Habit* (IRS); Les Rita Mitsouko *Presentent The No Comprendo* (Virgin); Madonna *You Can Dance* (Sire cassette); Magazine 60 *Costa del sol* (Baja); Sonic Youth *Sister* (SST); Tiffany *Tiffany* (MCA); Various *The History of the House Sound of Chicago* (BCM Germany box set).

1986: Beastie Boys *Licensed to Ill* (Def Jam); Boney M *Eye Dance* (Atlantic Canada); Bon Jovi *Slippery When Wet* (Mercury); Oran "Juice" Jones *Juice* (Def Jam); Lime *The Greatest Hits* (Unidisc Canada); Mantronix *The Album* (Sleeping Bag); Teena Marie *Emerald City* (Epic); Peter and the Test Tube Babies *Peter and the Test Tube Babies* (Profile); Poison *Look What the Cat Dragged In* (Enigma); Stacey Q *Better Than Heaven* (Atlantic); Salt 'N Pepa *Hot, Cool & Vicious* (Next Plateau); Schoolly D *Saturday Night* (Schoolly D); Slade *You Boyz Make Big Noize* (CBS Associated); Various *The Best of Italo Disco Vol. III* (ZYX Germany); Various *Dance Traxx* (Atlantic).

1985: DeBarge *Rhythm of the Night* (Gordy); The Fall *Hip Priest and Kamerads* (Situation 2 U.K.); The Flirts *Blondes Brunettes & Redheads* (CBS Associated); Billy Joel *Greatest Hits Volume I & Volume II* (Columbia); Kix *Midnite Dynamite* (Atlantic); Frank Kogan/Red Dark Sweet/The Pillowmakers *Stars Vomit Coffee Shop* (Stereo cassette); Lady Pank *Drop Everything* (MCA); L.L. Cool J *Radio* (Def Jam); John Cougar Mellencamp *Scarecrow* (Riva); The Nomads *Outburst* (Homestead); Pogues *Rum Sodomy and the Lash* (Stiff U.K.); Quarterflash *Back Into Blue* (Geffen); Alexander Robotnik *Ce n'est qu'un début* (Materiali Sonori Italy); Various *Fuzzdance* (Sire EP); Various *Vision Quest* (Geffen).

1984: John Anderson *Greatest Hits* (Warner Bros.); Boney M *Ten Thousand Light Years* (Ariola Spain); DeBarge *In A Special Way* (Gordy); Fun Fun *Have Fun!* (Energy); Hanoi Rocks *Back to Mystery City* (PVC); Cyndi Lauper *She's So Unusual* (Portrait); Billy Ocean *Suddenly* (Jive); Run-D.M.C. *Run-D.M.C.* (Profile); Slade *Keep Your Hands off My Power Supply* (CBS Associated); Bruce Springsteen *Born in the U.S.A.* (Columbia); Treacherous Three *Whip It* (Vogue/Sugarhill France); Two Sisters *Two Sisters* (Sugarscoop); Van Halen *1984* (Warner Bros.); Various *Get Up: 16 High Energy Dance Hits* (Hansa Germany); Various *The Perfect Beat Compilation* (21/Polydor U.K.).

1983: The Beat *What Is Beat?: The Best Of* (Go-Feet U.K.); John Conlee *Greatest Hits* (MCA); The Charlie Daniels Band *A Decade of Hits* (Epic); DFX2 *Emotion* (MCA EP); Ian Dury & the Blockheads *Exitòs Dury* (Stiff Spain); Hall and Oates *Rock 'N Soul Part 1* (RCA); Joan Jett and the Blackhearts *Album* (Epic); Kix *Cool Kids* (Atlantic); Huey Lewis and the

News *Sports* (Chrysalis); Madonna *Madonna* (Sire); John Cougar Mellencamp *Uh-Huh* (Riva); Quarterflash *Take Another Picture* (Geffen); Lionel Richie *Can't Slow Down* (Motown); Trio *Trio And Error* (Mercury); Wham! U.K. *Fantastic* (Columbia).

1982: Angry Samoans *Back From Samoa* (Bad Trip); Bellamy Brothers *Greatest Hits* (Curb); Boney M *Boonoonoonoos* (Dynamic Jamaica); Charlene *I've Never Been To Me* (Motown); John Cougar *American Fool* (Riva); The Fall *Hex Enduction Hour* (Kamera U.K.); Girlschool *Screaming Blue Murder* (Mercury); Michael Jackson *Thriller* (Epic); Grandmaster Flash and the Furious Five *The Message* (Sugarhill); Olivia Newton-John *Greatest Hits, Vol. 2* (MCA); Nichts *Tango 2000* (Schall/WEA Germany); Ray Parker Jr. *The Other Woman* (Arista); Ray Parker Jr. *The Very Best of* (Arista); Trouble Funk *Drop the Bomb* (Sugarhill); Two Man Sound *Capitol Tropical* (TSR).

1981: Abba *The Magic of Abba* (K-Tel); Boney M *The Magic of Boney M* (Gallo); Cepillin *Rock infantil* (Orfeon Mexico); The J. Geils Band *Freeze-Frame* (EMI America); Girlschool *Hit And Run* (Bronze U.K.); Rick James *Street Songs* (Gordy); Joan Jett *Bad Reputation* (Boardwalk); Kix *Kix* (Atlantic); Loverboy *Get Lucky* (Columbia); Teena Marie *It Must Be Magic* (Gordy); Ted Nugent *Great Gonzos: The Best of* (Epic); Quarterflash *Quarterflash* (Geffen); The Romantics *National Breakout* (Nemporer); Rose Tattoo *Assault and Battery* (Mirage); Various *Greatest Rap Hits Vol. 2* (Sugarhill).

1980: Angel City *Face to Face* (Epic); Boney M *Oceans of Fantasy* (WEA Canada); The Brains *The Brains* (Mercury); Change *The Glow of Love* (Warner Bros.); Cheap Trick *All Shook Up* (Epic); Hounds *Puttin' On The Dog* (Columbia); Loverboy *Loverboy* (Columbia); Pearl Harbor and the Explosions *Pearl Harbor and the Explosions* (415); Prince *Dirty Mind* (Warner Bros.); Public Image Ltd. *Second Edition* (Island); REO Speedwagon *Hi Infidelity* (Epic); The Rolling Stones *Emotional Rescue* (Rolling Stones); The Specials *The Specials* (Chrysalis); Tantra *The Double Album* (Importe/12); Various *The Great Rap Hits* (Sugarhill).

1979: The Boomtown Rats *A Tonic for the Troops* (Columbia); The Cars *Candy-O* (Elektra); The Clash *The Clash* (Epic); Cory Daye *Cory and Me* (New York International); The Fall *Live at the Witch Trials* (I.R.S.); Foreigner *Head Games* (Atlantic); The Gibson Brothers *Cuba* (Island); Joe Jackson *Look Sharp* (A&M); Michael Jackson *Off the Wall* (Epic); The Knack *Get the Knack* (Capitol); Barbara Mandrell *The Best Of* (MCA); Skatt Bros. *Strange Spirits* (Casablanca); Squeeze *Cool For Cats* (A&M); Streetheart *Under Heaven Over Hell* (Atlantic); Donna Summer *Bad Girls* (Casablanca).

1978: Boney M *Nightflight to Venus* (Sire); Cheap Trick *Heaven Tonight* (Epic); Chic *C'Est Chic* (Atlantic); David Allan Coe *Human Emotions* (Columbia); Elvis Costello and the Attractions *This Year's Model* (Columbia); Gruppo Sportivo *Mistakes* (Sire); D.C. Larue *Confessions* (Casablanca); Pere Ubu *Dub Housing* (Chrysalis U.K.); Pere Ubu *The Modern Dance* (Blank); Don Ray *The Garden of Love* (Polydor); The Rolling Stones *Some Girls* (Rolling Stones); Bob Seger & the Silver Bullet Band *Stranger in Town* (Capitol); The Spinners *The Best of the Spinners* (Atlantic); Village People *Macho Man* (Casablanca); Various *No New York* (Antilles).

1977: Boney M *Love For Sale* (Hansa Germany); Cerrone *Supernature* (Cotillion); Fleetwood Mac *Rumours* (Warner Bros); Foreigner *Foreigner* (Atlantic); Heartbreakers *L.A.M.F.* (Track/Polydor U.K.); Richard Hell and the Voidoids *Blank Generation* (Sire); Hot Chocolate *XIV Greatest Hits* (RAK Germany); Plastic Bertrand *Ça plane pour moi* (Vogue France); Santa Esmeralda *Don't Let Me Be Misunderstood* (Casablanca); Sex Pistols *Never Mind the Bullocks Here's the Sex Pistols* (Warner Bros.); Starz *Violation* (Capitol); Donna Summer *I Remember Yesterday* (Casablanca); Donna Summer *Once Upon a Time* (Casablanca); The Vibrators *Pure Mania* (Epic); Various *Saturday Night Fever* (RSO).

1976: AC/DC *Dirty Deeds Done Dirt Cheap* (Atlantic Australia); AC/DC *High Voltage* (Atco); Bachman-Turner Overdrive *Best of B.T.O. (So Far)* (Mercury); Jorge Ben *Africa Brasil* (Philips Brazil); Blue Öyster Cult *Agents of Fortune* (Columbia); Boston *Boston* (Epic); David Bowie *Changesonebowie* (RCA Victor); Dr. Buzzard's Original Savannah Band *Dr. Buz-*

zard's *Original Savannah Band* (RCA); The Eagles *Hotel California* (Asylum); The Eagles *Their Greatest Hits 1971–1975* (Asylum); Michael Hurley, the Unholy Modal Rounders, Jeffrey Fredericks & the Clamtones *Have Moicy!* (Rounder); Linda Ronstadt *Greatest Hits* (Asylum); The Runaways *The Runaways* (Mercury); Bob Seger and the Silver Bullet Band *Night Moves* (Capitol); Silver Convention *Madhouse* (Midland International).

1975: Aerosmith *Toys in the Attic* (Columbia); Canned Heat *The Very Best Of* (United Artists); Crack the Sky *Crack the Sky* (Lifesong); The Dictators *Go Girl Crazy* (Epic); Disco Tex and his Sex-O-Lettes *Disco Tex and his Sex-O-Lettes* (Chelsea); Bob Dylan *Blood on the Tracks* (Columbia); Fleetwood Mac *Fleetwood Mac* (Reprise); Led Zeppelin *Physical Graffiti* (Swan Song); Nazareth *Hair of the Dog* (A&M); Helen Reddy *Greatest Hits* (Capitol); Patti Smith *Horses* (Arista); Bruce Springsteen *Born to Run* (Columbia); Donna Summer *Love to Love You Baby* (Oasis); Sweet *Desolation Boulevard* (Capitol); The Tubes *The Tubes* (A&M).

1974: Aerosmith *Get Your Wings* (Columbia); Cher *Greatest Hits* (Warner Bros.); Eric Clapton *461 Ocean Boulevard* (RSO); Alice Cooper *Greatest Hits* (Warner Bros.); Golden Earring *Moontan* (MCA); Kraftwerk *Autobahn* (Vertigo); Lynyrd Skynyrd *Second Helping* (MCA); Joni Mitchell *Court and Spark* (Asylum); New York Dolls *In Too Much Too Soon* (Mercury); Pink Fairies *Kings of Oblivion* (Polydor U.K.); Suzi Quatro *Suzi Quatro* (Bell); Sparks *Kimono My House* (Island); The Stylistics *The Best of* (Avco U.K.); 10cc *Sheet Music* (UK); Various *This is Reggae Music* (Island).

1973: Babe Ruth *First Base* (Harvest); Brownsville Station *Say Yeah!* (Big Tree); The Carpenters *The Singles 1969–1973* (A&M); Iggy and the Stooges *Raw Power* (Columbia); Elton John *Goodbye Yellow Brick Road* (MCA); Janis Joplin *Greatest Hits* (Columbia); Led Zeppelin *Houses of the Holy* (Atlantic); Lynyrd Skynyrd *Pronounced Leh'-nerd Skin'-nerd* (MCA); Mott the Hoople *Mott* (Columbia); Nazareth *Loud 'N' Proud* (A&M); Nazareth *Razamanaz* (A&M); New York Dolls *New York Dolls* (Mercury); Slade *Sladest* (Reprise); 10cc *10cc* (UK); Various *The Harder They Come* (Mango).

1972: The Belmonts *Cigars Acappella Candy* (Buddah); Jimmy Castor Bunch *Phase Two* (RCA Victor); Miles Davis *On the Corner* (Columbia); Fanny *Fanny Hill* (Reprise); Giorgio *Son of my Father* (ABC/Dunhill); Curtis Mayfield *Super Fly* (Curtom); Mott the Hoople *All the Young Dudes* (Columbia); Louis Prima *The Prima Generation '72* (Brunswick); REO Speedwagon *R.E.O./T.W.O.* (Epic); Rolling Stones *Exile on Main St.* (Rolling Stones); Roxy Music *Roxy Music* (Reprise); Simon and Garfunkel *Greatest Hits* (Columbia); Slade *Slayed?* (Polydor); Sparks *A Woofer in Tweeter's Clothing* (Bearsville); Steely Dan *Can't Buy a Thrill* (ABC).

1971: Glen Campbell *Greatest Hits* (Capitol); Alice Cooper *Killer* (Warner Bros.); Alice Cooper *Love it to Death* (Straight); The Faces *A Nod is as Good as a Wink ... to a Blind Horse* (Warner Bros.); Marvin Gaye *What's Going On* (Tamla); The Guess Who *The Best Of* (RCA); Tom T. Hall *In Search of a Song* (Mercury); Jackson 5 *Greatest Hits* (Motown); Carole King *Tapestry* (Ode); The Kinks *Lola* (Hallmark U.K.); Led Zeppelin *Zoso* (Atlantic); Nilsson *Nilsson Schmilsson* (RCA Victor); The Rolling Stones *Sticky Fingers* (Rolling Stones); Rod Stewart *Every Picture Tells a Story* (Mercury); The Who *Meaty Beaty Big and Bouncy* (Decca).

1970: Black Sabbath *Paranoid* (Warner Bros.); David Bowie *The Man Who Sold the World* (Mercury); Creedence Clearwater Revival *Cosmo's Factory* (Fantasy); Fairport Convention *Unhalfbricking* (A&M); James Gang *Rides Again* (ABC); The J. Geils Band *The J. Geils Band* (Atlantic); Led Zeppelin *III* (Atlantic); MC5 *Back in the U.S.A.* (Atlantic); Anne Murray *Snowbird* (Capitol); Santana *Abraxas* (Columbia); Simon and Garfunkel *Bridge Over Troubled Water* (A&M); Sly and the Family Stone *Greatest Hits* (Epic); The Stooges *Fun House* (Elektra); Temptations *Greatest Hits, Volume 2* (Gordy); Velvet Underground *Loaded* (Cotillion).

1969: The Bee Gees *Best Of* (Atco); Cream *Best Of* (Atco); Creedence Clearwater Revival *Green River* (Fantasy); Isaac Hayes *Hot Buttered Soul* (Enterprise); Jimi Hendrix Experience *Smash Hits* (Reprise); Led Zeppelin *Led Zeppelin* (Atlantic); Led Zeppelin *II* (Atlantic); The Monkees *Greatest Hits*

(Arista); The Rolling Stones *Let It Bleed* (London); The Stooges *The Stooges* (Elektra).

1968: Big Brother and the Holding Company *Cheap Thrills* (Columbia); The Joe Cuba Sextet *Wanted Dead or Alive: Se busca muerto o vivo* (Tico); Great Society with Grace Slick *Conspicuous Only in its Absence* (Columbia); Hombres *Let it Out* (Verve/Forecast); Prince Buster *Fabulous Greatest Hits* (Fab/Melodisc U.K.); Smokey Robinson and the Miracles *Greatest Hits, Vol. 2* (Tamla); Merilee Rush *Angel of the Morning/That Kind of Woman* (Bell); Mitch Ryder and the Detroit Wheels *Greatest Hits* (Virgo); The Swinging World of Johnny Rios *Neuvo Boog-a-loos* (Mic-Tone); Velvet Underground *White Light/White Heat* (Verve).

1967: The Byrds *Greatest Hits* (Columbia); Count Five *Psychotic Reaction* (Double Shot); Joe Cuba Sextet *Estamos hacieno algo bien!: We Must Be Doing Something Right!* (Tico); The Doors *The Doors* (Elektra); Jefferson Airplane *Surrealistic Pillow* (RCA Victor); Moby Grape *Moby Grape* (Columbia); Perez Prado *The Best Of* (RCA Victor); Sam the Sham and the Pharoahs *The Best Of* (MGM); Velvet Underground *The Velvet Underground and Nico* (Verve); The Who *Sell Out* (Decca).

1966: The Animals *The Best Of* (MGM); Neil Diamond *The Feel of Neil Diamond* (Bang); Bob Dylan *Blonde on Blonde* (Columbia); The Lovin' Spoonful *The Best Of* (Kama Sutra); Paul Revere and the Raiders *Just Like Us!* (Columbia); The Rolling Stones *Aftermath* (London); The Rolling Stones *Big Hits (High Tide and Green Grass)* (London); The Shangri-Las *Golden Hits* (Mercury); Frankie Yankovic and his Yanks *Greatest Hits* (Columbia); The Yardbirds *Over Under Sideways Down* (Epic).

1964–1965: Bob Dylan *Another Side of Bob Dylan* (Columbia); Bob Dylan *Bringing it All Back Home* (Columbia); Bob Dylan *Highway 61 Revisited* (Columbia); Bob Dylan *The Times They Are a-Changin'* (Columbia); Shirley Ellis *The Name Game* (Congress); The Holy Modal Rounders *The Holy Modal Rounders* (Prestige); Tom Lehrer *That Was the Year That Was* (Reprise); The Rolling Stones *Now!* (London); The Rolling Stones *Out of Our Heads* (London); Dusty Springfield *Stay Awhile–I Only Want to Be With You* (Philips).

1960–1963: Sam Cooke *The Best Of* (RCA Victor); Joey Dee and the Starlighters *The Pepperment Twisters* (Scepter); Bob Dylan *The Freewheelin' Bob Dylan* (Columbia); The Kingston Trio *College Concert* (Capitol); The Limeliters *The Slightly Fabulous Limeliters* (RCA Victor); The Limeliters *Tonight: In Person* (RCA Victor); The Matys Bros *Who Stole the Keeshka?* (Select); Dee Dee Sharp *All the Hits* (Cameo/Parkway); The Shirelles *Greatest Hits* (Scepter); Various *A Christmas Gift For You From Phil Spector* (Philles).

1950–1959: Perry Como *Como's Golden Records* (RCA Victor); The Kingston Trio *From the Hungry i* (Captiol); The Kingston Trio *The Kingston Trio* (Capitol); New Lost City Ramblers *Old Timey Songs for Children* (Folkways 10"); Louis Prima *Digs Keely Smith* (Coronet); Victor Zembruski and his Orchestra *Dance Polkas* (Remington 10" EP); Various *Dance the Mambo* (Epic 10" EP); Various *Kiss Me Kate* (RCA Victor); Various *My Fair Lady* (Columbia); Various *West Side Story* (Columbia).

Reissue Archives

'70s Music: The Allman Brothers Band *The Best Of* (Polydor 1980); Babe Ruth *Grand Slam: The Best Of* (EMI/Harvest Canada 1994); The Jimmy Castor Bunch *The Best Of: The Everything Man* (Rhino 1995); The Chi-Lites *Greatest Hits* (Epic 1983); The Marshall Tucker Band *Greatest Hits* (Capricorn 1978); Van Morrison *The Best Of* (Polydor 1990); Pere Ubu *Terminal Tower: An Archival Collection* (Twin/Tone 1985); Suzi Quatro *The Wild One: Classic Quatro* (Razor & Tie 1996); Shocking Blue *Venus* (Piccadilly 1980); Steely Dan *A Decade of Steely Dan* (MCA 1985); Three Dog Night *The Golden Greats Of* (Pickwick 1979); War *The Best of War . . . And More* (Rhino 1992); Wire *And Here It is . . . Again . . . Wire* (Sneaky Pete Germany 1984); Various *Burning Ambitions: A History of Punk* (Cherry Red U.K. 1981); Various *The Disco Years, Volume One: Turn the Beat Around* (Rhino 1990); Various *Even More Dazed and Confused* (Medicine 1994); Various *The Great Glam-Rock Explosion* (Biff U.K. c. 1984); Various *Mega-Hits Dance Classics, Vols. One–Seven* (Priority 1989); Various *Punk You Vol. 1 (Music For the Discerning Slacker Punk)* (EMI 1995); Various *Super Hits of the '70s: Have a Nice Day, Vols. One–Fifteen* (Rhino 1990).

'60s Music: The Beach Boys *Endless Summer* (Capitol 1974); The Beatles *1962–1966* (Capitol 1973); James Brown *Star Time* (Polydor 1991); Chocolate Watchband *The Best Of* (Rhino 1983); Desmond Dekker *Rockin' Steady: The Best Of* (Rhino 1992); The Doors *Greatest Hits* (Elektra 1980); Merle Haggard *Songs I'll Always Sing* (Capitol 1977); Tommy James & the Shondells *The Very Best Of* (Rhino 1993); Jefferson Airplane *2400 Fulton Street–An Anthology* (RCA Victor 1987); Diana Ross and the Supremes *Anthology* (Motown 1974); Frankie Valli and the Four Seasons *Greatest Hits, Volume Two* (Rhino/Warner Special Products 1991); Dionne Warwick *20 Greatest Hits* (Phoenix 20 1981); The Yardbirds *Great Hits* (Epic 1977); Various *The Best of the 1910 Fruitgum Company/Ohio Express and other Bubblegum Smashes, Vols. One and Two* (Rhino 1983); Various *The British Invasion: The History of British Rock, Vols. Seven–Nine* (Rhino 1991); Various *Frat*

Rock!: The Greatest Rock'n'Roll Party Tunes of All Time (Rhino 1987); Various *Nuggets: Vols. One, Two, Six, and Twelve* (Rhino 1984); Various *Soul Train Hall of Fame* (Adam VIII 1973); Various *Super Bubble* (Warner Special Products 1977); Various *Wonder Women: The History of the Girl Group Sound, Vols. One and Two* (Rhino 1982–1984.)

'50s Music: Chuck Berry *The Chess Box* (Chess/MCA box set 1988); The Coasters *Young Blood* (Atlantic 1982); Bo Diddley *His Greatest Sides, Vol. One* (Chess 1984); Dion and the Belmonts *24 Original Classics* (Arista 1984); The Drifters *1959–1965 All Time Greatest Hits and More* (Atlantic 1988); Louis Jordan *The Best Of* (MCA 1975); Jerry Lee Lewis *Milestones* (Rhino 1989); Little Richard *The Original Little Richard* (GRT 1977); Elvis Presley *The Top 10 Hits* (RCA Victor 1987); Elvis Presley *The Sun Sessions* (RCA Victor 1976); Louis Prima *Collectors Series* (Capitol 1991); Hank Williams *40 Greatest Hits* (Polydor 1978); Various *American Graffiti* (MCA 1973); Various *Appalachian Stomp: Bluegrass Classics* (Rhino 1995); Various *Aunt Carmela's Italian Favorites* (RCA Special Products 1975); Various *The Best of Doo Wop Ballads, Vols. One and Two* (Rhino 1987–89); Various *The Best of Doo Wop Uptempo, Vols. One and Two* (Rhino 1987–89); Various *Stardust: Capitol Sings Hoagy Carmichael* (Capitol 1995); Various *A History of New Orleans Rhythm & Blues, Vols. One–Three* (Rhino 1987); Various *The History of Rock Instrumentals, Vols. One and Two* (Rhino 1987).

Pre-'50s Music: Les Brown *And His Great Vocalists* (Legacy/Columbia 1995); Duke Ellington *And His Great Vocalists* (Legacy/Columbia 1995); Hoosier Hot Shots *Rural Rhythm 1935–1942* (Columbia/Legacy 1992); Memphis Jug Band *Double Album* (Yazoo 1982); Emmett Miller *The Minstrel Man From Georgia* (Columbia/Legacy 1996); Charley Patton *Founder of the Delta Blues* (Yazoo c. 1980); Charlie Poole *And His North Carolina Ramblers* (County c. 1980); Bob Wills and his Texas Playboys *The Tiffany Transcriptions Vols. One, Two, Three, and Six* (Rhino 1987); Smokey Wood *The Houston Hipster: Western Swing 1937* (Rambler 1982); Various *The Anthology of American Folk Music* (Folkways box set 1953); Various *The Envelope Please: Academy Award Winning Songs Vol. One*

(1934–1956) (Rhino promo cassette 1995); Various *Jazz the World Forgot: Jazz Classics of the 1920's Vols. One and Two* (Yazoo 1996); Various *Minstrels and Tunesmiths: The Commerical Roots of Early Country Music* (JEMF 1981); Various *Mister Charlie's Blues 1926–1938* (Yazoo cassette 1989); Various *Okeh Western Swing* (Okeh/Epic 1982); Various *The Roots of Rap: Classic Recordings from the 1920's and 1930's* (Yazoo 1996); Various *Roots of Rock* (Yazoo 1982); Various *The Secret Museum of Mankind: Ethnic Music Classics Vols. One and Two* (Yazoo 1995); Various *When I Was A Cowboy: Early American Songs of the West—Classic Recordings from the 1920's & 30's Vol. Two* (Yazoo 1996); Various *White Country Blues 1926–1938: A Lighter Shade of Blue* (Columbia/Legacy 1993).

Acknowledgments

The first person I have to thank, if I know what's good for me, is my wife Martina, who makes more money than I do, thus enabling me to indulge in such childish pursuits as writing about teenage music. She's also given me hundreds of opinions to claim as my own over all these years, and she and her lazy good-for-nothing brother Marvin Kominiarek (he told me I could call him that) perused every word in a version of this book you'll never see, locating 4000 or so dumb ones I got rid of.

Editors did some editing, too. Several of the half-sentences and quarter-paragraphs strewn and shuffled throughout this tome were initially submitted to and published (usually in pre-strewn-and-shuffled form) by *Request, Rolling Stone, L.A. Weekly, Entertainment Weekly, Spin, Creem, B.A.M., Huh?, Millenium Pop, City Pages, Harper's, Option, Vibe, Graffiti, the Village Voice, Boston Phoenix, Bay Guardian, City Paper, Wire,* and sundry other outlets. Greg Boyd and Bill Reynolds at Toronto's *Eye Weekly*, especially, were open to printing a number of subchapters when Harmony Books (who initially contracted me to write it) chickened out of publishing the thing. Still, I do owe gratitude to Harmony refugee Kathy Belden for helping me get the ball rolling in the first place, not to mention Da Capo's Yuval Taylor for deciding my lunatic B.S. belonged in bookstores after all, and for helping me turn the final draft into something vaguely comprehensible.

I owe debts to too many other brainstorm-helpers, sanity-salvagers, co-conspirators, and social directors to list, and I'm bound to miss some given my lack of a Rolodex, but I'll try anyway. Here are a few: Don Allred, Jill Blardinelli, Robert Christgau, Chris Cook, Regina DeAngelo, Coco Eddy, Linus Eddy, Sherman Eddy, Michael Freedberg, Yvonne Gomez, Mariluz Gonzales, Jennie Inglis, Rita Johnson, John Kordosh, Anne Leighton, Rob Michaels, Laura Morgan, Arsenio Orteza, Jeff Pike, Molly Priesmeyer, Marusa Reyes, Richard Riegel, Mike Saunders, Rob Sheffield, Sara Sherr, Adam

Sobolak, Jack Thompson, Richard C. Walls, Eric Weisbard, Marc Weisblott, and Scott Woods.

The chart positions I've quoted almost all come from Joel Whitburn's indispensable *Billboard Book of Top 40 Hits*, which was on my desk nearly the entire time I was doing my research. As was Richard Meltzer's *The Aesthetics of Rock*, which more than 25 years after its birth increasingly strikes me as the most useful volume ever written about the topic, if only because almost nobody has done anything with its ideas since—until now, I hope. Yet I've been equally inspired by Phil Dellio's annual Top 40 fanzine *Radio On* (124 Eighth St., Apt. 2, Etobicoke ONT Canada M8V 3C4), and a truly obscene amount of music I praise herein, not to mention the methodology I use to dissect it, reflects a slavish devotion to the scribblings (published and unpublished) and tapings of Frank Kogan, who puts out *Why Music Sucks* (1449 Valencia, San Francisco CA 94110). For wit, honesty, insight, and courage, no other '90s music magazines come remotely close to these two. Mail them $7 each for copies right now.

Index

339

341

Gilder, Nick, 45, 106, 284
Gillespie, Dizzy, 203
Gillette, 51, 200, 324
Ginsberg, Allen, 159
Gipsy Kings, 13, 109, 121, 187
Girard, Mike, 70
Girls, 221
Girls Against Boys, 43, 227
Girlschool, 44, 205, 251, 302, 328
Glass, Philip, 37, 54
Glasses, 225
Gleason, Jackie, 22
Glitter, Gary, 192–196, 284, 290–292
Globetrotters, 199
Glosson, Lonnie, 125–126
Go-Gos, 193
Goings, Jimmy, 153
Gold, Andrew, 30, 208
Golden Earring, 56, 145, 190, 194, 330
Goldsboro, Bobby, 24, 29
Gonzalez, Juan, 198
Goodman, Benny, 68
Goombay Dance Band, 290
Gordy, Berry, 297
Gore, Lesley, 23, 68, 87
Gramm, Lou, 23, 82, 268
Grand Funk, 190
Grandmaster Flash (and the Furious Five), 16, 45, 74, 79, 100, 111, 126, 129, 136, 178–179, 198, 204, 246, 251, 261, 282, 297–298, 308, 328
Grant, Amy, 13, 25, 28, 33, 65, 74, 325
Grant, Eddy, 290
Grass Roots, 149
Grayson, G.B., 159
Great Society, 324, 332
Green Day, 8, 67, 103, 208, 241, 306, 324
Green, Jerome, 192
Greenbaum, Norman, 190
Griffith, Nanci, 21
Grupo Exterminador, 249

Gruppo Sportivo, 329
Guess Who, 190, 331
Guided by Voices, 137
Guns N' Roses, 13, 22, 29, 72, 75, 129, 167, 192, 217, 224, 236, 249, 251, 254, 264, 282, 294, 305–307, 319, 324, 326
Guthrie, Arlo, 126
Guthrie, Woody, 18, 53, 126, 178, 297

Haan, Jennie, 182
Hagen, Nina, 154
Haggard, Merle, 31, 33, 231–232, 298, 334
Hall and Oates, 327
Hall, Tom T., 178, 308, 331
Hambone, Beans, 64
Hammond, Albert, 306
Hancock, Herbie, 66–67, 275
Hanoi Rocks, 228, 327
Happy Mondays, 194
Harbor, Pearl (and the Explosions), 250, 328
Harding, Tonya, 318
Harmonica Frank, 123, 126
Harptones, 96
Harrelson, Ken, 198
Hart, Corey, 84
Hartman, Dan, 110
Harvey, P.J., 200, 248, 325
Havens, Richie, 59
Hawkins, Edwin, 131
Hawkins, Sophie B., 28
Hawkwind, 39, 277–279, 283
Hayes, Isaac, 21, 31, 38–39, 110, 124, 217, 299, 331
Hayzi Fantayzee, 128
Haza, Ofra, 129
Hazlewood, Lee, 28, 161, 262
Heart, 97, 146, 236, 314
Heartbeats, 276
Heartbreakers (with Johnny Thunders), 329
Heat, Rev. Horton, 174
Heatwave, 175

Mas, Jeanne, 253
Mascis, J., 43
Mason, Vaughan, 7
Matthews, Ian, 77
Matys Bros., 202, 333
Mayfield, Curtis, 161, 280, 331
Mayonaise, Patty, 194
Mays, Willie, 197
Mbuti Pygmies of the Ituri Rainforest, 250
McCall, C.W., 127
McCartney, Paul, 83, 107, 142, 286
McClintock, Lil, 178
McCoy, Van, 188, 190, 217
McCoys, 45, 190, 203
McDowell, Black Jack, 201
McDuffie, Sean, 169
McEntire, Reba, 21–22, 27
McFerrin, Bobby, 120
MC5, 63, 189, 220, 240, 278, 280, 331
M.C. Hammer, 66, 318
McKinley, William, 178
McLaren, Malcolm, 128, 137, 142
McLean, Don, 46, 175, 199
McLeese, Don, 240
Mead, Sister Janet, 149
Meat Beat Manifesto, 137
Meat Loaf, 59, 164, 197, 217, 252, 273
Mecano, 155, 180
Mekanïk Destructïw̄Komandöh, 252
Mekons, 289
Mel and Tim, 199, 250
Melanie, 266
Melle Mel, 178
Mellencamp, John Cougar, 39, 45, 49–50, 63, 66, 88, 176, 179, 199, 207, 230, 299, 302, 308, 319, 327–328
Meltzer, Richard, 28, 34, 40, 130, 242, 338
Melvins, 6
Membranes, 289

Memphis Jug Band, 16–17, 63–64, 175, 307, 335
Memphis Shieks, 64
Men At Work, 82, 208, 312
Mercury, Freddie, 50
Metallica, 6, 50, 67, 101, 151–153, 225, 227, 255, 319
Michael, George, 28, 87, 101
Michaels, Bret, 31, 227–228, 275
Michaels, Elin, 93
Mickey and Sylvia, 193
Midi Maxi & Efti, 312, 325
Midnight Oil, 205
Miller, Emmett, 126, 335
Miller, Glen, 260
Miller, Roger, 127
Miller, Steve, 287
Milli Vanilli, 29, 61, 77, 101, 235
Mills Brothers, 52
Ministry, 67, 137, 244
Minor Threat, 70–71, 269
Minoso, Minnie, 201
Mississippi Shieks, 309
Mr. Big, 57–58
Mr. Mister, 56
Mr. Wizard, 227
Mitchell, Joni, 53, 77, 196, 330
Mitsou, 255
Moby, 38
Moby Grape, 332
Moles, 311
Molinari, Dave, 196
Mona Lisa, 135
Money, Eddie, 33, 58, 87, 229
Monfou, 212
Monkees, 72, 80–81, 98, 161, 265, 332
Monotones, 134
Montez, Chris, 182
Moody Blues, 141, 143
Moonglows, 276
Moore, Rudy Ray, 122
Moore, Sampson, 213
Moore, Thurston, 243
Mordred, 137
Morford, Emily, 318
Morgan, Lorrie, 26

Pilot, 146
Pink Fairies, 266, 301, 330
Pink Floyd, 135–136, 250, 252, 277–278, 283
Pinnochio, 236
Pipkins, 123–124
Pitney, Gene, 298, 300
Plant, Robert, 168
Plastic Bertrand, 107, 286, 329
Plato, 200
Platters, 52, 207
Pogues, 294, 327
Pointed Sticks, 54, 324
Poison, 31, 33, 55–56, 103, 227–228, 266, 275, 302, 307, 326–327
Police, 53–54, 56, 82–84, 118, 290, 303, 315, 318
Ponichielli, 141
Pooh Sticks, 107
Poole, Charlie (and his North Carolina Ramblers), 103, 178, 335
Pop Group, 127, 137
Pop, Iggy, 28, 45, 194, 225, 240, 249, 259, 265, 301, 330
Pope Gregory I, 148
Pope Gregory XIII, 148
Popeye, 106
Poppy Family, 51
Porter, Cole, 11
Positive Force, 205
Positive K, 17
Prado, Perez, 206, 332
Precious Metal, 302
Premiers, 204
Presidents of the United States of America, 274
Presley, Elvis, 44–45, 51, 54, 61, 65, 113, 135, 140, 159, 185, 193, 201, 229, 235, 243, 276, 290, 335
Pretenders, 7, 71, 266
Price, Lloyd, 296
Prick, 220
Pride, Charlie, 198

Prima, Louis, 130–131, 134, 202, 244, 261, 276, 331, 333, 335
Primus, 67
Prince, 28, 30, 42, 146, 162, 189, 191, 212, 228, 253, 280, 328
Prince Buster, 170, 253, 266, 288–289, 332
Principle, Jamie, 267
Prisioneros, Los, 155, 251, 325
Prism, 249, 284, 296
Proby, P.J., 189
Procol Harum, 143, 145
Professor Longhair, 69, 120, 184
Propaganda, 38
Pryor, Richard, 122
Public Enemy, 16, 36, 73, 142, 164, 235, 244
Public Image Ltd. (PiL), 37–38, 43, 70, 80–81, 114, 255, 289, 302, 328
Puccini, Giacomo, 142
Puchalski, Tanya, 22
Pull My Daisy, 326
Pulp, 83, 250, 265
Punjabis (oi! band), 292

Q, Stacey, 44, 89, 98, 241, 326–327
Quad City DJs, 265
Quarterflash, 25, 46, 206, 274, 327–328
Quatro, Suzi, 105, 182, 194, 241, 330, 334
Quayle, Dan, 177
Queen, 62, 128–129, 135, 141, 146, 150, 197, 199, 266, 275, 290
Queensrÿche, 129, 138
? and the Mysterians, 162, 182, 189
Quinn, Dann, 244–245

Rabbit, Eddie, 255
Rachmaninoff, Serge, 53
Radiohead, 284
Rage Against the Machine, 67, 177

357

Other titles of interest

THE AESTHETICS OF ROCK
Richard Meltzer
New introd. by Greil Marcus
360 pp., 14 illus.
80287-2 $11.95

ANTI-ROCK
The Opposition to Rock'n'Roll
Linda Martin and Kerry Segrave
382 pp.
80502-2 $14.95

ARE YOU EXPERIENCED?
The Inside Story of the
Jimi Hendrix Experience
Noel Redding and Carol Appleby
258 pp., 28 photos
80681-9 $13.95

AWOPBOPALOOBOP
ALOPBAMBOOM
The Golden Age of Rock
Nik Cohn
New preface by the author
272 pp., 12 pp. of photos
80709-2 $13.95

THE BOWIE COMPANION
Edited by Elizabeth Thomson and
David Gutman
304 pp., 15 illus.
80707-6 $14.95

BRIAN ENO
His Music and the
Vertical Color of Sound
Eric Tamm
242 pp.
80649-5 $14.95

CHRISTGAU'S RECORD GUIDE
The '80s
Robert Christgau
525 pp.
80582-0 $17.95

THE DARK STUFF
Selected Writings on Rock Music,
1972–1995
Nick Kent
Foreword by Iggy Pop
365 pp.
80646-0 $14.95

GIANTS OF ROCK MUSIC
Edited by Pauline Rivelli
and Robert Levin
125 pp., 24 photos
80148-5 $7.95

IT CRAWLED FROM
THE SOUTH
An R.E.M. Companion
Fully Revised and Updated
Marcus Gray
560 pp., 48 illus.
80751-3 $17.95

THE LIFE AND TIMES OF
LITTLE RICHARD
Updated Edition
Charles White
337 pp., 70 photos
80552-9 $13.95

NO COMMERCIAL POTENTIAL
The Saga of Frank Zappa
Updated Edition
David Walley
240 pp., 28 photos
80710-6 $13.95

PET SHOP BOYS, LITERALLY
Chris Heath
368 pp., 44 photos
80494-8 $14.95

PIECE OF MY HEART
A Portrait of Janis Joplin
David Dalton
287 pp., 91 illus.
80446-8 $14.95

REMEMBERING BUDDY
The Definitive Biography
of Buddy Holly
John Goldrosen and John Beecher
210 pp., 160 illustrations,
including 4 pp. in color
80715-7 $18.95

ROCK ALBUMS OF THE 70s
A Critical Guide
Robert Christgau
480 pp.
80409-3 $15.95

THE SOUND OF THE CITY
The Rise of Rock and Roll
Newly illustrated and expanded
Charlie Gillett
604 pp., 64 pp. of illus.
80683-5 $16.95

STRANDED
Rock and Roll for a Desert Island
Edited and with a new preface by
Greil Marcus
New foreword by Robert Christgau
320 pp.
80682-7 $14.95

TRANSFORMER
The Lou Reed Story
Victor Bockris
464 pp., 32 photos
80752-1 $15.95

COUNTRY
The Twisted Roots of Rock 'n' Roll
New preface and appendix
Nick Tosches
290 pp., 54 illus.
80713-0 $13.95

THE DA CAPO COMPANION
TO 20th-CENTURY
POPULAR MUSIC
Phil Hardy and Dave Laing
1,168 pp.
80640-1 $29.50

HEROES AND VILLAINS
The True Story of the Beach Boys
Steven Gaines
432 pp., 66 photos
80647-9 $14.95

SOUL MUSIC A-Z
Revised Edition
Hugh Gregory
390 pp., 48 photos
80643-6 $17.95

PENNIES FROM HEAVEN
The American Popular Music
Business in the Twentieth Century
Russell Sanjek
Updated by David Sanjek
800 pp.
80706-8 $21.50

NOWHERE TO RUN
The Story of Soul Music
Gerri Hirshey
416 pp., 26 photos
80581-2 $14.95

BOB DYLAN: THE EARLY YEARS
A Retrospective
Edited by Craig McGregor
New preface by Nat Hentoff
424 pp., 15 illus.
80416-6 $13.95

Available at your bookstore

OR ORDER DIRECTLY FROM

DA CAPO PRESS, INC.

1-800-321-0050